AMERICAN STATESMEN

EDITED BY

JOHN T. MORSE, JR.

VOL. XX.

DOMESTIC POLITICS: THE TARIFF
AND SLAVERY

HENRY CLAY

AMS PRESS
NEW YORK

American Statesmen

STANDARD LIBRARY EDITION

The Home of Henry Clay

HOUGHTON, MIFFLIN & CO.

American Statesmen

HENRY CLAY

BY

CARL SCHURZ

IN TWO VOLUMES
VOL. II.

BOSTON AND NEW YORK
HOUGHTON, MIFFLIN AND COMPANY
The Riverside Press, Cambridge

Library of Congress Cataloging in Publication Data

Schurz, Carl, 1829-1906.
  Henry Clay.

  (American statesmen, v. 19-20)
  First published under title: Life of Henry Clay.
  Reprint of the 1899 ed.
  1. Clay, Henry, 1777-1852. I. Title: Life of
Henry Clay. II. Series.
 E340.C6S425   973.6'3'0924 [B]   70-128965
 ISBN 0-404-50891-X

Reprinted from the edition of: 1899, Boston, New York
First AMS edition published in 1972
Manufactured in the United States of America

International Standard Book Number:
Complete Set: 0-404-50891-X
Volume II: 0-404-50870-7

AMS PRESS INC.
NEW YORK, N.Y.   10003

CONTENTS

CHAP.		PAGE
XIV.	The Compromise of 1833	1
XV.	The Removal of the Deposits	24
XVI.	French Difficulties.—Indians.—Patronage	53
XVII.	Slavery	70
XVIII.	The Exit of President Jackson	96
XIX.	The Crisis of 1837	114
XX.	Clay and Van Buren	129
XXI.	Slavery again	153
XXII.	The Election of 1840	172
XXIII.	Clay and Tyler	199
XXIV.	The Election of 1844	229
XXV.	1844–1849	269
XXVI.	The Compromise of 1850	316
XXVII.	The End	374
Index		417

ILLUSTRATIONS

John J. Crittenden . . . . *Frontispiece*
   From a daguerreotype in the possession of the Century Company.
   Autograph from the Chamberlain collection, Boston Public Library.
   The vignette of "Ashland," Mr. Clay's home, near Lexington, Ky., is from a photograph of an engraving, kindly furnished by H. C. McDowell, Esq., the present owner of the estate.

Page

Thomas Ewing . . . . *facing* 102
   From a portrait painted in 1856, by Israel Quick, in the possession of Mrs. Thomas Ewing, Yonkers, N. Y.
   Autograph from a letter in the possession of his grandson, Thomas Ewing, Jr., New York, N. Y.

Henry Clay delivering his Farewell Address before the United States Senate, March 31, 1842 *facing* 226
   After an engraving from the original painting by Peter Frederick Rothermel.

David Wilmot . . . . *facing* 286
   From a painting by Marchant in the possession of Wilmot's niece, Mrs. George W. Merrick, Wellsboro, Pa
   Autograph from a MS. in the possession of Andrew H. Allen, Esq., Washington, D. C.

Thomas Corwin . . . . *facing* 356
   From a photograph by Brady in the Library of the State Department at Washington.
   Autograph from the Chamberlain collection, Boston Public Library.

HENRY CLAY

CHAPTER XIV

THE COMPROMISE OF 1833.

THE election of 1832 seemed to bury Henry Clay in defeat. But it was followed by events which made him again one of the most conspicuous actors on the public stage. The tariff act of 1828 had greatly intensified the dissatisfaction with the protective system long existing in the planting States. They complained that they had to bear all the burdens of that system without enjoying any of its benefits; that the things they had to buy had become dearer, while the things they produced and exported found a less profitable market, and that therefore ruin stared them in the face. This was in a great measure true. They further argued that, in a federative republic which cannot rest upon force alone, the concerns and wishes of any portion of the confederacy, even if that part be only a minority, should be carefully consulted; that laws calculated seriously to affect the material interests of any part of the country should be agreed upon in a spirit of mutual accommodation; and that the majority should not insist upon the execution of measures injurious to the minority simply because it had the power to do so.

Such reasoning would have commended itself at least to the candid and respectful consideration of fair-minded men, had it aimed only at constitutional means for its enforcement. But when it was accompanied with threats of the nullification of laws, and the eventual secession of States from the Union, it assumed the character of aggressive hostility to the republic.

The excitement on account of the tariff of 1828 was kept under a certain restraint so long as it was expected that Jackson, although at first favoring protection, would, as a Southern man, be mindful of Southern interests. He had, indeed, in his messages gradually abandoned the doctrine advanced in his Coleman letter, and recommended a revision of the tariff to the end of reducing the revenue and of giving up high protective duties as a system. But he signed the tariff act of 1832, which kept the protective system virtually intact. The agitation in the South then received a new impulse, and in South Carolina the nullifiers, for the first time, won complete possession of the state government.

Calhoun, anticipating the acquiescence of Jackson in the continuance of the protective system, had elaborately formulated the doctrine of nullification in an "Address to the People of South Carolina," published in the summer of 1831. It embodied the well known propositions that the Constitution is a mere compact between sovereign States; that the general government is the mere agent of the same sovereign States; that whenever any one of the parties to the compact — any State — considers any law made by the general government to be unconstitutional, it may "nullify" that law, — that is, declare and treat it as void and of no force. This, as Calhoun affirmed, was not inimical to the Union, but rather calculated to promote a good understanding among the States composing it; for, if that right of nullification were recognized, the majority would be more apt to listen to reason, and nullification would really be equivalent only to a suspension of the offensive law in the nullifying State or States, until the mistake committed by the majority should be rectified. If that mistake be not rectified, then the aggrieved State or States should have the constitutional right to secede from the Union.

This doctrine, which in our days would scarcely find a serious advocate in the country, was then argued with a great display of political metaphysics, and sincerely believed in by a very large number of people in South Carolina and other Southern States. In August, 1832, Calhoun put forth another manifesto, developing his constitutional theory to the highest degree of perfection it ever attained, and urging an immediate issue on account of the oppressive tariff legislation under which the South was then suffering.

The legislature of South Carolina was convened by the governor to meet on October 22, for the purpose of calling a convention "to consider the character and extent of the usurpations of the general government." The convention met on November 19, and adopted without delay an "ordinance" declaring that the tariff act of 1828 and the amendments thereto passed in 1832 were null and void; that it should be held unlawful to enforce the payment of duties thereunder within the State of South Carolina; that it should be the duty of the legislature to make laws giving effect to the ordinance; that all officers of the State should take an oath to obey and execute the ordinance and the laws made to enforce it; that no appeal from a state court to the federal Supreme Court should be allowed in any case arising under any law made in pursuance of the ordinance; and that, if the general government should attempt to use force to maintain the authority of the federal law, the State of South Carolina would secede from the Union, — the ordinance to go into full effect on February 1, 1833. The legislature, which met again on November 19, passed the "appropriate" laws. But these enactments were not very fierce; as Webster said, they "limped far behind the ordinance." Some preparation, although little, was made for a conflict of arms.

There was an anti-nullification movement in

South Carolina which caused some demonstrations against these proceedings. But the great families of the State, and with them the strongest influences, were overwhelmingly on the side of nullification. The nullifiers doubtless hoped for active sympathy in other Southern States. Webster, indeed, had as early as December, 1828, become " thoroughly convinced " that " the plan of a Southern Confederacy had been received with favor by a great many of the public men of the South." But when South Carolina actually put forth her nullifying ordinance, there seemed to be little eagerness outside of her borders to coöperate with her. Some Southern legislatures denounced the tariff as unconstitutional, without, however, recommending nullification and resistance. By some nullification was denounced. Virginia favored nullification, but offered to mediate between South Carolina and the general government. What would have happened in case of a conflict of arms between the general government and the nullifying State is a matter of conjecture. It was apprehended by many that several Southern States would have been drawn into the conflict on the Carolinian side.

President Jackson's annual message, which went to Congress on December 4, 1832, was remarkably quiet in tone. He congratulated the country upon extinction of the public debt. "The protection to the manufactures," he said, "should not exceed what may be necessary to counteract the regulations of foreign nations, and to secure a supply of those articles of manufacture essential to the national independence in time of war." Beyond that he recommended a gradual diminution of duties to the revenue standard "as soon as a just regard to the faith of the government and to the preservation of the large capital invested in establishments of domestic industry will permit." He alluded to the discontent created by the high tariff, adding that the people could not be expected to pay high taxes for the benefit of the manufacturers, when the revenue was not required for the administration of the government. He also mentioned the opposition to the collection of the revenue in one quarter of the United States, but hoped that the laws would be found adequate to the suppression thereof.

The message did not foreshadow a strong policy. John Quincy Adams wrote in his Diary: "It goes to dissolve the Union into its original elements, and is in substance a complete surrender to the nullifiers of South Carolina." Neither did it alarm the nullifiers. They saw reason to think that Jackson, who in the case of the Georgia Indians had acquiesced in the most extravagant pretensions of the State, even refusing to enforce a decision of the Supreme Court of the United States, did not materially differ from them as to the doctrine of state-rights. But both Mr. Adams and the nullifiers were mistaken.

Six days later, on December 10, came out Jackson's famous proclamation against the nullifiers, which spoke thus: —

"The Constitution of the United States forms a government, not a league; and whether it be formed by compact between the States, or in any other manner, its character is the same. . . . I consider the power to annul a law of the United States incompatible with the existence of the Union, contradicted expressly by the letter of the Constitution, and destructive of the great object for which it was formed. . . . Our Constitution does not contain the absurdity of giving power to make laws, and another power to resist them. To say that any State may at pleasure secede from the Union is to say that the United States are not a nation."

He appealed to the people of South Carolina, in the tone of a father, to desist from their ruinous enterprise; but he gave them also clearly to understand that, if they resisted by force, the whole power of the Union would be exerted to maintain its authority.

All over the North, even where Jackson had been least popular, the proclamation was hailed with unbounded enthusiasm. Meetings were held to give voice to the universal feeling. In many Southern States, such as Louisiana, Missouri, Tennessee, Kentucky, North Carolina, Maryland, Delaware, and even Virginia, it was widely approved as to its object, although much exception was taken to the "Federalist" character of its doctrines. Clay was not among those opponents of Jackson who hailed this manifesto with unqualified satisfaction.

"One short week," he wrote to Brooke, "produced the message and the proclamation, — the former ultra on the side of state-rights, the latter ultra on the side of consolidation. How they can be reconciled I leave to our Virginia friends. As to the proclamation, although there are good things in it, especially what relates to the judiciary, there are some entirely too ultra for me, and which I cannot stomach." It was perhaps not unnatural, after so painful a defeat, that Clay should be inclined to find fault with whatever Jackson might do. But there was, in truth, nothing "too ultra" for him in Jackson's proclamation.

The nullifiers in South Carolina received the presidential manifesto apparently with defiance. The governor of the State issued a counter-proclamation. Calhoun resigned the vice-presidency, and was immediately sent to the Senate to fight the battle for nullification there.

Now it was time for Congress to act. On December 27 a tariff bill, substantially in accord with the views expressed by the secretary of the treasury in his report, was reported in the House of Representatives from the Committee of Ways and Means, by Mr. Verplanck. It was looked upon as an administration measure. It contemplated a sweeping reduction of tariff duties down to the standard of the tariff of 1816, — " carrying back," as Benton says, "the protective system to the year of its commencement," — the reduction to take place in the course of two years. The protectionists loudly protested against it, but it might have satisfied the nullifiers, as it virtually conceded in that direction all they could hope for.

But another demonstration from the President intervened. The counter-proclamation of the governor of South Carolina had irritated him. He now uttered emphatic threats against the nullifiers, and sent a message to Congress asking for such an enlargement of the executive powers as would enable him to close ports of entry, remove customhouses that were interfered with, employ military force in holding goods for customs dues, and so on. He recommended also that the jurisdiction of the federal courts be extended over all revenue cases. The bill embodying these objects was currently called the " Force Bill," or, by South Carolinians, the " Bloody Bill."

Thus the administration offered a timely reform with one hand, and a vigorous enforcement of the law with the other. South Carolina, too, less eager than before to bring on the decisive crisis, put off the day when nullification should practically begin. Both sides secretly desired and hoped to escape a conflict. But one day after another passed, and the end of the short session approached without anything being accomplished in the way of legislation. The Senate lost itself in seemingly endless talk about the various theories of the Constitution as applicable to the " Force Bill," while the House appeared to be utterly unable to arrive at any conclusion on the tariff bill reported by Verplanck.

It was then that Clay took the matter into his hands. On February 12, only twenty days before the final adjournment of the twenty-second Congress, he offered in the Senate a tariff bill of his own, avowedly as a compromise measure. As it was finally shaped, it provided that, in all cases where the duties on foreign imports exceeded twenty per cent. ad valorem, they should be reduced by one tenth of such excess after September 30, 1833; by another tenth after September 30, 1835; and by another tenth every second year thereafter until September 30, 1841; then one half of the remaining excess should be taken off, and in 1842, the remaining half, which would leave a general rate of twenty per cent. on dutiable goods. The free list also was to be much enlarged; the duties were to be paid in cash, the credit system to be abolished. Home valuation — valuation of imported goods at the port of entry — was added by amendment, much against the wish of Calhoun.

The introduction of such a bill by the champion of the "American system" was a great surprise to the public. The same Henry Clay who had so violently denounced Albert Gallatin as "an alien at heart," for having suggested a reduction of duties to about twenty-five per cent., himself now proposed a reduction to twenty per cent., and called it a protective measure. Most of the protectionists stood aghast. The faithful Niles cried out in agony: "Mr. Clay's new tariff project will be received like a crash of thunder in the winter season, and some will hardly trust the evidence of their senses on a first examination of it, so radical and sudden is the change of policy proposed." This, no doubt, expressed the feelings of all protectionists except those with whom Clay had confidentially consulted.

The measure proposed was not a sudden contrivance on Clay's part. He himself subsequently said that he had conceived the plan while on a visit in Philadelphia, before the opening of the session, where he had conferences concerning it with several manufacturers, who concurred. It was communicated to Webster, who did not approve of it. Upon his return to Washington, Clay had interviews with Calhoun, who agreed to his scheme. Then and there a singular coalition was formed between the champion of protection and the most absolute free-trader; the chief of the latitudinarians and the strictest of strict constructionists; the emancipationist at heart and the devotee of the divine right of slavery; the most enthusiastic Union man and the apostle of the right of nullification and secession.

The motives avowed by Clay for his course were plausible: that the majority in the next Congress already elected was known to be hostile to the protective system, and likely to resort to an immediate reduction of the tariff to a strict revenue basis; that, if the present Congress should pass a law providing for moderate and gradual reductions as a solemn compromise, which would appeal for its maintenance to the honor and good faith of all parties to it, that would be so much gain to the protected interests; that at the same time the measure would serve to avert the dangers threatening the Union, — for he feared seriously, that if in some way a conflict of arms should take place in South Carolina, other Southern States might, by the contagion of excitement following the shedding of blood, be drawn into revolt and civil war. His biographer, Epes Sargent, who had the advantage of Clay's supervision of his work, mentions in addition a secret and very probable motive: "An invincible repugnance to placing under the command of General Jackson such vast military power as might be necessary to enforce the laws, and put down any resistance to them in South Carolina, and which might extend he knew not where. He could not think, without the most serious apprehensions, of intrusting a man of his vehement passions with such an immense power." These apprehensions became the more intense as he thought " he perceived, with some, a desire to push matters to extremities." Finally his constant inclination to lead in everything naturally pushed him forward.

But why did Calhoun assent to Clay's compromise measure rather than wait for the much more thorough tariff bill of Verplanck? Although as earnest in his nullification movement as ever, Calhoun had begun to be seriously troubled as to the outcome of it in case things were carried to extremes. The story that Jackson had threatened to cause Calhoun to be arrested and hanged for treason as soon as the authority of the United States should be resisted by force in South Carolina, and that Calhoun, hearing this, was thrown into a paroxysm of fear, was mere gossip. But the enthusiastic reception of Jackson's proclamation by the people convinced Calhoun that nullification, as well as secession, would be met by force. He grew anxious to end the trouble on the best terms he could obtain. But did not Verplanck's bill offer the best terms? In one respect, yes; in another respect, no. Verplanck's bill, although aiming at the greatest and speediest reduction of tariff duties, was not offered as a compromise measure. It was introduced as a simple fiscal scheme to reduce the revenue, as foreshadowed by Jackson's message, and as recommended in the report of the secretary of the treasury. It was represented to be an administration measure. It would probably have been introduced if the nullification ordinance had never been adopted in South Carolina. Its passage, therefore, would not have been ostensibly a concession to the nullifiers. Moreover, it was by no means certain to pass.

On the other hand, Clay's bill, although not carrying the reduction of tariff duties so far, was professedly a compromise. It was offered by the foremost champion of that protective system against which South Carolina had risen up, for the avowed purpose of conciliating the nullifiers by concession. Its enactment might therefore be looked upon as something extorted from Congress by the nullification movement, and thus as a victory by nullification. Calhoun, for this reason, was willing, and even eager, to sacrifice the possibility of some material advantage for the honor and the future of his cause.

To quiet the alarm of the frightened manufacturers, Clay, when introducing his bill, labored hard to prove that it was a protection measure. Some of the arguments he employed to this end were very curious.

"There are four modes [he said] by which the industry of the country can be protected: First, the absolute prohibition of rival foreign articles; second, the imposition of duties in such a manner as to have no reference to any object but revenue; third, the raising as much revenue as is wanted for the use of the government and no more, but raising it from the protected and not from the unprotected articles; and, fourth, the admission, free of duty, of every article which aided the operations of the manufacturers."

"These," he said, "are the four modes for protecting our industry; and to those who say that the bill abandons the power of protection, I reply that it does not touch that power, and that the fourth mode, so far from being abandoned, is extended and upheld by the bill." He would, as he said, have preferred the third mode as a general policy, but he recognized that the manufacturing industries could be protected by putting the raw

THE COMPROMISE OF 1833

material on the free list while reducing duties on everything else. He further set forth that what the manufacturers needed was stability in legislation, certainty at least for a fixed period of time. Such certainty, he argued, was given by his bill for the period of nine years; for, although the present Congress could not bind its successors, yet every honorable man would consider himself in conscience bound to respect as inviolable the terms of a compromise.

He felt the awkwardness of his position in offering a compromise to a party standing in an attitude of defiance to the authority of the United States. He confessed to have felt "a strong repugnance to any legislation at the commencement of the session," principally because he had "misconceived, as he found from subsequent observation, the purposes which South Carolina had in view." He had supposed that the State had "arrogantly required the immediate abandonment of a system which had long been the settled policy of the country." Supposing this, he had "felt a disposition to hurl defiance back again." But since his arrival at Washington he had found that South Carolina "did not contemplate force," for she disclaimed it, and asserted that she was merely making an experiment, namely, "by a change in her fundamental laws, by a course of state legislation, and by her civil tribunals to prevent the general government from carrying the laws of the United States into operation within her limits." This, he admitted, was indeed rash and unjustifiable enough, but it was not so wicked as a direct appeal to force would have been. South Carolina was still open to reason, and it would therefore be wrong to precipitate a conflict.

This was very light reasoning; the only ground he had for it was that South Carolina had permitted the 1st of February to pass by without executing her threats.

The compromise bill found much opposition in the Senate. Webster, especially, would not admit that it was a measure in accord with the principle of protection. Neither would he admit that this was an occasion for compromise. He thought it was time to test the strength of the government; and he therefore stood sturdily by the President, their party differences notwithstanding. To reconcile discordant opinions, the compromise bill was referred to a select committee, of which Clay was chairman. The manufacturers had assembled a powerful lobby at Washington to oppose the bill as first framed. They insisted upon several amendments, upon which, however, the committee could not agree. One of these, the provision for home valuation, was especially distasteful to Calhoun. But the manufacturing interest, which was strongly represented in the Senate, would not consent to the passage of the bill without it. Clay, therefore, undertook to move and support it in the Senate. This he did. Still Calhoun opposed the amendment as unconstitutional, and oppressive to the

South. Then Clayton of Delaware, an earnest protectionist, and so far a warm advocate of the compromise, moved to lay the bill on the table; giving Calhoun and his friends to understand that, unless they all voted for that amendment, and finally for the bill with the amendment added to it, he would defeat the measure. Calhoun's friends begged for themselves and their chief to be spared the humiliation of such a vote. Even Clay generously interceded for them. But Clayton remained firm, saying, "If they cannot vote for a bill to save their necks from a halter, their necks may stretch." He insisted especially that Calhoun himself should vote for it, not without reason; for Calhoun, as it was proved beyond doubt by several circumstances, desired the compromise to pass without his own vote, so that he might be at liberty afterwards to repudiate such parts of it as did not suit his doctrines and aims. At last, when he saw that the compromise was doomed unless he consented to vote for the amendment, he promised to do so. Clayton withdrew his motion to lay on the table, and the amendment passed with the support of the nullifiers.

Meanwhile the Force Bill, vigorously advocated by Webster, had, after a long discussion, passed the Senate, — John Tyler having made himself its conspicuous opponent. On February 25 Clay made a final appeal to the Senate for his measure of peace. Once more he assured the manufacturers that his compromise was their only salvation;

that "the true theory of protection supposed, too, that after a certain time the protected arts would have acquired such strength and protection as would enable them subsequently to stand up against foreign competition." Then, in his most captivating, heart-winning strains, he sought to persuade the Senate that the Force Bill and the bill of peace should go together for the good of the country: the one to "demonstrate the power and the disposition to vindicate the authority and the supremacy of the laws of the Union;" the other, to "offer that which, accepted in the fraternal spirit in which it was tendered, would supersede the necessity of the employment of all force." He closed with a remarkable outburst of personal feeling. "I have been accused of ambition in presenting this measure. Ambition! inordinate ambition! Low, groveling souls, who are utterly incapable of elevating themselves to the higher and nobler duties of pure patriotism, — beings who, forever keeping their own selfish aims in view, decide all public measures by their presumed influence on their aggrandizement, — judge me by the venal rule which they prescribe for themselves. I am no candidate for any office in the gift of these States, united or separated. I never wish, never expect, to be. Pass this bill, tranquillize the country, restore confidence and affection in the Union, and I am willing to go to Ashland and renounce public service forever. Yes, I have ambition. But it is the ambition of

THE COMPROMISE OF 1833

being the humble instrument, in the hands of Providence, to reconcile a divided people, once more to revive concord and harmony in a distracted land, — the pleasing ambition of contemplating the glorious spectacle of a free, united, prosperous, and fraternal people." It was the chronic candidate for the presidency who found it necessary to assure his hearers that his measure was in truth an inspiration of patriotism, and not a mere electioneering trick.

One objection to the compromise bill — that a bill to raise revenue could not originate in the Senate — was overcome, at the very moment he made this moving appeal, by a stroke of shrewd management. The House of Representatives had been long and drearily wrangling over the Verplanck bill, when suddenly, on February 25, Letcher of Kentucky, Clay's intimate friend and ally, moved to amend the Verplanck bill by striking out all after the enacting clause, and inserting a new set of provisions agreeing literally with Clay's compromise bill as then shaped in the Senate. Clay's and Calhoun's friends in the House having been secretly instructed as to what was to come, and the opposition being taken by surprise, the amendment was adopted, and the bill so amended passed to a third reading the same day, "while members were putting on their overcoats to go to their dinners." The next day the bill passed the House by 119 to 85, and thus Clay's compromise was sent to the Senate in the shape of a House bill. The last objection being thus removed, the bill was adopted in the Senate by 29 to 16. President Jackson signed it on the same day with the Force Bill, which had meanwhile passed the House, and thus the compromise of 1833 was consummated.

The first object of the measure was attained: South Carolina repealed her nullification ordinance. The manufacturers, too, gradually persuaded themselves that Clay, in view of the anti-protection character of the next Congress, had averted from them a more unwelcome fate. The compromise was received by the country, on the whole, with great favor; as Benton expresses it, "it was received as a deliverance, and the ostensible authors of it greeted as benefactors, and their work declared by legislatures to be sacred and inviolable, and every citizen doomed to political outlawry that did not give in his adhesion and bind himself to the perfecting of the act." Clay had once more won the proud title of "pacificator."

But before long it became clear that, beyond the repeal of the nullification ordinance, the compromise had settled nothing. The nullifiers strenuously denied that they had in any sense given up their peculiar doctrine. They denounced the Force Bill as a flagrant act of usurpation, which must be wiped from the statute book. While at heart they were glad of their escape from a perilous situation, they assumed the attitude of having only graciously accepted the terms of capitulation proposed by a distressed foe. Even the postponement of the day when nullification was practically to begin was, in appearance, yielded only to the friendly anxiety of Virginia, which had sent a "commissioner" to South Carolina to ask that favor. They treated the assertion, that the compromise act was a protection measure, as little better than a joke. They represented the reduction of the tariff duties as a concession extorted by a threat, — as a palpable triumph of the nullification movement. In one word, not only the compromise did not include the abandonment of the doctrine that a State could constitutionally nullify a law of the United States, but it rather served to give the believers in that doctrine a higher opinion of its efficacy. In fact, attempts to terrorize the rest of the Union into compliance with the behests of the South became a settled policy when the slavery question came to the foreground; and this was owing in a large measure to the encouragement given to the spirit of resistance in 1833.

Clay evidently failed to understand at the time that there was something more potent and imperious than mere discontent with a tariff at the bottom of the chronic trouble, — the necessities of slavery; and that a mere tariff compromise could only adjourn, but by no means avert, the coming crisis, nor touch the true cause of it. In later years, however, he is reported to have often said to his friends, when speaking of the events of

1833, that, "in looking back upon the whole case, he had come seriously to doubt the policy of his interference."

One thing was, indeed, gained for the Union. Jackson by his proclamation, and Congress by passing the Force Bill, had strongly asserted the supremacy of the general government in all national concerns, and the principle that the republic cannot be dissolved in a constitutional way, or by anything short of a revolutionary act; and the popular mind had familiarized itself with the idea that the Union was to be maintained by all the power at the command of the general government. Clay also, in his compromise speeches, had affirmed this principle in emphatic language; but the stronger impulse was given by those who, like Jackson and Webster, declared themselves ready to test the strength of the government, rather than by him who sought to preserve the Union by concession under a threat.

It was during the debate on the compromise bill that Clay and John Randolph met for the last time. Randolph, in the last stage of consumption, was on his way to Philadelphia, seeking medical aid. Passing through Washington, he desired to be carried to the senate chamber. At the moment he arrived there, Clay obtained the floor to speak for conciliation. Randolph, stretched on a lounge, raised his head and said, "I came here to hear that voice once more." When Clay had finished his remarks he approached his old antagonist, who was soon to die, and they shook hands.

Immediately before the adjournment Clay's Land Bill, providing for the distribution of the proceeds of land sales among the States, passed both houses. Jackson neither signed it, nor did he return it with his veto. Taking advantage of the shortness of the time before the adjournment, he permitted the bill to die unsigned, by a so-called pocket veto; and then he sent to Congress at its next session his reasons for disapproving it.

CHAPTER XV

THE REMOVAL OF THE DEPOSITS

In June, 1833, General Jackson made a "presidential tour" from Washington by way of Philadelphia to New York and the New England States. His proclamation against the nullifiers was still fresh in men's minds, and the people received him everywhere with demonstrative and sincere enthusiasm. Clay was meanwhile at Ashland; and how he enjoyed his rural life is pleasingly portrayed in a letter to Brooke, in May, 1833: —

"Since my return from Washington, I have been principally occupied with the operations of my farm, which have more and more interest for me. There is a great difference, I think, between a farm employed in raising dead produce for market and one which is applied, as mine is, to the rearing of all kinds of live stock. I have the Maltese ass, the Arabian horse, the Merino and the Saxe-Merino sheep, the English Hereford and Durham cattle, the goat, the mule, and the hog. The progress of these animals from their infancy to maturity presents a constantly varying subject of interest, and I never go out of my house without meeting with some one of them to engage agreeably my attention. Then our fine greensward, our natural parks, our beautiful undulating country, everywhere exhibiting combinations of grass and trees or luxuriant crops, all conspire to render home delightful."

But in spite of all this he informed Brooke that in July he would set out on a journey through Ohio to Buffalo, thence to Canada and New England. He "intended" to travel "with as much privacy as possible." He wanted "repose." He wanted it so much that he had not yet decided whether he would return to the Senate. Only the situation of his Land Bill might determine him to do so.

So Clay had his "progress," too, and after his return he wrote to Brooke: —

"My journey was full of gratification. In spite of my constant protestations that it was undertaken with objects of a private nature exclusively, and my uniformly declining public dinners, the people everywhere, and at most places without discrimination of parties, took possession of me, and gave enthusiastic demonstrations of respect, attachment, and confidence. In looking back on the scenes through which I passed, they seem to me to have resembled those of enchantment more than of real life."

But as to the appearance of the two rivals before the people that summer, Jackson had, no doubt, the advantage. With the old lustre of military heroship, he had the new lustre of the "savior of the Union," the "conqueror of nullification." Clay, indeed, was the "great pacificator," but Jackson was the strong man. However, Clay was delighted with the new evidences of his popularity, and, when he returned to Washington at the opening of the twenty-third Congress, his bucolic pleasures and his yearning for repose were readily forgotten. The session beginning in December, 1833, was to bring the two leaders face to face in a struggle fiercer than any before.

Great things had happened during the summer. As soon as the issue between him and the Bank of the United States was declared, Jackson resolved that the bank must be utterly destroyed. The method was suggested by Kendall and Blair of the kitchen cabinet. It was to cripple the available means of the bank by withdrawing from it and its branches the deposits of public funds. In the message of December, 1832, Jackson had expressed his doubt as to the safety of the government deposits in the bank, and recommended an investigation. The House, after inquiry, resolved on March 2, by 109 to 46 votes, that the deposits were safe. The bank was at that period undoubtedly solvent, and there seemed to be no reason to fear for the safety of the public money in its custody. But Jackson had made up his mind that the bank was financially rotten; that it had been employing its means to defeat his reëlection; that it was using the public funds in buying up members of Congress for the purposes of securing a renewal of its charter and of breaking down the administration; and that thus it had become a dangerous agency of corruption and a public enemy. Therefore the public funds must be withdrawn, without regard to consequences.

But the law provided that the public funds should be deposited in the Bank of the United States or its branches, unless the secretary of the treasury should otherwise " order and direct," and in that case the secretary should report his reasons for such direction to Congress. A willing secretary of the treasury was therefore needed. In May, 1833, Jackson reconstructed his cabinet for the second time. Livingston, the secretary of state, was sent as minister of the United States to France. McLane, the secretary of the treasury, the same who in December, 1831, had made a report favorable to the bank, was made secretary of state. For the Treasury Department Jackson selected William J. Duane of Philadelphia, who was known as an opponent of the bank. Jackson, no doubt, expected him to be ready for any measure necessary to destroy it. In this he was mistaken. Duane earnestly disapproved of the removal of the deposits as unnecessary, and highly dangerous to the business interests of the country. He also believed that so important a change in the fiscal system of the government was a matter of which the executive should not dispose without the concurrence of Congress. Nor was his opinion without support in the administration. A majority of the members of the cabinet thought the removal of the deposits unwise. Even one of the members of the kitchen cabinet, Colonel Lewis, Jackson's oldest friend, entertained the same opinion. In fact, it was held by almost every public man who was consulted upon the subject. The exceptions were very few. In the business community there seemed to be but one voice about it. The mere rumor that the removal of the deposits was in contemplation greatly disturbed the money market.

But all this failed to stagger Jackson's resolution. The important question, what to do with the public funds after the removal from the United States Bank, — whether state banks could be found to which they could be intrusted safely and upon proper conditions, — puzzled and disquieted others, but not him. He was firm in the belief that the United States Bank used the public money to break down the government, and must therefore be stripped of it without unnecessary delay. But Duane refused. Jackson argued with him in vain. Duane knew that his position was at stake. He knew, as he afterwards said, that there was an "irresponsible cabal" at work, an "influence unknown to the Constitution and to the people," which took advantage of President Jackson's hot impulses. He would not become a party to a scheme the execution of which, in his opinion, would plunge the fiscal concerns of the country into "chaos."

On September 18 Jackson caused to be read to the assembled cabinet a paper, setting forth why the deposits should be removed, and declaring that he was firmly resolved upon that step as necessary to preserve the morals of the people, the freedom of the press, and the purity of the elective franchise. He announced the measure to be his own; he would take the responsibility. This paper was written by Taney, and evidently intended not only for the members of the administration, but for the public. The cabinet, with the exception of the secretary of the treasury, bowed to Jackson's will. But Duane would not shelter himself behind the President's assumed responsibility to do an act which, under the law, was to be his act. He also refused to resign. If he had to obey or go, he insisted upon being removed. Jackson then formally dismissed him, and transferred Roger B. Taney from the attorney-generalship to the treasury. Benjamin F. Butler of New York, a friend of Van Buren, was made attorney-general.

Taney forthwith ordered the removal of the deposits from the Bank of the United States; that is to say, the public funds then in the bank were to be drawn out as the government required them, and no new deposits to be made in that institution. The new deposits were to be distributed among a certain number of selected state banks, which became known as the "pet banks." The amount of government money at that time in the United States Bank, which was to be gradually drawn out and not to be replaced by new government deposits, was $9,891,000. The bank resolved to curtail its loans to the extent of nearly $7,000,000, which sum had been the average of government deposits for several years. The money market became stringent. Many failures occurred. The general feeling in business circles approached a panic. The whole country was in a state of excitement.

The twenty-third Congress, which met under these circumstances on December 2, 1833, became distinguished by the unusual array of talent in its ranks, as well as the stormy character of its proceedings. It was then that the great duel between Clay and Jackson, as the leaders of the opposing forces, reached its culmination; and by Clay's side stood, — now for the first time united in open opposition to Jackson, — Webster and Calhoun. Jackson's supporters were in the minority in the Senate, but commanded a large majority in the House of Representatives. In his annual message the President announced that he had urged upon the Treasury Department the propriety of removing the deposits from the Bank of the United States, and that accordingly it had been done. He denounced the bank as having attempted to corrupt the elections with money, and as being "converted into a permanent electioneering machine." The question was presented, he said, whether true representatives of the people or the influence of the bank should govern the country. He accused the bank of attempting to force a restoration of the deposits, and to extort from Congress a renewal of its charter, by curtailing accommodations and hoarding specie, thus creating artificial embarrassment and panic.

The secretary of the treasury, Taney, in his report to Congress, argued that under the law he had the right to remove the deposits whenever in his opinion the public interest would be benefited by it, no matter whether the deposits were safe or not, and that Congress had divested itself of all right to interfere. He had, as an executive officer of the government, subject to the direction of the President, removed the deposits for reasons of public interest. By implication he admitted that the bank was solvent and the deposits safe. But, he argued, the bank, by asking Congress four years before the expiration of its charter for a renewal thereof, had submitted itself to the popular judgment at the presidential election which was then impending. The people had pronounced against the bank. A renewal of the charter being therefore out of the question, it was best to begin with the removal of the deposits at once, instead of leaving it to the last moment of the legal existence of the depository. He enlarged upon the President's message in criticising the conduct of the bank. Finally, he preferred state banks as depositories.

Clay opened the attack on December 10. He offered a resolution calling upon the President to inform the Senate whether a paper concerning the removal of the deposits, purporting to have been read to the cabinet on September 18, 1833, and alleged to have been published by the President's authority, was genuine or not, and, if genuine, to furnish a copy of it to the Senate. The resolution passed. This was an ill-considered movement, for it gave Jackson an opportunity for administering a smart snub to the Senate without leaving the Senate anything to reply. "I have yet to learn," he said in his special message, "under what constitutional authority that branch of the legislature [the Senate] has a right to require of me an account of any communication, either verbally or in writing, made to the heads of departments acting as a cabinet council." He added: "Feeling my responsibility to the American people, I am willing upon all occasions to explain to them the grounds of my conduct," — a sentiment which, since his reëlection, appeared frequently, and, as we shall see, in a much more significant form. The statesmen of the Senate shook their heads, but Jackson had altogether the best of the encounter in the eyes of the masses.

This, however, was merely a preliminary skirmish. On December 26 Clay introduced two resolutions, one declaring that, by dismissing a secretary of the treasury because that officer would not, contrary to his sense of duty, remove the deposits, and by appointing another for the purpose of effecting that removal, the President had "assumed the exercise of a power over the Treasury of the United States not granted to him by the Constitution and laws, and dangerous to the liberties of the people;" and the other declaring that the reasons assigned by the secretary of the treasury for the removal of the deposits were "unsatisfactory and insufficient."

The speech with which he opened the debate on these resolutions deserves to be studied as a piece of good debating, although the constitutional theory set forth in it was based upon a fiction. "We are," he began, "in the midst of a revolution, hitherto bloodless, but rapidly tending toward a total change of the pure republican character of the government, and the concentration of all power in the hands of one man." This he sought to prove by showing that President Jackson had assumed power over the Treasury which the Constitution had withheld from the executive and expressly conferred upon Congress.

During the Revolutionary period, and among the men who had grown up under the influence of its reminiscences, the great danger threatening free institutions in America was thought to be that the republic would be turned into a monarchy by a change in the character of the executive. The spectre of a "king" haunted their imaginations in a variety of shapes. In Jefferson's mind, it was a sort of British king of Hamiltonian pattern. Clay's king was a successful military chieftain like Jackson; and Benton's a "money king," with a monster bank at his command. In the writings and speeches of that time we constantly meet dismal predictions that, if this or that were done or permitted, the king would surely come. In the legislation of the first Congress under the Constitution, organizing the government, there were also traces of an anxious desire to withdraw all financial concerns as much as possible from the influence of the executive, — sprung, perhaps, from the memories, familiar to all Americans, of the struggles in England against the royal pretension to hold both the sword and the purse, as well as of the Revolutionary fight against taxation without representation. Thus it was not only provided in the Constitution that Congress should have the exclusive power to lay and collect taxes, duties, imposts, and excises, to pay debts, and to borrow money on the credit of the United States, to coin money and regulate the value thereof, but the first Congress, creating the State, War, and Treasury Departments, made a remarkable distinction between them. While the State and the War Departments were, in the language of the law, called "executive departments," the Treasury Department received no such designation. The secretaries of state and of war were commanded by the law "to perform and execute such duties as shall, from time to time, be enjoined on or intrusted to them by the President of the United States." The secretary of the treasury was not commanded by the law to perform such duties as might be intrusted to him by the President, but was commanded to perform certain duties enumerated in the act, and to make report, not to the President, but directly to Congress.

The theory was, therefore, adhered to by many that the secretary of the treasury was not, like the heads of other departments, under the direc-

THE REMOVAL OF THE DEPOSITS 35

tion of the executive, but that he was the agent of Congress, and that Congress substantially should control the Treasury Department. Clay held to this theory; and, as the law creating the Bank of the United States provided that the public funds should be deposited in that institution, "unless the secretary of the treasury should otherwise order and direct," and that, if he did otherwise order, he should promptly report the reasons to Congress, Clay concluded that the matter was left exclusively to the secretary of the treasury under the supervision of Congress; and that, if the President interfered with the secretary's conception of his duty in the premises, it was an unwarranted interference with a department which the Constitution had placed under the special supervision of Congress, and therefore a revolutionary attempt to overthrow the constitutional system.

The answer suggesting itself was that, after all, the Constitution had intrusted the power of appointing the secretary of the treasury, not to Congress, but to the President; that the law, as construed, recognized the power of the President to remove that officer, giving the President in these respects the same power over the secretary of the treasury as over other officers of the government; that, therefore, the President, having the power to remove the secretary of the treasury for reasons of his own, was practically intrusted with a supervision over the official conduct of that officer, and that, in effectually exercising that supervision through the power of removal, Jackson had technically acted within his constitutional authority.

On the other hand, Congress, when making the law by which the Bank of the United States was created, had undoubtedly intended that the bank should have the public deposits; that the secretary of the treasury should be empowered to remove them only for weighty reasons; that those reasons should be as promptly as possible reported to Congress, not to satisfy mere curiosity, but to enable Congress to judge of them and to sanction or disapprove the act; that it was certainly not contemplated to give, either to the President or to the secretary, power to effect so great a change in the fiscal system of the government as was involved in the transfer of the public deposits from the United States Bank to a number of hastily selected state banks, without consulting Congress; and that in these respects the action of President Jackson in removing the deposits was a very high-handed proceeding. Clay's review of the reasons given by the secretary for the removal was crushing, and remained in almost all points entirely unanswered.

It is interesting that in the course of his speech Clay quoted Gallatin as authority, adding, "who, whatever I said of him on a former occasion, — and that I do not mean to retract, — possessed more practical knowledge of currency, banks, and finance than any man I have ever met in the public councils." He did not retract what he had said

THE REMOVAL OF THE DEPOSITS 37

before, but it looked as if he had become ashamed of it.

The debate on Clay's resolutions lasted, with some interruptions, three months, calling out on Clay's side the best debating talent of the Senate, — Webster, Calhoun, Ewing, Southard, and others. The resolutions had to undergo some changes, to the end of obviating constitutional scruples, and were finally, on March 28, adopted, the one declaring the reasons given by the secretary of the treasury for the removal of the deposits " unsatisfactory and insufficient," by 28 to 18; and the other, " that the President, in the late executive proceeding in relation to the public revenue has assumed upon himself authority and power not conferred by the Constitution and laws, but in derogation of both," by 26 to 20. Clay subsequently offered a joint resolution requiring the public deposits to be restored to the Bank of the United States, which passed the Senate, but failed in the House of Representatives.

Meanwhile petitions had been pouring in from all sides setting forth that production and transportation were hampered; that an enormous number of laboring men were without work; that business was suffering fearfully from the inability of business men to obtain the necessary bank accommodations; that there was general distress; and that all this was attributable to the derangement of the banking business by the removal of the deposits. In the Senate these " distress petitions," which formed a great feature of the session, were presented with great pomp of eloquence, especially by Webster and Clay.

An extraordinary scene occurred on March 7, when Clay, presenting a petition of workingmen of Philadelphia, the "builders' memorial," and speaking of the President's power to afford relief, suddenly turned upon the Vice-President, Van Buren, in the chair, and, as if involuntarily, moving down to the Vice-President's desk, apostrophized him personally in a most impressive burst of eloquence: —

" Those who in this chamber support the administration [he said] could not render a better service than to repair to the executive mansion, and, placing before the chief magistrate the naked and undisguised truth, prevail upon him to retrace his steps and abandon his fatal experiment. No one, sir, can perform that duty with more propriety than yourself. You can, if you will, induce him to change his course. To you, then, sir, in no unfriendly spirit, but with feelings softened and subdued by the deep distress which pervades every class of our countrymen, I make the appeal. Go to him and tell him, without exaggeration, but in the language of truth and sincerity, the actual condition of his bleeding country. Tell him it is nearly ruined and undone by the measures which he has been induced to put in operation. Tell him that in a single city more than sixty bankruptcies, involving a loss of upward of fifteen millions of dollars, have occurred. Tell him of the alarming decline of all property, of the depreciation of all the products of industry, of the stagnation in every branch of business, and of the close of numerous manufacturing establishments which, a few short months ago, were in active and flourishing operation. Depict to him, if you can find language to portray, the heart-rending wretchedness of thousands of the working classes cast out of employment. · Tell him of the tears of helpless widows, no longer able to earn their bread; and of unclad and unfed orphans who have been driven by his policy out of an honest livelihood."

So he went on, through the whole catalogue of misery, with increasing urgency impressing upon the Vice-President the solemn message. It would have been a deeply affecting scene but for the circumstance that it was Martin Van Buren who received the pathetic commission. Benton describes it thus: —

"During the delivery of this apostrophe the Vice-President maintained the utmost decorum of countenance, looking respectfully and even innocently at the speaker all the while, as if treasuring up every word he said, to be faithfully repeated to the President. After it was over and the Vice-President had called some senator to the chair, he went up to Mr. Clay and asked him for a pinch of his fine maccaboy snuff, and, having received it, walked away."

But elsewhere the matter was taken more seriously. At a public meeting in Philadelphia a resolution was adopted "that Martin Van Buren deserves and will receive the execration of all good men, should he shrink from the responsibility of conveying to Andrew Jackson the message sent by the Hon. Henry Clay."

This storm of hostile demonstrations did not stagger Jackson's indomitable spirit in the least. Having been made to believe that the business disturbances in the country were wholly owing to the malicious curtailment of bank accommodations by the "monster," he met "distress delegations" which waited upon him, sometimes with cold courtesy, sometimes with explosions of wrath, telling them that, if they wanted money to set the business of the country moving again, they should go to Nicholas Biddle, who was treacherously shutting up millions upon millions in his bank. Clay's resolutions of censure, adopted by the Senate, he answered by sending, on April 17, 1834, a formal "protest," which he demanded should be entered upon the journal.

It was an extraordinary document. He denounced not only the adoption, but also the discussion, of the resolutions by the Senate, as "unauthorized by the Constitution," and in every respect improper, because it was, in his opinion, in the nature of an impeachment trial without the observance of any of the prescribed constitutional rules and forms. He censured particularly, for having supported the resolutions, the senators from States whose legislatures had approved the conduct of the administration. He affirmed that the President was the "direct representative of the American people;" that he was responsible for the entire action of the executive department, and must therefore have a free choice of his agents and power to

THE REMOVAL OF THE DEPOSITS 41

direct and control their doings; that it was his sworn duty to protect the Constitution, if it must be, for the people against the Senate; and that, if the people allowed "the practice by the Senate of the unconstitutional power of arraigning and censuring the official conduct of the executive," it would "unsettle the foundations of the government," and "the real power of the government would fall into the hands of a body holding their offices for long terms, not elected by the people, and not to them directly responsible."

The protest was at once denounced as a gross breach of the privilege of the Senate, and a resolution pronouncing it to be such, and declaring that it should not be entered upon the journal of the Senate, was offered by Poindexter of Mississippi. Jackson, no doubt, believed in all sincerity that by destroying the United States Bank he was doing the American people a great service, and that he was fully warranted by the Constitution in all he had done. He therefore felt himself very much aggrieved by the resolution of censure adopted in the Senate. But the pretension set up in his protest, that the Senate, because it might have to sit as a judicial body in case of impeachment, had, as a legislative body, no constitutional right to express an unfavorable opinion about an act of the executive, — nay, that neither house of Congress had such a right except in case of impeachment, — was altogether incompatible with the fundamental principles of representative government. The Constitution, indeed, authorizes the President to do certain things in his discretion; but this fact does certainly not take from the legislature, or from either house, the right to inquire whether in a given case the President has acted within that constitutional discretion, or whether that discretion has been wisely exercised for the public good. The Senate is, indeed, a judicial body when it tries impeachments. But it is also a legislative body, and as such it can certainly not be stripped of the necessary privilege of discussing and criticising the conduct of public officers on the ground that such officers might possibly be impeached for the acts criticised.

Equally startling was the assumption that "the President is the direct representative of the American people;" that he possesses original executive powers, and absorbs in himself all executive functions and responsibilities; and that it is his especial office to protect the liberties and rights of the people and the integrity of the Constitution against the Senate or the House of Representatives, or both together.

It is more than probable that Jackson, although at the moment giving full rein to his hot impulses, never understood all the bearings of the doctrines to which he put his name; but it may certainly be said that in the history of the republic no document has ever come from any president so inconsistent in its tendency with republican institutions as was Jackson's "protest." Clay did not go much too far when, in a fiery speech which he made on the occasion, he described Jackson as animated by "the genuine spirit of conquerors and conquest," which "lives by perpetual, agitating excitement, and would die in a state of perfect repose and tranquillity," — a spirit attacking in turn "the Indians, the Indian policy, internal improvements, the colonial trade, the Supreme Court, Congress, the bank, and now presenting himself " as a dictator to rebuke a refractory Senate," and preparing to attack and annihilate the Senate itself.

After a debate of three weeks, which called forth the heaviest thunders of Clay, Webster, and Calhoun on one side, and of Benton and Silas Wright on the other, the resolutions condemning the protest as an unconstitutional assertion of power and a breach of the privileges of the Senate, and refusing to put it on the journal, passed by 27 to 16 votes.

The war between the President and the majority of the Senate was carried on with unprecedented bitterness and all available weapons. In one of the short addresses with which he presented "distress petitions," Clay laid down certain rules to be followed by senators who meant to oppose to all encroachments, and to all corruption, a manly, resolute, and uncompromising resistance," in acting upon nominations for office. He said : —

"In the first place, to preserve untarnished and unsuspected the purity of Congress, let us negative the nomination of every member for office, high or low, foreign or domestic, until the authority of the Constitution and laws is fully restored. And, in the next place, let us approve of the original nomination of no notorious, brawling politician and electioneerer, but especially of the reappointment of no officer presented to us who shall have prostituted the influence of his office to partisan and electioneering purposes."

With alacrity the Senate rejected the nomination for reappointment of four government directors of the Bank of the United States. Jackson repeated the same nominations, roundly scolding the Senate for having rejected them; but they were rejected again. The speaker of the House of Representatives, Stephenson of Virginia, was nominated for the mission to England, apparently as a reward for ardent partisanship, and was sternly voted down. Roger B. Taney had been put into the Treasury Department more than two months before the meeting of Congress, and Jackson did not send in his nomination until six months after the opening of the session. It was promptly rejected, which infuriated Jackson beyond measure. He nominated Levi Woodbury in Taney's place, and Taney was subsequently put on the bench of the Supreme Court.

Congress adjourned in June. Few sessions had ever been so prolific of exciting debates. Crowds of people, gathered from far and near, went day after day to the galleries of the Senate as they would go to a play. But few sessions also had been so barren of practical results. The brilliant

THE REMOVAL OF THE DEPOSITS 45

arraignment of the President's course, combined with the business depression, was indeed not altogether without effect. In the spring of 1834 there seemed to be a strong current of popular sentiment running against the administration. The anti-Jackson men won in several local elections. It was at this period that the opposition began to call itself the Whig party. "In New York and Connecticut," wrote Niles in April, "the term Whigs is now used by the opponents of the administration when speaking of themselves, and they call the Jackson men by the offensive name of Tories." Clay had used the term with great emphasis already in March, in one of his "distress" speeches, commenting upon an anti-administration success in a municipal election in New York city.

"It was a brilliant and signal triumph of the Whigs [he said]. And they have assumed for themselves, and bestowed on their opponents, a denomination which, according to all the analogy of history, is strictly correct. It deserves to be extended throughout the whole country. What was the origin among our British ancestors of these appellations? The Tories were the supporters of executive power, of royal prerogative, of the maxim that the king could do no wrong, of the detestable doctrine of passive obedience and non-resistance. The Whigs were the champions of liberty, the friends of the people, and the defenders of their representatives in the House of Commons. During the Revolutionary war the Tories took sides with the king against liberty, the Whigs against royal executive power and for freedom and independence. And what is the present but the same contest in another form? The partisans of the present executive sustain his power in the most boundless extent. The Whigs are opposing executive encroachment, and a most alarming extension of executive power and prerogative. They are contending for the rights of the people, for free institutions, for the supremacy of the Constitution and the laws."

The name of "Whig" remained, but Clay did not succeed in fastening the name of "Tory" upon their adversaries. The Whig party was strengthened by the accession of men from the Democratic side who were alarmed at Jackson's proceedings and sought refuge among the opposition. Thus it received in its ranks a mixture of incongruous elements which were destined, in the course of events, to break out in distracting divergences of opinion. Moreover, the common opposition to Jackson had brought them into relations of alliance with Calhoun and his following of nullifiers. This was a source of great discomfort to Clay. On every possible occasion Calhoun pushed his nullification principles to the foreground, and began to taunt Clay with having been obliged to fall back upon the aid of the nullifiers to save protection. Clay treated Calhoun with great courtesy, but the companionship galled him. "The nullifiers are doing us no good," he wrote to Brooke, in April, 1834. The alliance was felt on both sides to be an unnatural one that could not endure.

The anti-Jackson current in the local elections, which cheered the Whigs so much, did not last long. The business panic caused by the removal of the deposits was for a time genuine and serious enough. But, as people became aware that the removal of the deposits did not mean the immediate breaking down of everything, the crisis gradually subsided, and the opposition lost much of their political capital. It became evident that the defection from Jackson, which his high-handed course had caused in the upper political circles, had not reached the masses. The spokesman of the Jackson party very adroitly persisted in representing the opposition of the leaders of the Senate to the President's policy as a mere incident of the great struggle going on between the "old hero" and the "monster." Clay saw this very clearly; "but," said he, "it was in vain that we protested, solemnly protested, that that [the bank] was not the question; that the true question comprehended the inviolability of the Constitution, the supremacy of the laws." Such protests were of no avail. It may then have dawned upon Clay's mind how unwise it had been to make the bank a political issue and to fasten it like a clog to his foot.

The very business distress, which at one time seemed to become so dangerous to Jackson, was at last made to tell against the bank. The great mass of mankind can easily be induced to believe evil of a powerful moneyed institution. It was not difficult, therefore, to spread the impression that the whole calamity had really been inflicted upon the country by the bank, the heartless monopoly, which without necessity curtailed its loans, pinched all business interests, and ruined merchants, manufacturers, and laborers, in order to bring an enormous pressure upon the President and Congress for the purpose of extorting from them the restoration of the deposits and the grant of a new charter. A monopoly so malicious and tyrannical must, of course, be in the highest degree dangerous to the public welfare and to popular liberty; it had to be put down, and there was nobody to put it down save the old hero; he was willing, and it was for this that the "minions of the money power," the "slaves of the monster monopoly," the "subjects of the bank," in the Senate, were persecuting him.

With the first session of the twenty-third Congress the struggle about the Bank of the United States was substantially decided. The great parliamentary cannonade in the Senate had availed nothing. The storm of distress petitions had been without effect. Jackson had remained firm. The House of Representatives had passed by large majorities a series of resolutions reported by James K. Polk, that the deposits should not be restored, and that the bank charter should not be renewed. Popular sentiment ran in the same direction. The bank was doomed. Jackson went on denouncing it in his messages, and distressing it with all sorts of hostile measures; but all energy of resistance was gone. It would have been well for Clay and his party had they recognized the fact that not

THE REMOVAL OF THE DEPOSITS

only this Bank of the United States could not be saved, but that no other great central bank, as the fiscal agent of the government, could be put in its place with benefit to the country.

When Jackson became President the bank was financially sound. The management was not faultless, but very fair. It did not meddle with politics. A financial institution of that kind is not naturally inclined to become a political agency. Its stockholders, who are anxious for the safety of their investments and desire to draw regular dividends, do not wish it to involve itself in the fortunes and struggles of political parties. This was the disposition of the United States Bank under Nicholas Biddle. Jackson's first attack upon the bank in that respect was therefore wanton and reckless. But it is also true that an institution whose interests depend upon the favor of the government is always apt to be driven into politics, be it by the exactions of its political friends or by the attacks of its political enemies. Its capacity for mischief will then be proportioned to the greatness of its power; and the power of a central bank, acting as the fiscal agent of the government, disposing of a large capital, and controlling branch banks all over the country, must necessarily be very large. Being able to encourage or embarrass business by expanding or curtailing bank accommodations, and to favor this and punish that locality by transferring its facilities, it may benefit or injure the interests of large masses of men, and thereby exercise an influence upon their political conduct, — not to speak of its opportunities for propitiating men in public position, as well as the press, by its substantial favors. So it was in the case of the Bank of the United States. Although Jackson's denunciations of its corrupting practices went far beyond the truth, there can be no doubt that, when it at last fought for the renewal of its charter and against the removal of the deposits, it did use its power for political effect.

It might be said that it did so in self-defense, and that, had there not been so violent a character in the presidential office, it would not have been obliged to defend itself. This would be an unsafe conjecture. A great central banking institution, a government agent, enjoying valuable privileges, will always have the flavor of monopoly about it, — and there is nothing more hateful than the idea of monopoly among a democratic people. It will always excite popular jealousy by the appearance of offering to a limited circle of persons superior opportunities of acquiring wealth at the public expense. It will always arouse popular apprehensions with regard to the harm it might do as a great concentrated money power. These apprehensions and jealousies will, in a democratic community, at any time be apt to break out, cause an attack upon the institution, and oblige it to "fight" in self-defense. Being attacked on the political field it will, in obedience to a natural impulse, try to protect itself on the political field, and thus easily become a dangerous and demoralizing factor in politics.

An institution like the Bank of the United States, whatever its temporary usefulness may have been, is therefore not a proper fiscal agent for the government of a democratic country; and the American people have reason to remember with gratitude Salmon P. Chase and the Congress of 1863 for having, in the greatest crisis of public affairs, given the country a national banking system equal to the United States Bank in efficiency, superior to it in safety, avoiding the evils of a concentrated money power, and, as subsequently perfected, entirely free from that flavor of monopoly which made the old bank in its time so odious.

Andrew Jackson's severest critics will have to admit that his war upon the United States Bank appealed to a sound democratic instinct, and negatively served a good end. But his most ardent admirers will hardly deny that the manner in which he accomplished the overthrow of the bank was utterly reckless, not only on account of the violence which was done to the spirit of the law, but also on account of the disposition which was made of the public funds. They were distributed among state banks, without any system, unless it be called a system that political favoritism had much to do with the selection, and that the deposit of the public funds became to a great extent a part of the executive patronage. Capital in the shape of bank deposits was arbitrarily located in different parts of the country, to be liberally used for bank accommodations, and this in constantly increasing sums as the public debt disappeared and the revenue surplus grew larger. Great rivalry sprang up among the state banks for a share of the deposits. New banks were started by aspiring individuals who hoped to be among the favored ones. Banks multiplied in all directions. Upon the business depression followed one of those expansions of credit which are so exhilarating in the beginning and so sure to end in disaster, and the scattering of the deposits served to make that expansion more and more reckless.

Thus the seed of a great disaster was sown broadcast. We shall see the harvest. But at first it looked like a suddenly growing crop of prosperity and wealth. Jackson was more popular and powerful than ever. Clay came out of the struggle about the United States Bank defeated, but with the honors of war. His friends clung to him with increased admiration of his courage and brilliant abilities, and he was ready for new conflicts.

CHAPTER XVI

FRENCH DIFFICULTIES. — INDIANS. — PATRONAGE

When the second session of the twenty-third Congress opened, in December, 1834, the United States found themselves in danger of a war with France. It was a curious entanglement. The United States had many and heavy claims against France for damages on account of the depredations committed upon American shipping by the French during the Napoleonic wars. Ever since 1815 these claims had been the subject of fruitless negotiation. In 1829 President Jackson caused them to be pressed with vigor, and in his first annual message he said that, if they were not satisfied, they would "continue to furnish a subject of unpleasant discussion and possible collision." The French government, Charles X. still being king, considered this "menacing" language, and, as such, a sufficient reason for doing nothing. But Louis Philippe, seated on the French throne by the Revolution of 1830, chose not to remember the menace; and on July 4, 1831, a treaty was concluded in Paris, by which France promised to pay the United States $5,000,000 in six installments, to begin one year after the ratification of the treaty, while the United States were to make certain reductions in the duties on French wines. Congress promptly passed a law accordingly. The treaty was ratified on February 2, 1832: the first French payment was therefore due on February 2, 1833. A draft was drawn upon the French government, and presented to the French minister of finance at Paris. But payment was refused on the ground that the French Chambers had made no appropriation for that purpose. There was at the time no American minister at Paris. Edward Livingston, whom we have met as secretary of state, vacating that office for McLane, was sent, with strong instructions, to fill that position. King Louis Philippe promised to do his best with the Chambers, but the appropriation failed again. The French king is said then to have confidentially intimated to Livingston that an earnest passage in the President's next message might serve to induce the French Chambers to give attention to the subject. Livingston reported something like this to his government. For earnest passages Jackson was the man. He put a paragraph into his annual message of December, 1834, in which, after recapitulating the whole story, he bluntly recommended that "a law be passed authorizing reprisals upon French property, in case provision shall not be made for the payment of the debt at the approaching session of the French Chambers."

That was undoubtedly more earnestness than King Louis Philippe had meant to suggest. What

Jackson asked of Congress fell little short of a declaration of war. When the message and the report of the diplomatic correspondence, published by the State Department, became known in Paris, the French press of all parties cried out against it as a wanton insult offered to the French nation; and the government, finding itself obliged to yield to the clamor, resolved to recall the French minister from Washington, and to tender Livingston his passports. It was a thoroughly Jacksonian situation.

There being neither telegraphs nor fast steamers in those days, the effect produced by Jackson's message in France, and the recall of the French minister, could not become known in Washington until late in February, 1835. But statesmen who had some knowledge of the manner in which governments speak of one another easily foresaw what impression President Jackson's spirited language would make. They foresaw, also, that the demonstrations of resentment excited in France by the President's message would be apt to be as offensive to the American people as the President's message had been to the French, and that then, both governments having assumed positions from which they could not honorably withdraw, the two countries might drift into war in spite of their inmost wish to remain at peace. It was therefore important that something be done to keep the possibility of friendly negotiation open, before the news of the reception in France of the President's message should arrive in the United States. This task was undertaken by Clay. He knew well how dangerous it would be to give to a man of Jackson's hot temper the power to make reprisals upon French property; and he felt, too, that it would be a shame and disgrace to go to war with a friendly nation upon a mere question of money, until the last resources of peaceable diplomacy should have been exhausted. He therefore took the matter promptly in hand.

That part of the President's message which related to the French business was referred to the Senate Committee on Foreign Relations, of which Clay was chairman. On January 6, 1835, he made a report on the subject, which he himself read to the Senate, and which had the rare fortune to call forth the applause of all parties. He gave a lucid review of the history of the case, and with dignified emphasis asserted the right of the United States to indemnity. He affirmed that, in their determination to protect the rights of the United States, the President, and the opposition, and the whole American people, stood inseparably together. He then pointed out the friendly disposition of Louis Philippe's government; the difficulties it had to contend with; the misapprehensions which in the course of the negotiation had arisen between the two governments, creating unnecessary irritation. He then explained President Jackson's position, how the President did not insist upon reprisals as the only remedy; how he suggested them only as an alternative, if Congress did not choose to wait longer for favorable action on the part of the French ; how he did not look upon reprisals under such circumstances as absolutely a measure of hostility, and expressly disclaimed his recommendation to have been intended as a menace. On the other hand, Clay admitted that it might easily be misunderstood as a menace, and that a resort to reprisals was apt to be regarded and resented as an act of war. It behooved the government of the United States not to anticipate a final breach by France of her solemn engagements, and, while firmly standing by our rights as set forth by the President, to treat her with confidence in her honor and good faith.

This was the drift of Clay's report. He also offered a resolution declaring it " inexpedient, at this time, to pass any law vesting in the President authority for making reprisals upon French property," etc. This resolution, modified, with Clay's consent, to spare Jackson's feelings, so as to read, " that it is inexpedient at present to adopt any legislative measures in regard to the state of affairs between the United States and France," was then adopted by a unanimous vote.

Thus Clay's point was gained. The existing irritation was soothed, and Jackson did not receive the means to force the country into a war with France whenever his temper might run away with his judgment. The sequel of the story is interesting. The French Chambers were so far pacified that in April they passed an appropriation for the three installments then due, — not to be paid, however, until after the French government should have received "satisfactory explanations" with regard to President Jackson's message of December, 1834. Jackson understood this to mean something like a demand for an apology, and an apology he would not give. He said so in his annual message of 1835, declaring however, at the same time, that he had never intended any "menace." The *chargé d'affaires*, left behind by Livingston, was instructed to make a formal demand for the money without the apology. Payment was refused. Both governments called home their diplomatic representatives. Jackson, in a special message in January, 1836, recommended that Congress pass a law that French ships and goods be excluded from American ports. Things looked more threatening than ever. Then Great Britain interposed with her good offices, which were accepted by both parties. The French government was induced to declare that Jackson's message, in which he had incidentally said that no menace had been intended, was a sufficient explanation: the money was paid and the trouble was over. It must be added that in popular estimation General Jackson had "beaten the French," and he was in the eyes of the masses a greater hero than ever, — not unnaturally so; for his style of diplomacy, no doubt, convinced all Europe that this republic could not safely be trifled with. But it was largely due to Clay's skillful interposition that the

French business did not take a warlike turn at the start, and that the United States carried their point, and raised their standing among the nations of the world, without firing a gun.

Returning to the second session of the twenty-third Congress, we find Clay advocating a just and generous treatment of the Indians, in a manner worthy of notice, because it proved how a man who had a low opinion of the Indian character, and believed the Indian race doomed to decay and extinction, still might recognize his duty to protect them in their rights. When Clay was secretary of state under John Quincy Adams, the question of incorporating the Indians in the general body of citizenship happened to be discussed at a cabinet meeting, when Clay, according to Adams's Diary, expressed these opinions: that it was impossible to civilize Indians; it was not in their nature; he believed they were destined to extinction; and, although he would never use or countenance inhumanity toward them, he did not think them, as a race, worth preserving.

It is scarcely possible to pronounce upon the Indians a more unfavorable judgment. We hear in it rather the voice of the frontiersman than of the philanthropist. But when the rights of the Indian were attacked, Clay vigorously entered his plea for justice.

This was the occasion. From some of the Cherokees in Georgia, who had attained a respectable degree of civilization, and then were driven away by the greed of the white man from their lands and churches and schools, Clay received a memorial praying Congress to aid them in emigrating from Georgia to the Indian Territory. Clay, in presenting the memorial to the Senate, told in burning words the story of the wrongs the Cherokees had to suffer, and then uttered these sentiments: —

"Shall I be told that the condition of the African slave is worse? No, sir, it is not worse. The interest of the master makes it at once his duty and his inclination to provide for the comfort and the health of his slave. But who, what human being, stands in the relation of master, or in any other relation which makes him interested in the preservation and protection of the poor Indian thus degraded and miserable? It is said that annihilation is the destiny of the Indian race. Perhaps it is, judging from the past. But shall we therefore hasten it? Death is the irreversible decree pronounced against the human race. Shall we accelerate its approach because it is inevitable? No, sir. Let us treat with the utmost kindness and the most perfect justice the aborigines whom Providence has committed to our guardianship. Let us confer upon them, if we can, the inestimable blessings of Christianity and civilization; and then, if they must sink beneath the progressive wave, we are free from all reproach, and stand acquitted in the sight of God and man."

With such remarks he introduced resolutions contemplating further provision by law to enable Indian tribes to defend and maintain in the courts of the United States their rights to lands secured to them by treaty, to set apart a district west of the Mississippi for Cherokees disposed to emigrate there, and to secure to them and their descendants in perpetuity the peaceful and undisturbed enjoyment thereof. His was the correct doctrine in regard to the Indians: let them have justice; and, if they cannot be made as civilized and useful citizens as white people, let them be made as civilized and useful as it is possible to make them.

During the same session an attempt was made to arrest by law the flagrant abuses which President Jackson's arbitrary course in making removals and appointments had spread in the machinery of the general government and on the field of national politics. The statesmen of the time felt keenly the growing danger. They were alarmed at the demoralization which the vicious doctrine, that public office should be treated as the spoil of party victory, was infusing into all the channels of political life. They looked for a remedy. Arbitrary removals for partisan reasons, scarcely ever known before, never thought possible in the extent to which Jackson carried them, were the first scandal, in his treatment of the public service, which startled thoughtful men. It was natural, therefore, that a limitation of the removing power should have been the first remedy thought of. On February 9, 1835, Calhoun made a report from a committee appointed to inquire into the extent of the executive patronage, and kindred subjects. The report portrayed the existing abuses in a startling picture, and recommended the passage of a bill repealing the act of 1820 limiting to four years the tenure of certain offices, and providing further "that, in all nominations made by the President to the Senate to fill vacancies occasioned by removal from office, the facts of the removal shall be stated to the Senate, with a statement of the reasons for such removal."

The debate, one of the most instructive on that subject in the history of Congress, was mainly carried on by Calhoun, Clay, Webster, and Ewing on the side of the report. They were all united in the opinion that the Constitution did not give to the President the absolute power of removal. The contrary construction put upon the Constitution by the first Congress was by no means overlooked by them. But they thought that the strength of argument had been then, as it was now, altogether on the other side; that it was impossible to read the debate in the first Congress "without being impressed with the conviction that the just confidence reposed in the Father of his Country, then at the head of the government, had great, if not decisive, influence in establishing" that construction of the Constitution. They held "that the power of appointment naturally and necessarily included the power of removal," both to be exercised by the President by and with the advice and consent of the Senate. They admitted, however, that the construction given to the Constitution in 1789 had become established by practice and recognized by subsequent laws. But they insisted, as Webster expressed it, that Congress clearly had the power "of regulating the condition, duration, qualification, and tenure of office in all cases where the Constitution has made no express provision on the subject;" and that, therefore, it was "competent for Congress to declare by law, as one qualification of office, that the incumbent shall remain in place till the President shall remove him for reasons to be stated to the Senate." This last proposition it is very difficult to controvert.

Clay went beyond the recommendation of the report. A year before, in March, 1834, he had proposed a series of resolutions, the gist of which he now moved by way of amendment, providing that in all instances of appointment to office by the President, with the consent of the Senate, the power of removal should be exercised only in concurrence with the Senate; but that during the vacation of the Senate the President should have the power to suspend any such officer, with the duty to communicate his reasons for the suspension to the Senate during the first month of its succeeding session, when, if the Senate concurred with him, the officer should be removed, and, if the Senate did not concur, the officer should be reinstated. Clay was induced not to urge his amendment, and he dropped it. But it was destined to come to life again more than thirty years later, when, during President Johnson's administration, Congress embodied its substance in the famous tenure-of-office act.

Clay supported with some pointed arguments the proposition of the committee that it should be the duty of the President to communicate to the Senate the reasons for the removals made. "It has been truly said," he remarked, "that the office was not made for the incumbent. Nor was it created for the incumbent of another office. In both and in all cases, public offices are created for the public; and the people have a right to know why and wherefore one of their servants dismisses another."

It was then, as it is now, argued that the absolute power of removal must be vested in the executive, because summary proceedings were sometimes required for the good of the service, and also because the responsibility for removals must definitely rest upon somebody. Concerning this part of the subject, as it had been discussed by Madison in 1789, Clay said: —

"He [Madison] says, 'The danger, then, merely consists in this: the President can displace from office a man whose merits require that he should be continued in it. What will be the motives which the President can feel for such an abuse of his power?' What motives! The pure heart of a Washington could have had none; the virtuous head of a Madison could conceive none; but let him ask General Jackson, and he will tell him of motives enough. He will tell him that he wishes his administration to be a unit; that he desires only one will to prevail in the executive branch of the government; that he cannot confide in men who opposed his

TENURE OF OFFICE

election; that he wants places to reward those who supported it; that the spoils belong to the victors. And what do you suppose are the securities against the abuse of this power on which Mr. Madison relied? 'In the first place,' he says, 'he will be impeachable by the House before the Senate for such an act of maladministration,' and so forth. Impeachment! It is a scarecrow. Impeach the President for dismissing a receiver or register of the land office, or a collector of the customs!"

Clay went on to show that the other "security" mentioned by Madison, "that the President, after displacing the meritorious officer, could not appoint another person without the concurrence of the Senate," could not at all be depended upon to prevent the abuse of the removing power by the executive, because the President alone would exercise the power of nomination, and weary the Senate finally into accepting somebody selected by the executive.

Clay apparently did not foresee what part the Senate itself would play in the development of "spoils" politics. At that period, indeed, the procuring of offices, the manipulation of the patronage, had not yet become an absorbing occupation among legislators. It was still thought that the legitimate business of statesmanship concerned other things. The "courtesy of the Senate," which, in acting upon nominations made by the President, puts personal considerations above all others and keeps in view the solidarity of senatorial advantages, had not yet risen to the dignity of a system.

The danger that "tenure of office laws" might become sources of corrupt practices in the Senate did not yet appear. The principal agency of evil was, therefore, still seen in the executive. Nor was this at all illogical. "Spoils" politics had indeed been carried to an alarming extent in some States before. The greed of office-seekers had been many a time complained of in Washington. But the wisdom and patriotic firmness of the men in the executive chair of the national government had successfully restrained the dangerous tendency down to the close of John Quincy Adams's administration. It was then, with Jackson's advent to power, the executive hand that opened the floodgates, against the judgment, and even against the indignant protest, of the first order of statesmen in Congress. Nothing could have been more natural, therefore, than that the executive should have been held wholly responsible for the mischief, and that in restraints to be put upon the executive the remedy should have been sought.

It is true, the aspect of the matter has since changed somewhat. The offices of the government having once been declared to be the "spoils" of the victorious party, senators and representatives in Congress seized upon the opportunities thus opened to them. They learned how to serve themselves by apparently serving their constituents. Then members of Congress found themselves set upon by a pressure of demand from partisan office-seekers, and presidents from members of Congress, which demand constantly grew in overbearing and tyrannical force as it gradually acquired the sanction of established custom. That is the "spoils system" as we know it in our days. We therefore no longer see the agency of the evil in the executive alone.

But even now no remedy has been devised the efficacy of which does not depend upon the action of the executive. No reform law has ever been suggested — unless it be one forbidding members of Congress to meddle with appointments to office — which has not for its object to restrain the executive in making arbitrary appointments and removals, or to serve the executive as a protecting bulwark against the pressure of the spoils politicians. Neither is the prevention of arbitrary removals less important now than it was then; for the facility of making arbitrary partisan removals will always encourage the making of appointments for mere personal or partisan ends. The statesmen of the twenty-third Congress were, therefore, not only right in their day, but they would be equally right in our day, in proposing a measure to prevent the arbitrary use of the removing and appointing power. Nor was the measure they advocated, although mild, unwisely chosen.

Clay readily admitted the "necessity of some more summary and less expensive and less dilatory mode of dismissing delinquents from subordinate offices than that of impeachment, which, strictly speaking, was perhaps the only one in the contemplation of the framers of the Constitution." Neither would the measure he recommended curtail the discretion of the executive in this respect. He said : —

"By the usage of the government, — not, I think, by the Constitution, — the President possesses the power to dismiss those who are unworthy of holding these offices. By no practice or usage, but that which he himself has created, has he the power to dismiss meritorious officers only because they differ from him in politics. The principal object of the bill is to require the President, in cases of dismission, to communicate the reasons which have induced him to dismiss the officer ; in other words, to make an arbitrary and despotic power a responsible power. It is not to be supposed that, if the President is bound publicly to state his reasons, he would act from passion or caprice, or without any reason. He would be ashamed to avow that he discharged the officer because he opposed his election."

Clay might have said more ; a president, or any officer intrusted with the power of removal, would find in such an obligation a most powerful protection against the urgency of those demanding removals, the reasons for which cannot honorably be avowed.

This proposition was vigorously supported by the statesmen whose names stand foremost in the political history of that period ; and it is a remarkable fact that the repeal of the four years' term act received in the Senate a vote of 31 to 16, and that among the majority we find the celebrities of both parties, such as Bell, Benton, Calhoun, Clay, Clayton, Ewing, Frelinghuysen, Mangum, Poindexter, Preston, Southard, Tyler, Webster, and White; while among those sustaining the four years' act there were, of well-known names, only Buchanan, Silas Wright, and King of Alabama. Even such friends of General Jackson as Benton and White voted for the repeal. But the reformatory effort did not go beyond the Senate, and was therefore fruitless.

CHAPTER XVII

SLAVERY

THE opening of the twenty-fourth Congress in December, 1835, found Clay greatly afflicted by the death of a favorite daughter. But he turned resolutely to his public duties. Early in the session he introduced his land bill again, which, as we have seen, had once passed Congress, but had been prevented from becoming a law by President Jackson's disapproval. Again he protested that the proposition to distribute the proceeds of the land sales among the States was "not founded upon any notion of a power in Congress to lay and collect taxes, and distribute the amount among the several States." The bill passed the Senate again later in the session, but failed in the House of Representatives.

But a bill did pass which carried into effect the worst feature of Clay's land bill, — providing that the money in the treasury on January 1, 1837, excepting $5,000,000, should be "deposited" with the several States in proportion to their representation in Congress, in four quarterly installments, to be returned on the call of Congress. This bill President Jackson signed, "reluctantly," he said, and we shall see the outcome of it.

SLAVERY

But now another problem pressed to the front, far more portentous than all the questions of banks and deposits and lands, which agitated the public mind under Jackson's turbulent presidency. In Benton's "Abridgment of the Debates of Congress" the following short foot-note is attached to the Senate proceedings of January 7, 1836: "At this session the slavery discussion became installed in Congress, and has too unhappily kept its place ever since." The slavery question had assumed a new character.

The great excitement called forth by the admission of Missouri had been allayed by compromise. During the decade which followed, the slaveholding interest had indeed made itself felt in politics, but usually in disguise. The subject of slavery in its large moral and political aspects had been the occasional topic of discussion, but only in a passing way, except among a class of people who soon were to rise into unlooked-for importance, — the "abolitionists."

A few old anti-slavery societies had continued a quiet existence, most of them in the South, without creating any alarm. Then appeared on the stage, with all his peculiar strength, that formidable revolutionary factor in human affairs, the man of one idea. Anti-slavery missionaries came forth, who carried the word, spoken and written, from place to place: first, Benjamin Lundy, a mild-mannered Quaker mechanic, whose "heart was deeply grieved at the gross abomination" when he "heard the wail of the captive;" then William Lloyd Garrison, a young printer and editor from Massachusetts, who was moved by Lundy's words, and put into his work the fierce energy of a fiery spirit revolting against a great wrong. With these came a host of men equally devoted. They taught that not only the slaveholders, but the people of the free States too, — in fact, all the citizens of this republic, — were responsible for the "crime of slavery;" and Garrison went so far as to insist that, not the colonization of free negroes, nor the gradual emancipation of the slaves, but the unconditional and immediate abolition of slavery was the duty enjoined by moral law upon all righteous men.

Such was the faith professed by the abolitionists who in 1831 began to organize the New England Anti-slavery Society, and started a movement which presently spread over the free States. Their principles and aims were most clearly put forth by the National Anti-slavery Convention held at Philadelphia in December, 1833. It declared that the American people were bound to "repent at once," to let the slaves go free, and to admit them to an equality of rights with all others; that there was, in point of principle, no difference between slaveholding and man-stealing; that no compensation should be given to slaveholders emancipating their slaves, because what they claimed as property was really not property, and because, if any compensation were to be given at all, it belonged justly to the slaves. They admitted that Congress had no constitutional power to abolish slavery in the States; but they insisted that Congress had power to suppress the domestic slave trade, and to abolish slavery "in the District of Columbia, and in those portions of our territory which the Constitution has placed under its exclusive jurisdiction;" and this power Congress was in duty bound to exercise. The methods of "working for the cause" recommended by the convention consisted in the organization of societies, in the sending out of missionaries to explain and exhort, in circulating anti-slavery tracts and periodicals, in enlisting the pulpit and the press in the work, in giving preference to the products of free labor over those of slave labor, — in one word, "in sparing no exertions nor means in bringing the whole nation to speedy repentance."

This agitation was carried on with singular devotion, but its startling radicalism did not at first enlist large numbers of converts, or result in the organization of a political force that might have made itself felt at the polls. It did, however, have the effect of exciting great irritation and alarm among the slaveholders, and among those in the North who feared that a searching discussion of the slavery question might disturb the peace of the country; and thus it started a commotion of grave consequences.

About that time the South was in an unusually nervous state of mind. In 1831 an insurrection of slaves broke out in Virginia under the leadership of Nat Turner, a religious fanatic. It was easily suppressed, but caused a widespread panic. In 1833 the emancipation of the slaves in the British West Indies made the slaveholders keenly sensible of the hostility of public opinion in the outside world, and increased their alarm. Events like these gave the agitation of the abolitionists a new significance. The slave power found it necessary to assert to the utmost, not only its constitutional rights, but also its moral position. Abandoning its apologetic attitude, it proclaimed its belief that slavery was not an evil, but economically, politically, and morally a positive good, and " the corner-stone of the republican edifice." It fiercely denounced the Northern abolitionists as reckless incendiaries, inciting the slaves to insurrection, rapine, and murder, — as enemies to the country, as fiends in human shape, who deserved the halter. What disturbed the slaveholders most was the instinctive feeling that now they had to meet an antagonist who was inspired by something akin to religious enthusiasm, which could neither be argued with nor cajoled nor frightened, but could be suppressed only with a strong hand, if it could be suppressed at all. They imperiously demanded of the people of the North that the abolitionists be silenced by force; that laws be made to imprison their orators, to stop their presses, to prevent the circulation of their tracts, and by every means to put down their agitation. They said that, unless this were done, the Union could not be maintained.

In the North their appeal did not remain unheeded. A fierce outcry arose in the free States against the abolitionists. Turbulent mobs, composed in part of men of property and prominent standing, broke up their meetings, destroyed their printing-offices, wrecked their houses, and threatened them with violent death. There were riotous attacks upon anti-slavery gatherings in Philadelphia, New York, Utica, and Montpelier. In Boston, William Lloyd Garrison was dragged through the streets with a halter round his body. In Connecticut and New Hampshire, schools which received colored pupils were sacked. In Cincinnati, a large meeting of citizens resolved that an anti-slavery paper published there must cease to appear, and that there must be "total silence on the subject of slavery." An excited mob executed the decree, threw the press into the Ohio, and looted the homes of colored people. Some time later, Pennsylvania Hall, the meeting house of the abolitionists, was burned in Philadelphia, and Elijah P. Lovejoy was murdered in Illinois.

It was a strange commotion. There was the timid citizen, who feared that the anti-slavery agitation might split the Union, and believed that the abolitionists were bent upon inciting slave insurrection; there was the politician, intent upon currying favor with the South; there was the merchant and manufacturer, anxious to protect his

Southern market against disturbance, and to please his Southern customer; there was the fanatic of stability, cursing everybody who, as he thought, "wanted to make trouble;" there was the man who "had always been opposed to slavery as much as anybody," but who detested the abolitionists because they would sacrifice the country to their one idea, presumed to sit in judgment upon other good people's motives, and accused them of "compounding with crime;" there was the rabble, bent upon keeping the negro still beneath them in the social scale, and delighting in riotous excesses as a congenial pastime, — all these elements coöperating in the persecution of a few men, who in all sincerity followed the dictates of their consciences, and, somewhat ahead of their time, demanded the general and immediate application of principles which, at the North, almost everybody had accepted in the abstract.

But this violent persecution could not accomplish its object. On the contrary, it could scarcely fail to strengthen the cause it was designed to put down. Many of the "intelligent and respectable citizens," who had countenanced it, remembered it with shame when the first heat was over. Who, after all, were the abolitionists, those "incendiaries," "fiends," "enemies of human society"? Who were the Lundys, Garrisons, and Tappans? They were men of pure lives who, believing slavery to be a great wrong which must be abolished, the great crime of the age which must be expiated, devoted themselves to an unpopular cause, and, serving it, suffered obloquy and social ostracism and mob violence without flinching. In doing what they did, they could win neither money nor popularity nor power. Their work was one of constant self-denial and sacrifice. It is true they were not, in the ordinary sense, statesmen. They did not weigh present possibilities. They did not measure immediate consequences. They did not calculate the relation between the means available and the ends to be accomplished. But theirs was after all the statesmanship of the prophets, which is seldom appreciated by the living generation. If it was true that the universal and immediate emancipation they preached could not be undertaken without great economic disturbance, pecuniary loss, social disorder, and perhaps bloodshed, it was equally true that the longer emancipation was put off the more inevitable and the greater would be the loss, disorder, and bloodshed. The abolitionists had a sublime belief in the justice of their cause, and in the sacredness of their duty to serve that cause. Thus they had the stuff in them of which the moral heroes in history are made. It is difficult to imagine a figure more heroic than William Lloyd Garrison with the rope about his body, the respectability of the town howling for his blood. The unselfishness of their devotion did not fail to extort respect. Such men could not be suppressed. They forced an unwilling people to hear them, and they were heard.

The number of abolition societies grew, not rapidly, but steadily. The leading abolitionists themselves never became popular with the multitude. With many men, the intrusive admonition of conscience is peculiarly irritating. But the immediate effect of their work has frequently been much underrated. The abolitionists served to keep alive in the Northern mind that secret trouble of conscience about slavery which later, in a ripe political situation, was to break out as a great force. They accomplished another immediate result of the highest importance. By the alarm they excited in the South they caused slavery to disclose to public view, more openly than ever before, those tendencies which made it incompatible with the fundamental conditions of free government.

The means which an institution or an interest needs for its defense, when attacked by the criticism of public opinion, may be taken as a test of its consistency with a democratic organization of society. When such an institution or interest cannot stand before the tribunal of free discussion, the question will soon arise which of the two shall give way. This question the abolitionists caused to be put before the American people with regard to slavery. While Northern mobs assaulted abolition conventions, and Northern meetings passed resolutions assuring the slaveholders of the sympathy of the Northern people, Southern journals, speakers, and legislatures demanded that, although occasional mobbings and anti-abolition resolutions were well in their way, the anti-slavery agitation, the publication of anti-slavery tracts, the delivery of anti-slavery speeches in the Northern States, should be put down by penal laws. But then it turned out that Northern men, who had favored the mobs and voted for the resolutions, instinctively recoiled from the enactment of laws clearly hostile to the freedom of speech and press. They felt the difference between the occasional violence of a mob — a passing occurrence — and a solemn act of legislation, the establishment of a permanent rule. They had been willing to do a lawless thing, but they were not willing to make that thing legal. There the slave power was asking too much. No Northern State made the laws demanded by it; and the Southern press was not slow to declare that the anti-abolition resolutions adopted by Northern meetings had no real value as to the safety of slavery, if the Northern States refused to clothe the sentiments professed with the strength of law.

It was under these circumstances that, as Benton expressed it, "the slavery discussion became installed in Congress," thenceforward to keep its place. For some years abolition societies had sent petitions to Congress praying for the abolition of slavery in the District of Columbia, and of the slave trade, without creating much excitement. The twenty-fourth Congress was flooded with them, and they were taken more seriously. In the Senate, Calhoun denounced them as incendiary documents and moved that they be not received. There was, then, slavery against the right of petition. Buchanan, to whom some of them had come from his Quaker constituents, — a circumstance which moved him to caution, — proposed that the petitions be received, but that the prayer they contained be at once rejected without further consideration. Thus, he thought, the right of petition would receive due respect without leaving any misapprehension as to the sentiment of the Senate concerning the subject-matter. Northern senators with anti-slavery leanings insisted that the petitions should be referred to the appropriate committee for consideration and report. Thus the issue was made up, causing a warm debate which ran over two months, as it happened, in both houses at the same time.

Clay's republican principles revolted at a curtailment of the right of petition. His old anti-slavery sentiments, too, were still strong enough to make him desire that anti-slavery petitions be treated at least with respect. He therefore opposed Calhoun's motion not to receive them. Neither did Buchanan's proposition to receive them, but to reject the prayer without consideration, find favor in his eyes. At the same time, true to his compromising disposition, he would not encourage the abolition movement by advocating the reference of the memorials to a committee with a view to a report thereon, to further discussion, and to legislation. A motion simply to receive the petitions was carried by a large majority, Clay

SLAVERY 81

voting in the affirmative. As to the further disposition to be made of them, he preferred a middle course between their immediate and simple rejection and their reference to a committee. He moved an amendment to Buchanan's motion which, while rejecting the prayer, would at least give polite reasons for the rejection, and also define his position on the subject of slavery in the District of Columbia. The amendment recited that "the Senate, without now affirming or denying the constitutional power of Congress to grant the prayer of the petition (*i. e.* to abolish slavery in the District of Columbia), believes, even supposing the power uncontested, which it is not, that the exercise of it is inexpedient: 1, because the people of the District of Columbia have not themselves petitioned for the abolition of slavery within the District; 2, because the States of Virginia and Maryland would be injuriously affected by it as long as the institution of slavery continues to subsist within their jurisdictions, and neither of these States would probably have ceded to the United States the territory forming the District, if it had anticipated the adoption of any such measure, without expressly guarding against it; and 3, because the injury which would be inflicted by exciting alarm and apprehension in the States tolerating slavery, and by disturbing the harmony between them and the other members of the confederacy, would far exceed any practical benefit which could possibly flow from the abolition of slavery within the District."

This weak device, throwing doubt upon everything and dealing in unwarranted historical assumptions, dissatisfied both sides and found no support. Clay saw himself compelled to vote for Buchanan's motion unamended. But, while he himself held that Congress did have the constitutional power to abolish slavery in the District, the views expressed in his amendment remained the burden of his utterances during his whole public life, whenever the subject came up for discussion.

In the House of Representatives the presentation of anti-slavery memorials bore still more significant fruit. It started John Quincy Adams in his heroic struggle for the freedom of petition, which for a long time engaged the wondering attention of the whole people. It led to the adoption of the "gag rules," designed to cut off all discussion about slavery. So there was slavery as the enemy of free debate in Congress. It caused all the agitation that the abolitionists might have wished to bring on.

But the slavery question appeared in a still more startling shape. The circulation of tracts and periodicals by the abolition societies provoked an outcry from the South that those publications were calculated to incite the slaves to insurrection. On July 29, 1835, the post-office of Charleston in South Carolina was invaded by a mob, who took out what anti-slavery documents they could find and destroyed them. A public meeting, at which the clergy of all denominations appeared in a body, ratified these proceedings. The postmaster of Charleston assumed the right to prevent the circulation of such literature, and wrote to the postmaster at New York, Samuel L. Gouverneur, to stop its transmission. Gouverneur asked the postmaster-general for instructions. The postmaster-general, Amos Kendall, late of the kitchen cabinet, answered that the law had not vested any power in his department to exclude any species of newspapers or pamphlets from the mail, for such a power would be "fearfully dangerous;" but if any postmaster took the responsibility of stopping those "inflammatory papers," he would "stand justified in that step before the country and all mankind." His instructions to the postmaster at Charleston were of the same tenor. It was patriotism, he said, to disregard the law if its observance would produce a public danger. "Entertaining these views," he added, "I cannot sanction, and will not condemn, the step you have taken."

In August, 1835, the Anti-slavery Society of Massachusetts published an "Address to the Public" in which, in the most emphatic terms, it protested against the "calumny" that it circulated incendiary publications among the slaves, or had any desire to incite them to revolt. But the charge was nevertheless repeated and believed. The Southern mind had become so sensitive upon this subject that a mere declaration that all men were born equal was in some slave States condemned as "incendiary."

President Jackson, in his message of December, 1835, sternly denounced the agitation carried on by the abolitionists, and suggested the passage of a law "prohibiting under severe penalties the circulation in the Southern States, through the mail, of incendiary publications intended to instigate the slaves to insurrection." This was far from satisfying Calhoun. He insisted that such a law would be unconstitutional, for the general government, including Congress, had not the right to determine what publications should be considered incendiary or not incendiary in the several States. This would concede the power of Congress to permit the circulation in the Southern States of such publications as it pleased, and thus Congress would be virtually clothed with the power of abolishing slavery in the States. The States themselves had to take care of their internal peace and security, and therefore to determine what was, and what was not, calculated to disturb that peace. The general government was simply bound to respect the measures thought necessary by the slaveholding States for their protection, and to coöperate in their execution as much as should be necessary. In other words, the slave States had to make the law, and it was the duty of the general government to help in enforcing it. If the general government failed to perform this duty, the slave States must look to themselves for their protection as independent communities. This was Calhoun's reasoning.

Accordingly he offered a bill providing that it should be unlawful for any postmaster knowingly to deliver to any one any printed paper touching slavery in any State or Territory where such publications were prohibited, and that any offending postmaster should be instantly removed; and that postmasters should from time to time advertise such publications, when received, for withdrawal by the senders, and destroy the detained mail matter if not withdrawn in one month. Thus slavery appeared as the enemy of the security of the mails.

Another hot slavery discussion followed. Calhoun's reasoning and bill were riddled with objections. It was eloquently set forth that here Calhoun was pushing his state-rights doctrines to an extreme never before heard of; that he attempted to make the laws of slave States, encroaching upon the freedom of the press, laws of the United States " by adoption; " that his bill subjected all mail matter to a censorship by the postmasters, constituting them the judges of other people's right of property in their papers, and so on.

Clay was especially outspoken. With great vigor he denounced the bill as uncalled for by public sentiment, unconstitutional, and dangerous to the liberties of the people. The action of the postmaster-general had alarmed him. Anti-slavery publications, he thought, did no harm while they were in the post-office. Only their circulation outside of it could have the dangerous effects complained of; and when they were so circulated in the slave States " it was perfectly competent for the state authorities to apply the remedy." But he could find nothing in the Constitution authorizing a federal law like the one proposed. He recognized the evil caused by incendiary publications. " But," he exclaimed, " it is too often in the condemnation of a particular evil that we are urged on to measures of dangerous tendency."

He hoped "never to see the time when the general government should undertake to correct the evil by such remedies." He declared himself opposed to it "from the first to the last." There was a tone of deep anxiety in the words of the old republican, whose heart began to be profoundly disquieted by the fear that in protecting slavery the free institutions of the country might suffer great and permanent harm.

Calhoun's bill was defeated in the Senate by a vote of 25 to 19. Of Northern senators, only Buchanan and the two senators from New York, Tallmadge and Silas Wright, voted for it. Van Buren, the vice-president, manifested his approval of it by his casting vote on some preliminary questions. He was the representative "Northern man with Southern principles." Seven Southern senators, led by Clay, voted against the bill.

A few days after this vote, George Tucker wrote to Clay that shortly before James Madison's death — Madison died on January 28, 1836 — he had

had a conversation with that veteran statesman about "the then agitating question of the efforts of the abolitionists," and that Madison had remarked: "Clay has been so successful in his compromising other disputes, I wish he could fall upon some plan of compromising this, and then all parties (or enough of all parties) might unite and make him president." It was just at that time, while listening to the extreme sentiments of Calhoun, that Clay expressed his first doubts as to the wisdom of his tariff compromise of 1833. But, as was usually the case with him, he did not reason out the why and wherefore to the end; he never learned that no compromise about slavery could last; and so he was indeed, as Madison hoped he would be, ready to compromise again whenever an occasion came.

After having given his vote against a measure which slavery demanded for its security, he had to play a part in the progress of another scheme which the slave power pushed forward for the same object, — the scheme having in view the eventual annexation of Texas.

Clay's "record" as to Texas was very curious. In 1820, as a member of the House of Representatives, he fiercely attacked the Monroe administration for having given up Texas in the Florida treaty, taking the ground that Texas was included in the Louisiana purchase, and therefore belonged to the United States. In March, 1827, when he was secretary of state under John Quincy Adams, he instructed Poinsett, the envoy of this republic to Mexico, to propose to the Mexican government the purchase of Texas for a sum of money; and, judging from the entries in Adams's Diary, the scheme was Clay's own. It was that Western ambition which wanted the republic to spread and to occupy a " big country." Now Clay was at the head of the Committee on Foreign Relations in the Senate, and the subject presented itself to him in an entirely new aspect.

Texas had in the mean time had a history. In the early part of this century American adventurers cast their eyes upon that country, and in 1819 one James Long attempted to make Texas an "independent republic." In 1821 an American citizen, Moses Austin, having obtained a large grant of land in Texas from the Mexican government, founded an American colony there, which, in its growth, recruited itself mainly from Louisiana, Mississippi, and Tennessee. The settlers brought their slaves with them, and continued to do so notwithstanding a decree of the Mexican Congress, issued in July, 1824, which forbade the importation into Mexican territory of slaves from foreign countries, and notwithstanding the Constitution adopted the same year, which declared free all children thereafter born of slaves.

About that time the slaveholders in the United States began to see in Texas an object of peculiar interest to them. The Missouri Compromise, admitting Missouri as a slave State and opening to slavery all that part of the Louisiana purchase south of 36° 30', seemed at first to give a great advantage to the slave power. But gradually it became apparent that the territory thus opened to slavery was, after all, too limited for the formation of many new slave States, while the area for the building up of free States was much larger. More territory for slavery was therefore needed to maintain the balance of power between the two sections.

At the same time the Mexican government, growing alarmed at the unruly spirit of the American colony in Texas, attached Texas to Coahuila, the two to form one State. The Constitution of Coahuila forbade the importation of slaves; and in 1829 the Republic of Mexico, by the decree of September 15, emancipated all the slaves within its boundaries. Then the American slave States found themselves flanked in the Southwest by a power not only not in sympathy with slavery, but threatening to become dangerous to its safety. The maintenance of slavery in Texas, and eventually the acquisition of that country, were thenceforth looked upon by the slaveholding interest in this republic as matters of very great importance, and the annexation project was pushed forward systematically.

First the American settlers in Texas refused to obey the Mexican decree of emancipation, and, in order to avoid an insurrection, the Mexican authorities permitted it to be understood that the decree did not embrace Texas. Thus one point was gained. Then the Southern press vigorously agitated the necessity of enlarging the area of slavery, while an interest in the North was created by organizing three land companies in New York, which used pretended Mexican land grants in Texas as the basis of issues of stock, promising to make people rich overnight, and thus drawing Texas within the circle of American business speculation. In 1830 President Jackson made another attempt to purchase Texas, offering five millions, but without success. The Mexican government, scenting the coming danger, prohibited the immigration of Americans into Texas. This, however, had no effect.

The American colony now received a capable and daring leader in Sam Houston of Tennessee, who had served with General Jackson in the Indian wars. He went to Texas for the distinct object of wresting that country from Mexico. There is reason for believing that President Jackson was not ignorant of his intentions. Revolutionary convulsions in Mexico gave the American colonists welcome opportunities for complaints, which led to collisions with the Mexican authorities. General Santa Anna, who by a successful revolutionary stroke had put himself at the head of the Mexican government, attempted to reduce the unruly Americans to obedience. In 1835 armed conflicts took place, in which the Americans frequently had the advantage. The Texans declared their independence from Mexico on March 2, 1836. The declaration was signed by about sixty men, among whom there were only two of Mexican nationality. The constitution of the new republic confirmed the existence of slavery under its jurisdiction, and surrounded it with all possible guaranties.

Meanwhile Santa Anna advanced at the head of a Mexican army to subdue the revolutionists. Atrocious butcheries marked the progress of his soldiery. On March 6 the American garrison of the Alamo was massacred, and on the 27th a large number of American prisoners at Goliad met a like fate. These atrocities created a great excitement in the United States. But on April 21 the Texans under Houston, about eight hundred strong, inflicted a crushing defeat upon Santa Anna's army of fifteen hundred men, at San Jacinto, taking Santa Anna himself prisoner. The captive Mexican president concluded an armistice with the victorious Texans, promising the evacuation of the country, and to procure the recognition of its independence; but this the Mexican Congress refused to ratify.

The government of the United States maintained, in appearance, a neutral position. President Jackson had indeed instructed General Gaines to march his troops into Texas, if he should see reason to apprehend Indian incursions. Gaines actually crossed the boundary line, and was recalled only after the Mexican minister at Washington had taken his passports. The organization of reinforcements for Houston, however, had been suffered to proceed on American soil without interference.

The news of the battle of San Jacinto was received in the United States, especially in the South, with a jubilant shout. Meetings were held and petitions sent to Congress urging the prompt recognition of Texas as an independent State. On May 23 Walker of Mississippi presented such a petition in the Senate, and moved its reference to the Committee on Foreign Relations. Calhoun, who had the necessity of increasing the number of slave States constantly in his mind, pronounced himself at once not only in favor of the immediate recognition of the independence of Texas, but of its annexation to the United States. Webster said that if the people of Texas had established a government *de facto*, it was the duty of the United States to recognize it. He was alarmed by rumors "that attempts would be made by some European government to obtain a cession of Texas from the government of Mexico." It has frequently been observed in the history of this republic that those who agitate for a territorial acquisition spread the rumor that European powers are coveting it. It is strange that Webster should have failed to penetrate that shallow device.

Clay was in no haste. Nearly four weeks later he reported from the Committee on Foreign Relations a resolution "that the independence of Texas ought to be acknowledged by the United States whenever satisfactory information shall be received that it has in successful operation a civil government capable of performing the duties and fulfilling the obligations of an independent power." This resolution he introduced by a speech in which he warned against precipitate action, and expressed the hope that further and more authentic information would soon render the recognition of Texan independence proper. But in his utterances there was nothing of that glow which had animated his speeches for the recognition of the South American republics and in behalf of Greece. He coldly suggested that it did not seem at all necessary to act upon his resolution at the present session. The reason for the conspicuous lack of ardor in all he said on this subject may without difficulty be conjectured. The man who had always shared the Western passion for territorial aggrandizement, and at a former period had strenuously insisted that Texas belonged to the United States, now was reluctant to touch it because at heart he recoiled from augmenting the political power of slavery. The very thing which made the acquisition of Texas so desirable to Calhoun, secretly alarmed Clay. His subsequent conduct with regard to the annexation of Texas fully justifies this explanation of his attitude.

His resolution, slightly amended, passed the Senate by a unanimous vote. The House took similar action a few days later, and there the matter rested for the time being. But the course of the administration in its dealings with Mexico can scarcely be explained on any other theory than that it desired to bring on a war between the two countries. The observations of the Mexican minister, concerning the aid openly given to the Texans by American citizens, were treated with a coolness little short of contemptuous irony. Claims were presented to the Mexican government, and satisfaction demanded, in language so insulting that, as John Quincy Adams said, "no true-hearted citizen of this Union" could witness the proceeding "without blushing for his country." In his annual message of December, 1836, Jackson saved appearances by adopting a comparatively temperate tone. But the number of American claims against Mexico, some of which were gotten up with the most scandalous disregard of decency, constantly increased, and with it the bullying virulence of the demand. In December, 1836, the American *chargé d'affaires* at Mexico precipitately took his passports and left for the United States. In February, 1837, President Jackson, in a special message to Congress, declared that Mexico, by neglecting to satisfy these claims, had given just cause for war, but that, mindful of the embarrassed condition of that country, he would recommend that another and last chance for atonement be given it, and that an act be passed authorizing the President to resort to reprisals in case of refusal.

The Senate Committee on Foreign Relations, which then had been reorganized with Buchanan as chairman, reported a resolution substantially confirming these views of the President concerning the conduct of Mexico, but providing that, in case satisfaction were not speedily given, Congress should then promptly consider what measures might be "required by the honor of the nation." Clay made a speech plainly betraying the misgivings which disturbed his mind. He could see no cause for war with Mexico; he considered the abrupt departure of the American *chargé* from Mexico harsh and unnecessary; he thought that the case against Mexico was by no means so strong as it was represented; he was for justice and moderation; however, he would vote for the resolution reported by the committee. When, a few days later, another resolution was acted upon, declaring that the condition of things in Texas was now such as to entitle that country to recognition as an independent state, Clay's name did not appear among those voting.

CHAPTER XVIII

THE EXIT OF PRESIDENT JACKSON

The presidential election of 1836 was to give a successor to President Jackson. He was not a candidate for a third term, but the power of his will in his party was so absolute that the candidate favored by him found no effective opposition. The Democratic party was in admirable drill. It might justly have been called Jackson's own party. The Democratic National Convention, largely composed of office-holders, was held as early as February, 1835. It nominated for the presidency Martin Van Buren, — a mere formality to ratify Jackson's command.

During Jackson's second administration the Whigs had fallen into a cheerless, if not despondent, state of mind. Until then it had been generally understood that the leader of the party should be its candidate. But Henry Clay's defeat in 1832 had changed many men's views in that respect. In the summer of 1835 the leading Whig politicians began to look about for some other "available man." Clay felt this keenly. He wrote in July, 1835:—

"The solicitations of other gentlemen, perhaps more

entitled than I am to be chosen chief magistrate, and the discouragement of the use of my name resulting from the issue of the last contest, have led respectable portions of the Whigs, in different States, to direct their views to other candidates than myself. The truth is that I was strongly disinclined to be presented as a candidate in 1832, fearing the issue which took place; but I was overruled by friends, some of whom have since thought it expedient, in consequence of that very event, that another name should be substituted for mine."

Such words revealed the bitterness of soul of the aspirant to the presidency, who discovered that he was no longer the only candidate thought of by his party. It may fairly be doubted whether it was only in yielding to the urgency of his friends that he had taken the nomination in 1832; for then he acted as the recognized leader of his party, and his candidacy was a matter of course. It was so no longer. He still expressed his belief that he could gather more votes than any other Whig, although, as he admitted, probably not enough to win the election. His correspondence of that period leaves the impression that he would have disliked to see the Whig party unite upon any other candidate, as that would have created a rival to him. He discussed competitors in the manner characteristic of presidential candidates, finding reasons why each of them would not answer. He would have been in favor of Webster, had there not been a "general persuasion" that Webster could not succeed. Some Whigs spoke of Senator Hugh L.

White of Tennessee, a very estimable man, who had been an intimate friend of General Jackson, and then turned away from him on account of his high-handed proceedings. Clay disliked White's candidacy because he was no Whig, although he would have preferred his election to that of Van Buren.

The Whig party finally went into the campaign of 1836 without holding a national convention, and without uniting upon a ticket. In several States Whig meetings were held which put forward General William H. Harrison, who was also nominated by the convention of Anti-Masons at Harrisburg. Clay favored him in preference to all others. Webster was presented by the legislature of Massachusetts. The legislature of Alabama and popular meetings in Tennessee nominated Hugh L. White. John Tyler and Francis Granger were candidates for the vice-presidency. The Whigs hoped, by putting several candidates of local strength into the field, to throw the election into the House of Representatives. But a party so utterly distracted could not make a vigorous campaign against the well-disciplined Democrats. Of the 294 electoral votes Van Buren obtained 170, — a clear majority of 46 votes over all his competitors. Thus Jackson's choice was ratified by the people.

Clay had been for more than a year in a dejected mood. The apparent fruitlessness of his struggle against Jackson's popularity seriously depressed his spirits. Again and again he spoke of retiring to private life for the rest of his days. "This is the thirtieth year," he wrote to a committee of citizens of Indiana in the spring of 1836, "since I first entered the service of the federal government. My labors for the public have been various and often arduous. I think they give me some title to repose. If I were persuaded that by remaining longer in the public service I could materially aid in arresting our downward progress, I should feel it my duty not to quit it. But I am not sure that my warning voice has not too often been raised. Perhaps that of my successors may be listened to with more effect." He added that he would serve until the end of his term, which was near at hand, but he "could conceive of no probable contingency which would reconcile" him to the acceptance of another.

There is no reason for doubting that he meant all he said at the time. Sanguine temperaments like his are subject to fits of despondency and a profound yearning for repose, — an overpowering desire to be done forever with all that tries and annoys them. But such fits seldom last long. When Clay was reëlected to the Senate the succeeding winter, the "improbable contingency" which reconciled him to the acceptance of another term of service had arrived. He did not decline.

The last session of Congress under Jackson's presidency opened on December 5, 1836. A large part of its time was given to discussions called forth by the famous "specie circular," which Jackson had issued during the last recess of Congress, and of which more will be said when we reach the story of the great business crisis of 1837.

Clay once more introduced his land bill, which again failed to pass. Presenting some memorials from living British authors, he earnestly declared himself in favor of the enactment of a law tendering to all foreign nations reciprocal security for literary property by granting copyrights.

The great political duel between Clay and Jackson came to a dramatic close. When Clay's resolution censuring President Jackson for assumptions of power " not conferred by the Constitution and laws, but in derogation of both," had passed the Senate on March 28, 1834, Benton forthwith announced his intention to move that this resolution be formally expunged from the records of the Senate. He repeated the motion session after session. Several state legislatures, in which the Jackson party was dominant, taking up the cry, sent memorials to the Senate pressing the measure, and passed resolutions instructing the Senators from their States to support it. When the Virginia legislature had passed such a resolution, John Tyler, recognizing the "doctrine of instruction," but unwilling to vote for a mutilation of the official records, resigned his seat in the Senate. But not until the winter of 1836–37 had there been a majority in the Senate obedient to Jackson's will. Now at last that majority was there.

The resolution offered by Benton contemplated

THE EXIT OF PRESIDENT JACKSON 101

that the record on the official journal of the vote of censure passed upon the President be encircled with large black lines, and crossed with the inscription, " Expunged by order of the Senate." If it had been intended merely to counteract whatever mischievous influence the vote of censure might have had as a precedent, some resolution simply rescinding it, or some declaration censuring the censor, would have served the purpose. But it was desired to make the senators, who by their votes had pronounced the censure upon Jackson, feel all the bitterness of humiliation. They were to be presented to the country as having done a thing too infamous to have a place on the records of the government. It was one of those coarse parades of the brutal power which, not satisfied with victory, delights in mortifying the defeated.

On January 12, 1837, Benton opened the debate with a highly characteristic speech. He presented himself as the voice of the popular will. The people had decided that the resolution censuring President Jackson must be expunged. He found conclusive proof of the popular will in the fact that many state legislatures had so instructed their senators; that a large majority of the States had elected Democratic senators and representatives favorable to the measure; that the Bank of the United States had become odious to the public mind; and that Jackson's friend, Martin Van Buren, who had openly approved the expunging resolution, had been elected president by a large majority. The popular will so manifested, Benton affirmed, was, "upon the principle of representative government, binding and obligatory" on the Senate, — one of those doctrines which Jacksonian orators were peculiarly fond of dwelling upon. After a fulsome panegyric on Jackson's public career, Benton wound up with a display of that frank and ingenuous egotism which distinguished him, saying: "Solitary and alone, and amidst the jeers and taunts of my opponents, I put this ball in motion. The people have taken it up and rolled it forward. I am no longer anything but a unit in the vast mass which now propels it. In the name of that mass I speak. I demand the execution of the edict of the people."

A great oratorical tournament followed, in which all the distinguished men of the Senate took part. Against the expunging resolution were Calhoun, Crittenden, Bayard, Clayton, Southard, Preston, White, Ewing of Ohio, Kent, Clay, and Webster; and for it spoke Benton, Buchanan, and Rives. The debate ranged once more over all the constitutional and legal questions bearing upon the removal of the deposits. The opposition proved to the satisfaction of all unbiased men that to expunge any recorded proceeding of the Senate would be a clear violation of the Constitution, which provided that "each house shall keep a record of its proceedings:" if the record was to be "kept," it could not be expunged. The evi-

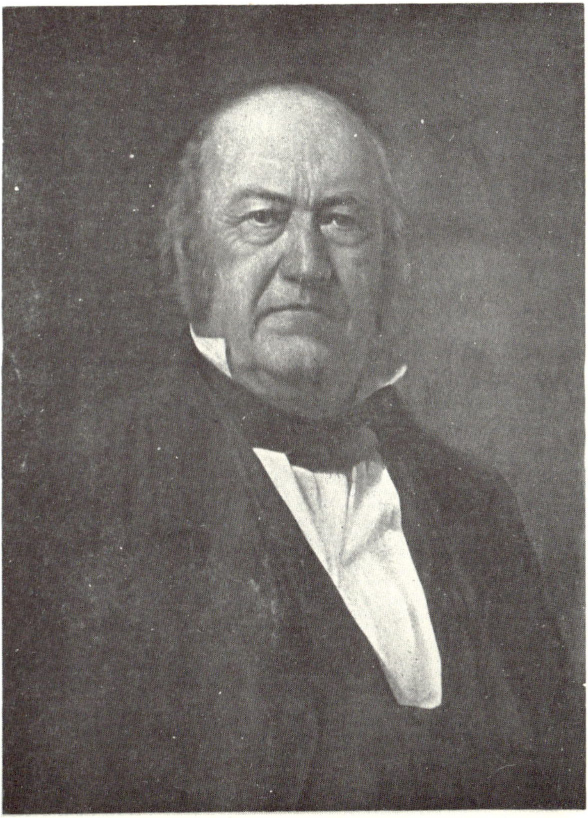

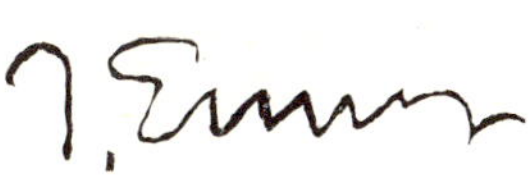

dent superiority of the argument on the side of the opposition was felt so keenly, even by some of the supporters of the resolution, that Ewing of Ohio, speaking of the expungers as the servants of a superior will, " compelled to go onward, against all those feelings and motives which should direct the actions of the legislator and the man," could add : " Why do I see around me so many pale features and downcast eyes, unless it be that repentance and remorse go hand in hand with the perpetration of the deed? "

Clay's speech was in his loftiest style. As the author of the resolution which was to be treated as unworthy of forming a part of the record, he once more summed up the whole case, and then, with irresistible force, he drove home the argument against the assumed power of blotting out anything from the official journals of the national legislature. He rose to his grandest tone in drawing a picture of Jackson's power, and in pouring out his contempt upon the slavish spirit of the expungers : —

"He is felt from one extremity to the other of this vast republic," he exclaimed. "By means of principles which he has introduced, and innovations which he has made in our institutions, alas but too much countenanced by Congress and a confiding people, he exercises uncontrolled the power of the state. In one hand he holds the purse, and in the other he brandishes the sword of the country. Myriads of dependents and partisans, scattered over the land, are ever ready to sing hosannas to him, and to laud to the skies whatever he does. He has swept over the government during the last eight years like a tropical tornado. Every department exhibits traces of the ravages of the storm. What object of his ambition is unsatisfied? When disabled from age any longer to hold the sceptre of power, he designates his successor, and transmits it to his favorite. What more does he want? Must we blot, deface, and mutilate the records of the country to punish the presumptuousness of expressing an opinion contrary to his own? What patriotic purpose is to be accomplished by this expunging resolution? Can you make that not to be which has been? Is it to appease the wrath and to heal the wounded pride of the chief magistrate? If he really be the hero that his friends represent him, he must despise all mean condescension, all groveling sycophancy, all self-degradation and self-abasement. He would reject with scorn and contempt, as unworthy of his fame, your black scratches and your baby lines in the fair records of his country."

Benton himself admitted Clay's speech to have "lacked nothing but verisimilitude" to render it "grand and affecting."

But such attacks had "verisimilitude" enough to make the leaders of the expunging movement feel somewhat uncomfortable as to the firmness of their followers. Jackson imposed upon his friends tasks which not all of them found it consistent with their self-respect to perform. Some had already dropped away from him, and others were inclined to do so. Benton confessed that "members of the party were in the process of separating from

THE EXIT OF PRESIDENT JACKSON 105

it and would require conciliation." The "pale features and downcast eyes" among the Democrats in the Senate seem to have alarmed him, for on Saturday, January 14, according to his own story, the Democratic senators had a night meeting at a restaurant, "giving the assemblage the air of a convivial entertainment," which "continued until midnight." On that occasion it "required all the moderation, tact, and skill of the prime movers to obtain and maintain the union upon details, on the success of which the fate of the [expunging] movement depended." The weak brethren were worked upon until they "severally pledged" themselves "that there should be no adjournment of the Senate, after the resolution ‘was called, until it was passed;" and, as this might make a protracted session necessary, and "knowing the difficulty of keeping men steady to their work and in good humor when tired and hungry, the mover of the proceeding gave orders that night to have an ample supply of cold hams, turkeys, rounds of beef, pickles, wines, and cups of hot coffee ready in a certain committee-room near the senate chamber."

This programme was faithfully carried out the following Monday. Late in the night, after a long debate and a solemn protest against the proceeding read by Daniel Webster, the expunging resolution was carried by a vote of 24 to 19. The secretary of the Senate executed at once the order to draw the required black lines and other marks on the Senate journal of March 28, 1834, whereupon the galleries broke out in groans and hisses; and, after a furious denunciation of the "bank ruffians" by Benton, the Senate adjourned. Thus "the deed was done," as the current saying was at the time. General Jackson did not act the hero depicted by Clay, who would " despise all sycophancy and self-abasement," and "reject with scorn, as unworthy of his fame, the black scratches." On the contrary, as Benton recorded, " the gratification of General Jackson was extreme," and " he gave a grand dinner to the expungers and their wives." Nothing could have imparted greater sweetness to his triumph than the reflection that the man whose work had been stamped by the act of the Senate with such unprecedented ignominy was Henry Clay, whom he hated more fiercely than any other human being. Indeed, that triumph could scarcely have been more complete. Incessantly attacked by Clay at the head of the most brilliant array of talent ever marshaled by any parliamentary leader in American history, Jackson had carried every one of his favorite measures, and been sustained by a most emphatic popular majority in a presidential election. Clay had only been able in two instances — in the nullification trouble and the French difficulty — to put Jackson's violent impulses under some restraint. But of his own favorite objects he had lost everything, — the bank, internal improvements, the protective tariff, the land bill; and finally, when so wanton a measure as the expunging resolution was forced through, Jackson celebrated his victory by trampling upon the prostrate bodies of his foes. Clay felt the humiliation so keenly that he wrote to one of his friends: " I shall hail with the greatest pleasure the occurrence of circumstances which will admit of my resignation without dishonor to myself. The Senate is no longer a place for a decent man. Yesterday Benton's expunging resolution passed, 24 to 19." And to another: " I shall escape from it [the Senate] as soon as I decently can, with the same pleasure that one would fly from a charnel-house."

On March 4, 1837, the " reign of Andrew Jackson," as Von Holst has very appropriately called it, came to an end. There had never been before, and fortunately there has never been since, so powerful and autocratic a will at the head of the government, and so phenomenal a popularity to support it. The passions excited by the vociferous contests of those days were so fierce and enduring that in Jackson's own time, and through a decade or two following, a large majority of American citizens might have been divided into two classes, — those who sincerely and inflexibly believed that Jackson was one of the greatest statesmen of all centuries, and certainly the greatest benefactor of the American people; and those who believed with equally inflexible sincerity that he was little better than a fiend in human shape. It required a new generation to do justice to him as well as to his opponents.

It is generally conceded now that he was a man

of incorruptible integrity and aggressive patriotism, and that he always meant to do right, always firmly believing himself to be in the right. It is also conceded that, as president, he rendered the country very valuable services. He obtained more satisfaction from foreign powers for American claims and grievances, and did more to enforce respect for the American flag abroad, than many other presidents. He asserted the national authority against attempts at nullification and the pretended right of secession, and proclaimed that the Union would be maintained at all hazards, with a patriotic fervor which electrified the popular heart, and gave national loyalty its battle-cry for all coming contests. Nor will any one now find fault with him for having been opposed to a great central bank as the fiscal agent of the government, or for having vetoed Clay's land bill with its distribution scheme, or for trying to keep questionable bank paper out of the public treasury.

But his opponents were certainly right in censuring him for pursuing some of these objects with a recklessness most hurtful to the public welfare, and in utter disregard of those principles which are the soul of constitutional republicanism. His autocratic nature saw only the end he was bent upon accomplishing, and he employed whatever means appeared available for putting down all obstacles in his path. Honestly believing his ends to be right, he felt as if no means that would serve them could be wrong. He never understood that, if constitutional government is to be preserved, the legality of the means used must be looked upon as no less important than the rightfulness of the ends pursued. His conception of the executive power, at least while he wielded it, was extravagant in the extreme. There is a constitutional theory growing up now — if it is not formulated, it is at least sometimes acted upon — that the general government possesses not only the powers granted and those incidental thereto, but all powers not expressly withheld from it by the Constitution. Jackson anticipated that doctrine as applied to the executive. He sincerely believed that as president he was authorized to do whatever the Constitution did not expressly forbid. The "original executive powers" mentioned in his "protest" contained an undefined fund upon which he could draw as occasion required. He held himself to be the sole "direct representative of the people," and in that character he found a source of authority for doing almost anything in the people's name. After his reëlection in 1832 he felt that the people had formally set the seal of their approval upon all his acts and thoughts, past, present, and future, so that his will was equivalent to a popular edict.

He treated the legislative power with a contempt almost revolutionary. Not only did he, in the absence of Congress, set on foot measures, especially of financial policy, which Congress had already disapproved beforehand, and which he was sure would be rejected if submitted to Congress, but he lost no opportunity to denounce, in his public utterances, especially the Senate, but also his opponents in the House, as a set of conspirators against popular rights and the public welfare. Nothing, certainly, could have been farther from Jackson's mind than the desire to overthrow republican government, and to put a personal despotism in its place. But if a president of the United States ever should conceive such a scheme, he would probably resort to the same tactics which Jackson employed. He would assume the character of the sole representative of all the people; he would tell the people that their laws, their rights, their liberties, were endangered by the unscrupulous usurpations of the other constituted authorities; he would try to excite popular distrust and resentment, especially against the legislative bodies; he would exhibit himself as unjustly and cruelly persecuted by those bodies for having vigilantly and fearlessly watched over the rights and interests of the people; he would assure the people that he would protect them if they would stand by him in his struggle with the conspirators, and so forth. These are the true Napoleonic tactics, in part employed by the first, and followed to the letter by the second, usurper of that name.

General Jackson, indeed, delivered the presidency to his constitutionally elected successor, and then retired to the Hermitage. But before he retired he had violently interrupted the good constitutional traditions, and infused into the government and into the whole body politic a spirit of lawlessness which lived after him, and of which the demoralizing influence is felt to this day. Our public life has not yet recovered from the example, which he was the first American president to set, of a chief magistrate breaking, without remorse, some of his most explicit pledges given when he was an aspirant, — thus encouraging that most baleful popular belief that in politics there is no conscience, and that in political jugglery and deceit the highest are no better than the lowest. The present generation has still to struggle with the barbarous habits he introduced on the field of national affairs, when his political followers, taking possession of the government as " spoil," presented the spectacle of a victorious soldiery looting a conquered town. There can be nothing of a more lawless tendency than the " spoils system " in politics, for it makes the coarsest instincts of selfishness the ruling motives of conduct, and inevitably brutalizes public life. It brought forth at once a crop of corruption which startled the country.

It is a remarkable fact that, during the latter part of Jackson's presidency, the general condition of society corresponded strikingly with the style in which the popular idol used to " take responsibilities," to disregard legal restraint, and to unchain his furious passions against his " enemies." Lawless ruffianism has perhaps never been as rampant in this country as in those days. " Many of the people of the United States are out of joint," wrote Niles in August, 1835. "A spirit of riot, and a disposition to 'take the law in their own hands,' prevails in every quarter." Mobs, riots, burnings, lynchings, shootings, tarrings, duels, and all sorts of violent excesses, perpetrated by all sorts of persons upon all sorts of occasions, seemed to be the order of the day. They occurred not only in the frontier districts of the West and South, but were reported from all quarters, mainly from the cities. Alarmingly great was the number of people who appeared to believe that they had a right to put down by force and violence all who displeased them by act or speech or belief, in politics, or religion, or business, or social life. It can unfortunately not be said that Jackson discountenanced this spirit of violence when it appeared in his immediate surroundings. Several members of Congress were, on the streets of Washington, "cruelly assaulted" and shot at for "words spoken in debate." Such proceedings, when the victims were anti-Jackson men, found no disapproval at Jackson's hands, who, on one occasion in 1832, said that, "after a few more examples of the same kind, members of Congress would learn to keep civil tongues in their heads;" and who on another occasion, when the assailant was fined by a court, promptly pardoned him. The excitement in Washington was at one time so great that a committee of citizens waited upon the President, asking him to order out the troops for the purpose of putting down the rioters, — a request which he answered with an emphatic "No."

THE EXIT OF PRESIDENT JACKSON

Scarcely had General Jackson left the presidential chair when that apparent prosperity which for a long period had kept the people in high spirits, and which by his friends had been attributed to the wisdom of his financial policy, broke down with a tremendous crash in the great crisis of 1837.

CHAPTER XIX

THE CRISIS OF 1837

THE financial measures of the Jackson régime, the crisis of 1837, and the party struggle brought forth by that event, will be made more intelligible by a brief review of the situation.

The time of Jackson's presidency was a period of great material progress. The completion of the Erie Canal had made the Northern lake regions easily accessible, and accelerated their settlement. Steamboat navigation on the Western rivers increased rapidly. Between 1830 and 1834 the number of steamboats rose from 130 to 230, and their tonnage nearly doubled, opening more widely the valleys of the Mississippi and of its great tributaries. Railroad building, too, began in earnest. In 1830 only 23 miles had been in operation; in 1835 there were 1098, and two years later 1497. The railroad did not yet pierce the "Great West," but railroad schemes were abundant there, and the imagination of bold speculators easily annihilated the distance between the Atlantic seaboard and the banks of the Mississippi. Canals for the transportation of goods were projected and begun everywhere. All these things naturally stimulated the desire of locomotion and the reach of enterprise. The fertile acres of Illinois, Missouri, and Wisconsin were drawn nearer and nearer to the great seaport markets, and their prospective value seemed to outrun all sober calculation. It was not surprising that the venturesome mind of the American should have turned to speculation in new lands. In the South and Southwest the speculative spirit found a special stimulus. The price of cotton, which had been 6 to 8 cents a pound, touched $13\frac{1}{2}$ in 1833, and vibrated between 14 and 20 in 1835. The value of cotton lands seemed, therefore, to leave far behind all previous estimates.

Under such conditions it required only some financial facilities to start the speculative spirit on its career. These facilities were not wanting. In England, owing partly to natural, partly to artificial circumstances, such as the establishment of many new banks of issue, large amounts of capital were ready to go into foreign investment and speculation. The United States were presenting the extraordinary spectacle of a nation extinguishing its public debt. The credit of the country rose, foreign capital was attracted, and American state bonds and other securities were easily sold on the European market in large quantities. Many American claims against foreign governments were settled at this period, and from this source, too, considerable sums of money flowed in. All this had a highly stimulating effect.

To the end of moderating the tendency to speculative enterprise, which is always apt to run into excess, nothing would have been more desirable than that the financial policy of the government should be even more than ordinarily circumspect and conservative. But it was just then that the government withdrew its funds from the United States Bank, an institution under a comparatively cautious management, naturally inclined to serve by preference the legitimate business of the country, and turned over the deposits to a number of favored state banks. But not only that. In order to reconcile the people to the change, the secretary of the treasury expressly admonished those " pet banks " to " afford increased facilities to commerce," and to expand their " accommodations to individuals," by means of the public money, — in other words, to lend out the public funds as freely as possible. This, of course, the deposit banks did with zest, by no means confining their favors to the "merchants engaged in foreign trade," whom the secretary had especially commended to them. As the public debt became extinguished and the treasury surplus grew in consequence, the amount of public money deposited in the " pet banks " and available for the " accommodation of individuals " increased rapidly. The United States Bank, too, was drawn into the whirl. From August, 1833, to June, 1834, the bank had contracted its loans, in part probably for the purpose of creating the impression that the war made upon it by the admin-

THE CRISIS OF 1837

istration was injuring the business of the country. But when it saw that the state banks were using this opportunity for efforts to draw its custom to themselves, it expanded again in order to keep its hold upon business.

But the prospect of the final downfall of the United States Bank, and the hope of getting for themselves some of the public deposits, encouraged greatly the establishment of new state banks. In 1830 there were about 330 in the country; there were 558 in 1835, and no less than 634 in 1837. Their capital rose from 61 millions in 1830 to 231 millions in 1835, and nearly 291 millions in 1837; their loans, from 200 millions in 1830 to 365 millions in 1835, and 525 millions in 1837; their note circulation, from 61 millions in 1830 to 103 millions in 1835, and to 149 millions in 1837, with respectively 22 millions, 44 millions, and 38 millions of specie behind the paper. The convertibility of the bank-note circulation was therefore very uncertain; the specie basis of many of the banks for their note issues ludicrously small. There was a perfect mania for establishing banks. As Niles reports, a bank was looked upon as a panacea to cure all kinds of troubles, as if it were the creation of capital by enchantment.

The expansion of the currency and the inflation of prices went hand in hand under the influence of unbridled speculation and reckless debt-making. The characteristic feature of the period was the speculation in wild lands. While the price of everything else rose, the government price of public land remained the same, say $1.25 an acre. In the light of the gorgeous future, land thus appeared ridiculously cheap; there could be no more promising investment. The land bought by the speculator was paid for in bank-notes. These bank-notes went from the land office as public funds to the deposit banks. The public funds so deposited were largely lent out again to speculators, who used them in buying more lands. The money paid for these new lands went back again as public funds to the deposit banks, to be lent out again and to return in the same way. Thus the money went round and round in the same circle, carrying larger and larger quantities of public lands from the government to the speculators, the government receiving for the land in fact only bank credits. No wonder the land speculation grew beyond all bounds. In 1832 the receipts from the sale of the public lands had been $2,623,000; in 1834 they were $4,857,000; in 1835 they rose to $14,757,000, and in 1836 to the amazing figure of $24,877,000. And all this increase swelled the treasury surplus at the disposal of the deposit banks for the "accommodation of individuals."

No sooner was a purchase made than the land, bought at $1.25 an acre, was estimated to be worth six, eight, ten times as much. The more a speculator had bought, and the more money he had borrowed to pay for the lands, the richer he thought himself to be. People were intoxicated with their imagined wealth won overnight. The fever of speculation remained by no means confined to the public lands. The contagion spread irresistibly. The insane expansion of credit was general. The frenzy raged from the cotton fields of the South to the pineries of Maine. In some cities the speculation in real estate assumed absurd proportions. At Mobile, a chief cotton mart, the assessed value of city property rose between 1831 and 1837 from $1,294,810 to $27,482,961; in New York, between 1831 and 1836, from $139,280,314 to $309,500,000. In other towns, large and small, similar things were going on. The importation of merchandise increased enormously during the same period, and there was the most reckless gambling in all things that could be bought and sold. It was a universal carnival in which people seemed to vie with one another in madness of venture and expectation.

Two government measures adopted in 1836 interfered with this crazy round dance, measures which, indeed, did not cause the explosion, — for there were other causes making it eventually inevitable, — but which hastened it, and probably rendered it more destructive. One proceeded from Congress, — the distribution of the surplus funds among the States. The idea of distributing among the States surplus funds accumulated in the national treasury was not a new one. Jefferson had suggested it; also Jackson in his annual message of 1829, though he afterwards repented of it. Clay's land bill, introduced, passed, and disapproved by Jackson in 1832, provided for the distribution of the proceeds of land sales. When, with the extinguishment of the public debt, the excess of revenue over regular expenditures lost its employment and simply accumulated, the question became more pressing, especially as not only the proceeds from land sales, but also, under the stimulus of general inflation, the customs revenue, increased amazingly, — between 1834 and 1836, from $16,200,000 to $23,400,000.

The public deposits amounted on January 1, 1835, to $10,223,000; on December 1, 1835, to $24,724,000; on March 1, 1836, to $33,700,000; and by June 1, 1836, they had risen to $41,500,000, distributed among thirty-five banks. This state of things created alarm, political as well as financial. The Whigs feared, not without reason, the enormous political power gathered in the hands of the administration by the control of banks in all parts of the country, which were to afford "accommodation to individuals" with so many millions of government money. As to the financial aspect of the case, it was seriously questioned whether the public funds were safe in the deposit banks, some of which were known to be weak; and that feeling of insecurity could not but be increased by the mad speculation which the public deposits, filtering through the banks, were so powerfully helping to keep up. Moreover, the existence of the surplus had its natural effect of stimulating jobbery and extravagance in Congress, as well as in other branches of the government. " We had a surplus which we knew not how to dispose of," said Preston of South Carolina, in September, 1837. " The departments were stimulated and goaded on to find out how much they could spend, while the majority in Congress seemed to be employed in finding out how much they could give." The surplus had to be disposed of, and Congress, at the session of 1835-36, finally agreed upon a method.

A bill was passed which provided that the deposits of public funds in any one bank should not exceed three fourths of its " paid-in " capital stock; that the banks should pay all drafts on the public deposits in specie, if required ; that no bank should have any public deposits that failed to redeem its notes in specie, and that circulated notes under five dollars ; and, finally, that the surplus funds at the disposal of the Treasury on January 1, 1837, reserving five millions, should be " deposited " with the several States in proportion to their representation in the Senate and the House of Representatives, to be paid back to the United States at the call of the secretary of the treasury. Jackson approved the bill in June, 1836, probably because, the presidential election impending, the failure of the popular distribution scheme through his veto might have injured Van Buren. In his message a few months later, he gave good reasons why he should not have signed it. Some of those who had supported the bill, — Calhoun, for instance, — holding a distribution of public funds as a gift among the States to be unconstitutional, but a deposit or loan to be constitutional, seriously thought that the States might be called upon at some time to refund the money. But generally the deposit was looked upon as a gift; and Clay, on his return to his constituents, said "he did not believe a single member of either house imagined that a dollar would be recalled." The Whigs represented the passage of the bill as a great victory on their side. It was a bad law in itself, but perhaps no worse than other available expedients, since the accumulation of the surplus had not been prevented by a timely reduction of the taxes.

The effect of the law was to hurry on a crisis. The distribution of the public deposits among the "pet banks" had served to place capital arbitrarily in different parts of the country, without much regard to the requirements of legitimate business. The regulations imposed upon the deposit banks by the new law, especially the provision that the public deposits in no one bank should exceed three fourths of its paid-up capital, led in some cases to an equally arbitrary dislocation of funds from banks which had an excess of deposits to other banks in other places which had less than the amount allowed. But the distribution of the treasury surplus among the several States produced this effect of arbitrary dislocation on a much greater scale. On January 1, 1837, the surplus available for distribution amounted to $37,468,859. That surplus was nominally in the banks, but really in the hands of borrowers who used it for legitimate business or speculation. Withdrawing it from the banks meant, therefore, withdrawing it from the business men or speculators who had borrowed it. The funds so withdrawn were made for some time unavailable. They passed under the control of the several States, some of which used them for public improvements, some for educational purposes, some for other objects. The money would, of course, gradually find its way back into the channels of business, but then into channels other than those from which it had been taken.

The distribution among the States was to take place in four quarterly installments; but the preparations for the transfer of large sums from one place to another — and a transfer, too, regardless of the condition of commerce, or of the money market, or of the needs of any economic interest, or of any person — had to be begun at once and vigorously. A fierce contraction of loans and discounts necessarily followed. The exchanges between different parts of the country were violently disturbed, so that when the first installment of the surplus was delivered to the States the bodily transportation of specie and bank-notes from place to place became necessary to an extraordinary degree. Millions upon millions of dollars went on their travels, North and South, East and West, being mere freight for the time being, while the business from which the money was withdrawn gasped for breath in its struggle with a fearfully stringent money market.

The trouble was aggravated by one of Jackson's own financial measures. For a while the enormous land sales struck Jackson's mind as something uncommonly fine. In his message of December, 1835, he spoke of them as "among the evidences of the increasing prosperity of the country," attesting "the rapidity with which agriculture, the first and most important occupation of man, advances, and contributes to the wealth and prosperity of our extended territory." Presently, however, he became aware that the land sales did not mean settlement and agriculture, but speculation. He learned also that the land sold was paid for generally in notes issued, in great part at least, by banks of very uncertain solvency and granting loans with great readiness. Banks in the old States would lend their small notes in large sums to speculators, who would carry them "out West" to buy land with them; these notes would thus get into circulation far away from their places of issue and redemption, — far enough to find their way back but slowly. The land sales were, indeed, in a great measure, "a conversion of public land into inconvertible paper." Jackson resolved that this must be stopped.

His confidential friend, Benton, introduced a resolution in the Senate that nothing but specie should be received in payment for public lands. The resolution had no support. Immediately after

THE CRISIS OF 1837

the adjournment of Congress, in July, 1836, President Jackson, although knowing that such a measure could not have passed either house of Congress, and also that a majority of his cabinet was against it, ordered the famous "specie circular" to be issued, — an instruction to the land officers to accept in payment for public lands only gold and silver coin, with an exception in favor of actual settlers until December 15 ensuing. This would have been an excellent measure to restrain the speculation in lands at its beginning. At the time when it came it did, indeed, as Benton said, "overtake some tens of millions of this bank paper on its way to the land offices to be changed into land, — which made the speculators rage." But it did more. As Clay at a later period said, it expressed the distrust of the executive in the solvency of the banks, and created an extraordinary demand for specie "at a moment when the banking operations were extended and stretched to their utmost tension," and when the banks "were almost all tottering and ready to fall, for the want of that metallic basis on which they all rested." It drew specie from the centres of commerce to transport it to the wilderness, where it found its way through the land offices into Western banks, in some of which, according to Jackson's message, there were already credits to the government "greatly beyond their immediate means of payment."

Here was again a violent dislocation of capital,

effected in the crudest way. As Webster described it, the specie circular "checked the use of bank-notes in the West, and made another loud call for specie. The specie, therefore, is transferred to the West to pay for lands. Being received for lands, it becomes public revenue, is brought to the East for expenditure, and passes, on its way, other quantities going West to buy lands also, and in the same way returns again to the East." Moreover, while specie was required at the land office, bank-notes passed at the custom-house.

All this was going on at the same time with the distribution of the treasury surplus, — a rare combination of measures to withdraw millions of capital from active employment, to enforce a violent contraction of loans, to keep large quantities of specie and bank-notes in aimless migration, and thus to produce a general confusion which set all calculations at naught. History shows few examples of wilder financiering. No wonder that the money market, which in times of inflation always suffers from spasmodic fits of tightness, became tight beyond measure, and that the signs of an approaching collapse multiplied from day to day. Business men and speculators cast about frantically for some means of relief. There was a loud cry for the withdrawal of the specie circular, and Congress, at the close of the session of 1836–37, passed by large majorities a bill rescinding it. But that bill Jackson refused to approve. It could have done no good.

THE CRISIS OF 1837

The first installment of the treasury surplus, amounting to $9,367,000, due on January 1, 1837, was taken from the deposit banks amid great agony, and transferred to the several States; also the second, about April 1. But before the third fell due the general collapse came. First the influx of capital from England ceased. The speculation, which had prevailed there during the same period, was brought to an end by financial embarrassments in the autumn of 1836. Discounts went up and prices down. Some banks were compelled to wind up, and three large business houses, which had been heavily engaged with America, failed. English creditors called in their dues. The manufacturing industries, which, carried along by the general whirl, had produced beyond demand, had to reduce their operations, and the price of cotton fell more rapidly than it had risen. In August, 1836, it had been from 15 to 20 cents a pound; in May, 1837, it was from 8 to 12. The cotton houses in the South went down. Nine tenths of the merchants of Mobile suspended. New Orleans was in a state of financial anarchy. Tobacco shared the fate of cotton. The whole South was bankrupt. It became painfully apparent that the speculation in public lands had anticipated the possible progress of settlement by many years. The imagined values of great possessions in the West vanished into thin air. The names of the paper towns located in the wilderness sounded like ghastly jests. Fortunes in city lots disappeared overnight. The accumulated masses of imported merchandise shrunk more than one third in their value. Stocks of all kinds dropped with a thump. Manufacturing establishments stopped. Tens of thousands of workingmen were thrown on the streets. Bankruptcies were announced by scores, by hundreds. "Everybody" was deeply in debt; there was a terrible scarcity of available assets. The banks, being crippled by the difficulty in collecting their dues, and by the sudden depreciation of the securities they held, could afford very little if any help. In May, 1837, while the preparatory steps for the distribution of the third surplus installment were in progress, the Dry Dock Bank of New York, one of the deposit banks, failed. Runs on other institutions followed; and on May 10 the New York banks in a body suspended specie payments, — the effect of the surplus distribution act and the heavy drafts for specie being given as the principal causes. All the banks throughout the country then adopted the same course. Confusion and distress could not have been more general.

CHAPTER XX

CLAY AND VAN BUREN

WHEN Andrew Jackson left office on March 4, 1837, the great financial explosion had not yet occurred. The old hero went out in a halo of glory; but the disastrous conflagration broke out immediately behind him, and seemed to singe his very heels. The man to whom he left his fearful legacy, Martin Van Buren, was the first trained "machine politician," in the modern sense of the term, elevated to the presidency. He had made his studies in the school of New York politics, and had become the ruling spirit of the renowned Albany Regency. His career gave color to the charge that he permitted no fixed principles to stand in the way of his personal advancement. He had been a Clinton and an anti-Clinton man. He had, as a legislator in New York, been in favor of giving colored citizens the right to vote; he had been against the admission of Missouri as a slave State; he had helped to elect Rufus King, a leader of the Antislavery Federalists, to the Senate of the United States; and then he became the foremost of the "Northern men with Southern principles." He had, in the New York Convention of 1821, opposed universal suffrage, and had then become an advocate of the extremest Democratic theories. He had been the finest pattern of the "baby-kissing" statesman, who, as one of his friends described him, "travels from county to county, from town to town, sees everybody, talks to everybody, comforts the disappointed, and flatters the expectant with hope of success." He had, as the "Democratic Review" said in 1848, by "party centralization at Albany, controlling offices as well as safety bank-charters, presidents, cashiers, and directors in all the counties, formed machinery which set every man's face towards Albany, as a political Mecca," and had thus "acquired his title to national honors." He had been a Crawford manager, and had become a Jackson manager. As a member of Jackson's cabinet, he had won the old hero's especial favor by supporting the cause of Mrs. Eaton; and Jackson selected him as his successor, employing all his tremendous energy in the advancement of the favorite. Every one knew that he owed the presidency solely to Jackson's power.

He was a man of scanty education, but of much native ability; smooth, affable, and good-humored; always on pleasant personal terms with his political enemies. As president, he promised "to tread generally in the footsteps of President Jackson;" and his inaugural address contained, by the side of some well-worn generalities, but one positive declaration, that he would inflexibly oppose the abolition of slavery in the District of Columbia against the wishes of the slaveholding States. This man had to take upon himself the troubles left behind by Jackson, — troubles which would have sorely tried the stoutest heart and the strongest mind. He confronted them with unexpected fortitude.

As is always the case under such circumstances, the distressed business community turned to the government for relief. It demanded the recall of the specie circular, which Van Buren firmly refused, and the speedy convocation of Congress in extra session, which he was obliged to grant. The deposit banks having suspended specie payments with the rest, the government funds were locked up, or had to be drawn from the banks in depreciated bank paper. The distribution of the first three installments of the treasury surplus had well-nigh exhausted the resources of the government, and there was a prospect of a deficit, instead of a surplus, before the end of the year. Congress met on September 4, 1837.

The business crisis had brought forth a strong reaction against the administration party, which showed itself in one local election after another. The Democratic members of Congress arrived at Washington in a somewhat dejected state of mind. The Whigs saw their opportunity for a successful opposition, and the spirit in which Clay was ready to lead that opposition had already been foreshadowed in a letter written to his friend Brooke shortly after Van Buren's election. "Undoubtedly," he wrote, "such an opposition should avail itself of the errors of the new administration; but it seems to me that it would acquire greater force by availing itself also of that fatal error in its origin, which resulted from the president-elect being the designated successor of the present incumbent. If a president may name his successor and bring the whole machinery of the government, including its one hundred thousand dependents, into the canvass, and if by such means he achieves a victory, such a fatal precedent as this must be rebuked and reversed, or there is an end of the freedom of election. Now I think that no wisdom or benefit, in the measures of the new administration, can compensate or atone for this vice in its origin." This evidently meant systematic opposition, just that kind of opposition which had been waged by the Jackson party against the administration of John Quincy Adams, also on account of its origin, which Clay had then considered extremely unjust.

The subject of the next presidential election, too, was already looming up. Van Buren had hardly slept a night in the White House when Clay's friends in New York held a meeting to consider the means by which Clay's election in 1840 could be secured. The proceedings of that meeting having been communicated to him, Clay wrote in August, 1837, as a reply, one of those stilted letters in which candidates for the presidency, made restless not only by their own ambition, but also by the importunate zeal of their "friends," vainly try to conceal the miseries of their existence. It was too early yet, he wrote, to speak of the presidential election. The popular mind, owing to the prevailing distress, was occupied with schemes of relief. To be sure, the only adequate remedy for existing evils would be a "change of rulers." Too much delay in considering how that change should be effected was as unadvisable as too great precipitancy. There ought to be a national convention to avoid division and lack of harmony; but all proper means should be used beforehand to concentrate public sentiment upon some candidate. He himself was not anxious — rather was "extremely unwilling"— to be "thrown into the turmoil of a presidential canvass." But if he "were persuaded" that a majority of his fellow citizens desired to make him president, his "sense of duty would exact obedience to their will." And so on. In short, Clay was an aspirant for the Whig nomination for the presidency in 1840, and he desired the preliminary campaign to begin without delay.

Van Buren's message in September, 1837, was a surprise to those who had not considered him a man of courage. He gave a clear exposition of the causes which had brought on the existing distress. He admitted that the policy of depositing the public funds in state banks had proved a failure. He declared himself against a continuation or repetition of the experiment, and as firmly against a restoration of the United States Bank as the fiscal agent of the government. He recommended that the government itself, through its own officers, do its fiscal business, consisting in "the collection, safekeeping, transfer, and disbursement of the public money." He further recommended the enactment of a bankrupt law applicable to "corporations and other bankers." He declared his determination not to withdraw the specie circular. Nothing but the constitutional currency, gold and silver, or "its equivalent," — notes convertible into specie on demand, — should be taken in payment by the government. He also urged that the distribution of the fourth surplus installment, due on October 1, should be withheld, as there was no available "surplus;" and that the prospective deficit in the Treasury be covered by the temporary issue of treasury notes.

Further measures of "relief" he did not propose, giving as a reason that it was not the office of the government under the Constitution to help people out of their business embarrassments. Neither did he think that the government had anything to do with the "management of domestic and foreign exchange." In his opinion, all the government could do was to furnish to the people a good "constitutional currency," to collect its taxes in good money, and to defray its expenses and pay its creditors in good money. In this respect he did not go far enough to "follow the footsteps of President Jackson," who had made most of his experiments of financial policy, professedly at least, with a view to improving the domestic exchanges. Van Buren recognized no duty of the government regarding these things beyond the mere regulation of the gold and silver coin.

Immediately after the reading of the message, Clay "could not forbear saying that he felt the deepest regret that the President, entertaining such views, had deemed it his duty to call an extra session of Congress at this inconvenient period of the year." This was characteristic of the spirit of the opposition. It found the recommendations of the President unacceptable or insufficient, but was not able, or did not choose, to offer propositions of its own. The administration party brought forward the President's programme in a series of bills, the first being a bill to postpone the distribution of the fourth surplus installment until further provision by law. The customs revenues, as well as the land sales, having suddenly fallen off, there was a deficit rather than a surplus of revenue in prospect. Indeed, the government could scarcely meet its obligations from day to day. It seems utterly absurd that under such circumstances the distribution of a surplus should have been demanded. Yet this demand the Whigs made under Clay's leadership, for it was Clay who, at a meeting of Whigs at the beginning of the session, had insisted upon the maintenance of the distribution policy. His conduct can be explained, but not justified.

The three surplus installments distributed among the States had in some of them been more or less usefully expended, in others squandered, and in several had led to engagements for future expenditures. In other words, some of the States, having received some money from the federal treasury, had run into debt in anticipation of more. The proposition not to distribute the fourth installment, therefore, called forth a great clamor. It was denounced as a breach of contract and an act of robbery, and the demand was made in all seriousness that, if the government had not the money to be distributed as a surplus, it was bound to borrow the required amount by way of a loan. All these outcries found voice in Congress. The bill to withhold the fourth installment finally passed; but the bulk of the Whig vote, including the names of Clay, Webster, Bayard, Crittenden, Clayton, Preston, and Southard, stand recorded against it. The bill passed with an amendment by which the power of recalling from the several States the distributed "deposits" was transferred from the secretary of the treasury to Congress, which was equivalent to an assurance that they would never be recalled. In fact, they have remained on the books of the Treasury down to our days as "unavailable funds." If ever a similar measure should be proposed again, the history of the moral and economic effects produced by the distribution of the treasury surplus in 1837, in the States which received the money, as well as throughout the general business community, may well be studied as a warning example.

The administration party then offered a bill to

issue ten millions of treasury notes. It gave the Whigs a welcome opportunity for ridiculing Jackson's financial experiments, which had flourished before the country high-sounding promises of a gold currency, and then resulted in a new issue of "government paper money." Such sarcastic thrusts were certainly not undeserved. But the government needed the money to keep its machinery running; and Clay's opposition to the bill, he preferring a loan, could not carry more than a handful of votes with it. The financial condition of the government was such that several new issues of treasury notes became necessary, continuing until 1843.

But the principal struggle of the session took place on the sub-treasury bill, at the time called the "Divorce Bill," as its purpose was to divorce the government from the banks. It provided simply that all officers receiving public moneys should safely keep them in their custody, without loaning or otherwise using them, until duly ordered to pay them out, or to transfer them either to the central treasury at Washington, or to its branches or sub-treasuries in different parts of the country; and that the officers concerned should be held to give sufficient bond, and to render their accounts periodically, — in one word, that the government revenues, to be collected in gold and silver, should be in the safekeeping no longer of banks, but of government officers. Calhoun moved as an amendment that the notes of specie-paying banks should be accepted in part payment of public dues, but in decreasing proportion from year to year, until a certain period, when the government should accept only specie.

With regard to the subject involved in the bill, both parties executed some curious marches and counter-marches. The Democrats had, under Jackson, approved of the transfer of the public deposits from the United States Bank to the selected state banks, the funds to be used for the accommodation of the business community. Now they proposed the withdrawal of the public funds from the banks, and the absolute prohibition of their use for private accommodation. The Whigs had violently denounced the " pet bank " system as unsafe and demoralizing; now they insisted that the withdrawal of the public money from the banks was an attack upon the banking system, and would be ruinous to business interests as well as dangerous to free institutions.

The debate on the sub-treasury scheme extended through four sessions. It was one of the most exciting in the history of Congress. At first popular sentiment, stimulated by the influence of the banks, ran strongly against the measure. In the extra session of 1837 the bill passed the Senate, but was defeated in the House. In the regular session of 1837-38 it failed again. Being pressed with great perseverance by the administration, it passed at last in the session of 1839-40.

Clay led the opposition to it from beginning to

end. In the debate his powers as an orator shone out in all their brilliancy, but they could hardly disguise the weakness of his reasoning. The whole cause of the economic disturbances, according to him, was to be found in Jackson's measures against the United States Bank. These measures, he argued, would have had no excuse had there been no treasury surplus; and there would have been no treasury surplus had not Jackson prevented his (Clay's) land bill, providing for the distribution of the proceeds of the land sales, from becoming a law. The enactment of the sub-treasury bill " must terminate in the total subversion of the state banks," and would place them all at the mercy of the general government. The " proposed substitution of a purely metallic currency for the mixed medium " would reduce all property in value by two thirds, obliging every debtor in effect " to pay three times as much as he had contracted for." Moreover, the public funds would be unsafe in the hands of the public officers. There would be favoritism, and a dangerous increase of the federal patronage. It would immensely strengthen the power of the executive, and " that perilous union of the purse and the sword, so justly dreaded by our British and Revolutionary ancestors, would become absolute and complete." The local banks being destroyed, " the government would monopolize the paper issues of the country; the federal treasury itself would become a vast bank, with the sub-treasuries for its branches; a combined and concentrated money power would then be beheld, equal to all the existing banks with the United States Bank superadded. This tremendous power would be wielded by the secretary of the treasury under the immediate command of the President. Here would be a perfect union of the sword and the purse, — an actual, visible consolidation of the moneyed power. Who or what could withstand it? These States themselves would become suppliants at the feet of the executive for a portion of the paper emissions. The day might come when the Senate of the United States would have "humbly to implore some future president to grant it money to pay the wages of its own sergeant-at-arms and doorkeeper." He firmly believed that the enactment of the sub-treasury bill would be "fatal to the best interests of this country, and ultimately subversive of its liberties."

In our days the sub-treasury system, in its essential features as originally designed, having so long been in practical operation, we find it difficult to understand how a mind like Clay's should have looked upon it with such extravagant apprehensions. But it is equally difficult to believe that these expressions of fear should have been mere dissimulation, or oratorical feint. Indeed, the solemnity with which he began his second speech on this subject, on February 19, 1838, stands perhaps without example in the annals of the Senate.

"I have seen some public service [he said], passed through troubled times, and often addressed public assemblies, in this capitol and elsewhere; but never before have I risen in a deliberative body under more oppressed feelings, or with a deeper sense of awful responsibility. Never before have I risen to express my opinions upon any public measure fraught with such tremendous consequences to the welfare and prosperity of the country, and so perilous to the liberties of the people, as I believe the bill under consideration will be. If you knew, sir, what sleepless hours reflecting upon it has cost me, if you knew with what fervor and sincerity I have implored Divine assistance to strengthen and sustain me in my opposition to it, I should have credit with you, at least, for the sincerity of my convictions. And I have thanked my God that he has prolonged my life until the present time to enable me to exert myself in the service of my country against a project far transcending in pernicious tendency any that I have ever had occasion to consider."

Such displays of emotion are so apt to appear ridiculous to the hearer, that a skilled parliamentary speaker will hardly venture upon them as an artifice, especially with so cool an audience as the Senate. Clay was then sixty years old, — too old for experiments in farce. His utterances must therefore be taken as evidence that he profoundly believed in all the horrors he predicted. The old cry about the " union of the purse and the sword " probably had so excited his imagination as to make him overlook the fact that what our " British ancestors " dreaded was that union of sword and purse which consisted in the levying of taxes without law, and the spending of public funds without an appropriation by parliament; and that Martin

Van Buren, in proposing the safekeeping of public funds by government officers, was very far from aiming at such a privilege.

In truth, the only objections of importance to the sub-treasury scheme were those brought forward by Webster in a series of speeches on the sub-treasury bill which discussed the subject of currency and exchange with remarkable grasp of thought, clearness of statement, and brilliancy of reasoning. Webster blamed the President for not recognizing in his recommendations the power as well as the duty of the government to secure to the people a safe and uniform currency, which would facilitate the domestic exchanges, and for not aiding the banks in their efforts to return to specie payments. He expressed the apprehension that the sub-treasury system would temporarily withdraw large amounts of money from active employment, — an evil which could be reduced to the smallest proportions by confining the revenues of the government to its current wants, thus avoiding the accumulation of a surplus. But Webster did not see in the sub-treasury system the downfall of republican institutions.

As to the question of remedy, however, Webster and Clay substantially agreed. Their invention did not go beyond the establishment of another United States Bank. That was their panacea. Clay confessed that he felt himself unable to suggest to his friends, who looked to him for a "healing measure," anything that did not " comprehend a national bank as an essential part." At the same time he frankly declared: "If a national bank be established, its stability and its utility will depend upon the general conviction which is felt of its necessity; and until such a conviction is deeply impressed upon the people, and clearly manifested by them, it would, in my judgment, be unwise even to propose a bank." That such a bank could be safe and useful only if the people were generally convinced of its necessity, was a statesmanlike observation; if Clay had only adhered to its true meaning when the time of temptation came! The Senate, as then constituted, certainly did not believe in that necessity, for it passed a resolution adverse to the establishment of a national bank by a majority of more than two thirds.

Neither was the conduct of the old Bank of the United States, which, after the expiration of its national charter, continued to exist under a charter obtained from the State of Pennsylvania, calculated to maintain the prestige of its name. When it was severed from the government, it drifted into unsound operations. In the efforts to resume specie payments, which were made mainly under the leadership of the venerable Albert Gallatin, then a bank president in New York, the United States Bank played an obstructive and in many respects questionable part. Clay offered a resolution in the Senate to promote resumption by making the notes of the resuming banks receivable in payment of all dues to the general government. The resolution was not adopted, but the New York banks resumed, without this aid, in May, 1838; the New England banks followed in July, and then also the Bank of the United States and those of the South and West. The strong, solvent banks maintained themselves without much difficulty. In October, 1839, the Bank of the United States suspended again, carrying the Southern and Western banks with it, while those of New York and New England remained firm. In 1841 the Bank of the United States broke down entirely. Its stockholders lost their whole investment. The catastrophe was charged to corrupt and reckless management. Nicholas Biddle, who had resigned the presidency already in March, 1839, was prosecuted for conspiracy and acquitted. He died in 1844, poor and broken-hearted.

At the time of the debates on the sub-treasury bill the United States Bank still held a powerful position, although its equivocal attitude as to the resumption of specie payments excited suspicions which subsequently turned out to have been but too well justified. It would be unjust to identify the conduct of that institution during its existence as a mere state bank with its conduct while it was the fiscal agent of the general government. Yet these two characters and periods were not kept apart in the popular mind; the final downfall of the institution cast its shadow over the name throughout its whole career, and it long remained a very general impression that the old Bank of the United States under "Nick Biddle" had always been a very corrupt and corrupting concern.

The contests on the sub-treasury bill and the other so-called relief measures brought into public view a rupture in the Democratic ranks. Several prominent Democrats in the Senate and House (Rives of Virginia and Tallmadge of New York, and others), who believed that the sub-treasury system would destroy the banking interest, joined the opposition and were called "Conservatives." But a more exciting event was the final breaking up of that alliance in which Clay and Calhoun had appeared as companions in arms against Jackson. While Jackson was president, Calhoun had zealously coöperated with the Whigs in their resistance to the "dangerous growth of executive power." Jackson gone, Calhoun appeared as a friend of the Democratic administration. He dissolved the old partnership with a formal manifesto, a public letter, in which he declared that the further coöperation of those who had been united in opposition to Jackson, namely, the state-rights party and the Whigs, might indeed succeed in overthrowing the administration, but that the victory would redound only to the benefit of the Whigs and their cause; that he and his followers could not consent to be absorbed by an organization "whose principles and policy," as he expressed it, "are so opposite to ours, and so dangerous to our institutions, as well as oppressive to us:" he could therefore not continue "to sustain those in opposition in whose wisdom, firmness, and patriotism he had no reason to confide." This was not only notice of a dissolved alliance: it was a declaration of war.

Such a challenge could not pass unanswered. A "personal debate" succeeded, one of those oratorical lance-breakings in which the statesmen of that period delighted, and which that generation of citizens listened to or followed in the printed reports with bated breath. This time it was a passage at arms between those who were called the giants, — Calhoun on one side, Clay and Webster on the other; but on his side Clay was so much more conspicuous than Webster that the debate was usually called "the great debate between Clay and Calhoun." It started in the shape of great orations, and then, subsiding and breaking out again, it ran fitfully along with the discussions on the sub-treasury and on Calhoun's land bill until January, 1840.

It was a curious spectacle, that of the two contracting parties to the compromise of 1833, now become enemies, settling their accounts in public. But, as is usually the case, these encounters, however dramatic and brilliant, added little to the stock of things worth knowing. They consisted mainly in arduous efforts of each combatant to set forth what he desired the world to think of himself and of his antagonist. Clay opened with a severe criticism of Calhoun's new alliance with the Van Buren administration. Calhoun was especially anxious to establish the consistency of his "record," which he tried to do with great elaborateness, and to prove that the compromise of 1833 had been his victory and Clay's defeat. He drew a picture of himself striking down the protective policy, the American system, by "state interposition," another name for nullification; and of Clay finding himself deserted by his friends and proposing the compromise to save his political life, the compromise then being accepted by Calhoun as the capitulation of a discomfited foe is accepted by the victor. Clay retorted with his version of the story. He had found Calhoun at that period in an untenable, miserable, and perilous situation; he held out the compromise to the unfortunate nullifier as a rope is thrown to a drowning man, almost from mere motives of pity; Calhoun eagerly grasped it as a last chance of escape from Jackson's clutches. He (Clay) desired, too, to save the protective system from greater damage, and the country from an exciting conflict.

This controversy, going through a variety of repetitions, at last culminated in an angry explosion. "Events had placed him (Clay) flat on his back," said Calhoun, "and he had no way to recover himself but by the compromise. He was forced by the action of the State, which I in part represent, against his system, by my counsel to compromise, in order to save himself. I had the mastery over him on that occasion." This set Clay's wrath aflame. "The senator from South

Carolina," he exclaimed, "has said that I was flat on my back, and that he was my master. He my master! I would not own him as a slave!" This retort, although neither witty nor elegant, was at least an emphatic expression of genuine feeling, and much enjoyed by Clay's friends.

On the whole, Clay appeared in this debate to much greater advantage than Calhoun. It was not only the readiness and brilliancy of his eloquence, with its captivating tones, its biting sarcasm, its stirring appeals, and the music of sonorous sentences, that appealed to the hearer and reader, while Calhoun's speech, although compact, precise, and well-arranged, was somewhat dry in tone, jerking and rapid in delivery, and without a gesture to enliven it; but Clay was also more truthful, more ingenuous, more chivalrous. His version of the compromise of 1833 certainly accorded more with the facts than did Calhoun's. Clay was, indeed, not justified in representing the compromise as a protection measure. He proposed it to save a little remnant of the "American system," and to settle a difficulty dangerous to the country without leaving the matter to Jackson's violent impulses. But to say that the compromise was dictated by Calhoun, and intended to save Clay, was utterly absurd. Calhoun accepted it, and assented to provisions very distasteful to him, in order to escape from a perilous situation without an entire sacrifice of pride and a total surrender of his cause. John Quincy Adams witnessed one of the encounters. "Clay," he wrote, "had manifestly the advantage in the debate. The truth and the victory were with Clay, who spoke of the South Carolina nullification with such insulting contempt that it brought out Preston, who complained of it bitterly. Preston's countenance was a portraiture of agonizing anguish."

To accuse Calhoun of tergiversation and treachery because he left the Whig alliance and went over to Van Buren was, indeed, unjust. Calhoun had never been a Whig. For many years he had not sworn allegiance to any party except his "state-rights party," and that he expected to take with him wherever he went. It was easily shown, as Clay and Webster did show, that Calhoun had in years long past advocated the United States Bank, internal improvements, a protective tariff, and generally a broad construction of constitutional powers. But he had done that as a young Republican, long before the existence of the Whig party. Since that period Calhoun's mind had gone through that process which became decisive for his whole career as a statesman. He had always been a pro-slavery man. But so long as slavery seemed secure he permitted himself to have opinions upon other subjects according to their own merits. All this changed so soon as he saw that slavery was in danger. From that time all the workings of his mind and all his political endeavors centred upon the preservation of slavery. State-rights principles, nullification, political alliances, all these were to him subservient to his one aim. He modified his theories, as well as his associations, as that one interest seemed to demand. In Jackson he had opposed assumptions of executive power hostile to the state-rights principle, which he considered the essential bulwark of slavery. The ascendency of the Whig party he feared, because it would strengthen the general government in a manner dangerous to slavery. He saw in the breaking up of the alliance with the Whigs "the chance of effecting the union of the whole South."

But there was something crafty and disingenuous in the manner in which Calhoun tried to prove the complete consistency of his political conduct during the first period with that during the second. He worked hard to show that, while he supported the tariff, internal improvements, the United States Bank, and a liberal construction of the Constitution, he never meant what he appeared to mean, — in fact, that he had really never been the man he had induced his associates to believe him to be. His own presentation of himself was calculated to characterize him as a man of mental reservations and secret purposes, with whom it was dangerous to coöperate in full confidence.

Clay, on the other hand, while defending his general consistency with his usual impulsiveness, did not hesitate frankly to admit that once, indeed, on an important subject, he had changed his opinion; and the dashing freedom with which he opened himself as to his career, his principles, and his aims could scarcely fail to draw to him the hearts of his hearers. One of his most noteworthy utterances in this debate was that upon the tariff: "No one, Mr. President," said he, "in the commencement of the protective policy, ever supposed that it was to be perpetual. We hoped and believed that temporary protection, extended to our infant manufactures, would bring them up, and enable them to withstand competition with those of Europe. If the protective policy were entirely to cease in 1842, it would have existed twenty-six years from 1816, or eighteen from 1824, — quite as long as, at either of those periods, its friends supposed might be necessary."

While the sub-treasury bill was passing through its various stages, Clay was ever active in discussing a variety of other subjects. In 1837 and 1838 there was going on in Upper Canada an insurrection called the "Patriot War," begun for the object of reforming the government of the province. Many citizens of the United States sympathized with the insurgents. A British force came over to the American side of Niagara River and destroyed the steamboat Caroline, which was suspected of being used for conveying men and stores to the Canadian revolutionists. Clay thundered vehemently against the "British outrage," and called for satisfaction, but strongly deprecated war.

When a territorial government for Oregon was

proposed, he advised cautious proceedings, in order to avoid complications with England; and as to the settlement of the disputed northwestern boundary, too, his voice was for arbitration and peace. He spoke on a resolution concerning the American claims against Mexico, counseling moderation and justice, and censuring the administration for its bullying attitude. He supported a bill against dueling in the District of Columbia. He opposed the reduction of the price of public lands according to a graduated scale, as well as the preëmption right of settlers, adhering to his old notion that the public lands should be sold at public auction, and be treated as a source of public revenue. But also another and greater question called him forth again, the overshadowing importance of which only gradually dawned upon his mind.

CHAPTER XXI

SLAVERY AGAIN

The anti-slavery agitation continued, and grew in strength. The petitions for the abolition of slavery in the District of Columbia, presented in the session of 1835-36, had borne 34,000 signatures. Those presented in 1837-38 bore 300,000. The number of anti-slavery societies in the Northern States had increased to 2000. The movement was no longer confined to little conventicles. In fact, some of the original abolitionists, as is often the case with men who give themselves to an idea far ahead of the common ways of thinking, began to run into abstract speculations, — in this case, a variety of theories concerning woman's rights, nonresistance, the wrongfulness of all government, and similar theories; and, drifting into polemics among themselves, they lost much of their immediate influence. But their cause now moved forward by its own impulse. The legislatures of Massachusetts and Vermont passed, by enormous majorities, resolutions censuring, as hostile to the Constitution, the action of Congress in refusing to receive, or to treat with respect, anti-slavery petitions, and affirming the power of Congress to abolish slavery in the District of Columbia. Vermont also protested against the annexation of Texas. The legislature of Connecticut repealed the "black laws." The anti-slavery movement began to make itself felt as a power on the political field.

At the same time the South became painfully sensible of the growing superiority of the North in population and wealth. In 1838 a "commercial convention" of the Southern States was held, which, after instituting some gloomy historical and statistical comparisons, formed the conclusion that the South was becoming impoverished and "tributary" to the North; that this was owing to the tariff, internal improvements, and abuses of government; and that, as a remedy, the South should "open a direct trade between Southern and foreign ports." The convention did not seem to suspect that slavery was at the bottom of it all, and that they pronounced the doom of slavery by their very complaints. On the contrary, the more fatal the evil became, the more blindly and passionately they hugged it.

In December, 1837, when petitions for the abolition of slavery in the District of Columbia were presented in the Senate, Clay, whose democratic instinct was keenly stirred, inquired of the senator presenting them " whether the feeling of abolition in the abstract was extending itself " in the States from which the petitions were arriving, " or whether it was not becoming mixed up with other matters, such, for instance, as the belief that the sacred right of petition had been assailed?" The answer was that there had been such a mixture of causes. Clay then, advancing a step from the position he had formerly taken, moved that the petitions be not only received, but that they be referred to the Committee on the District of Columbia, "to act on them as they pleased." When it was objected that such a course would provoke that most undesirable thing, argument on the slavery question, Clay answered: —

"It has been said that this is not a case for argument. Not a case for argument! What is it that lies at the bottom of all our free institutions? Argument, inquiry, reasoning, consideration, deliberation. What question is there in human affairs so weak or so strong that it cannot be approached by argument and reason? This country will, in every emergency, appeal to its enlightened judgment and its spirit of union and harmony, and the appeal will not be unsuccessful."

These words were spoken while the extreme pro-slavery men cried out against the reception of every anti-slavery petition in the Senate, and muzzled the House with gag rules, feeling instinctively that free argument was just the thing slavery could not endure. Free argument on slavery was what the abolitionists demanded, and Clay, advocating the same thing, soon found himself denounced as one of them.

In the nineteenth century slavery could live only if surrounded by silence. Calhoun knew this well, but, as if impelled by the evil fate of his cause, he could not remain silent himself. While insisting that no petition hostile to slavery should be received and discussed by the Senate, he invited the discussion of the subject by offering a series of resolutions which set forth his theory of the relations between slavery and the Union. They affirmed that the several States entered the Union as independent and sovereign States, with the view to "increased security against all dangers, domestic as well as foreign;" that "any intermeddling of any one or more States, or a combination of their citizens, with the domestic institutions or police of the others, on any ground, political, moral, or religious," was unconstitutional, insulting, and tending to destroy the Union; that the general government was instituted by the several States as "a common agent" to use the powers delegated to it to give "increased stability and security to the domestic institutions of the States," and to resist all attempts to attack, weaken, or destroy them; that slavery was an important part of the domestic institutions referred to; that the intermeddling to abolish slavery in the District of Columbia or in any of the territories, under the pretext that slavery was "immoral or sinful," would be "a dangerous attack on the institutions of all the slaveholding States;" and, finally, that resistance to annexation of new slave territory (pointing at Texas), on the assumption that slavery was "immoral, or sinful, or otherwise obnoxious," would be contrary to the equality of rights and advantages of the several

SLAVERY AGAIN

States under the Constitution, and a virtual disfranchisement of the slave States. In other words, every attack on slavery anywhere was to be considered unconstitutional in spirit; state rights must be maintained for the slave States, and the general government must be part of the police force to give "increased stability and security" to slavery.

The vote on these resolutions, Calhoun said, would be "a test." By rejecting them the Senate would say to the South, "Come here no longer for protection." If the Senate adopted them, "it would be a holy pledge of that body to protect the South from further aggression." The postponement or evasion of a vote on them "must be considered a silent acquiescence in the insults offered to Southern rights and Southern feelings."

Calhoun's instinct was correct. Slavery was in danger — indeed, it was lost — if people were permitted to attack it as "an immoral and sinful institution." But could he force people, by a resolution adopted in the Senate, to believe that slavery was not sinful and immoral? Could he hope thus to disarm the ruling sentiment of the nineteenth century? He himself had grave doubts. "He was not sanguine," he said, "of the success of the measure, even if it should be adopted. He had presented it as the most likely to do good, and in the desire to do anything to avert the approaching catastrophe, which he was most anxious to avoid." He desired to preserve the Union, provided he could make slavery secure within it. "This [the slavery question] was the only question of sufficient potency," he said, "to divide the Union, and divide it it would, or drench the country in blood if not arrested." He saw the danger clearly. He felt instinctively that a people differing essentially in their notions of right and wrong cannot permanently remain bound together by voluntary union. But could he hope to avert the danger by the promulgation of mere abstractions? What he actually accomplished was to put the incompatibility of slavery with free institutions again in the strongest light.

A senator from Indiana, Smith, promptly moved to add a proviso to Calhoun's resolutions, that nothing therein should be construed as expressing an opinion of the Senate adverse to the fundamental principles of this government: that "all men are created equal;" that the freedom of speech and of the press, and the rights of peaceable meeting and of petition, should never be abridged; that "error of opinion may be tolerated while reason is left free to combat it;" and that "the Union must be preserved." He showed conclusively that, if the prohibition of "intermeddling" were enforced by effective legislation, all these fundamental principles of free government would have to yield. Here was again the logic of liberty put face to face with the logic of slavery.

Calhoun might have read the ultimate fate of his cause in the troubled faces of the "Northern senators with Southern principles." They looked at him beseechingly. They wished to support him and stand by the South; they would go as far as they could; but he must not put upon them loads too heavy for them to carry in their States; he must not threaten the right of petition; he must not impose upon the general government the duty of "strengthening" slavery, and of "increasing its stability;" he must not insist upon condemning as dangerous fanatics all those among their constituents who believed slavery to be "immoral and sinful." He was indeed asking too much of them. Their embarrassment was pitiable to behold.

Clay stepped in with an intermediate proposition, after the debate had proceeded for several days, and the first resolutions of Calhoun's series, modified and amended, had been adopted. Clay had voted for them, "not," as he said, "from any confidence in their healing virtues;" on the contrary, he thought, they were calculated, especially at the North, "to increase and exasperate, instead of diminishing and assuaging, the existing agitation." What he thought necessary was to strengthen the Union sentiment. Calhoun was trying, by his resolutions, to rally the state-rights party. In Clay's opinion, the interests of the South should not be put in the exclusive safekeeping of any one party, but of them all. He believed in the healing power of argument, reasoning, friendly discussion.

"Mr. President," he exclaimed, "I have no apprehension for the safety of the Union from any state of things now existing. I will not answer for the consequences which may issue from indiscretion and harshness on the part of individuals or of Congress, here or elsewhere. We allow ourselves to speak too frequently, and with too much levity, of a separation of this Union. It is a terrible word, to which our ears should not be familiarized. I desire to see in continued safety and prosperity *this* Union, and no other Union. I go for this Union as it is, one and indivisible, without diminution. I will neither voluntarily leave it, nor be driven out of it by force. Here, in my place, I shall contend for all the rights of the State which sent me here. I shall contend for them with undoubting confidence, and with the perfect conviction that they are safer in the Union than they would be out of the Union."

Then he offered a series of resolutions as substitutes for those of Calhoun, affirming: 1. That slavery in the States was exclusively under the control of the several States, and not to be interfered with; 2. That petitions touching slavery in the States should be rejected as praying for something "palpably beyond the scope of the constitutional power of Congress;" 3. That the abolition of slavery in the District of Columbia would be a violation of the good faith "implied in the cession" of the District, that it could not take place without indemnifying the slave owners, and would alarm the slave States; 4. That, on the other hand, the Senate, recognizing its "duty in respect to the constitutional right of petition," should hold itself bound to receive and treat with respect petitions touching slavery in the District; 5. That such petitions should be referred to the appropriate committees; 6. That it would be "highly inexpedient to abolish slavery in Florida, the only territory of the United States in which it now exists," because it would excite alarm in the South, because the people of Florida had not asked for it, and because they would be exclusively entitled to decide the question when admitted as a State; 7. That Congress had no power to abolish the slave trade between slave States; 8. That the agitation of the abolition question was to be regretted, that the Union should be cherished, and that the prevailing attachment to the Union was beheld "with the deepest satisfaction."

Calhoun was exasperated. "The difference between me and the senator from Kentucky," he said, "is as wide as the poles." No doubt it was. Calhoun would have preserved the Union if slavery could have been made secure in it. But he would willingly have sacrificed the Union to save slavery. Clay tried to pacify the slaveholders, and opposed the abolitionists, to avert from the Union a threatening danger. But he would have sacrificed slavery to save the Union. To him it was "not expedient" to abolish slavery in the District of Columbia and in Florida. Calhoun would hear nothing of "expediency." He insisted on placing the constitutional duty of protecting slavery on "the high ground of principle." He would hear nothing of concession. "Shall we yield, or stand firm? That is the question," he said. "If we yield an inch, we are gone." He was certainly right. But to be entirely right he should have added: "If we stand firm, we are gone likewise."

Clay was more hopeful, because he saw the real nature of the trouble less clearly. A natural compromiser, he believed in the efficacy of compromise in all cases. His resolutions were intended to be a compromise between slavery and the principles of republican government. The greatest stress he laid upon those referring to the District of Columbia and to Florida, in which he neither affirmed nor denied the power of Congress to abolish slavery, but deprecated its exercise as "inexpedient." They were offered to replace those of Calhoun concerning the territories and the annexation of Texas, and Clay actually succeeded in securing their adoption as substitutes. The rest of Calhoun's resolutions, the keenest edges of which had been much blunted by amendments, passed the Senate by a large vote.

The practical result was nothing, except more agitation of the slavery question. Calhoun had forgotten that senate resolutions will not determine public sentiment, but that public sentiment will at last determine the action of senates; and also that the struggle about slavery was to be, in the last resort, a struggle of moral and material forces, and not of constitutional theories. The greatest thinker among the champions of slavery tried to fight fate with paper balls.

Clay suspected Calhoun of personal ambition in this movement. He wrote to his friend Brooke: "They [Calhoun's resolutions] are at last disposed of. Their professed object is slavery; their real aim, to advance the political interest of the mover, and to affect mine." That was the suspicion of a presidential candidate watching a supposed rival. Calhoun certainly could not expect to win any political capital by his resolutions. They could never be popular at the North, and even a good many Southern men considered their introduction extremely impolitic. A speech delivered by Clay about a year later was more justly suspected to be a part of a presidential campaign.

The Senate continued to lay anti-slavery petitions on the table without that reference and respectful consideration which Clay had asked for them. The House adopted more gag rules to silence anti-slavery members. But all these things served only to strengthen the movement among the people. It began seriously to alarm the politicians, for they found themselves confronted by a force which could neither be conciliated by the offer of offices, nor be frightened by exclusion from them. To the managing politician the man who wants nothing is the most embarrassing problem. The anti-slavery men began to catechise candidates, and to work against those they did not find "sound" on the slavery question. And, as is apt to happen, they worked most bitterly against those who in their opinion ought to have been sound and were not. By them a Democrat might be forgiven for being a pro-slavery man, but a Whig could not be forgiven.

"In Ohio the abolitionists are alleged to have gone against us almost to a man," Clay wrote in November, 1838. "The introduction of this new element of abolition into our elections cannot fail to excite, with all reflecting men, the deepest solicitude. Although their numbers are not very great, they are sufficiently numerous in several States to turn the scale. I have now before me a letter from the secretary of the American Anti-slavery Society in New York, in which he says: 'I should consider' (as in all candor I acknowledge I would) 'the election of a slaveholder to the presidency a great calamity to the country.' The danger is that the contagion may spread until it reaches all the free States. My own position touching slavery, at the present time, is singular enough. The abolitionists are denouncing me as a slaveholder, and slaveholders as an abolitionist, while both unite on Mr. Van Buren."

The opinion that the abolitionists were a dangerous class of people grew very strong in Clay's mind. The half way man usually considers those who insist upon the last logical consequences of his own feelings or principles very inconvenient, and even very obnoxious, persons. On the other hand, Clay's course with regard to the anti-slavery petitions, as well as his occasional professions of sentiments unfriendly to slavery, had injured his popularity with the slaveholders. This he felt, as his correspondence indicates; and it is probable that Southern Whigs, many of whom, while his friends, were fierce pro-slavery men, suggested to him the policy of "setting himself right" with the South. In February, 1839, he made a speech which had all the appearance of an attempt on his part to do this. It was not in the course of a debate on some practical measure, but in presenting a petition of inhabitants of Washington *against* the abolition of slavery in the District of Columbia. Gossip had it that he himself had written the petition; and there is good ground for believing that, contrary to his habit, he carefully wrote out the whole speech, and read it, before its delivery in the Senate, to Senator Preston from South Carolina, an ardent pro-slavery man, in company with several other friends. The speech bears all the marks of that careful weighing of words characteristic of a candidate "defining his position" on a delicate subject.

It may perhaps be called his least creditable performance. Many of his friends and admirers must have witnessed it with regret. It was an apology for his better self. Formerly he had spoken as a born anti-slavery man, who to his profound regret found himself compelled to make concessions to slavery. Now he appeared as one inclined to deplore the attacks on slavery no less, if not more, than the existence of slavery itself. He divided the abolitionists into three classes: the conscientious and peaceful philanthropists, such as the Quakers; those who coöperated with the abolitionists because they thought the right of petition had been violated; and finally, the real ultra-abolitionists, who would resort to the ballot, and also to the bayonet, to effect a revolution in the South, and hurry the country "down a dreadful precipice." The principal cause of the present excitement he found in the example of emancipation in the British West Indies, and in the existence of "persons in both parts of the Union who have sought to mingle abolition with politics, and to array one part of the Union against another." He recited all his old arguments against the abolition of slavery in the District of Columbia and the Territory of Florida, as well as against the power of Congress to prohibit the slave trade between the slave States.

The immediate object of the abolitionists, he asserted, was to liberate, at one stroke, all the three millions of slaves in the slave States. Of this he denied the power as well as the morality. If there were no slavery in the country, he would resolutely oppose its introduction. But in the slave States the alternative was that the white man must govern the black, or the black the white. "In such an alternative," he said, "who can hesitate? Is it not better for both parties that the existing state should be preserved? This is our true ground of defense. It is that which our Revolutionary ancestors assumed. It is that which, in my opinion, forms our justification in the eyes of all Christendom."

There was a visionary dogma that negro slaves

were not property. "That is property which the law declares property." That species of property was worth twelve hundred millions. Would the abolitionists raise that sum to indemnify the owners? The abolition movement had set back for half a century the prospect of any kind of emancipation, and "increased the rigors of legislation against the slaves." Kentucky had once thought of gradual emancipation, but did so no longer. He himself had then favored it, because the number of slaves was much smaller than that of the whites. "But," he added, "if I had been then, or were now, a citizen of any of the planting States, I should have opposed, and would continue to oppose, any scheme of emancipation, gradual or immediate, because of the danger of an ultimate ascendency of the black race, or of a civil contest which might terminate in the extinction of one race or the other." He drew a gloomy picture of the dangers threatening the Union, of disruption, hatred, strife, and carnage, from which the abolitionists themselves would shrink back.

This was the highest flight upon which his old anti-slavery spirit ventured: —

"I am no friend of slavery. The Searcher of all hearts knows that every pulsation of mine beats high and strong in the cause of civil liberty. Wherever it is safe and practicable, I desire to see every portion of the human family in the enjoyment of it. But I prefer the liberty of my own country to that of any other people, and the liberty of my own race to that of any other race.

The liberty of the descendants of Africa in the United States is incompatible with the liberty and safety of the European descendants. Their slavery forms an exception — an exception resulting from a stern and inexorable necessity — to the general liberty in the United States. We did not originate, nor are we responsible for, this necessity. Their liberty, if it were possible, could only be established by violating the incontestable powers of the States and subverting the Union; and beneath the ruins of the Union would be buried, sooner or later, the liberty of both races."

He closed with a beseeching appeal to the abolitionists to desist.

Clay received his reward — or punishment — immediately. No sooner had he finished his speech than Calhoun rose as if to accept his surrender. When he turned his eyes back for the last twelve months, Calhoun said, and compared what he then heard with what was now said in the same quarter, he was forcibly struck, and he might say pleasurably, with the change. He recalled to the memory of the Senate the debate on his resolutions, and Clay's part in it. "Sir," he added, "this is a great epoch in our political history. Of all the dangers to which we have ever been exposed, this has been the greatest. We may now consider it passed. The resolutions to which I referred, with the following movements, gave the fatal blow, to which the position now assumed by the senator from Kentucky has given the finishing stroke." And, as if this had not been enough of humiliation to Clay, he went on: —

SLAVERY AGAIN 169

"What has been done will be followed by a great moral revolution of feeling and thinking in reference to the domestic institutions of the South. Already the discussion has effected a great change among ourselves. There were many, very many, in the slaveholding States, who, at the commencement of the controversy, believed that slavery was an evil to be tolerated, because we could not escape from it, but not to be defended. That has passed away. We now believe that it has been a great blessing to both of the races — the European and African — which, by a mysterious Providence, have been brought together in the southern section of this Union. I heard the senator from Kentucky with pleasure. His speech will have a happy effect, and will do much to consummate what had already been so happily begun and successfully carried on to a completion."

How would the proud and fiery spirit of Clay have blazed forth at this haughty assumption of superiority and leadership, had he not been a candidate for the presidency! But the candidate for the presidency, having said what he did not feel to win the favor of the slaveholders, bore his humiliation in silence. Calhoun assigned to him a place in his church on the bench of the penitents, and the candidate for the presidency took the insult without wincing.

Not long after these occurrences Senator Preston of South Carolina, with whom Clay had consulted before delivering his speech against the abolitionists, addressed a Whig meeting in Philadelphia, and said in the course of an eloquent eulogy on

Clay: "On one occasion Mr. Clay did me the honor to consult me in reference to a step he was about to take, and which will, perhaps, occur to your minds without a more direct allusion. After stating what he proposed, it was remarked that such a step might be offensive to the ultras of both parties, in the excitement which then existed. To this Mr. Clay replied: 'I trust the sentiments and opinions are correct; I had rather be right than be president.'"

This was a fine saying. But, alas! Clay wanted very much to be president, and men who want very much to be president are often not fully conscious of their motives. What he called "right" on this occasion he would not have called right at other periods of his life. He said it with the presidency in his mind. But it did not make him president after all.

He repeated something feebly resembling the sentiments expressed in his speech against the abolitionists, when presenting an anti-slavery petition a year later, in February, 1840. But he showed again that he had by no means lost the appreciation of the moral feelings of mankind with regard to slavery. In April, 1840, when discussing a set of resolutions offered by Calhoun protesting against the liberation of slaves on the American brig Enterprise, which had been forced by stress of weather into a British West Indian port, Clay expressed regret that such resolutions had been offered, for he thought "that prudence and discretion should admonish us not too often to throw before the world " questions in relation to slave property. It was repugnant to him to see his country appear among the nations of the civilized world as the champion of slavery. But as a politician he voted for Calhoun's resolution.

CHAPTER XXII

THE ELECTION OF 1840

THE opposition to Van Buren's administration consisted of heterogeneous elements. There were the original "National Republicans," organized while John Quincy Adams was president; there were various groups of Democrats, who had been driven into opposition during the "reign of Andrew Jackson," partly by the removal of the deposits, partly by the specie circular, partly by disgust at the expunging resolution; and there were, finally, the "Conservatives," who revolted at Van Buren's sub-treasury scheme, in which they saw a systematic war upon the banks of the country. These elements had an object of attack in common; but they disagreed among themselves, more or less, about everything that would constitute the positive part of a party programme. It is true the old National Republicans, forming the bulk of the Whig party, were among themselves in tolerable accord about the construction of constitutional powers, the tariff, internal improvements, and, in a less degree, about the National Bank question. But among the auxiliary forces, the "wings" of the party, there were many strict constructionists, anti-bank men, anti-tariff men, anti-internal-improvement men; and these forces had to be consulted, for, without their aid, a victory in a national election could scarcely be hoped for. As to the slavery question, a large number, if not a large majority, of the Northern Whigs were conscientiously opposed to slavery, while many of the Southern Whigs figured among the most ardent devotees of the peculiar " institution."

Clay undertook the task of making himself, as a candidate for the presidency, acceptable, if not to all, at least to most, of these divergent elements. As to the tariff, he declared in his letters to political friends that he would adhere to the compromise measure of 1833. He also repeated that the protective policy had never been intended to be permanent. As to internal improvements, Congress, he insisted, possessed the required power, but should no longer exercise it, considering what had been done for the States by the distribution act, and what they had severally done for themselves; he wished only to pass his bill distributing the proceeds of public land sales. As to the bank question, he repeated that the establishment of another United States Bank would be inexpedient until it should be clearly demanded by an undoubted majority of the people. He further reaffirmed his belief that the use of the government patronage was dangerous to republican institutions, and that the power of removal should be regulated by legislation. As to the slavery question, we have seen what position he took in his speech against the abolitionists. He was also anxious to strengthen the party by attaching those who had ceased to be administration Democrats without at once becoming Whigs. "It is manifest," he wrote to Brooke, "that if we repel the advances of all the former members of the Jackson party to unite with us, under whatever name they may adopt, we must remain in a perpetual and helpless minority." To encourage that element he favored, in a somewhat occult way, the reëlection of Senator Rives of Virginia, who had, as a zealous Jackson man, voted for the expunging resolution, but then opposed Van Buren's sub-treasury measure, and thus dropped out of the Democratic communion. This involved the defeat of Rives's competitor, John Tyler, who had sacrificed his seat in the Senate because he would not obey the Virginia legislature, which instructed him to vote for the expunging resolution. When Tyler's defeat was brought home to Clay's influence, the wrath of some of Tyler's friends was great; and it is reported that, to appease this wrath, the parties concerned agreed to open to Tyler the way to the vice-presidency.

But all these contrivances did not suffice to smooth his path. Rival ambitions confronted him. Webster had for years been burning to be president. His support outside of Massachusetts was, indeed, so slender that in June, 1839, he formally withdrew his candidacy. But his influence could be a formidable obstacle in Clay's way, and, as

John Quincy Adams wrote, there was "no good-will lost between Clay and Webster." Their disagreement on the compromise measures of 1833, and still more their constant rivalry as to the presidency, had estranged them. Even after his withdrawal, many of Webster's friends continued very actively to oppose Clay's pretensions, especially in the important State of New York. Directly and indirectly, their influence was exerted for General William H. Harrison of Ohio, as Clay was believed to have favored Harrison rather than Webster in 1836. It seems to be one of the weaknesses of great men, in the competition for the highest honors, to prefer comparatively small men to one another.

Harrison possessed the advantage of being a "military hero." A quarter of a century before, he had beaten the Indians at Tippecanoe, and also won the "battle of the Thames," where Tecumseh was killed. He had filled the territorial governorship of Indiana, and a seat in the House of Representatives and in the Senate, with quiet respectability. His "claims" as a statesman were, in his own opinion, not very exalted. "In relation to politics," he wrote to Clay in September, 1839, "I can only say that my position in relation to yourself is to me distressing and embarrassing. How little can we judge of our future destinies! A few years ago I could not have believed in the possibility of my being placed in a position of apparent rivalry to you, particularly in relation to the presidency, an office which I never dreamed of attaining, and which I had ardently desired to see you occupy. I confess that I did covet the second, but never the first, office in the gift of my fellow citizens. Fate, as Bonaparte would say, has placed me where I am, and I wait the result which time will determine." When a man put forward as a candidate for the presidency sees no particular reason why he should be made the chief of a great state, he may still discover in himself the mysterious qualification of being a man of "fate." It was upon him that Clay's opponents in the Whig party united, because he had elements of popularity which lay outside of politics and aroused no hostility.

The opposition to Clay came from several classes, — the Anti-Masons, of whom there were remnants mainly in Pennsylvania and New York; some of the anti-slavery Whigs, whom Clay displeased as a slaveholder, and whom his speech against the abolitionists had irritated; some of Webster's friends, for reasons largely personal; and the political managers, who wanted to win at any price, and in whose eyes Clay had, by his defeats in former campaigns, been marked as an "unlucky candidate." These politicians went to work systematically to compass his defeat.

The Whig National Convention was to meet at Harrisburg, in Pennsylvania, on December 4, 1839. In February, 1839, Clay was advised by one of his confidential friends, General Porter, that a major-

THE ELECTION OF 1840

ity of the Whigs in New York decidedly preferred him as a candidate; that the Whigs in the legislature were ready to give him a preliminary nomination, but that they were restrained by a class of politicians "calling themselves Whigs, but who thought that no political victory was worth achieving if not gained by stratagem. The governor [Seward]," he added, "and Thurlow Weed, who at this moment is decidedly the most important man, politically speaking, in the State, are not only friendly to your election, but warmly and zealously so; but they deem it inexpedient to make public declaration of their preference at this time."

This had a fair sound, but Clay was not without misgivings. Although he had, the year before, declined the invitation of enthusiastic friends who desired him to visit New York, on the ground that it might look like an attempt to "attract the current of public feeling to him," he accepted a similar invitation in the summer of 1839. He was splendidly received, and great popular enthusiasm accompanied his "progress" through the State. But at Saratoga Thurlow Weed, who had been reported as "not only friendly, but warmly and zealously so," waited upon him with the suggestion, thinly if at all disguised, that, as he (Clay) could probably not carry the State of New York, he should withdraw in favor of another candidate more likely to be elected. "Nothing could be more courteous and kind than Mr. Clay's bearing throughout the conversation," says Thurlow Weed in his autobiography. But such a suggestion was not what Clay had expected from a "warm and zealous" friend. He had gone through the whole gamut of doubt and hope which enlivens the existence of a presidential candidate. He had been sanguine in the spring of 1838; he had been despondent in November, when the elections turned out unfavorably to the Whigs, and had spoken of promulgating that he would under no circumstances be a candidate. He felt again in 1839 that the current in his favor would break forth "with accumulated strength." He was determined now to remain in the field, and Thurlow Weed could not shake that determination. Neither did Clay's courteous and kind bearing shake Thurlow Weed's determination that not Clay, but Harrison, should be nominated.

If the story told by Henry A. Wise in his "Seven Decades" may be believed, the Whig managers in New York opposed to Clay's nomination played a shrewd game, called "the triangular correspondence," by which the election of Clay delegates to the national convention was to be prevented. Three of them, located say at New York city, Utica, and Rochester, would write to one another: "Do all you can for Clay in your district, for I am sorry to say he has no strength in this." These letters from pretended friends of Clay, being handed round in each of the districts, would enable the conspirators to say everywhere: "It is useless for us to send delegates favorable to Mr. Clay from here, for he has no strength anywhere else." But whether the matter was really managed in this manner or not, it turned out that, of the delegates to the Harrisburg Convention, only ten were for Clay, twenty for General Scott, and two for Harrison. General Scott, no doubt, had been made to believe himself a serious candidate. In February, 1839, he had written a friendly letter to Clay, informing him that he (Scott) had been "approached" with assurances of eventual support for the office of president by "persons of more or less consideration," and deprecating all feelings of jealousy. Thurlow Weed admitted that the name of General Scott, who had some popularity in New York, was used merely "to keep New York away from Clay." At Harrisburg the Scott delegates were at the proper moment to be transferred to Harrison.

Nothing could excel the shrewdness and audacity with which the convention itself was managed to insure Clay's defeat. When it met, Clay's friends had an undoubted plurality of votes. It was probable that, if Clay's name were brought before the convention in a clever speech, its charm would be irresistible. Such a risk his opponents would not run. To avoid it, a resolution was carried providing that each state delegation should appoint a committee of three to "receive the views and opinions of each delegation, and communicate the same to the assembled committees of all the delegations;"

the delegations should then, each for itself, ballot for presidential candidates, and thereupon compare notes in general committee through their committees of three; and then, if no majority was at once apparent, ballot again and compare notes, and so on, until a majority should be obtained, which fact should then be reported to the convention. Thus all the important business was to be done in secret by a select body of men, and the convention, in its public session, was only to ratify what had been "cut and dried" for it. This contrivance worked as desired. On the first balloting, Clay received 102 votes, Harrison 91, and Scott 57. After several secret decoctions and filtrations occupying several days, a majority for Harrison was evolved. The bulk of the Scott vote, embodying a large part of the Webster influence, had gone over to Harrison, according to programme. Scott himself discovered that the "assurances of eventual support," with which he had been "approached," had not made him as serious a candidate as he had imagined; and Clay found, on the decisive ballot, little more on his side than votes from slaveholding States.

When the result was determined, Clay's friends were not only "disappointed and grieved, even to tears," but also indignant. The managers became alarmed. Speeches praising Clay to the skies were made by men who had voted against him, and it was at once determined that the nomination for the vice-presidency must be given to one of Clay's

THE ELECTION OF 1840

most pronounced friends. Watkins Leigh of Virginia, a very honorable and able man, was pointed out by the Clay delegates, but he declined. Clayton, Tallmadge, and Southard declined likewise, until finally John Tyler was nominated, as Thurlow Weed said, "because we could get nobody else to accept," but probably because the convention remembered that something was due to the man who had sacrificed his seat in the Senate rather than vote for the expunging resolution, and then been set aside in favor of a late comer in the opposition.

In the convention, after Harrison had been nominated, a letter from Clay to the Kentucky delegation was read, in which he assured them that, while he should highly appreciate the honor of a nomination, yet, if it were thought wise to nominate somebody else, he would, "far from feeling any discontent," give the nominee his best wishes and cordial support, and admonishing his friends not to hesitate if they found it necessary to select some other candidate than himself in order to unite the party. He was, however, when he wrote that letter, far from anticipating such an emergency. The news of his defeat threw him into paroxysms of rage. As Henry A. Wise, who was with Clay at the moment when the tidings from Harrisburg arrived at Washington, tells the story, Clay, who had been drinking freely in the excitement of expectation, "rose from his chair, and, walking backwards and forwards rapidly, lifting his feet like a horse string-halted in both legs, stamped his steps upon the floor, exclaiming: 'My friends are not worth the powder and shot it would take to kill them!'" He added: "If there were two Henry Clays, one of them would make the other president of the United States." And when Wise reminded him that he had been warned of the intrigues going on, he replied: "It is a diabolical intrigue, I know now, which has betrayed me. I am the most unfortunate man in the history of parties: always run by my friends when sure to be defeated, and now betrayed for a nomination when I, or any one, would be sure of an election."

The lack of dignity in this explosion of wrath was certainly unbecoming a great leader. But there can be no doubt that Clay had reason for being angry. He was the chief of the Whig party. He had always been its foremost champion in the field. He had fought its battles, and received the blows struck at it. His personal integrity was clear. If it could be said that its honors were due to any one, they were due to him. He found himself cast aside for a man whose significance could not be compared to his. And more; the methods employed to defeat him had been those of intrigue, designed to falsify the feelings of the masses and to muzzle the enthusiasm of his friends, — unscrupulous, crafty, without precedent in American politics. All this was true.

On the other hand, Clay had himself done much, if not most, to make the Whig party what it was in 1839 and 1840, — a coalition rather than a party, without common principles and definite aims beyond the mere overthrow of those in power. Such a temporary combination will always be apt to look, not for candidates who represent well defined objects and measures, but rather for mere availabilities, who repel nobody because they represent nothing with distinctness. By his anti-abolition speech and his explanatory letters, Clay had tried to lower himself to the level of a mere availability, but he had a past career which spoke loudly for itself. It was, perhaps, the consciousness of having sacrificed much of his dignity in vain that fanned his fury when he heard of his defeat.

He was right in speaking of the election of 1840 as one in which he or any other Whig candidate would be sure of success. The Democrats renominated Van Buren. Even had Van Buren been a popular man, which he was not, the force of circumstances would have overwhelmed him. The crisis of 1837 had produced a strong political current against the ruling party. An apparent improvement in business in 1838 enabled the Democrats to recover some of the lost ground. But in 1839 the renewed suspension of the United States Bank, and of a host of banks in the South and West, cast new gloom upon the country, and, as usually, the bad times turned the minds of the people against those in power.

Moreover, the "spoils system," introduced in

national politics by Jackson, had developed some of its most repulsive attributes. Not only were the officers of the government permitted to become active workers in party politics, but they were made to understand that active partisanship was one — perhaps the principal one — of their duties. Political assessments upon office-holders, with all the inseparable scandals, became at once a part of the system. The spoils politician in office grasped almost everywhere the reins of local leadership in the party. The influence of party spirit upon the public business went so far, as Clay related in one of his speeches, that two officers of the army were "put upon their solemn trial on the charge of prejudicing the Democratic party by making purchases for the supply of the army from members of the Whig party. And this trial was commenced at the instance of a committee of a Democratic convention, and conducted and prosecuted by them."

The "spoils system" bore a crop of corruption such as had never been known before. Swartwout, the collector of customs at New York, one of General Jackson's favorites, was discovered to be a defaulter to the amount of nearly $1,250,000, and the district attorney of the United States at New York to the amount of $72,000. Almost all the land officers were defaulters. Investigations instituted by the House of Representatives proved the administration to have been incredibly lax, not only in supervising the conduct of the public business, but in holding the delinquents in the service

THE ELECTION OF 1840

to an account. Officials seemed to "help themselves" to the public money, not only without shame, but in many cases apparently without any fear of punishment. In Congress, too, the habit of lavish expenditures had grown to an unprecedented extent. The contingent expenses for the stationery of members, when disclosed, fairly startled the country. No wonder the Van Buren party was styled the "spoils party"!

Nor was this all. Party discipline under Jackson and Van Buren had become so tyrannical that a reaction was inevitable. Jackson's high-handed proceedings had driven off many men of independent impulses, while his prestige and immense popularity prevented the secession of large masses. But when the imposing figure of Jackson disappeared from the place of command, — when that fierce party despotism was wielded no longer by the lion, but by the "fox," and the painful throes of the business crisis had produced a general disposition to be dissatisfied with the government, — the revolt against party tyranny could not fail to become formidable.

These were the circumstances which brought forth the phenomenal commotion of 1840. The Whig National Convention had adopted no platform, passed no resolutions, issued no address, put forth no programme of policy. It had simply nominated in General Harrison a candidate for the presidential office whose "record" might have fitted him for a Democratic as well as for a Whig candidacy. He was of the old Jeffersonian Republican school. His public utterances had not clearly identified him with any distinctively Whig principles or measures. He was a state-rights man. As to the tariff, he, like many old Republicans, had once been warmly in favor of the protective system, but was now for the compromise of 1833, and against any alteration of it. As to the United States Bank, he thought there was "no express grant of power" in the fundamental law to charter a national bank, and "it never could be constitutional to exercise that power, save in the event that the powers granted to Congress could not be carried into effect without resorting to such an institution." As to the slavery question, he had in his official capacities generally supported what the slaveholding interest asked for. His political wisdom consisted in some general maxims which were very good in themselves, and would benefit the republic if well applied. He was an honest man, who had been harshly removed from a foreign mission by General Jackson, and then retired to a small farm in Ohio. His fancied log cabin and hard cider contrasted strikingly with Van Buren's aristocratic "gold spoons." He was just the man whom the popular imagination would invest with that homely common sense and rugged virtue thought to be required for putting an end to the hard times, and restoring the good, frugal, honest government of the fathers. There was a vague and widespread feeling that any change would be for the better. A change, therefore, was wanted. General Harrison represented that change, and the future would take care of itself.

There has probably never been a presidential campaign of more enthusiasm and less thought than the Whig campaign of 1840. As soon as it was fairly started, it resolved itself into a popular frolic. There was no end of monster mass meetings, with log cabins, raccoons, and hard cider. One half of the American people seemed to have stopped work to march in processions behind brass bands or drum and fife, to attend huge picnics, and to sing campaign doggerel about "Tippecanoe and Tyler too." The array of speakers on the Whig side was most imposing: Clay, Webster, Corwin, Ewing, Clayton, Preston, Choate, Wise, Reverdy Johnson, Everett, Prentiss, Thompson of Indiana, and a host of lesser lights. But the immense multitudes gathered at the meetings came to be amused, not to be instructed. They met, not to think and deliberate, but to laugh and shout and sing.

Clay, faithful to his promise, supported the Whig candidates with much energy, speaking at many places. In one of his addresses — a speech delivered at Taylorsville in Virginia — he undertook to "sound the keynote of the campaign" by laying down an elaborate and carefully prepared programme for future action in case of a Whig victory. At the start, however, he declared that he " did not pretend to announce the purposes of the new president," of which he had "no knowledge other than that accessible to every citizen. He spoke only for himself." His programme, in many points, especially those relating to the veto power and the treasury, thoroughly characteristic of his impressionable and impulsive statesmanship, was this: The executive power should be circumscribed by such limitations and safeguards as would render it no longer dangerous to the public liberties. There should be a constitutional provision limiting the President to a single term. The veto power should be more precisely defined, and be subjected to further limitations; for instance, that a veto might be overruled by a simple majority of all the members of the Senate and the House of Representatives. The power of dismission from office should be restricted, and its exercise be rendered responsible; the President should be bound to communicate fully the grounds and motives of the dismission. The control of the treasury should be confided exclusively to Congress, and the President should no longer have the power of dismissing the secretary of the treasury, or other persons having the immediate charge of it. The appointment of members of Congress to any office, or any but a few specific offices, during their continuance in Congress, and for one year thereafter, should be prohibited. As to "matters of an administrative nature," Congress should exert all its power to establish and maintain a currency of stability and uniform value. Whether this were to be done by the means of state banks carefully selected, or of a new United States Bank, "should be left to the arbitrament of an enlightened public opinion." He feared that without a United States Bank there could be no sound currency; but if it could be obtained otherwise, he would be satisfied. Manufacturing industries should be protected, but he was contented with the tariff duties provided for in the compromise act of 1833. The public lands should be treated as a source of revenue, in accordance with his land bill. The building of roads and canals should be left to the States; and they should receive from the general government, for internal improvements, no more than the fourth installment under the distribution law, and their share of the proceeds of public land sales. There should be a reduction of expenses and a diminution of offices. The right to slave property "should be left where the Constitution had placed it, undisturbed and unagitated by Congress."

We shall remember some parts of this programme when we hear its author on the meaning of the victory.

Harrison was elected by 234 electoral votes against 60 for Van Buren. The Whigs carried nineteen, the Democrats only seven, States. In the popular vote, Harrison's majority reached nearly 150,000. The Whigs were wild with delight. They regarded their success as a great deliverance, the greatest event of their time. Few of them would have admitted that an occurrence which had happened two and a half years before — the first crossing of the ocean by a steamship, the bringing to one another's doors of the old and the new world — was far more important in its consequences; and perhaps fewer still that the seven thousand votes cast for Birney and Lemoyne, the candidates of an anti-slavery convention which had been almost entirely lost sight of in the turmoil of the "hard-cider campaign," bore in themselves the germ of infinitely greater developments.

Soon after the election, Clay and Harrison had an interview, which Harrison had in vain tried to avoid. The lucky mediocrity seems to have felt some discomfort in the thought of meeting the imperious party chief, to whom the honors which he himself wore were known to be really due. Harrison offered to Clay the first place in his cabinet, intending to summon Webster also. This was prudent. A second-rate man elected to the presidency will act wisely in taking the able and ambitious leaders of his party, if they are honest men, from Congress into the cabinet. They may then try to serve their own ambitions, but, in doing so, they will feel themselves under honorable obligation and restraint; they will scarcely seek to overthrow the administration. When the real leaders of the party are not identified with the administration and strive to control it from the outside, dissension and strife are almost inevitable.

But Clay declined Harrison's offer. He desired

to be independent in his leadership, and preferred the Senate as his field of action. He informed Harrison that his confidence in Webster had been somewhat shaken during the last eight years; but with proud condescension he assured the President-elect that the appointment of Webster to a place in the cabinet would not diminish his interest in the administration, nor his zeal in its support, if it were conducted on the principles he hoped it would be. In parting, Clay cautioned Harrison, if any efforts were made by any one to create distrust or ill-feeling between them, to listen to no reports in regard to his opinions, or intended course concerning this or that act or measure of the administration, but to depend upon his frankness, — which Harrison promised. In the cabinet, subsequently appointed by Harrison, Clay had four strong friends: Ewing of Ohio, secretary of the treasury; Badger of North Carolina, secretary of the navy; Bell of Tennessee, secretary of war; and Crittenden of Kentucky, attorney-general. Webster was secretary of state, and his friend Granger postmaster-general.

Congress had hardly met, in December, 1840, for the last session under Van Buren, when Clay offered a resolution in the Senate that the sub-treasury act "ought to be forthwith repealed." The speech with which he accompanied it sounded like a wild shout of triumph. He would not make an argument, he said. He would "as lief argue to a convicted criminal with a rope around his neck, and the cart about to leave his body, to prove to him that his conviction was according to law and justice, as to prove that this sub-treasury measure ought to be abandoned." It was sufficient for him to say that "the nation wills the repeal of the measure, the nation decrees the repeal of the measure, the nation commands the repeal of the measure, and the representatives of nineteen States were sent there instructed to repeal it." This had been almost exactly Benton's language in passing the expunging resolution four years before.

Silas Wright answered with keen irony that, after a campaign such as the country had witnessed, the presidential election might be interpreted as meaning that the Capitol should be taken down, and a log cabin ornamented with coon-skins put in its place, as well as that the sub-treasury law should be repealed. The Democrats still had a majority in the Senate, and Clay's resolution failed. The same fate had his land bill, which he urged in an elaborate speech. The session remained without any result of importance. But Clay lost no opportunity to make his opponents understand that soon both houses would be in the hands of the Whigs, and that then all his measures would be speedily consummated. "Clay crows too much over a fallen foe," John Quincy Adams wrote in his Diary. He would have "crowed" less had he known the disappointments in store for him.

First those trials came upon him which he who

THE ELECTION OF 1840

is regarded as a potential man with a new administration cannot escape. The Whigs had denounced the Democrats as the "spoils party." Their victory was to inaugurate an era of reform. But no sooner was that victory won than it turned out that the victors had taken the infection. "We have nothing new here in politics," wrote Horace Greeley, who in the campaign had distinguished himself as the editor of the "Log Cabin" newspaper in New York, "but large and numerous swarms of office-hunting locusts sweeping on to Washington daily. All the rotten land speculators, broken bank directors, swindling cashiers, etc., are in full cry for office, office; and even so humble a man as I am is run down for letters, letters. 'None of your half-way things. Write strong!' Curse their nauseous impudence!"

This picture exaggerated nothing. Clay was overwhelmed with applications for his "influence." Some of them glaringly illustrated the understanding of the word "reform" which prevailed among a powerful class of Whig politicians. General Porter, late secretary of war under John Quincy Adams, wrote to Clay that he had been requested by Thurlow Weed to secure Clay's support for the appointment of Mr. Edward Curtis as collector of customs in New York, Curtis being represented as "not personally popular," but as "possessing an extraordinary share of tact or stratagem," and as being able, "by his skill in planning and combining, and his untiring industry in executing, to produce the most astonishing political results; that, with the office of collector, he could on all important occasions command the vote of the city of New York, and *par consequence* of the State." Curtis, as a warm partisan of Webster, had with great industry and zeal helped to defeat Clay at the Harrisburg Convention. But seeing now that Webster had no chance, Curtis would persuade Webster to give up his presidential aspirations forever, and henceforth Clay would be Curtis's candidate. Clay contemptuously suggested that this information be communicated to Webster. But Thurlow Weed took the matter very seriously, and wrote to a friend that, if Curtis now failed because he had opposed Clay's nomination, "such a condition of things would destroy us."

Clay resolved to have nothing to do with the distribution of the spoils. A month before Harrison's inauguration he informed his friend Brooke: "I have been constrained, after a full consideration, to adopt the principle of non-interference with the new administration as to new appointments. Without it, if the day had a duration of forty-eight hours, I should be unable to attend to the applications I receive."

But, while he did not ask for appointments, he no doubt sought to exercise a controlling influence as to the policies and measures of the new administration; and, as he felt himself to be the true chief of the Whig party, it is not unlikely that his advice was given with that air and tone of command to which he had become accustomed. Harrison, a much weaker man, could easily be made to feel that his dignity would fatally suffer if he permitted it to be believed that he was under Clay's dictation. It is reported that on one occasion he sharply turned on Clay, saying: "Mr. Clay, you forget that I am president." Clay's influence was still visible in Harrison's inaugural address, which, at the request of prominent Whigs, was submitted to him. It was also mainly Clay's impatient urgency which prevailed upon Harrison to call an extra session of Congress to meet on May 31, 1841. But Harrison had not been president ten days when something very like a rupture of friendly relations occurred between them.

Nathan Sargent, as he tells us in his "Public Men and Events," one day found Clay in his room greatly agitated. "He had received an intimation from the President that whatever suggestion or communication he wished to make to the President he should make in writing, as frequent personal interviews between them might give occasion for remark, or excite the jealousy of others." The indignation of the proud man was, no doubt, much toned down in the farewell note he addressed to Harrison on March 15, on the eve of his departure from Washington. He would not trouble the President again by a personal visit.

"I was mortified," he continued, "by the suggestion you made to me on Saturday, that I had been represented as dictating to you or to the new administration, — mortified, because it is unfounded in fact, as well as because there is danger of the fears that I intimated to you at Frankfort of my enemies poisoning your mind against me. In what, in truth, can they allege a dictation, or even interference, on my part? In the formation of your cabinet? You can contradict them. In the administration of the public patronage? The whole cabinet as well as yourself can say that I have recommended nobody for any office. I have sought none for myself or my friends. I desire none. I learned to-day, with infinite surprise, that I had been represented as saying that Mr. Curtis *should not* be appointed collector of New York. It is utterly unfounded. I never uttered such expressions in relation to that or any office, of the humblest grade, within your gift. I have never gone beyond expressing the opinion that he is faithless and perfidious, and, in my judgment, unworthy of the place. It is one of the artifices by which he expects to succeed."

He added that if, as a citizen and a senator, he could not express his opinions without being accused of dictation, he would prefer retirement to private life, which he desired; and he would promptly gratify that desire, did he not hope to render some public service by staying in the Senate a little longer. "I do not wish to trouble you with answering this note," he said, in closing. " I could not reconcile it to my feelings to abstain from writing it. Your heart, in which I have the greatest confidence, will justly appreciate the motives of, whatever others may say or insinuate, your true and faithful friend, H. Clay." It is by no means improbable that those who pushed the appointment of Curtis, the man of "tact and stratagem," to the collectorship of New York, precipitated the rupture between Clay and Harrison in order to remove an adverse influence. If so, they succeeded, for Curtis was soon afterwards appointed.

As soon as he had sent his farewell letter to the President, Clay left Washington. He and Harrison never met again. It was a terrible disappointment, — first to be thrown aside by the convention of his party for a second-rate man, and then to be thrown aside by that second-rate man to gratify the jealousy or greed of small politicians. For twelve years he had struggled against the tremendous power of Jackson and the cunning of Van Buren. Now at last his party was in power, and he was shown the door. He was then sixty-four years old, and had reached that age when such slights cut deeply. He turned his back on Washington much embittered. At Baltimore he fell ill, and for a week was unable to continue his homeward journey.

Harrison entered upon his office with a sincere intention to keep his promise of reform. On March 20, Webster, as secretary of state, issued in the President's name a circular to the heads of the executive departments, informing them that the President considered it " a great abuse to bring the patronage of the government into conflict with the freedom of elections;" and that he would regard "partisan interference in popular elections," or "the payment of any contribution or assessment on salaries or official compensation for party or election purposes," on the part of any officer or employee of the government, as cause for removal. But this did not accord with the views and objects of a large class of active Whig politicians like Thurlow Weed, who wanted public officers of "skill in planning and combining, and untiring industry in executing," to help them carry elections. The rush for place continued, and the party managers were busy in organizing a Whig "machine," determined to overcome the reform tendencies of the administration.

President Harrison died, after a short illness, on April 4, 1841, one month after his inauguration. The presidential office devolved upon the Vice-President, John Tyler of Virginia. Grievous as Clay's disappointment had been at the beginning of Harrison's administration, worse was now to come.

CHAPTER XXIII

CLAY AND TYLER

JOHN TYLER had always been a strict-constructionist of the Virginia school. The position he took on the bank question in 1816, and on the admission of Missouri in 1820, was in accord with its doctrines. In 1824 he supported Crawford for the presidency, but preferred Adams to Jackson, and wrote a letter approving Clay's conduct at that memorable period. But, finding fault with the latitudinarian principles of Adams, he joined, with many of Crawford's friends, the opposition camp. Elected to the Senate in 1827, he continued to act on strict-construction principles, approved Jackson's position adverse to internal improvements, and opposed high protection as well as the re-charter of the United States Bank, on constitutional grounds. He disapproved Jackson's attitude with regard to nullification, and voted against the Force Bill. He disapproved also the removal of the deposits, and voted for Clay's resolutions censuring Jackson. He refused to vote for the expunging resolution which the Virginia legislature had instructed him to support, and, recognizing the " power of instruction," he resigned his seat in the Senate. Thus he became a martyr to his convictions. Then he was sacrificed by the Whigs to a competitor for a seat in the Senate, Rives, to attract the "Conservatives," and he acquiesced. This gave him a "claim" upon the consideration of the Whig party. He also tried to promote Clay's interest in the Harrisburg Convention, and was grieved at his defeat.

This was his "record" when the Harrisburg Convention nominated him as the Whig candidate for the vice-presidency, and there is no ground for believing that this record was not known. Clay himself had reason to remember that Tyler was his friend with a mental reservation; for, in a letter written before the Harrisburg Convention, Tyler had said to him that he regarded him as "a Republican of the old school, who had indulged, when the public good seemed to require it, somewhat too much in a broad interpretation to suit our Southern notions." Henry A. Wise says that Tyler "was put into the vice-presidency by the friends of state-rights and strict construction avowedly for the purpose of casting any tie vote in the Senate in their favor." This may have been in the minds of some of the delegates, while the majority, no doubt, voted for him without considering the future beyond the election. He was a Whig only inasmuch as he belonged to one of those heterogeneous elements combined in opposition to the Jackson-Van-Buren party.

Now the unexpected, the unthought-of, happened.

CLAY AND TYLER 201

For the first time a president died in office, and the Vice-President was called to the head of the government. It was an entirely novel situation, and at first there seemed to be some doubt whether the Vice-President, so promoted, was to be considered a full president at all. The cabinet ministers, announcing to him President Harrison's death, addressed Tyler as "Vice-President." Clay, in a letter to a friend, called him a mere "regent." John Quincy Adams thought his official title should be, not "President," but "Vice-President acting as President." But Tyler, as soon as he assumed his new station, styled himself "President of the United States," and by common consent the title was at once recognized as legitimate, — fortunately so, for it is important in a republic that the title of the supreme executive power should always be full and unqualified.

This, however, was not the only matter of doubt. Much speculation arose as to what kind of a Whig president this Virginian strict-constructionist would make. As Henry A. Wise reports, immediately upon the news of Harrison's death, Tyler's state-rights friends quickly gathered around him with the advice "at once to form a new cabinet; to hasten a settlement with Great Britain, and, with that view, to retain Mr. Webster at the head of the new cabinet; to annex Texas as soon as possible; to veto any re-charter of the United States Bank, any tariff for protection, and any bill for the distribution of the proceeds of the sales of the public lands." As Wise says, "he concurred in every proposition except that of dismissing the then existing cabinet. His disposition was always for conciliation, and he dreaded to offend anybody." On April 19 Tyler issued an address to the people, in which he freely used the Whig phraseology about the "complete separation between the purse and the sword," about subjecting the power of removal to "just restraint," and ending the "war between the government and the currency." He promised promptly to give his "sanction to any constitutional measure" having in view the securing to industry its just rewards, and the "restoration of a sound constitutional medium;" and as to the question of expediency as well as constitutionality, he would "resort to the fathers of the great Republican school for advice and instruction." This could be interpreted as meaning that he favored a protective tariff, and that he would follow either those Republican fathers who, like Madison and Gallatin, put aside all constitutional scruples on account of public expediency in accepting a United States Bank, or those other Republican fathers who rejected the bank as unconstitutional and dangerous. On the whole, the address was Whiggish in sound, but open to different constructions.

Clay was at Ashland. He had his misgivings, and addressed a letter to Tyler in order to elicit more clearly his views and intentions on the principal subjects. Tyler answered on April 30 that he had no matured plans. The repeal of the sub-treasury law he looked upon as inevitable. The "relief of the treasury" might call for "additional burdens." The state of the military defenses, he thought, "required immediate attention." If Congress attended only to these subjects, great good would be done. But Congress would have to decide whether other measures should claim its attention. He favored the distribution of the proceeds of public land sales only if the annual appropriations for rivers and harbors were abandoned. As to the establishment of a United States Bank, he gave several good reasons — not calculated, however, to convince Clay's mind — why it should not be urged. He asked Clay to consider whether he could not "so frame a bank as to obviate all constitutional objections." But he would leave Congress "to its own action," and in the end resolve his doubts, if he entertained any, "by the character of the measure proposed."

With regard to the bank question, this had a decidedly uncertain sound. The message which Tyler addressed on June 1, 1841, to Congress assembled in extra session, was no clearer. It spoke encouragingly of the distribution of the proceeds of land sales, which were to aid the States in paying their debts, provided, however, they did not oblige Congress to increase tariff duties beyond the level fixed in the compromise of 1833. The President thought a "fiscal agent" desirable to facilitate the collection and disbursement of the revenue, to keep the funds secure, and to aid in the establishment of a safe currency. This might have meant a United States Bank. But the President was sure that Jackson in putting his veto upon the renewal of the charter, and Van Buren in opposing a revival of the United States Bank, had been "sustained by the popular voice." He was equally sure that the pet-bank system and the sub-treasury had been condemned in the same way. But what the "judgment of the American people on that whole subject" was, he did not pretend to know. The representatives of the people should tell him. He only knew that "the late contest, which terminated in the election of General Harrison, was decided upon principles well known and openly declared." What were those principles? He could say only that "the sub-treasury received the most emphatic condemnation," but "no other scheme of finance seemed to be concurred in." He would, therefore, concur with Congress "in the adoption of such a system" as Congress might propose, reserving to himself "the ultimate power of rejecting any measure" which, in his view, should "conflict with the Constitution," or otherwise "jeopard the prosperity of the country;" but he would not believe that the exercise of that power would be called into requisition.

This was by no means lucid. But if Tyler equivocated, Clay did not. The Whigs had in the twenty-seventh Congress a majority of seven in the Senate, and of nearly fifty in the House of Representatives. A majority of the cabinet, too, were Clay's friends. He felt himself in a position of command. Anticipating the disagreement between himself and the President, he is reported to have said: " Tyler dares not resist. I will drive him before me." He entered the Senate as a captain of a ship would step on deck to give his orders. Forthwith in a resolution he offered, he designated the subjects which at the extra session should be acted upon. They were: 1. The repeal of the sub-treasury law; 2. The incorporation of a bank adapted to the wants of the people and of the government; 3. The provision of an adequate revenue by the imposition of tariff duties, and a temporary loan; 4. The prospective distribution of the proceeds of public land sales; 5. The passage of the necessary appropriations; 6. Some modifications of the banking system of the District of Columbia. This was Clay's general order to Congress. He took for himself the chairmanships of the Committee on Finance and of a special committee on the bank question.

The repeal of the sub-treasury act was the measure first advanced, and urged with Clay's characteristic impetuosity. It passed both houses and Tyler promptly signed it. The incorporation of a new United States Bank was next in order. It was the measure nearest to Clay's heart. Ewing, the secretary of the treasury, sent a report to Congress recommending the establishment of a bank as the fiscal agent of the government, with a capital of thirty millions, to be incorporated in the District of Columbia, branches to be established in the several States, only with the assent of the States concerned. It was to be called the "Fiscal Bank of the United States." Clay reported a bill from his committee conforming in its main features to the secretary's plan, with the exception of the requirement that the establishment of branches should depend on the expressed assent of the respective States. But, as it was generally believed that the President would not sign any bill without such a clause, an amendment was adopted providing that such assent should be assumed unless dissent were expressed by the legislature of the State concerned at its session next ensuing. So amended, the bill passed, although it commanded in neither house the full vote of the party.

Then the crisis came. Rumors had long been current that the President would refuse to sign the bill. The excitement caused by the anticipation of a veto was so intense as to interfere with the amenities of official as well as social intercourse. At last, on August 16, the veto appeared. The President reminded Congress of the fact that he had always pronounced himself against the assumption by Congress of the power to create a national bank that would "operate *per se* over the Union." He thought he had a right to assume that the people had elected him vice-president "with a full knowledge of the opinions thus entertained." He could not satisfy himself that a bank was necessary for the fiscal operations of the government. He objected to the bill especially because it contemplated a bank of discount, and branches to be established in the several States with or without their assent, — "a principle," he added, "to which I have always heretofore been opposed, and which can never obtain my sanction."

The Whigs were extremely angry. In the evening a crowd assembled before the White House, demonstrating their disapproval of the President's conduct with disorderly noises. But a very different scene was enacted within. Many of the Democratic senators could not restrain their exultation. In a body they called upon President Tyler to congratulate him upon the "courageous and patriotic" step he had taken, and the congratulations gradually degenerated into convivial hilarity. A few days afterwards, an inquiry into the disorderly demonstrations before the White House having been moved, Clay availed himself of the opportunity to dramatize the congratulatory meeting inside in a very clever satire. He recited the speeches he supposed to have been delivered on that occasion by Democratic senators to the Whig President, imitating the style of the different orators, especially of Calhoun, Benton, and Buchanan, in so striking and artistic a way as to win the involuntary applause even of some of the victims.

Of a more serious nature was the speech in

which he answered Tyler's veto message. There was a forced and somewhat contemptuous moderation in its tone which made the severe thrusts all the more stinging. But the argument was more important. He had, before and during the campaign of 1840, taken the position that the establishment of a new United States Bank would not be safe unless a decided majority of the people recognized it as necessary. Now he asserted, in the most positive tone, that the question of "bank or no bank" had been the main issue of the last presidential canvass, and that a large majority of the people had pronounced in favor of a bank. It was an astounding assertion. During the campaign he himself had said again and again that, while he considered a bank necessary, a difference of opinion upon that subject was admissible, and people might vote for Harrison without voting for a bank; and there could be no doubt that Harrison had received many votes from anti-bank men. His experiences in Jackson's time should have made him cautious in interpreting the special meanings of presidential elections, but he was, if possible, even more emphatic than Benton had been after the elections of 1832 and 1836.

Equally rash was his assertion that he had come to Washington at the beginning of the session with the full confidence that all the great Whig measures, including the bank, would have Tyler's hearty approval. Tyler's letter to him was certainly not such as to justify that confidence. It might have given him reason to hope, but not to trust. His confidence, if it existed at all, must have been in his own power of persuasion, or his energy of leadership, or the overawing party pressure which Tyler would not be able to withstand, but certainly not in anything Tyler had said to him.

But, upon the assumption of a popular command, Clay argued that Tyler, with all his constitutional scruples, should have obeyed, either by signing the bill, or by permitting it to become a law without his signature, or by following the precedent set by Tyler himself in resigning when he thought he could not do what his constituents demanded. Clay declared, in conclusion, that if, as rumor had it, a bill could be framed to obviate the President's objections, that bill would not be opposed by him, although he could not share the responsibility of bringing it forward.

Indeed, on the very day when Tyler had sent his veto to the Senate, negotiations began between him and members of the cabinet and members of Congress with a view to the shaping of some measure that would prevent a breach between the President and the Whig majority in Congress. Tyler authorized Webster and Ewing of the cabinet to confer with Berrien of the Senate and Sergeant of the House about the details of a bill, the principle of which he was understood to have accepted. A bill providing for a "Fiscal Corporation" — the term "bank" being especially offensive to Tyler —

was agreed upon between the negotiators, and, with the expectation that it would have the approval of the President, it was rushed through the House in hot haste. But, while it hung in the Senate, rumors were abroad that President Tyler had again changed his mind. It passed the Senate on September 3, and on the 9th came a veto message prepared, as Henry A. Wise says, in a conference with friends outside of the cabinet, by one of them. It criticised some of the provisions of the bill, indicated that the President would not approve the incorporation of a national bank in any form, and expressed an anxious desire for "harmony."

The verdict of impartial history will probably be that John Tyler, when preventing by his veto the incorporation of another United States Bank, rendered his country a valuable service. Had Clay's bill become a law, the new bank would at once have been attacked by the Democratic opposition seeking to compass the repeal of its charter, — a purpose openly avowed by them. It is very doubtful whether, with such a prospect, capitalists would have been found willing to venture their means in such an enterprise. In any event, the existence of the greatest financial institution in the country would have depended on the fortunes of a political party, and with it, in a great measure, the currency and the credit system. Being the subject of party struggles, the bank would have been driven by the force of circumstances to become a political agency, and thus a hotbed of corruption, financially unsafe and politically dangerous. Something like this idea was probably in Clay's mind when, before the election of 1840, he declared that a United States Bank should not again be incorporated unless emphatically demanded by a majority of the people. In that case it was all the more unstatesmanlike to assume in 1841 that a majority did demand it, and to forget that a strong and determined minority would ordinarily be sufficient to endanger the credit and stability of a financial institution. The only excuse the Whig statesmen of that period had for thinking at all of the establishment of a new United States Bank was that they knew of no other means to secure to the country a well-regulated currency of uniform value. Even that was hardly an excuse, for, under the circumstances then existing, an uncertain bank experiment would only have produced new commotions and disorders. It is a significant fact that, after Tyler's bank vetoes, the scheme of a great United States Bank never regained vitality, and that the Whig party itself treated it in subsequent campaigns as an "obsolete idea."

Tyler would have rendered another service to the country had he put his veto upon another of Clay's measures, — the distribution of the proceeds of the public land sales, which at the extra session of 1841 passed both houses, and became a law on September 4. This time Clay had pressed his bill especially on the ground that many of the States were grievously in debt, and that the distribution urged by him would to some extent relieve them. The several States had run into debt to the amount of nearly two hundred millions. Mississippi was the first to pronounce the word "repudiation." Michigan, Indiana, Illinois, Louisiana, and even Pennsylvania, were staggering under the consequences of their improvidence. The credit of the country abroad was profoundly shaken. Foreign creditors asked whether the national government was not bound to protect American honor by seeing the state debts paid. The question of "assumption" was gravely considered, but Congress adopted an adverse resolution. Under such circumstances, the plan of relieving the distress by a distribution of funds had more than ordinary plausibility. But it was nevertheless fundamentally vicious. Several of the States had increased their indebtedness under the stimulus administered by the distribution of the treasury surplus. Another distribution, far from freeing them from debt, would only have been calculated to make them more reckless in spending, for it would have deadened their sense of responsibility by holding up before them the picture of an immensely rich uncle ever ready to pay their bills.

A distribution of any sort of public funds seemed especially absurd at a time when the government was obliged to borrow money for its running expenses, and could raise a loan only with difficulty. This absurdity was indirectly recognized by the adoption, against Clay's opposition, of an amendment to his bill, providing that the distribution should be suspended whenever the necessities of the treasury required an increase of the tariff duties above the twenty per cent. fixed by the compromise of 1833. Even in this shape the bill would probably have failed had it not been coupled, by a skillful piece of log-rolling, with a general bankruptcy law — a measure for the relief of insolvent debtors — which was not in Clay's original programme, but which he supported. As the tariff rates were raised above twenty per cent. before the time when, according to the terms of the compromise of 1833, the twenty per cent. level was reached, the distribution measure remained a dead letter.

On the evening of the day that brought Tyler's second bank veto, the members of the cabinet were invited to meet at the house of Badger, the secretary of the navy, to consult among themselves and with Clay. Webster absented himself when he heard that Clay was to be there. Four of the cabinet ministers being devoted to him, Clay again took command. It was agreed that the members of the cabinet should, one after another, resign their places on Saturday, September 11, Congress having resolved to adjourn on Monday the 13th. It has been charged that this was artfully contrived to embarrass the President by obliging him to find a new cabinet between Saturday and Monday. But there is no doubt that, if they had not resigned, they would soon have been dismissed. Webster was an exception. Having consulted the members of Congress from Massachusetts, he resolved to remain in his place if he could. He was with the President when Ewing's letter of resignation was brought in. John Tyler, Jr., who acted as the President's private secretary, gives the following account of what happened: —

"He (Webster) then, in his deep toned voice, asked: 'Where am I to go, Mr. President?' The President's reply was only in these words: 'You must decide that for yourself, Mr. Webster.' At this Mr. Webster instantly caught, and said: 'If you leave it to me, Mr. President, I will stay where I am.' Whereupon President Tyler, rising from his seat and extending his hand to Mr. Webster, warmly rejoined: 'Give me your hand on that, and now I will say to you that Henry Clay is a doomed man from this hour.'"

What he meant was that the alliance between Webster and himself would serve to detach the Northern Whigs from Clay's following, and leave him in a hopeless minority. John Tyler forgot that Clay was what Webster was not, — a leader. When Clay cut loose from the administration, he resolved to take the whole Whig party with him.

The quarrel between Tyler and his party created the intensest excitement at the time, and has remained one of the sensational chapters of our political history. It was wrong to accuse Tyler of breaking his pledges in disapproving the bank bills. He had never promised to aid in establishing a national bank, and there were very good reasons for refusing to do so. But his conduct, when the disagreement between him and his party became critical, was that of a small, if not a tricky, man. He dealt in equivocations which seemed to mean one thing and turned out to mean the opposite. He appeared to accept and then rejected the same propositions in rapid succession. He authorized members of his cabinet to confer with members of Congress about measures which he had permitted them to consider and to represent as acceptable to him, and then turned his back upon them. This is the way in which a public man easily makes himself contemptible. He was surrounded by a kitchen cabinet mainly composed of Virginians, and led by Henry A. Wise, a man of ability, but in a high degree flighty and erratic, who interfered in everything, and constantly pulled him back whenever an approach between him and leading Whigs in Congress seemed to be in progress. That coterie inflamed Tyler's brain, which was never one of the strongest, and easily turned by flattery, with gorgeous visions of future greatness, promising to gather a party around him strong enough to keep him in the presidential chair for a second term or more. Few things are more hateful to men interested in public affairs than to see the head of the state controlled by secret influence. On the whole, there was in the spectacle of "Captain" Tyler, as he was derisively called, and his little personal party, dubbed by Clay "the corporal's guard," much that provoked disdain and ridicule.

It is by no means probable, as some partisans of John Tyler have asserted, that the leading Whigs were bound to quarrel with him in any event. Had he approved their favorite measures, there would probably have been no outbreak of ill-feeling. But when he refused to do so, and a breach became certain, it was Clay's instinct as a leader to save the party by making that breach so wide and so irreparable that no Whig could safely stay with the President and remain a Whig. The prompt resignation of the cabinet, excepting Webster, was no doubt Clay's work. Webster was indeed right when, in publicly announcing his continuance in office, he said that, even if he had seen reasons for resigning, he would not have done so without giving the President due notice, affording him time to select a successor. It would have been proper for the other cabinet ministers to do so, but it would have impaired the dramatic effect which was thought necessary to startle the Whig masses; and, besides, they had to anticipate their removal. The formation of a new cabinet had evidently been considered by Tyler and his political body-guard while the old one was still in office. Tyler promptly nominated five men who, like himself, had been Jackson Democrats once, and left the Democratic party for the same reasons for which he had left it. "Like myself," he wrote to a friend, "they are all original Jackson men, and mean to act upon republican principles." Webster, remaining as secretary of state, found himself, therefore, in somewhat unaccustomed company.

This change in the political character of the cabinet could only aid the rallying of the Whigs on Clay's side. Nothing was left undone to drive Tyler away as far as possible. The members of the old cabinet published their reasons for resigning in elaborate letters addressed to President Tyler, mercilessly exposing his tricky conduct to the contempt of the people. Even that was not enough. After the second veto, a general meeting of the Whig senators and representatives was held, which issued a solemn address to the people denouncing Tyler as having betrayed the just expectations of the Whig party for selfish purposes, and as being unworthy of its confidence. A chorus of Whig papers all over the country echoed and reëchoed these denunciations, and attacked Tyler with a fury unheard of except during the hottest excitement of a presidential campaign. Indignation meetings and burnings in effigy were the order of the day.

Tyler was utterly disappointed in his expectation that Webster's remaining in the cabinet would isolate Clay. It did indeed produce the effect of causing a few Northern Whigs to protest against what they called "the dictatorship of the caucus," meaning Clay and a few more, to observe a cautious moderation in their utterances. But the principal effect was to excite the suspicions of the great mass of Whigs as to Webster's motives for not resigning with his colleagues. The concerted withdrawal of the cabinet being Clay's work, Webster was naturally disinclined to fall into line. That motive could not well be avowed. But he had another and a very proper and patriotic reason for his conduct. He was, as secretary of state, engaged in an important negotiation with the British government concerning the northeastern boundary line, and the complications on the northern frontier caused by the Canadian troubles. These negotiations, which finally resulted in the Ashburton treaty, were at that time in a precarious condition, and Webster very properly resolved not to abandon them. But his position was one of great difficulty in two respects. He was neither liked nor trusted by Tyler's kitchen cabinet. As early as the 29th of August, Henry A. Wise wrote to Beverly Tucker: "We can part friendly with Webster by sending him to England. Let us, for God's sake, get rid of him the best way we can." When such influences surrounded him, Webster's situation in the cabinet would necessarily become very uncomfortable. On the other hand, the current of sentiment in the Whig ranks was set. Webster's plea as to his duty to continue the British negotiations was sullenly accepted. As a martyr to duty, he could stand before the Whigs; but when he took Tyler's part in any other respect, he found himself in a hopeless defensive. Only a few Whigs in New

England stood by him in his isolation. Wrath against John Tyler seemed to be the great inspiration of the Whig party in those days of disappointment following so closely upon the thoughtless enthusiasm of 1840. Clay remained the idol of the Whig masses, and it was then already generally taken for granted that he would be, without competition, the Whig candidate for the presidency in 1844.

Clay's parliamentary leadership during that famous extra session proved that, with advancing age, his imperious temper grew more and more impatient. As he had at the beginning of the session prescribed to Congress its business by a sort of general order, so he tried to govern in detail the action of both houses by words of command. When the Democratic opposition sought to obstruct the progress of his measures, he thought at once of interfering with the freedom of debate. It was during this extra session that the rule limiting the speeches of members to one hour was adopted in the House of Representatives. In the Senate, too, Clay threatened repeatedly to propose " the adoption of a rule which would place the business of the Senate under the control of a majority of the Senate," that is, enable the majority to stop debate and muzzle the minority. But the resistance he met was so indignant and formidable that he gave up the attempt. And it is well that he failed. However tedious and useless, and however obstructive to the expedition of business, unrestrained debate in the Senate may sometimes appear, yet infinitely more important than the expedition of business is it that there should be one deliberate body in the government in which every question may receive the fullest discussion, and the smallest minority can make itself heard without restraint.

How far Clay was carried by the impetuosity of his temper appeared most strikingly in his attempt to treat petitions and memorials against his measures as the extreme pro-slavery men were in the habit of treating anti-slavery petitions, — laying them on the table unprinted, unreferred, and unconsidered. But again he soon saw his mistake and retreated. Notwithstanding all the fascinations of his manner, the dictatorial spirit of his leadership became not seldom so demonstrative that his followers had not a little to suffer for their submissiveness from the taunts and jeers of the opposition.

Clay succeeded in isolating Tyler, and in holding the bulk of the Whig party together. But he could not lead it to victory in the autumn elections of 1841. The Democrats recovered several States which in 1840 had given large Whig majorities, and were in high spirits. Clay, in his letters to his friends, attributed this result to the discouraging effect of Tyler's conduct. But it was not that alone. The outcome of the great Whig victory had been disappointing in all respects. The business interests of the country were still lamentably depressed. The manufacturing industries had not yet risen from their paralysis. The government found itself in a pitiable condition. During the year the public debt increased from $6,700,000 to $15,000,000. The public credit was so bad that a loan of twelve millions, authorized by Congress, could be placed only slowly and with great difficulty. The treasury had sometimes not money enough for the pay of the army and navy, and the salaries of the civil service. The expenditures were constantly and largely outrunning the regular revenues. This was the situation the twenty-seventh Congress had to deal with when it met in December, 1841, for its second session. President Tyler in his message recommended a revision of the tariff " with a view to discriminate as to the articles on which the duty shall be laid, as well as the amount," the rates of duty not to exceed the amount fixed in the compromise act of 1833. As to the regulation of the currency and of domestic exchanges, he proposed an " exchequer system," which, however, did not find serious consideration in Congress. The secretary of the treasury, Walter Forward of Pennsylvania, suggested in his report that the public interest would, as to the tariff, scarcely permit a strict adherence to the terms of the compromise act of 1833.

It was no longer as the leader of a majority party, hopeful of carrying all his favorite measures, that Clay stepped upon the scene in December, 1841. He was now fully determined to retire from the Senate. "I want rest, and my private affairs want attention," he wrote to Brooke. "Nevertheless, I would make any personal sacrifice, if, by remaining here, I could do any good; but my belief is I can effect nothing, and perhaps my absence may remove an obstacle to something being done by others. I shall, therefore, go home in the spring." His retirement from the Senate was, however, by no means to be an abandonment of public life; it was simply the withdrawal of a candidate for the presidency from a position beset with extraordinary difficulties. This resolution being fixed, his speeches in the Senate began to bear the character, not of efforts for the accomplishment of immediate results, but of admonitions for the future guidance of his followers.

He made a plea against the repeal of the bankrupt act, but in vain. That act was destined to be revoked by the same Congress which had made it. He then offered three amendments to the Constitution, all designed to reduce the authority of the executive. One embodied his old proposition that the veto of the President — which, with singular infatuation, he called in a letter "that parent and fruitful source of all our ills" — should be subject to be overruled by a simple majority of all the members of each house of Congress. The second provided that the secretary of the treasury and the treasurer of the United States should be appointed by Congress; and the third prohibited the appointment to office of any member of Congress during the term for which he was elected. These amendments formed an important part of the programme laid down by Clay in his principal speech in the campaign of 1840. They illustrate the dangerous tendency of that impulsive statesmanship which will resort to permanent changes in the Constitution of the State in order to accomplish temporary objects. It is more than probable that the same Clay who saw in the veto power " the parent of all ills," when his favorite measures were defeated by Jackson's and Tyler's vetoes, would have thought very differently had he himself been put into the executive chair and confronted by a hostile Congress. Neither has the experience of the American people in any manner justified Clay's apprehensions as to the danger which the veto power without further restriction would bring upon the country. That power has, on the whole, been exercised with remarkable discretion and with salutary effect, especially as regards the financial concerns of the government, which throughout have been treated by the executive with better judgment and a higher sense of honor than by Congress. The proposition to confer the power of appointing the secretary of the treasury and the treasurer upon Congress, instead of the President, is hardly intelligible in our days. Neither can we understand why a president should not be permitted to take proper men from the two houses of Congress into his cabinet. Clay had become so completely preoccupied by fears of executive encroachment that he was utterly unmindful of the dangers which might arise from arrogations of power by the legislature. But, as he himself admitted, there was no immediate prospect of the adoption of such constitutional amendments, and he only commended the questions involved in them to the consideration of his countrymen.

On March 1, 1842, he introduced with an elaborate argument a series of resolutions laying down certain rules for the reduction of current expenses, and for the raising of a revenue sufficient to meet them. June 30, 1842, the day upon which, according to his compromise act of 1833, all tariff duties should be reduced to twenty per cent. ad valorem, was near at hand. Clay had to recognize the fact that, even without that final reduction, the tariff as it was then arranged did not yield sufficient revenue; and the manufacturers told him that it did not afford sufficient protection. He was thus obliged to admit that in these respects his compromise measure had not fulfilled his predictions. He recommended, therefore, that the duties, which on June 30 should have been reduced to twenty, be raised to thirty per cent. on the ground of necessity. But at the same time, while struggling for revenue, he insisted that the provision of law, which suspended the distribution of the proceeds of land sales while the tariff duties were above twenty per cent., be repealed. His resolutions were referred to the appropriate committee, to come to light again after he should have left the scene of action.

On March 31, at last he took leave of the Senate, and his farewell again became one of those dramatic incidents in which his life abounded. A rumor had spread that he intended to deliver a valedictory speech when presenting the credentials of his successor. An eager audience crowded the galleries as well as the floor of the Senate. In a flow of stately sentences he pictured the grandeur of the Senate of the United States; he spoke of his long career of public service, of his unselfish endeavors, of the enmities to which he had been exposed, and of the fidelity of his friends. In touching words he expressed his gratitude to the State that had been so faithful to him. He could not refrain from defending himself against the most recent charge brought against him, that he had played the dictator. He owned that his nature was warm and his temper ardent; and if he had ever, in the heat of debate, wounded the feelings of any of his brother senators, he offered them the sincerest apology, and the assurance that he carried not a single resentment with him. After a few words of warm and graceful tribute to his successor, John J. Crittenden, he invoked Heaven's blessings upon them all and closed. The Senate sat silent for a moment, when Preston of South Carolina rose and said that what had just taken place was an epoch in their legislative history, and, from the feeling which was evinced, he saw that there was little disposition to attend to business. He therefore moved an adjournment, which was unanimously agreed to. The senators pressed around Clay to respond to his touching words. In leaving the chamber he met Calhoun, and the two aged statesmen shook hands for the first time after many years of estrangement. This valedictory, says Benton in his "Thirty Years," was "the first occasion of the kind, and, thus far, has been the last; and it might not be recommendable for any one except another Henry Clay — if another should ever appear — to attempt its imitation."

"Clay's leaving Congress was something like the soul's quitting the body," wrote Crittenden to Governor Letcher. "His departure has had (at least I feel it so) an enervating effect." But the Whig majority in Congress endeavored to follow his precepts, although it made slow progress. The 30th of June, with its reduction of the tariff under the compromise act, was rapidly approaching; and on June 7 only a provisional tariff bill was reported in the House to tide the country over the 30th, and thus to give time for further deliberation. But that provisional bill provided also that, while the distribution of the proceeds of the public land sales should be suspended for the month of July, they should go into force on August 1. Tyler returned the bill with his veto, mainly for the avowed reason that it provided for the distribution of the proceeds of land sales while the tariff rate exceeded twenty per cent. After a violent explosion of wrath, the Whig majority passed a tariff bill of a permanent character, which con-

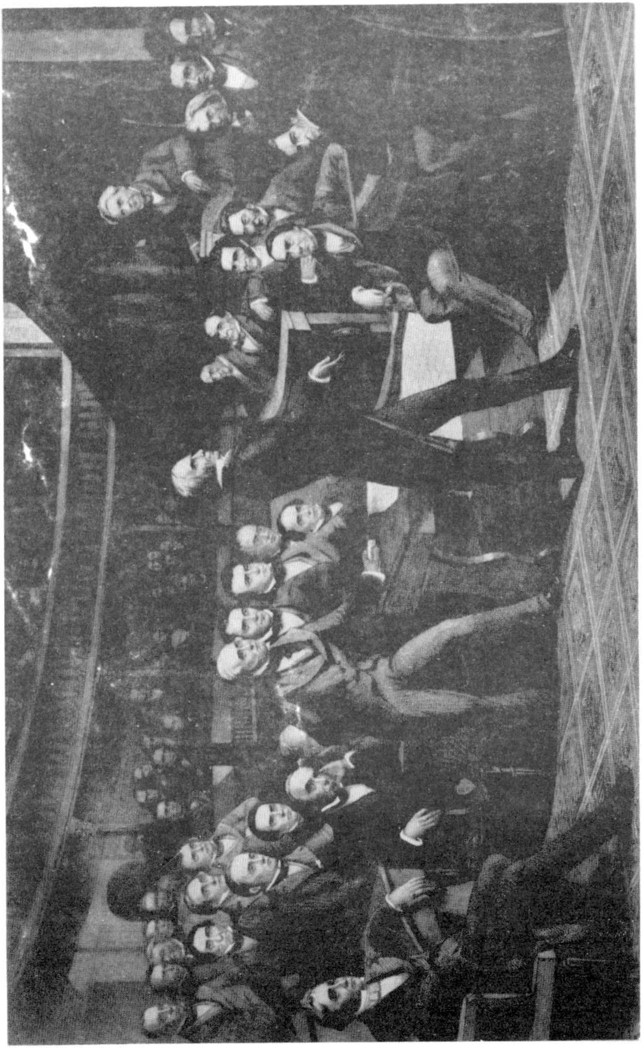

tained the same clause providing for the distribution of the proceeds of land sales. On August 6 this too came back with the President's disapproval. The veto was referred to a special committee, with John Quincy Adams as chairman, who made a report lashing Tyler with terrible severity.

But now the Whig majority stood before the clear alternative of either giving up the distribution scheme, or adjourning without provision for the necessary revenue, as well as for the protective duties which their friends, the manufacturers, urgently demanded. What should they do? Clay had written to Crittenden on July 16, after the first veto: —

"I think you cannot give up distribution without a disgraceful sacrifice of independence. The moral prejudice of such a surrender upon the character of the party, and upon our institutions, would be worse than the disorder and confusion incident to the failure to pass a tariff. It would be to give up the legislative power into the hands of the President, and would expose you to the scorn, contempt, and derision of the people, and of our opponents. Do not apprehend that the people will desert you and take part with Mr. Tyler. In my view of it, I think our friends ought to stand firmly and resolutely for distribution. The more vetoes the better now! — assuming that the measures vetoed are right."

John Quincy Adams, whose passions were fully roused, was of the same opinion. It is difficult to understand how patriotic and experienced statesmen, unless under the influence of blinding excitement, could have advised their party to commit so foolish and grave a blunder as to adjourn without passing a revenue measure which they themselves thought absolutely necessary.

Fortunately for them, the advice was not heeded by all their party friends. The business community grew restless and urgent. At last a sufficient number of Whigs, alarmed at the consequences of "standing firm," united with a sufficient number of Democrats in passing a tariff bill not containing the provision concerning the proceeds of land sales objected to by Tyler's veto. Thus Clay's distribution scheme was irretrievably defeated. Of all his great measures, nothing was saved but a moderate tariff, and that at the sacrifice of the compromise of 1833.

CHAPTER XXIV

THE ELECTION OF 1844

No sooner had Clay declared his determination to withdraw from the Senate than invitations poured upon him from all sides to show himself to the people. He replied to them in letters burning with wrath at the "weak, vacillating, and faithless chief magistrate," the "President vainly seeking, by a culpable administration of the patronage of the government, to create a third party." Clay's Kentucky constituency welcomed him to his home with boundless enthusiasm. He was honored with a grand open-air feast attended by a large multitude. The toast with which the chairman greeted him was a fair specimen of the language in which the ardent Whig of the time was in the habit of expressing his feelings about his gallant leader on festive occasions: —

"Henry Clay, farmer of Ashland, patriot and philanthropist, the American statesman and unrivaled orator of the age, illustrious abroad, beloved at home: in a long career of eminent public service, often, like Aristides, he breasted the raging storm of passion and delusion, and, by offering himself a sacrifice, saved the republic; and now, like Cincinnatus and Washington, having voluntarily retired to the tranquil walks of private life, the grateful hearts of his countrymen will do him ample justice. But, come what may, Kentucky will stand by him, and still continue to cherish and defend, as her own, the fame of a son who has emblazoned her escutcheon with immortal renown."

The nomination of the "Old Prince" — a name by which some of his friends proudly called him — as the Whig candidate for the presidency in 1844 was treated as a matter of "justice to Henry Clay." Too impatient to wait for a national convention, the Whigs of North Carolina brought forward his name as early as April, 1842; Georgia and Maine followed. The Whig members of the legislature of New York, the State which in 1840 had abandoned him, sent him a glowing address. In August the Whig State Convention of Maryland formally nominated him amid "tremendous enthusiasm," supplemented with a salute of one hundred guns. Even the Whigs of Massachusetts, Webster's influence notwithstanding, could not be restrained. In September he was invited to a great Whig convention at Dayton, in Ohio, where nearly one hundred thousand people were assembled, and where resolutions were adopted nominating Henry Clay and John Davis of Massachusetts as the Whig candidates for 1844. Wherever he appeared, he was greeted with extravagant demonstrations of affection. From Dayton he continued his triumphal "progress" into Indiana. It was there, in the town of Richmond, that an incident occurred the significance of which was scarcely understood by him. At an unexpected moment, when all around him seemed to be admiring devotion, the slavery question threw again its dark shadow across his path.

While he was addressing an enthusiastic Whig gathering, a Quaker by the name of Mendenhall presented to him a petition, bearing many signatures, in which Henry Clay was respectfully requested to emancipate his slaves. Clay's answer was a masterpiece of oratorical skill. He characterized the presentation of the petition as a breach of hospitality, and then he took Mendenhall generously under his protection, against the indignant cries of the crowd. He declared slavery to be a "great evil;" he deeply lamented that we had "derived it from the parental government and from our ancestors;" he wished every slave in the United States were in Africa; if slavery did not exist here, he would oppose its introduction with all his might. But, slavery existing, how could it be dealt with? Great as its evils were, would not the evils sure to flow from sudden emancipation be greater, — a "contest between the two races, civil war, carnage, pillage, conflagration, devastation, and the ultimate extermination or expulsion of the blacks?" The only safe method was gradual emancipation, and that had been postponed half a century by the reckless agitation of the abolitionists. As to himself, should he liberate his slaves forthwith? There were those among them whom age and infirmity made a heavy charge upon him. Should he turn them, and the infants, upon the cold charities of the world? There were those who would not leave him: should he drive them away? He recommended to Mr. Mendenhall the benevolent example of other Quakers who, while in principle firmly opposed to slavery, would not resort to revolution and disunion for its abolition. He expressed his respect for the "rational abolitionists," among whom he had many friends. They were not monomaniacs, but knew that they had duties to perform towards the white man as well as the black. Finally, he put to Mr. Mendenhall a practical question. If he (Clay) liberated his fifty slaves, worth about $15,000, would Mendenhall and his friends undertake to contribute an equal sum to take care of the slaves after their liberation? Then he dismissed Mendenhall with the admonition to begin the work of benevolence at home: "Dry up the tears of the afflicted widows around you; console and comfort the helpless orphan; clothe the naked, and feed and help the poor, black and white, who need succor, and you will be a better and a wiser man than you have this day shown yourself."

The assembled multitude was lost in admiration. Poor Mendenhall withdrew, discomfited and laughed at. Clay's speech was triumphantly published in the newspapers all over the country. But many thousands of Mendenhalls were to rise up in the campaign of 1844; and it was the cause represented by that humble Quaker that was to prove the absorbing question of the time, and the fatal stumbling-block of the great orator's highest ambition.

To mark the development of the slavery question, a short retrospect is required. In the House of Representatives, the struggle about the famous twenty-first rule — the rule excluding anti-slavery petitions — began afresh when, in the twenty-seventh Congress, the House was controlled by a Whig majority. Upon Adams's motion the rule was dropped, and the great controversy about the right of petition might have been wisely ended. But the representatives of the slave power, Whigs as well as Democrats, would not rest until it was revived. They insisted that "the hydra of abolitionism must be crushed." With blind infatuation, they kept slavery before the people as the enemy of the right of petition. They did more. In January, 1842, John Quincy Adams presented a memorial of some citizens of Massachusetts praying Congress " to adopt measures for the peaceful dissolution of the union of these States," and he moved that the petition be referred to a committee with instruction to report why the prayer could not be granted. Southern members, some of whom were in the habit of threatening the dissolution of the Union on all possible occasions, thought they saw an opportunity for crushing the fearless old champion of the right of petition, and moved that he be censured with the utmost severity for having presented a petition of such tenor. The right of defending himself could not be denied him, and the old statesman, summoning all his powers, exposed the character of slavery and the slaveholding aristocracy with so unsparing a force that, after several days of torture, his accusers, with a sigh of relief, permitted the resolution of censure to be laid on the table. Even the exciting quarrel between Tyler and Congress attracted scarcely more of popular attention than this "trial of John Quincy Adams."

But this experience did not teach the pro-slavery men prudence. Soon afterwards Joshua R. Giddings of Ohio offered in the House a series of resolutions concerning the case of the Creole, a brig, which, sailing with a cargo of slaves from Norfolk bound for New Orleans, had been taken possession of by the slaves, some of whom had risen in insurrection, overpowered the crew, killed a supercargo, and run the brig into the harbor of Nassau, where the British authorities had liberated the unoffending slaves and refused to surrender the mutineers. The resolutions of Giddings declared that slavery existed only by local municipal law; that the jurisdiction of the municipal law did not extend over the high seas; that the negroes on the Creole had not violated any law of the United States by claiming their natural right to individual freedom on the high seas, and that any attempt to make them slaves again by an exertion of the national power was unauthorized by the Constitution, and prejudicial to the national character. These resolutions caused another explosion of wrath. Debate was cut off by the previous question. Without giving Giddings an opportunity to defend himself, a vote of censure was passed, declaring that he deserved "the severest condemnation of the people of this country." Whereupon Giddings promptly announced his resignation as a member of the House. In leaving the hall he met Clay, who had witnessed the scene. To see a man condemned unheard, and a representative of the people cut off from the right of expressing his opinions, revolted Clay's heart. He held out his hand to Giddings, thanked him for the firmness with which he had met the outrage perpetrated upon him, and said that no man would ever doubt his perfect right to state his views. Giddings returned to his constituents, issued an address, was reëlected by a larger majority than before, and returned to the same Congress strengthened by the enthusiastic applause of his neighbors and of popular meetings held all over the North. In constantly widening circles the Northern mind began to doubt whether slavery could be "got along with" in a republic. The anti-slavery movement was gradually invading the masses.

Although the attacks upon the right of petition and the freedom of speech by the advocates of slavery greatly offended Clay's democratic instincts, there seemed still to remain in his mind a lingering impression that the greatest danger to the Union came, not from slavery, but from abolitionism. This misconception was no doubt nourished by the attacks made upon him by the abolitionists, and he in turn made every possible effort to discredit them with the Northern people. There is among his preserved correspondence a curious letter in which he suggested to a pamphleteer arguments to be addressed to the laboring men of the North, — how immediate emancipation would bring the labor of the blacks into competition with the labor of the whites; how it would degrade labor generally; and how the tendency would be toward the social intermingling and intermarrying of white and black laboring people, and so on. While he made such preposterous attempts to stem the current, the great event which, in its consequences, was to bring the slavery question to its final crisis, and which final opened Clay's eyes too as to the true source of danger, was pressing toward its consummation.

In 1837 the Texan government proposed to Van Buren the annexation of Texas to the United States, but Van Buren declined. Eight Northern legislatures formally protested against annexation. For the settlement of the claims against Mexico an arbitration treaty was concluded in 1839; but when in 1842 the term of the arbitration commission expired, many claims were still unadjusted. It was suspected that they were purposely kept an open sore.

The annexation of Texas became one of Tyler's

ruling ambitions. In October, 1841, he wrote to Webster: "I gave you a hint as to the probability of acquiring Texas by treaty. Could the North be reconciled to it, could anything throw so bright a lustre around us? Slavery, — I know that is the objection, and it would be well founded if it did not already exist among us." In March, 1842, the Texan minister at Washington renewed the offer of annexation, but Webster strongly opposed it. It was also considered certain that no annexation treaty could then obtain the consent of the Senate. The treaty with Great Britain called the Ashburton treaty was concluded that summer, assented to by the Senate in August, and ratified by the British government in October. Thus dangers of warlike complications with England were averted.

The congressional elections of 1842 resulted in a crushing defeat of the Whigs. The Democrats won a very large majority in the House of Representatives. Late in October Tyler consulted his friends as to whether he would not do well to throw himself into the arms of the Democrats, as he thought himself entitled to their gratitude. In May, 1843, Webster resigned the office of secretary of state. It is probable that Tyler, whose main purposes he did not serve, had ceased to treat him with confidence and cordiality; and the Whigs, even in Massachusetts, were greatly dissatisfied with him because he had stayed too long in office. Tyler reorganized his cabinet, taking three Democrats into it, and transferring Upshur of Virginia, who had been secretary of the navy, to the State Department. Upshur, an ardent state-rights and pro-slavery man, took up the Texan business with energy. The problem was not only to conclude a treaty, but to make annexation palatable to the country. Rumors were spread that Great Britain was endeavoring to obtain a controlling influence over Texas, — this to neutralize the adverse current of feeling at the North; and also that England was planning to bring about the abolition of slavery in Texas, — this to convince the South that there was extreme danger in delay. There was some plausibility in this. The Texan republic labored under extreme financial embarrassments. It was heavily in debt to England. Would not England take advantage of those financial difficulties to obtain a foothold there, and to use its influence for the abolition of slavery? England did, in fact, recommend to the Mexican government, when recognizing the independence of Texas, to make the abolition of slavery in Texas a consideration. This, however, remained without result. But the South was continually agitated with rumors of a plot of American and English abolitionists to disturb slavery in Texas, and thus the impression grew stronger that, in order to save slavery, prompt action was needed.

Tyler directed Upshur to inform the Texan minister that the United States were ready for the annexation. This proposition was kept secret, but preparations for the event went forward. A letter in favor of annexation was obtained from Andrew Jackson. A canvass of the Senate was made, to ascertain the chances of an annexation treaty in that body. The patronage was not spared to propitiate senators. We learn from John Tyler's eulogistic biographer, Lyon G. Tyler, that "an expedition was fitted out for Oregon in the summer of 1843; and the conciliation of Benton was one of the reasons which induced the administration to make John C. Fremont, apart from his own preëminent fitness for the place, the commander of the enterprise."

The Mexican government, scenting in the air what was coming, in August, 1843, declared to the American minister that it would consider the annexation of Texas by the United States a declaration of war. This did not deter Tyler and Upshur. They formally proposed to the Texan government a treaty of annexation. The Texan government hesitated. The friendly offices of France and England had brought about a cessation of hostilities between Mexico and Texas, which was a great relief to the exhausted Texan people, and not lightly to be jeoparded. The Texan president, Houston, calculated correctly that, should the fact of serious negotiations for annexation become known, Mexico might resume warlike operations. He therefore desired to be informed whether the United States could be depended upon to protect Texas *vi et armis* against all comers while the negotiations were pending. As a constitutional lawyer Upshur could not say "Yes," and he would not say "No." He did not answer that question at all, but caused the Texan government to be informed that the Senate had been canvassed, and that there was not the slightest doubt of the necessary two thirds majority being in favor of the annexation treaty. But the Texan government, anxious to obtain assurances of protection, addressed the same question which Upshur had left unanswered to Murphy, the diplomatic agent of the United States in Texas. Murphy replied without hesitation, in the name of his government, that neither Mexico nor any other power would be permitted by the United States to invade Texas on account of the negotiation. This satisfied the Texan government, which informed Murphy that a special envoy, General Henderson, would forthwith be sent to Washington with full power to conclude the treaty. A few days afterwards President Houston rejected, for a reason of punctilio, an armistice which had been concluded between the Texan and Mexican commissioners.

But before the Texan envoy, Henderson, reached Washington, Upshur had lost his life by the explosion of the gun "Peacemaker" on board the United States frigate Princeton. The attorney-general, Nelson, who was temporarily charged with the State Department, informed Murphy that the President, without being authorized to that effect by Congress, had no constitutional power to employ the army and navy against a foreign nation

THE ELECTION OF 1844

with whom the United States were at peace; that, therefore, he (Murphy) had gone too far in his promises; but that the President was "not indisposed to concentrate in the Gulf of Mexico and on the southern borders of the United States a naval and military force to be directed to the defense of the inhabitants and territory of Texas, at a proper time."

Tyler offered the secretaryship of state to Calhoun, who accepted it, declaring that he would resign as soon as the annexation of Texas should be accomplished. He entered upon his duties on March 29, 1844. The following day the Texan envoy, Henderson, arrived at Washington. Nothing stood in the way of the conclusion of the treaty but the question whether the United States would protect Texas during the pendency of the treaty before its final consummation. Calhoun's constitutional conscience was troubled, but he finally replied that the concentration of the naval and military forces promised by Murphy and Nelson would be made, and that the President, during the pendency of the treaty of annexation, "would deem it his duty to use all the means placed within his power by the Constitution to protect Texas from all foreign invasion." This was an equivocation. Calhoun knew that, Congress alone possessing the power to declare war, the means placed by the Constitution within the power of the President were not the means required for protecting a foreign state from invasion. He knew that the executive had, indeed, the right to initiate a treaty, but that by initiating a treaty the President could not transfer from Congress to himself the power to declare war, — that is to say, the power to determine whether war should be made against a foreign state for any cause. The Texans suffered themselves to be deceived in this respect, as they had been deceived by the assurance that there was in the Senate a two thirds majority in favor of the scheme. On April 12, 1844, the treaty of annexation was signed, to be sent to the Senate for approval ten days later. It was at this period that Clay found himself obliged to address the American people upon this momentous subject.

We left him at Richmond, in Indiana, where in October, 1842, he discomfited poor Mendenhall. His clever speech found so much applause in the press that he may have thought it sufficient to banish the slavery question from the coming presidential campaign. The following winter, combining business with politics, he visited New Orleans and all the prominent places of the Southwest, and, after taking a rest at Ashland during the summer of 1843, resumed his peregrinations during the winter of 1843–44, then touching all the important points in the Southeast, like a general riding along the line, giving instructions and encouragement to the subordinate commanders, and stirring the rank and file with his inspiring presence. His journeys were again public "progresses" in grand style, with no end of enthusiastic ovations and speech-making to and fro. He expressed himself sonorously upon all the old Whig principles and measures, repeating his view of the protective tariff as a temporary arrangement, which the infant industries, rapidly growing up to manhood, would not much longer require, and denouncing in vigorous terms the treacherous conduct of Tyler. When he rested at Ashland, tokens of esteem and affection poured in upon him in the shape of presents, ranging from barrels of American-made salt to bottles of American-made cologne water; and a flood of letters, inviting him to visit every county and town East and West, and asking for expressions of his views on public problems. Distinguished guests, too, from Europe as well as the United States, sought the renowned statesman at home. The political skies also looked brighter again. In the elections of 1843 the Whigs recovered much of the ground lost in 1842.

But the "old Whig policies" no longer absorbed the interest of the people. The Texas question pressed more and more to the foreground, an unwelcome intruder. The story goes — and was believed at the time — that a unique arrangement to prevent the Texas question from becoming an issue in the presidential canvass had been made by the two gentlemen likely to be nominated as the candidates of the contesting parties, — Henry Clay and Martin Van Buren. There had always been pleasant personal relations between them. However fiercely Clay might attack Van Buren's party or policies, he had always had a kind word to say for the man. When Van Buren, after leaving the presidential office, traveled in the South and West, Clay invited him to Ashland, and Van Buren, in May, 1842, heartily enjoyed for a few days the hospitality of his old adversary's roof. There they had, as Clay wrote to Crittenden, " a great deal of agreeable conversation, but not much of politics." A little conversation on politics, however, may possibly have sufficed for their purpose. The annexation of Texas was an unwelcome subject to both of them. Clay, in a large sense a Southern man with Northern principles, disliked annexation because his instinct told him that it meant the propagation of slavery, and that it endangered the Union. Van Buren, a Northern man with Southern principles, was afraid of it, because it was intensely unpopular at the North, and threatened to bring on a war. They agreed, therefore, if it should become necessary, both publicly to take position against it.

Until late in 1843, Clay hoped it would not be necessary. On December 5 he said, in a letter to Crittenden, that he did not "think it right, unnecessarily, to present new questions to the public," and "to allow Mr. Tyler, for his own selfish purposes, to introduce an exciting topic, and add to the other subjects of contention before the country." But the negotiations going on between the administration and the Texan government did in their progress not remain secret, and the rising excitement created a louder demand for the voice of the leaders. In his southeastern "progress" Clay arrived at Raleigh, in North Carolina, on April 12, the same day the treaty of annexation was signed by Calhoun and the Texan plenipotentiaries. Clay, who felt that he could remain silent no longer, wrote a public letter to the editor of the "National Intelligencer" known as his Raleigh letter of April 17, 1844.

Reviewing his connection with the Texas question in the past, he said he had believed and contended that the United States had acquired a title to Texas by the Louisiana purchase. But that title had been formally relinquished to Spain by the treaty of 1819. Texas had been sacrificed for Florida. Having thus "fairly alienated our title to Texas by solemn national compacts," it was as "perfectly idle and ridiculous, if not dishonorable, to talk of resuming our title to Texas," as it would be for Spain to talk of resuming her title to Florida, or France to Louisiana. Under the administration of John Quincy Adams he had attempted to repurchase Texas from Mexico, but without success. The extent to which the revolt in Texas had been aided by citizens of the United States had laid us open to the imputation of selfish designs. Our recognition of the independence of Texas had not impaired the rights of Mexico; and if Mexico still persevered in asserting her rights to Texas by force of arms, we should, in acquiring Texas, also acquire the war with Mexico. And he would not plunge the country into a war for the acquisition of Texas. Another objection to the annexation of Texas he found in the decided opposition it met with in a large part of the Union. He thought it wise rather to harmonize the confederacy as it existed than to introduce into it a new element of discord and distraction. Neither did he favor the acquisition of new territory for the purpose of maintaining the balance of power between the two great sections of the Union. If Texas were acquired to strengthen the South, Canada would be acquired to strengthen the North, and finally the weaker section would be the loser. If British North America should separate from England, the happiness of all parties would be best promoted by the existence of three separate and independent republics — Canada, the United States, and Texas — natural allies. Finally, he considered the annexation of Texas without the assent of Mexico as a measure compromising the national character, involving the country certainly in a war with Mexico, probably with other powers, dangerous to the integrity of the Union, and not called for by any general expression of public opinion.

This letter naturally displeased the annexationists of the South, who clamored for Texas at any cost. Neither was it satisfactory to the extreme anti-slavery men at the North, because it did not put forward slavery as the main reason for repelling Texas. It would have pleased them better

THE ELECTION OF 1844

had he repeated in his public manifesto what he had said in his letter to Crittenden of the 5th of December, 1843, that the establishment of British influence in Texas " would not be regarded with so much detestation by the civilized world as would the conduct of the United States in seeking to effect annexation," because the motive that would be attributed to the United States, " and with too much justice, would be that of propagating, instead of terminating, slavery." But in the manifesto, while not reasoning distinctly from the anti-slavery point of view, he did, indeed, emphatically object to the main reason, — the restoration, or rather the guaranty, of the balance of power, for which Texas was desirable to the slaveholding interest. The bulk of the Whig party in the free States accepted the document as substantially in accord with their views.

A public letter from Van Buren appeared at the same time in the Democratic organ at Washington, the " Globe." The coincidence was noticed as remarkable. Van Buren questioned the constitutionality of admitting Texas as a new State by treaty; it could only be done by Congress. He, too, believed that annexation meant war with Mexico. Whether we could " hope to stand justified in the eyes of mankind for entering into " such a war, was a grave question, " in respect to which no American statesman or citizen could possibly be indifferent," especially as nothing was more true or more extensively known than that

Texas was wrested from Mexico through the instrumentality of citizens of the United States. He warned against treating lightly the sacred obligations of treaties. As to the matter of slavery, he hinted that he might be trusted, not being a man "influenced by local or sectional feelings." Finally, if Congress in a constitutional manner should acquire Texas, he would, as president, execute the legislative will.

It was significant that Andrew Jackson, whose favorite candidate Van Buren was, hurried upon the scene with a second letter, expressing his unshaken confidence in the man who would undoubtedly change his mind when he considered "the probability of a dangerous interference with the affairs of Texas by a foreign power."

The letters of the presumptive candidates for the presidency went before the people at the same time that the annexation treaty was submitted to the Senate. Calhoun communicated together with the treaty an answer he had written to a dispatch from Lord Aberdeen, which had been received several weeks before. That answer contained his reasons why the annexation of Texas had become necessary. Lord Aberdeen had, in that dispatch, incidentally mentioned the well-known desire and constant exertion of Great Britain to procure the general abolition of slavery throughout the world, earnestly disclaiming, however, any intention directly or indirectly, openly or secretly, to interfere with the tranquillity and prosperity of the United

THE ELECTION OF 1844

States. Treating this as a new revelation, Calhoun, the same man who had declared in 1836 the annexation of Texas necessary, now pretended that, in view of such avowals by Lord Aberdeen, annexation had become immediately indispensable for the salvation of slavery, and, therefore, for the safety of the people of the United States. Tyler's message, which accompanied the treaty, had, indeed, much to say of the commercial advantages which the "re-annexation" of Texas would confer upon the American people; but it laid also great stress upon the "anxiety of other powers to induce Mexico to enter into terms of reconciliation with Texas, which, affecting the domestic institutions of Texas, would operate most injuriously upon the United States, and might most seriously threaten the existence of this happy Union." Nor did he omit to mention that "formidable associations of persons were directing their utmost efforts" to the overthrow of slavery in Texas. In other words, the United States were bound to risk a war and annex a country for fear that slavery might be abolished in that country; the United States must possess that country for the avowed purpose of preserving slavery there. This was the argument of the President and the secretary of state before the Senate, and this was the position in which they placed the great American republic before the world.

The Whig National Convention met at Baltimore on May 1. Almost all the notables of the

Whig party were there, Webster included. The nomination of Clay as the Whig candidate for the presidency required no ballot. It was carried with a great shout that shook the building. Theodore Frelinghuysen of New Jersey was nominated for the vice-presidency. The following day a "ratifying convention" was held, — an immense assemblage, — before which Webster solemnly renewed his allegiance to the Whig party.

Webster had, since he left Tyler's cabinet, lived in gloomy political isolation. His question, "Where shall I go?" had not been answered by the Whig leaders. He had to answer it himself. So he returned to the Whig party, and, as Clay was the recognized chief of the Whig party, to Clay. In the summer of 1843 some of Webster's intimates made overtures for a resumption of friendly relations. The chief received the approach somewhat grandly. "I approve in the main," Clay wrote to Peter B. Porter, "of the answer you gave to Mr. Webster's friend. I have done him [Mr. Webster] no wrong, and have therefore no reconciliation to seek. Should I be a candidate for the presidency, I shall be glad to receive his support, or that of any other American citizen; but I can enter into no arrangements, make no promises, offer no pledges, to obtain it." Porter answered: "Our friends were delighted with this reply, and even the Webster men were obliged to acknowledge that it was perfectly correct and proper." Webster came to Baltimore knowing that Clay's nomination was certain. In his ratification speech he spoke of Clay in terms of warm eulogy, extolling the services that eminent citizen had rendered to his country at home and abroad ; he rejoiced in presenting his name to the country as a candidate for the presidency; they had, indeed, differed upon some points of policy, but there was now no public question before the country upon which there was any difference between himself and that great leader of the Whig party. The cheering which responded to this speech was immense. The Whig party appeared to be as firmly united as ever, and its members congratulated one another upon the prospect of certain success.

These sanguine expectations seemed to be well justified by the dissensions disturbing the Democratic party. It was known that, of the delegates elected to the Democratic National Convention, a majority were for Van Buren, very many of them instructed by their constituents. But the ardent annexationists were bound to have a man in the presidential chair whom they could trust to go to extremes in insuring the acquisition of Texas. Systematically they went to work to compass Van Buren's defeat. They had at their disposal the whole power of Calhoun, Van Buren's old enemy. They appointed a committee of correspondence at Washington to organize the anti-Van Buren movement throughout the country. All over the South meetings were held to agitate the annexation of Texas, and to inflame the pro-slavery feeling. In South Carolina the cry, "Texas or disunion!" began to be heard. Calhoun's organs in the press loudly declared Van Buren's nomination impossible. Here and there steps were taken to rescind instructions in his favor. When the convention met, on May 27, Van Buren had still a majority of the delegates on his side, professedly at least. But as soon as, upon the motion of a Southern delegate, the rule was sustained that a majority of two thirds should be required for effecting a nomination, Van Buren was lost. On the first ballot he still had twelve more than a majority, but he lacked twenty-six of two thirds. On the ninth ballot the opposition to Van Buren combined with a rush upon James K. Polk of Tennessee, a warm advocate of the annexation of Texas. The two thirds rule, which had been applied in the conventions of 1832 and 1836, when there were hardly any contests, was, after 1844, recognized by the slave power as the surest means of controlling presidential nominations, or rather of preventing nominations obnoxious to its interests, and it remained the standing practice of Democratic national conventions.

For the vice-presidency, George M. Dallas of Pennsylvania was nominated, after Silas Wright, the friend of Van Buren, had peremptorily declined. A resolution was adopted recommending to the cordial support of the Democracy of the Union "the reoccupation of Oregon and the reannexation of Texas at the earliest practicable

THE ELECTION OF 1844

period" as great American measures, — Texas for the South, and Oregon ostensibly for the North.

The Democratic National Convention of 1844 marks an epoch in American history in two respects: it designated as the leading issue of the presidential election the annexation of Texas, the beginning of the end of slavery; and it was the first deliberative assemblage the proceedings of which were reported by the electric telegraph, the most striking exponent of modern civilization, Morse having, with the aid of the government, just completed his first line between Baltimore and Washington.

Another nominating convention was held in Baltimore at the same time. John Tyler had attempted to purchase the support of the Democrats with patronage, but received only ironical compliments. He had persuaded himself that the people believed him to be a very great man, and waited only for an opportunity to rise up for him *en masse*. This grand uprising of the American people for John Tyler had for a long time been the standing jest of the newspapers, but Tyler's faith could not be shaken. He therefore gravely posed as a candidate for the presidency, and assembled a convention consisting mainly of office-holders. The convention solemnly nominated him, and he responded with an equally solemn letter of acceptance. But before long it dawned upon him that he had no support whatever, and he withdrew in favor of the Democratic candidate.

Still another convention had been held months before, on August 30, 1843, at Buffalo, which the politicians of the two great organizations probably thought at the time of less practical importance even than Tyler's corporal's guard. It was the convention of the "Liberty party." Its presidential candidates were James G. Birney and Thomas Morris. The Liberty party consisted of earnest anti-slavery men who pursued their objects by political action. They were not in sympathy with those abolitionists who lost themselves in no "government" theories, who denounced the Union and the Constitution as a "covenant with death and an agreement with hell," and who abhorred the exercise of the suffrage under the Constitution as a participation in sin. In the language of Birney, they regarded the national Constitution "with unabated affection." They interpreted it as an anti-slavery document, and declared that they had "nothing to ask except what the Constitution authorizes, no change to desire except that the Constitution be restored to its primitive purity."

Their first practical step was to interrogate the candidates of the existing parties concerning their views on slavery, in order to throw the weight of their votes accordingly. Then they attempted a party organization of their own, to furnish a nucleus around which future political anti-slavery movements might gather. Their first presidential candidates, as we have seen, were offered to the people in the election of 1840, when they received about seven thousand votes. The popular excitement caused by the Texas question augmented their strength; and their national convention at Buffalo in August, 1843, was unexpectedly large in numbers, strong in character, and enthusiastic in spirit. Salmon P. Chase of Ohio, a man cast in a grand mould, who had already rendered conspicuous service in the anti-slavery cause, was one of its most prominent members. Birney, its candidate for the presidency, was a native of Kentucky. A slaveholder by inheritance, he liberated his slaves and provided generously for them. He was a lawyer of ability, a gentleman of culture, and a vigorous and graceful speaker. Obeying a high sense of duty, he sacrificed the comforts of wealth, home, and position to the cause of universal freedom, — not as a wild enthusiast or unreasoning fanatic, but as a calm thinker, temperate in language, and firm in maintaining his conclusions. His principal conclusion was that slavery and free institutions could not exist together. He has been charged with committing an act of personal faithlessness in opposing Clay in 1844. This charge was utterly unjust. He had never given Clay or Clay's friends any promise of support. It is true, Clay and Birney had maintained a friendly intercourse until 1834; but in June of that year they had a conference on the subject of slavery which produced upon Birney a discouraging effect. From that time their friendly intercourse ceased, and Clay found in Birney only a severe critic.

The defeat of Van Buren in the Democratic National Convention was a disappointment to the Whigs, as it baffled the hope of keeping the annexation question out of the presidential campaign. But Polk, although he had been speaker of the National House of Representatives, was comparatively so obscure a man, that a contest for the highest honors of the republic between him and the great Henry Clay appeared almost grotesque. The Democrats themselves were at first somewhat embarrassed by the contrast. The question, "Who is Polk?" was asked on all sides, to be answered by the Whigs with a jeering laugh. Indeed, had nothing happened to overshadow the old issues, the personal question would have appeared as the most important. For about the tariff and the bank the Democratic and the Whig platforms differed very little.

Of a United States Bank the Whig platform said nothing. It spoke only of a "well-regulated currency." Clay himself, returning to the position he had taken during the campaign of 1840, remarked at Raleigh that, while his views about the bank question remained the same, he did "not seek to enforce them upon any others;" he did not desire a bank unless it was imperatively demanded by the people. Among the Whigs generally, the United States Bank had been given up as an "obsolete idea." That point, therefore, was substantially yielded by them. As to the tariff, the Democrats had made a fresh record. In the session of

THE ELECTION OF 1844

1843-44, when they controlled the House by a very large majority, they laid a bill modifying the tariff of 1842 on the table; and in their platform, while denying the right of government to raise more than the necessary revenue, and to foster one branch of industry to the detriment of another, they did not even mention the tariff by name. They evidently did not mean to take the field as an anti-protection party. The manner in which, on the contrary, they continued to steal Clay's thunder was amazing in its boldness.

The tariff of 1842 was very popular in Pennsylvania, and, indeed, much favored by the manufacturing interests in various Northern States. It had also many friends among the Democrats of Kentucky and Louisiana. Polk enjoyed the reputation of being a free-trader. The problem to be solved was to make him acceptable to both sides. Three weeks after the Democratic convention he addressed a letter to J. K. Kane of Philadelphia, in which he first set forth his votes in Congress against the tariff of 1828, the "tariff of abominations," his vote for the tariff of 1832 effecting a reduction of duties, and his vote for the compromise tariff of 1833. This was for the free-traders. Then he declared that, in his judgment, it was "the duty of the government to extend, so far as practicable, by its revenue laws and all other means within its power, fair and just protection to all the great interests of the whole Union, embracing agriculture, manufactures, the mechanic arts, commerce, and navigation." This was for everybody, the protectionists included. No sooner had the "Kane letter" been published, than the cry was raised: "Polk, Dallas, and the tariff of 1842." In Pennsylvania at every mass meeting, in every procession, banners appeared bearing that legend, — not seldom with the addition, "We dare the Whigs to repeal it." But even that was not enough. While Polk and the Democratic party were paraded as the special champions of the tariff of 1842, Clay, the father of the "American system," was systematically cried down as a dangerous enemy of protection; and, in the name of protection to American industry, the voters of Pennsylvania were invoked to vote against him. It was one of the most audacious political frauds in our history. That it should have been possible to carry on such a palpable deception, through a campaign lasting several months, is truly astonishing. And what an opening of eyes there was in Pennsylvania when in 1846 the Polk Democrats did repeal the tariff of 1842, which the Clay Whigs vainly struggled to sustain!

While this trick cost him the vote of Pennsylvania, Clay had more dangerous enemies to encounter elsewhere. The campaign had hardly begun when the "old hero" at the Hermitage, on the brink of the grave, sent forth his last bugle-blast to summon his friends against the man he hated most. Andrew Jackson wrote a letter again affirming his belief in the story that Clay and

Adams had by bargain and corruption defrauded him of his right to the presidency in 1825, and again the old cry resounded in all the Democratic presses and in numberless speeches. Again Clay thought it necessary to call upon his friends for testimony to prove that he had given an uncorrupted vote for Adams twenty years before. But, in spite of Andrew Jackson's still potent hostility, he would have won the day had he not found his most dangerous enemy in himself.

The Texas question was, after all, the real issue of the campaign. In this respect Polk's position was perfectly clear. As a declared advocate of annexation, he could count upon a majority of the Southern States; but in the North he was for the same reason in danger of losing not a few Democratic votes. New York was looked upon as the decisive battle-ground. To prevent the loss of that State, Silas Wright, the friend of Van Buren and an opponent of annexation, was prevailed upon to accept the Democratic candidacy for the governorship. A secret circular was issued by prominent Democrats of anti-slavery feelings, — among them William Cullen Bryant, the editor of the "Evening Post," David Dudley Field, and Theodore Sedgwick, — censuring the Democratic National Convention for adopting a resolution in favor of annexing Texas, and recommending to Democrats to support only such candidates for Congress as were opposed to annexation, but to vote for the Democratic presidential ticket: a poor device, indicating, however, that there was ominous wavering in the Democratic ranks.

Clay's letter on the annexation question, while not reaching up to the standard of the Liberty party, had the approval of anti-slavery men of more moderate views, and was well calculated to attract to his support anti-slavery Democrats who were not willing to deceive themselves by voting for a candidate while protesting against that which he represented. Clay had, therefore, reason to hope that he would receive votes beyond the regular strength of his party, and this especially in the important State of New York. He had only to let his Raleigh letter produce its natural effect.

But in the planting States the excitement about the Texas question rose from day to day. It was still more inflamed by the news that the Senate, after a long and warm debate, had, on June 8, by a large majority (35 to 16), refused to assent to the treaty of annexation; that then Tyler had sent a message to the House asking that annexation be accomplished by "some other form of proceeding," but that Congress had adjourned without further action. The Southern Whigs became anxious, and some of them earnestly insisted that Clay should modify the expression of his views on the vexed question. In an evil hour Clay yielded to their entreaties, and ventured upon that most perilous of manœuvres on the political as well as the military field, — a change of front under the fire of the enemy. On July 1 he wrote a letter to Stephen

F. Miller of Tuscaloosa, Alabama, in which he disclaimed that, when speaking in his Raleigh letter of a "considerable and respectable portion of the confederacy" against whose wishes Texas should not be annexed, he had meant the abolitionists. "As to the idea of my courting the abolitionists," he said, "it is perfectly absurd. No man in the United States has been half as much abused by them as I have been." "Personally," he added, "I could have no objection to the annexation of Texas; but I certainly should be unwilling to see the existing Union dissolved or seriously jeoparded for the sake of acquiring Texas. If any one desires to know the leading and paramount object of my public life, the preservation of the Union will furnish him the key."

This might have passed without much harm, but his Southern friends demanded more, and he gave more. "I do not think it right," he wrote to Miller on July 27, "to announce in advance what will be the course of a future administration in respect to a question with a foreign power. I have, however, no hesitation in saying that, far from having any personal objection to the annexation of Texas, I should be glad to see it, without dishonor, without war, with the common consent of the Union, and upon just and fair terms. I do not think that the subject of slavery ought to affect the question, one way or the other. Whether Texas be independent, or incorporated in the United States, I do not think it will shorten or prolong the duration of that institution. It is destined to become extinct at some distant day, in my opinion, by the operation of the inevitable laws of population. It would be unwise to refuse a permanent acquisition, which will exist as long as the globe remains, on account of a temporary institution."

Whether these letters were extorted from him by the cry of the extreme annexationists, "Texas or disunion!" or whether they were merely a bid for Southern votes, in either case Clay could not, as to their effect upon the election, have committed a greater blunder. They could not strengthen him where he was weak: they could only weaken him where he was strong. They could not induce the annexationists to trust him: they could only make the opponents of annexation doubtful as to whether he deserved to be trusted by them. They could only repel the anti-slavery vote, for they declared that the anti-slavery argument against the annexation of Texas was without value.

The Liberty party suddenly rose to a practical importance in the canvass which it had not enjoyed before. Some of its speakers and writers had, indeed, attacked Clay, from the beginning of the campaign, as a "slaveholder and a gambler." True, Polk was a slaveholder, too; Polk and his party were pledged to do what the anti-slavery men held most in abhorrence, — enlarge the area of slavery. The Whig party contained a much larger element congenial to the anti-slavery men than did the Democracy, and the election of Clay was perhaps the only thing that could prevent the annexation of Texas: there were, therefore, many reasons why the anti-slavery men should have supported Clay. Yet their opposition to him was not without logic. They did not expect to decide the contest between the two great parties. Their work was, as they conceived it, missionary work. They simply desired to strengthen their organization for future action, and naturally endeavored to draw recruits from that party in which they had the largest number of sympathizers, — the Whigs. To that end they endeavored to make the anti-slavery Whigs dissatisfied with their party and their candidate. Hence the vigor of their warfare upon Clay. And that warfare was undoubtedly inspired also by a tendency always prevailing among men who are struggling for the realization of ideas in advance of their time, — the tendency to censure more bitterly those from whom they expect sympathy and aid, if that sympathy and aid do not come, than those from whom they expect and receive nothing but hostility. Thus the Liberty party gave up the Democrats as hopeless, and severely castigated the Whigs for not rising to its own standard.

Had Clay abstained from disturbing the impression produced by his Raleigh letter, that he would firmly oppose the annexation of Texas, those attacks of the Liberty party would not have become dangerous to him, because they would have appeared unreasonable. But his Alabama letters made him appear like one of those trimming politicians who have no fixed principles and aims. Then the assaults of the Liberty party began to tell, for they seemed unreasonable no longer. No more Democratic anti-annexation men would come to him, for they did not know whether he could be trusted. While a large majority of the anti-slavery Whigs remained with their party, they felt themselves reduced to an embarrassed defensive. Their enthusiasm was chilled, and their ability to make converts gone. The number of anti-slavery Whigs who left their party, and ranged themselves under Birney's banners, was comparatively small, but large enough to turn the scale.

The effect of the "Alabama letter" became so apparent that Clay, in the course of the campaign, tried to explain again and again, and to return to his first position; but in vain. The spell was broken. As Horace Greeley expressed it, the previous hold of his advocates on the moral convictions of the more considerate and conscientious voters of the free States was irretrievably gone. The Whigs did, indeed, not give up their efforts. They continued their displays of external enthusiasm, although in a far less hopeful mood. They called Cassius M. Clay, then in the first bloom of his fame as an anti-slavery champion, from meeting to meeting, to explain the true status and bearing of the Texas question from his point of view. All in vain. Washington Hunt wrote to Thurlow Weed: "We had the abolitionists in a good way, but Mr. Clay seems determined that they shall not be allowed to vote for him. I believe his letter will lose us more than two hundred votes in this county (Niagara). Cassius Clay's powerful usefulness is much weakened by the last letter of Mr. Clay. I dread with all his efforts he may not counteract the influence of the letter, coming as it does at this critical moment, when half the abolitionists were on a pivot."

Polk carried the State of New York over Clay by a majority of 5080 votes. Birney, the candidate of the Liberty party, received in the same State 15,812 votes, more than twice as many as had been cast for him in 1840 in the whole Union. There is no reasonable doubt that more than half of Birney's vote in New York — two thousand more than were required to give him the State — would have been cast for Clay but for his Alabama letter: and that would have made him president of the United States; for, with Massachusetts, Rhode Island, Connecticut, Vermont, New Jersey, Ohio, Delaware, Maryland, North Carolina, Kentucky, and Tennessee, which he carried, New York would have given him a majority of the electoral college. "The abolition vote lost you the election," wrote Ambrose Spencer of New York to Clay, "as three fourths of them were firm Whigs converted into abolitionists," The perpetration of gross and extensive election frauds was charged upon the Democratic party, especially in New York and in Louisiana, through fraudulent naturalizations, organized repeating, and ballot-box stuffing; and there was much to prove the justice of these complaints. It was also said that the excitement produced by the war of the "Native Americans" against the Catholics, which in May had led to bloody riots in Philadelphia, had driven the whole "foreign vote" upon the Democratic side, and thereby injured Clay, — especially through the unpopularity in that quarter of the Whig candidate for the vice-presidency, Theodore Frelinghuysen, who was a stern anti-Catholic. But all these causes would not have been sufficient to defeat Clay had he held on his side that anti-slavery vote which his Alabama letter drove from the Whigs to Birney. It is absurd to attribute the result of an election to accident, when it clearly appears that a number of voters sufficient to turn the scale were determined in their action by the character or conduct of one of the candidates with regard to the principal matter at issue. The object of Clay's highest ambition escaped him because, at the decisive moment, he was untrue to himself.

The masses of the Whig party, while the managers noticed the adverse current, firmly expected success to the very last. It seemed impossible to them that Henry Clay could be defeated by James K. Polk. Everything hung on New York. The returns from the interior of the State came slowly. There seemed to be still a possibility that heavy Whig majorities in the western counties might overcome the large Democratic vote in the eastern.

THE ELECTION OF 1844 267

The suspense was painful. People did not go to bed, watching for the mails. When at last the decisive news went forth which left no doubt of the result, the Whigs broke out in a wail of agony all over the land. "It was," says Nathan Sargent, "as if the first-born of every family had been stricken down." The descriptions we have of the grief manifested are almost incredible. Tears flowed in abundance from the eyes of men and women. In the cities and villages the business places were almost deserted for a day or two, people gathering together in groups to discuss in low tones what had happened. Neither did the victorious Democrats indulge in the usual demonstrations of triumph. There was a feeling as if a great wrong had been done. The Whigs were fairly stunned by their defeat. Not a few expressed the apprehension that their party would dissolve. Many despaired of the republic, sincerely believing that the experiment of popular government had failed forever. Others insisted that the naturalization laws must be forthwith repealed. Almost all agreed that the great statesmen of the country would thenceforth always remain excluded from the presidency, and that the highest office would be the prize only of secondrate politicians. Clay himself was in a gloomy state of mind. "The late blow that has fallen upon our country is very heavy," he wrote to a friend. "I hope that she may recover from it, but I confess that the prospect ahead is dark and discouraging. I am afraid that it will be yet a long time, if ever, that the people recover from the corrupting influence and effects of Jacksonism. I pray God to give them a happy deliverance."

CHAPTER XXV

1844-1849

During the autumn and early part of the winter of 1844-45 Clay remained at Ashland, receiving and answering a flood of letters from all parts of the United States, and even from Europe, which conveyed to him expressions of condolence and sympathy, — many of them most touching by the evident sincerity of their sorrowful lamentations. The electors of Kentucky, after having cast their votes for him, visited Ashland to assure the defeated man of the affection and faithful attachment of his State.

Private cares had meanwhile gathered in addition to his public disappointments. He had for some time been laboring under great pecuniary embarrassment, owing partly to the drafts which are always made upon the purse of a prominent public man, partly to the business failure of one of his sons. Aside from other pressing debts, there was a heavy mortgage resting on Ashland, and, as an old man of sixty-seven, Clay found himself forced to consider whether, in order to satisfy his creditors, it would not be necessary to part with his beloved home. Relief came to him suddenly, and in an unexpected form. When offering a payment to the bank at Lexington, the president of the institution informed him that sums of money had arrived from different parts of the country to pay off Henry Clay's debts, and that all the notes and the mortgage were cancelled. Clay was deeply moved. "Who did this?" he asked the banker. All the answer he received was that the givers were unknown, but they were presumably "not his enemies." Clay doubted whether he should accept the gift, and consulted some of his friends. They reminded him of the many persons of historic renown who had not refused tokens of admiration and gratitude from their countrymen; and added that, as he could not discover the unknown givers, he could not return the gift; and, as the gift appeared in the shape of a discharged obligation, he could not force the renewal of the debt. At last he consented to accept, and thus was Ashland saved to him.

In January, 1845, Clay attended a meeting of the American Colonization Society at Washington, which was held in the hall of the House of Representatives. "Last night Mr. Clay made a show on the colonization question, and such a show I never saw," wrote Alexander H. Stephens to his brother. "Men came from Baltimore, Philadelphia, and New York, to say nothing of Alexandria and this city. The house and galleries were jammed and crammed before five o'clock." Stephens then describes how he himself had to scheme and struggle to get in through a side door; how Clay appeared about seven o'clock, and could hardly force his way in; how the vast meeting would cheer him again and again at the top of their voices; how they would not let anybody speak before him; how " whole acres " of people had to go away without getting in at all; and how Shepperd of North Carolina, being " more Whiggish than Clayish," remarked, " rather snappishly," that " Clay could get more men to run after him to hear him speak, and fewer to vote for him, than any man in America."

In the mean time grave events were preparing themselves in Congress. In his annual message of December, 1844, President Tyler stoutly asserted that, through the late presidential election, "a controlling majority of the people and a large majority of the States " had declared in favor of the immediate annexation of Texas, and that both branches of Congress had thus been instructed by their respective constituents to that effect. William Cullen Bryant and his friends, who had made themselves believe that they could vote for Polk and at the same time against the annexation of Texas, might have taken this audacious statement as a personal affront. But the Whigs could hardly repel the doctrine of special instructions to Congress by presidential election, since they had pretended that the election of 1840 was a special instruction to Congress to create a new United States Bank. There was still opposition enough in the

Senate to render it doubtful whether another annexation treaty would obtain the necessary two thirds vote. The expedient was therefore adopted of annexing Texas by joint resolution, which required only a simple majority of each house. On January 25 a resolution annexing Texas passed the House of Representatives, with an amendment, championed by Stephen A. Douglas of Illinois, that, in such State or States as should be formed out of the territory of Texas north of the Missouri compromise line of 36° 30', slavery should be prohibited, the formation of four slave States being contemplated south of that line. All the Whigs, with the exception of eight from the South, voted against the resolution.

In the Senate it found opposition from those who insisted that foreign territory could not be constitutionally incorporated with the United States except by treaty. It would probably have been defeated, had not Walker of Mississippi offered, as an amendment, an addition to the resolution giving the President the option between submitting to the Texan government the joint resolution for its acceptance, or beginning new negotiations for an annexation treaty. Five of those who thought the original resolution unconstitutional accepted Walker's amendment, thus authorizing the President to violate the Constitution or not, as he might think most convenient. One of the five was Benton, who afterwards protested that, according to a secret understanding, the option was not to be exercised by

Tyler, but to be left to Polk, and that Polk would resume negotiations for a treaty. If there was such an understanding, Benton found himself cheated; for when the joint resolution so amended had passed both houses, and been signed by Tyler, a messenger was dispatched, on March 3, to the Texan government to offer annexation by joint resolution. On March 4 Polk was inaugurated as president. In his inaugural address he said that the enlargement of the Union would be the extension of " the dominions of peace over additional territories and increasing millions." He made James Buchanan secretary of state. Neither he nor Buchanan thought of recalling the messenger sent to Texas with the joint resolution, and of reopening negotiations for a new treaty.

Texas had, after the failure of the annexation treaty in the Senate, sought her salvation in another direction again, and, with the aid of England and France, negotiated a preliminary peace with Mexico. The peace was signed by the Texan agent on March 29. It contained the recognition of Texan independence, and a promise that Texas should not be annexed to any foreign State. On April 21 the Mexican Congress assented to the treaty. The Texan Congress met on June 16. The joint resolution passed by the Congress of the United States was submitted to it, and also the peace with Mexico. The Texan Senate unanimously rejected the peace with Mexico, and two days later the resolution of annexation was adopted by both houses. On July 4 a convention of the people of Texas met and ratified annexation.

Thus Mexico and Texas were still at war; and Clay's prediction, that with the annexation of Texas the United States would inevitably annex that war, seemed to be verified. Indeed, upon the passage of the joint resolution to annex Texas, the Mexican minister left Washington, and the American minister the city of Mexico. Still, actual war might have been avoided had the United States been satisfied with Texas as then occupied by Texans, or sought to acquire the line of the Rio Grande as the boundary line by patient negotiation. The joint resolution annexing "the territory properly included within, and rightfully belonging to, the Republic of Texas," and speaking of "an adjustment by this government of all questions of boundary that may arise with other governments," evidently looked to such negotiation. The question of boundary was whether Texas extended only as far as the Texan settlements extended, to the Nueces River, or beyond the Texan settlements to the Rio Grande, the eastern bank of which was dotted with Mexican villages and military posts. The country between the Nueces and the Rio Grande had, indeed, been wildly "claimed" by the Texans, although really looked upon as, at most, disputed territory. But Polk's administration assumed to decide the boundary question by force.

On July 30 General Taylor was ordered, with

the troops concentrated on the Sabine, to occupy, protect, and defend Texas as far as occupied by the Texans, and to approach the Rio Grande, which was "claimed to be the boundary between the two countries" (Texas and Mexico), but to remain away from Mexican settlements and military posts. In August, Taylor camped at Corpus Christi, on the Nueces. On August 23 he was informed that, if a large Mexican army should cross the Rio Grande, the President would regard that act as an invasion of the United States and the beginning of hostilities; and on August 30 he was instructed that an *attempt* to cross on the part of a large Mexican force should "be regarded in the same light," and that in such case he should consider himself authorized, in his discretion, to defend Texas by crossing the Rio Grande himself, driving the Mexicans from their positions on either bank, and occupying Matamoras. Before receiving this instruction General Taylor reported to the War Department that there were no concentrations of Mexican troops on the Rio Grande, and no expectation of war; he could hear only of small parties to be sent across the river by the Mexicans to prevent Indian depredations and illicit trade. On October 16, however, Taylor was again instructed to approach the Rio Grande, and to repel "any attempted invasion." This instruction was crossed on its way by a dispatch from Taylor, who had meanwhile begun to understand what was desired of him, saying that, if the Rio Grande boundary was really the ultimatum of the United States, a prompt advance was indeed advisable; but in that case, as Mexico had neither declared war nor committed any overt act of hostility, he wanted definite authority from the War Department for a forward movement. This seems to have been an unwelcome request. Definite orders did not come for months. Meanwhile operations on another line were going on.

In September Buchanan had inquired of the Mexican government, through the American consul, whether it would "receive an envoy from the United States, intrusted with full powers to adjust all questions in dispute between the two governments." The Mexican government promptly declared itself ready to receive a "commissioner" with full power to settle "the present dispute," meaning the dispute about Texas. Polk then appointed Slidell of Louisiana as "envoy extraordinary and minister plenipotentiary" to enter into negotiations about a variety of matters. It was not only Texas the administration had in mind, but also the Mexican province, California. While this was going on, Commodore Sloat, commanding the Pacific squadron of the American navy, was under instructions, as soon as he should ascertain with certainty that Mexico had declared war against the United States, at once to possess himself of the port of San Francisco, and to blockade or occupy such other ports as his force would permit; also to maintain friendly relations with the inhabitants. Everything indicates that, in the event of hostilities, California was to be occupied with a view to permanent possession. Thus the army and the navy were ready to seize by force what the administration coveted, in case Slidell did not succeed in buying it. He was instructed to offer the Mexican government the assumption by the United States of the American claims against Mexico, and five million dollars, for the Rio Grande line and New Mexico, or the assumption of the claims and twenty-five millions for New Mexico and California.

When Slidell appeared on Mexican soil, the Mexican president, Herrera, peaceably disposed, but fearing that he could not sustain himself against the popular temper if he opened negotiations forthwith, wished him to delay his arrival in the capital. But Slidell did not delay. He sent at once his letter of credence to the minister of foreign affairs. After some hesitation the minister declared that Slidell's credentials were not according to the understanding; that he was not a special "commissioner" sent to dispose of the Texas dispute only, but a regular minister plenipotentiary; and that therefore the question of his reception must be submitted to the government council. Slidell insisted, but the Mexican government repeated that he could be received only as commissioner to treat about Texas. Slidell replied in a haughty and insulting note, and announced his return to the United States, without, however, being really in haste to go. "In anticipation" of the refusal of the Mexican government to receive Slidell, and before his report had reached Washington, on January 13, 1846, General Taylor was directed, by an instruction which was kept secret, to advance with his whole command to the Rio Grande, and a strong naval force was ordered to the Gulf of Mexico, to give emphasis to Slidell's demands. Meantime Herrera's government was overthrown by a revolution. But on the Mexican side of the Rio Grande no military movements were perceptible. The Mexican government was in a condition of utter bankruptcy and confusion. Slidell was instructed to present his letter of credence to the new Mexican president, Paredes. If he, too, declined to receive him, the matter would then have to be submitted to Congress.

There was great excitement in Congress meanwhile, — not, however, about Mexico, but about another complication threatening war with England. It will be remembered that Oregon and Texas were linked together in the Democratic platform. The treaty of Ghent had left the conflicting claims of the United States and Great Britain concerning the Columbia or Oregon valley unsettled. The Convention of 1818 provided for a joint occupation. The value of the country was not known. The Americans had there the trading-post Astoria, and the British Hudson Bay Company its trappers and fur traders. Negotiations to determine the relative right of possession were carried on languidly and without result. In 1818 and 1820 the United States offered, as a compromise, the forty-ninth parallel as the dividing line, the British insisting on the line of the Columbia River down from the point where the forty-ninth parallel intersected its northeastern branch. But they agreed on nothing except to extend the joint occupation indefinitely, subject to notice of termination. In 1832 a small agricultural settlement was established by Americans on the Willamette, an affluent of the Columbia. In 1836 President Jackson ordered an exploration of that region, which attracted much interest. In 1838 the settlers on the Willamette petitioned Congress for the establishment of a territorial government, but without success. New petitions came, together with the report that the Hudson Bay Company, too, were introducing settlers. Oregon grew more important in the eyes of the people and the politicians. Tyler mentioned the subject in his messages, but in the negotiations between Webster and Lord Ashburton it was ignored. Six months after the conclusion of the Ashburton treaty, a missionary, Dr. Marcus Whitman, coming directly from Oregon, gave valuable information about the magnificent resources of that country. He soon led a caravan of two hundred wagons from the Missouri to the Columbia, demonstrating its accessibility by land. Fremont at the same period made his discoveries of practicable passes through the Rocky Mountains. The project of a trans-continental railway was not long afterwards suggested by Asa Whitney. In the Western States a clamor arose for the enforcement of the American right to Oregon. Western senators demanded that notice of the termination of the joint occupancy be served on Great Britain. The subject became fit for the manufacture of political capital, and could no longer be ignored.

Negotiations were resumed under Tyler's administration between Calhoun and Pakenham, the British minister, Calhoun repeating the offer of the forty-ninth parallel, but the British government insisting upon the Columbia as the boundary line. The British minister suggested arbitration, but Calhoun declined. The Democratic National Convention of 1844 took up the question, demanding the "reoccupation" of the whole of Oregon, which was made to include the country up to 54° 40′, a line which had been fixed twenty years before as the southern boundary of the Russian possessions in America. Polk, in his inaugural address, repeating very nearly the language of the Democratic platform, spoke of "the American title to the country of the Oregon" as "clear and unquestionable." Lord John Russell called this a "blustering announcement," and the reply of the American Democrats was "Fifty-four forty or fight!"

On July 12, 1845, Buchanan, while affirming the American right to "the whole of Oregon," admitted, in a note to the British minister, that the President felt himself "embarrassed by the acts of his predecessors," and offered once more the forty-ninth parallel as a compromise. When the British minister again declined, Buchanan withdrew the offer, and announced that the President would now insist on "the whole of Oregon." Polk, in his annual message of December, 1845, confirmed this, and recommended that one year's notice be given to Great Britain of the termination of the joint occupancy, and that provision be made for the protection of American settlers in Oregon. He declared himself convinced that no acceptable compromise could be effected, and threw the responsibility on England. This foreboded war. The business community became alarmed; stocks fell in Wall Street. On December 9 Cass moved in the Senate an inquiry into the condition of the army and navy. The "notice" to be served on Great Britain became the subject of exciting debates. The British minister once more proposed arbitration, which Polk again declined, affirming that he would not accept anything less than the whole territory, "unless the Senate should otherwise determine." The administration, having its eye on Mexico, desired no war with England, but tried to shift the responsibility for a compromise on the Senate.

The extremists, the "fifty-four forties," clamored for immediate "notice." They would not leave the matter to the Senate, quoting Clay's utterance in the debate on the Florida treaty in 1820, that no

territory belonging to the United States could be
ceded to a foreign power, or "alienated," without
the assent of both houses of Congress. But the
Southern leaders, Calhoun foremost, who on account of slavery dreaded a war with England, and
did not very warmly favor territorial expansion
northward, began to advocate a pacific course.
The Western Democrats did not fail to accuse the
Southerners of bad faith because, having acquired
Texas to strengthen their peculiar interests, they
would not go to extremes in carrying out the Northern part of the Democratic platform. But this did
not prevent the confidential spokesmen of the President in the Senate from familiarizing the public
mind with the abandonment of 54° 40'. It became
apparent that the administration wished to avoid
extremities. The popular temper sobered down.
The cry of "54° 40' or fight" gradually died away.
On April 16, 1846, "notice" in a very conciliatory
form passed the Senate. Public opinion in England was favorably affected. The British government itself then proposed the forty-ninth parallel.
Polk, still desirous of shifting the responsibility,
would not directly accept. Resuming a practice of
the early times of the republic, he consulted the
Senate in advance about a treaty yet to be made,
submitting a mere draft of it, and announced that,
according to the advice of the Senate, he would
either accept or reject the British proposition. The
Senate, by a majority of three to one, the Whigs
voting with the majority, advised the President to

accept, and the treaty was promptly concluded and ratified. Thus the Oregon question, which produced so much noisy excitement, was put out of the way, while the cloud on the southern horizon silently rose and grew blacker.

The American minister in London reported that the British government would hardly have been so forward in proposing the forty-ninth parallel had it known what at that period was passing on the Rio Grande.

On March 1 Slidell demanded that the new Mexican president, Paredes, should declare whether he would receive him in the character of a minister plenipotentiary or not. Paredes replied that the threatening attitude of the United States made the reception impossible. On March 11 General Taylor began his movement from Corpus Christi to the Rio Grande. On the 28th he arrived opposite Matamoras, and planted a battery commanding the public square of that town. With some vessels of the United States near at hand he blockaded the mouth of the Rio Grande to cut off all supplies from Matamoras, to the end of forcing the Mexican troops stationed there either to withdraw or to take the offensive. On April 24 the Mexican general, Arista, declared that he considered hostilities thus begun, and the following day a detachment of American dragoons became engaged on the eastern bank of the Rio Grande with a superior force of Mexicans, and lost sixteen men. General Taylor reported to the government that hostilities might now be deemed opened, and that he was going to carry the war into the enemy's country.

Taylor's dispatch arrived in Washington on May 9, a Saturday, and on Monday, the 11th, Polk sent a message to Congress accusing Mexico of having invaded the territory of the United States, and announcing that war existed, notwithstanding the efforts of the government of the United States to avoid it. The same day the House of Representatives, without taking time to have the reports and dispatches read, and almost without debate, passed a bill declaring that war existed " by the act of Mexico," authorizing the President to call out fifty thousand volunteers, and appropriating $10,000,-000. Only fourteen votes were cast against the bill, at their head that of John Quincy Adams. The Senate passed the bill on the 12th by a vote of forty to two. The contrast between the treatment of the Oregon question and that of the difficulty with Mexico could not have been more glaring.

At the same session of Congress the famous tariff of 1846 was passed, substantially stripping duties on imports of their high-protective character. The cries of the Pennsylvanians who had voted for " Polk, Dallas, and the tariff of 1842 " were pitiable in the extreme, but of no avail. Also the sub-treasury system was reëstablished, to remain ; and Polk put his veto upon a river and harbor bill.

On the Rio Grande events progressed rapidly.

Before his dispatch reached Washington, on May 8, General Taylor with his small force defeated the Mexicans at Palo Alto, and on the 9th he won a still more important success at Resaca de la Palma. On the 18th he crossed the Rio Grande and occupied Matamoras. General Kearney was ordered to conquer New Mexico, which he did without firing a gun. He was to push forward to California. But there his services were not needed. Captain Fremont, engaged in an exploring expedition, with the aid of his companions and of American settlers, and with the coöperation of American men-of-war on the Pacific coast, set up a provisional government in California, and brought the country under the control of the United States.

During the summer of 1846 there was a pause in the war and an "intrigue for peace." The administration had put itself in communication with Santa Anna, who, banished from Mexico, lived at the Havana. He created the impression that, if returned to power in his country, he would favor peace. The blockading squadron of the United States off Vera Cruz was instructed to let him pass into Mexico, which it did on August 8. President Polk asked of Congress an appropriation of $2,000,000 for purposes of negotiation, the intended result of which was understood to consist in territorial cessions by Mexico to the United States. Then something happened which marked the beginning of the final struggle about slavery in the United States. David Wilmot of Pennsylvania, a Democrat, moved in the House of Representatives an amendment to the $2,000,000 bill, providing that in all territories to be acquired from Mexico slavery should be forever prohibited. This was the renowned "Wilmot Proviso." The bill, with the proviso, passed the House, but failed in the Senate.

When Congress met in December, 1846, the American forces virtually controlled the larger part of the Mexican dominions. General Taylor had on September 22 and 23 assaulted Monterey, and on the 24th accepted the capitulation of General Ampudia. A great enterprise against Vera Cruz under General Scott was preparing. Polk, having received no money for his peace intrigue at the previous session, repeated the attempt. A bill appropriating $3,000,000 for purposes of negotiation was introduced in the House. Again the Wilmot Proviso was added to it. The contest grew warmer. Pro-slavery men in Congress, and Southern legislatures, proclaimed that this was a "Southern war;" that it was made to acquire more territory for slavery, and that they wanted the war to stop if, by the restriction of slavery, its object was to be defeated. Free state legislatures, on the other hand, one after another, men of both parties uniting, instructed their senators and requested their representatives to sustain the Wilmot Proviso. The Senate again struck out the proviso, and the House finally adopted the bill without it, many Northern members, however, with the mental re-

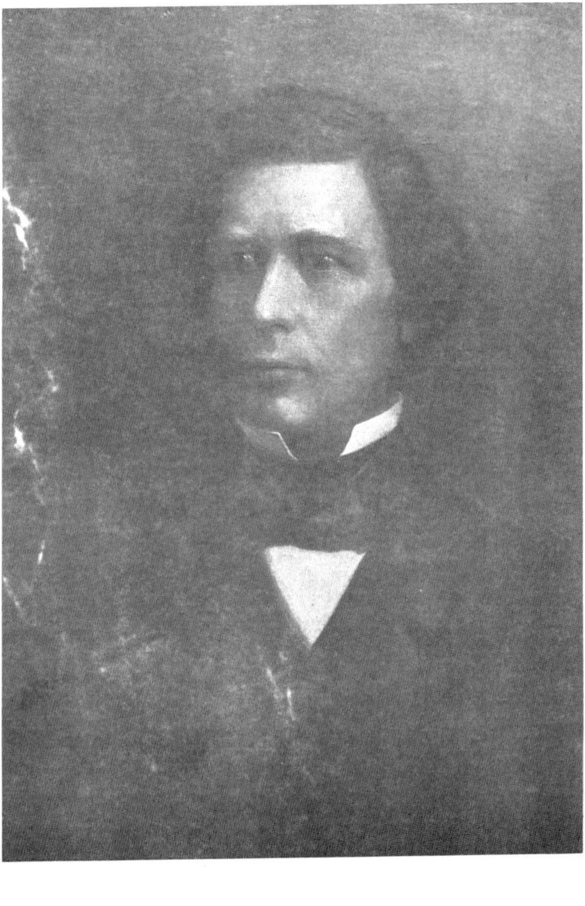

D Wilmot

servation that the proviso should be revived at a later stage of the proceedings. Thus the question was only adjourned.

Victories came thick and fast on the theatre of war. While great preparations were made by General Scott for an attack on Vera Cruz, and an expedition from that point on the city of Mexico, Santa Anna became provisional president of Mexico, and, instead of making peace, put himself at the head of the army for a supreme effort. In February, 1847, he fell with a greatly superior force upon General Taylor at Buena Vista, but was defeated. General Scott occupied Vera Cruz on March 29, beat Santa Anna at Cerro Gordo on April 18, and after a series of successes at Pueblo, Contreras, Churubusco, Molino del Rey, and Chapultepec, entered the city of Mexico on September 14.

While these great events were taking place, Clay spent his days in retirement at Ashland, or visiting his friends here and there, especially at New Orleans. He continued to receive testimonials of popular esteem and attachment. The Whig ladies of Virginia provided the means for erecting his statue at Richmond. Those of Tennessee presented him with a costly vase. Wherever he went he was greeted with warm demonstrations of friendship. But the war brought him a profound sorrow. His son, Colonel Henry Clay, the most gifted of all his children, and his favorite, who had joined Taylor's command with a regiment of Kentucky volunteers, fell at Buena Vista. This blow struck him very deeply. "My life has been full of domestic afflictions," he wrote to a friend, alluding to the loss of all his daughters by death, "but this last is the severest among them." Not long after the arrival of these sad tidings Clay became a member of the Episcopal Church, and was baptized according to its rites in the presence of his family. He never pretended to be a pious man, but always showed much respect for religious beliefs and observances. With advancing age he grew more meditative, and also more regular in his attendance upon Sunday services.

The political situation during that period could not be cheering to him. All the Whig principles and policies had been overthrown, and in the great crisis the conduct of the Whigs in Congress had lacked courage and dignity. They had denounced the war policy as unjust and dishonorable before the war was begun; afterward only fourteen of them in the House and two in the Senate voted firmly to the last against the declaration that war existed by the act of Mexico, which they believed to be a lie; and then, the war having been made its own by Congress, they denounced it as "Polk's war," and sought to belittle and discredit it as an unrighteous, partisan enterprise. It was Polk's war until Congress had assumed Polk's responsibility. Then it was the war of the American people, made so with the concurrence of a large majority of the Whig votes in Congress. To oppose the war policy until war was declared; in good faith to support the war as soon as it had become the war of the American people; and to strive for a just and beneficent peace as the contest was decided, — that was the course, if frankly and faithfully followed by the Whigs, to secure to the opposition party a consistent, patriotic, and strong position.

In spite of the vacillation and weakness of their conduct, the Whigs won a remarkable success in the congressional elections of 1846. In the twenty-ninth Congress the Democrats had a majority exceeding sixty votes in the House of Representatives. The elections of 1846 transformed that majority into a minority of eight; and this while the party in power was carrying on a victorious war. It was strange, but not inexplicable. Although the bulletins from the theatre of operations reported victory after victory, the popular conscience, at least in the North, was uneasy, and the shouts of triumph could not silence its voice, which said that the war was unjust in its origin, and that slavery was its object. Moreover, the shuffling character of Polk's diplomacy, and his apparent consciousness of guilt, urging him incessantly in his public utterances to defend the government as to the causes of the war, repelled the popular heart; and thus an administration victorious in the field was defeated at the ballot-box. There were among the new members elected in 1846 two men destined to fame, — Abraham Lincoln of

Illinois, a Whig; and Andrew Johnson of Tennessee, a Democrat.

Late in the autumn of 1847, before the thirtieth Congress met, Clay's voice was heard again. Scott was then in the city of Mexico. There were no more Mexican armies to combat. Neither was there a generally recognized Mexican government with which to conclude a peace of binding force, and sure to command general acceptance. Democratic meetings pronounced in favor of the permanent occupation and eventual annexation of the whole of the Mexican republic. Men of standing and influence countenanced the same idea. The " manifest destiny" cry stirred up the wildest schemes of aggrandizement. While this agitation was going on Clay addressed a public meeting at Lexington, hoping to be heard by the whole American people. He traced the origin of the war to the annexation of Texas, but showed how hostilities might after all have been avoided by prudence, moderation, and wise statesmanship. As to the action of Congress, he would not discredit the motives of any one, but, referring to the declaration that " war existed by the act of Mexico," he added " that no earthly consideration would ever have tempted or provoked him to vote for a bill with a palpable falsehood stamped upon its face." Solemnly he warned the American people of the dangers which would inevitably follow if they abandoned themselves to the ambition of conquest, pictured in glowing colors the evils which necessarily must come if such a country and such a people as Mexico and the Mexicans were incorporated with the political system of the United States, and admonished his countrymen to beware of trifling with the national honor. "I am afraid," he said, "that we do not now stand well in the opinion of other parts of Christendom. Repudiation has brought upon us much reproach. All the nations, I apprehend, look upon us, in the prosecution of the present war, as being actuated by a spirit of rapacity, and an inordinate desire for territorial aggrandizement.

He summed up his argument in a series of resolutions. They set forth that the war had been brought on by an unrighteous policy, but that, "Congress having, by subsequent acts, recognized the war thus brought into existence, the prosecution of it thereby became national;" that it was the right of Congress to declare, by some authoritative act, for what purposes and objects the existing war ought to be further prosecuted; that it was the duty of the President to conform to such a declaration of Congress; that the purpose of annexing Mexico to the United States in any mode, and especially by conquest, could not be contemplated without the most serious alarm; that a union of Mexico with the United States should be deprecated, because it could not be effected and carried on in peace, but would lead to despotic sway in the one and then in both countries; that there should be a generous peace, requiring no dismemberment of the Mexican republic, but "only a just and proper fixation of the limits of Texas;" and then "that we do positively and emphatically disclaim and disavow any wish or desire on our part to acquire any foreign territory whatever for the purpose of propagating slavery, or of introducing slaves from the United States into such foreign territory."

This speech found an immediate response. Public meetings were held in various quarters adopting Clay's resolutions. In New York great demonstrations took place, one at the Tabernacle and another at Castle Garden, one of the largest meetings ever assembled, which passed resolves and issued addresses echoing Clay's sentiments, and praising him to the skies.

That Lexington speech, with its vigorous reproof of the national ambition of aggrandizement, and especially with its uncompromising declaration against the acquisition of territory for the spread of slavery, little resembled the prudent style of utterance usual with aspirants to the presidency. But Clay was again an aspirant to the presidency at that time. It was not only the inveterate ambition that gave him no rest, but he had friends who constantly stimulated that ambition with flattering perspectives of success. Immediately after his defeat in 1844 he was "spoken of" again for "the next time;" and, when the Whig triumphs in the congressional elections of 1846 had infused new spirit into the party, he was, as appears from his correspondence, " often addressed " on the subject of the presidency; but he thought it was "too soon to agitate the question." He had suffered disappointments enough to make him cautious, and for that caution there was now peculiar reason. The number of Whigs who, while still loving and admiring him, had grown tired of being defeated with him, had increased rapidly since 1844. Among them were, no doubt, many who looked for their own preferment, who to that end desired party success at any price, and who were impatient with the old chief for standing in the way of their interests. But there were also others who, remaining his faithful friends, would not expose him, and at the same time their party, to more disasters. John J. Crittenden, a most honorable man, and Clay's lifelong brother-in-arms in all his struggles, was one of these. " I prefer Mr. Clay to all men for the presidency," he wrote to a friend; " but my conviction, my involuntary conviction, is that he cannot be elected." He was undoubtedly right. No man in public life was more idolized by his admirers, but no one had more unrelenting and active enemies, to whom his long career presented an abundance of vulnerable points. Moreover, he had grown stale as a presidential candidate. All the ingenuity of defense, and all the ardor of panegyric, had time and again been exhausted for him, and always in vain. There were no fresh resources to draw upon for a new campaign. The spokesmen of the party were naturally reluctant to undertake the same task again, and many of them therefore joined in the quiet protest against his renomination. This feeling had grown to especial strength where Clay had least expected it, and where it was most painful to him, — in Kentucky. Many of the Whigs of that State had reached the conclusion that Kentucky, after the experiences of the past, ought not to impose upon the Whig party Clay's candidacy for the presidency as a permanent burden. They were, therefore, among the first to look for a new man around whom to rally. They found that man in the person of a military chieftain.

Immediately after the news of the fights of Palo Alto and Resaca de la Palma had arrived in the United States, in May, 1846, some Whig politicians, Thurlow Weed among others, cast their eyes upon the victorious captain as a presidential possibility. Thurlow Weed learned from General Taylor's brother that the general had always been an admirer of Henry Clay, and preferred home-made goods to foreign importations. This was sufficient in his eyes to qualify the general as a good enough Whig for a presidential candidate. The general had never voted. He had spent the best part of his life in camps and at frontier posts, and never expressed, nor even entertained, a very decided preference for either of the two political parties. When the proposition of making him a candidate for the highest civil office was first broached to him, he promptly pronounced it as too absurd to be thought of for a moment. But there are very few American citizens, however prudent and modest, who, when repeatedly told that the people insist upon putting them into the presidential chair, will not finally believe that the people are right and must be obeyed. General Taylor, too, gradually came to that conclusion. On November 4, 1847, he wrote to Clay that he should be glad if his (Clay's) nomination, or the nomination of some other Whig by the party, would permit him (Taylor) to stand aside. But these sentiments gradually suffered a decided change. There was, indeed, something like a popular demand for him. As early as June, 1846, meetings had been held in Trenton, N. J., and in New York, recommending Taylor's nomination for the presidency. The movement spread rapidly, and became especially active in Kentucky, Clay's formerly faithful State.

These demonstrations were by no means confined to the Whig party. "People's" meetings, "Native American" meetings, and even some Democratic meetings, expressed the opinion that General Taylor was the man of the hour. The honest and simple-minded old soldier, once persuaded that the talk of making him president was serious, thought it but natural that, as he had never been a partisan, and as the call upon him was not confined to any political organization, he should consider himself as the people's candidate, and, if elected, as the people's president. He put forth these sentiments, at the same time confessing that he had only "crude impressions on matters of policy," in several letters which became public and astonished the politicians. His sponsors among the Whig leaders grew alarmed lest his unguarded utterances should endanger his nomination by a regular Whig party convention. They, therefore, took him in training, and composed a letter for him which should soothe the partisan mind. But they could not make him say more than that he was a Whig, "although not an ultra one;" that "he would not be president of a party," but "would endeavor to act independent of party domination," and "untrammeled by party schemes;" that he would not use the veto power "except in cases of clear violation of the Constitution, or manifest haste or want of consideration by Congress;" that, as to the tariff, the currency, and internal improvements, "the will of the people, as expressed through their representatives in Congress, ought to be respected and carried out by the executive;" and that he was in favor of peace, and opposed "to the subjugation of other nations and the dismemberment of other countries by conquest." With this the Whig politicians had to be satisfied.

Clay observed this movement in favor of General Taylor with extreme displeasure, which found vent in his letters to his friends. Up to the battle of Buena Vista he thought the Whig masses were determined to stand by him. He insisted that the Whig party had always been committed against mere military officers for the presidency, and that, if a man like General Taylor, absolutely without experience in civil affairs, were elected, the presidency would fall to a succession of military chieftains. At the same time he told his friends that he would be a candidate only if there was a general popular call for him, and in the mean time he would maintain a passive attitude. But of sustaining that passive attitude he seems not to have been capable. In the winter of 1847-48 he visited Washington to appear in a case before the Supreme Court, and to take part in a meeting of the Colonization Society. But that was not all. "The only news is," wrote Alexander H. Stephens, "that Mr. Clay has produced a great impression here. I expect he will give the Whigs some trouble. I think he will be flattered into the belief that he can be elected." A few days later he wrote: "I am now well satisfied that Mr. Clay will not allow his name to be used in the convention." Clay did not understand it so. He wrote to his friends that the strongest appeals were made to him against the withdrawal of his name. He complained bitterly of the Taylor movement in Kentucky. "Why is it?" he wrote. "After the long period of time during which I have had the happiness to enjoy the friendship and confidence of that State, what have I done, it is inquired, to lose it?" The opposition to him, and especially the circumstance that General Taylor, a man whom he thought utterly unfit for the presidency, was his competitor, seems to have sharpened his desire. A series of ovations elsewhere was in store for him, to test the popular temper. But before Clay left Washington he had to witness a solemn scene which might have sobered his ambition. On February 25 John Quincy Adams was stricken down by paralysis in the House of Representatives. The grand old hero of duty, the grim warrior of conscience, fell, as he had hoped to fall, in the service of his country. When he lay in the speaker's room unconscious, Clay was taken to him: he held the hand of the dying man in his, and the tears streamed down his face. From the scene of death he went forth, himself an old man of nearly seventy-one, to the last struggle for that which, as an object of ambition, as he might well have learned from Adams's life, was valueless. At Baltimore, Philadelphia, and New York he was received with great demonstrations of enthusiasm which filled the newspapers with gorgeous descriptions. At New York, where the city authorities took him in charge, the festivities lasted several days. There was no end of hand-shaking and cheers. The people seemed to think of nothing but Henry Clay.

Until then he had maintained what he called a passive attitude, — weighing chances with apparent coolness of judgment, but always ready to be deceived when the truth did not accord with his wishes. The assurances of friends in New York that, if nominated, he would triumphantly carry that State, and information equally flattering from influential Whigs in Ohio, the most prominent and urgent among whom was Governor Bebb, finally decided him to proclaim what he had probably long before determined in his heart. Early in April he published a letter assenting to the "use of his name" in the Whig National Convention. And then he had to learn a piece of startling news from General Taylor himself. Clay had expected that, if he were nominated by the Whig Convention, General Taylor, as a matter of course, would quietly leave the field. He had carried on some secret hope, perhaps, of dissuading him from being a candidate at all. But now the general, in a public letter of April 20, 1848, declared, and in a letter addressed to Clay himself on April 30, affirmed, that, having been nominated by "the people called together in primary assemblies in several of the States," he considered himself "in the hands of the people," and was determined to remain a candidate, whoever else might be in the field. Such a declaration would, under ordinary circumstances, have provoked the resentment of a party conscious of its strength, and thus defeated the pretensions of the man making it. It produced a different effect upon the Whigs of 1848. Those who desired a party victory at any price calculated that, if Taylor remained a candidate under any circumstances, the Whigs could win only by accepting, but would surely lose by opposing him. There was also another class who actually preferred him because he was not a party man. This was not surprising at a time when the question which most engaged people's minds and feelings did not form a clear issue between the political parties, but rather divided the parties within themselves.

Clay did not appreciate this. In a letter of August 4, 1847, to Daniel Ullmann he had still expressed the opinion that, with the exception of the United States Bank, — which he, too, by that time had dropped as no longer available, — the old issues would still be good for another campaign, such as the principle of protection, and internal improvements, and the "alarming increase of the vetoes," and, added to these subjects, " the Mexican war, its causes, the manner of conducting it, and the great national debt" fastened by it on the country. But he was mistaken. The " free-trade " tariff of 1846 had not produced the destruction of prosperity which its opponents had predicted. The hard times, beginning with the crash of 1837, had at last been followed by a revival of business. This was, indeed, ascribed by many to the effect of the famine in Europe; but, whatever the cause, there was in point of fact no distress in America that would have justified a cry for a reversal of economic policy. Neither would the people excite themselves about a veto killing a river and harbor bill. Nor would the distribution of the proceeds of sales of public land stir the popular heart. As to the Mexican war, the unrighteousness of its cause, and the conduct of the administration in managing it, might, indeed, furnish material for discussion; but the main point, the decision of the question what should be the outcome of it, was before the country in the shape of an accomplished fact before the presidential campaign opened.

In February, 1848, the treaty of Guadaloupe Hidalgo was concluded. By its terms Mexico recognized the Rio Grande as the western boundary of Texas, and ceded to the United States New Mexico and California, in consideration of which the United States were to pay to Mexico fifteen millions, and assume the payment of the claims of American citizens to a limited amount. Whatever their feelings about the origin of the war might have been, a large majority of the American people were well enough satisfied with the acquisition of New Mexico and California. The only question which seriously troubled them was whether, in the newly acquired territories, slavery should exist or not. That question loomed up in a portentous shape, and with regard to it neither party was at peace within itself. The main force of the Democratic party was in the South, and therefore leaned toward the interests of slavery; but in order to win in presidential elections the Northern States necessary for party success, it had to make occasional concession to the anti-slavery spirit prevailing there. The main force of the Whig party was in the North, and therefore leaned toward general freedom; but in order to secure the Southern States necessary for success, it had to make occasional concession to the demands of slavery. Thus both found the slavery question an exceedingly troublesome and dangerous one, and both were afraid of it. But, whatever might be done to hold it back, it pressed irresistibly forward.

The Wilmot Proviso, aiming at the total exclusion of slavery from the newly acquired territories, although defeated in the Senate, was certain to rise up again. It served as a rallying cry all over the North, and profoundly alarmed the South. Southern statesmen, and, more clearly than any of them, Calhoun saw the greatness of their danger, and resolved to make a final stand against it. In February, 1847, Calhoun, true to his method of fighting fate with constitutional theories, introduced a set of resolutions declaring that the territories belonged to the several States in common; that any law depriving any citizen of a State of the right to emigrate with his property (slaves included) into any of the territories, would be a violation of the Constitution; and that no condition could be imposed upon new States to be admitted, other than that they should have a republican form of government. In other words, Calhoun, who advanced his positions step by step as the dangers to slavery increased, affirmed now substantially that the Constitution by its own force carried slavery into the territories of the United States. These resolutions were never voted upon in the Senate. But Southern legislatures adopted them as their doctrine, and an attempt was made in Congress to establish that doctrine by practical application.

In the last session of the twenty-ninth Congress, the House passed a bill giving Oregon a territorial government, with a provision excluding slavery, but the Senate laid the bill on the table. When in the succeeding session the subject reappeared, the exclusion of slavery was resisted by Southern senators and representatives with the utmost energy. Practically to establish slavery in Oregon, whose inhabitants, in giving themselves a provisional government, had already voted against its admission, might have seemed hopeless. But the assertion of the principle with regard to Oregon would facilitate its future application to California and New Mexico; or, perhaps, a final yielding as to Oregon might become a valuable consideration in a compromise touching the other more promising territories. It was then that Daniel S. Dickinson of New York addressed a long speech to the Senate, in which he endeavored to prove that it would be according to the principles of self-government and the spirit of the Constitution to leave the question, whether slavery should be admitted or excluded, to the territorial legislatures for decision. This was the principle of "squatter sovereignty," which reappeared again six years later in a new application. Calhoun and his followers rejected it unhesitatingly, on the ground, that if Congress could not legislate on slavery in the territories, the territorial legislatures, which derived their authority from Congress, certainly could not. They insisted emphatically on the right of the slaveholder under the Constitution to take his slaves into the territories.

It is a remarkable fact that the same Congress, which thus discussed the right of slavery in the great American republic to go where it had not been before, passed eloquent resolutions congratulating the nations of Europe upon the triumphs of freedom achieved by the uprisings of 1848.

The struggle about the admission of slavery in Oregon was still going on, and the more portentous struggle about New Mexico and California was impending, when the two parties held their national conventions to nominate candidates for the presidency. The Democratic Convention met first on May 22 at Baltimore. The first business it had to deal with was a contest of two rival delegations from New York, one representing the "Hunkers," whose principal chiefs were Marcy, then secretary of war, and Daniel S. Dickinson, the senator; and the other the "Barnburners," who counted among their leading men such Democrats as John A. Dix and Preston King, with Martin Van Buren in the background. The State Convention which sent the Hunker delegation had laid on the table a resolution approving the Wilmot Proviso. The Barnburner Convention had declared itself warmly against the admission of slavery in the territories. The Hunkers pledged themselves to support the Democratic nominees, whoever they might be. The Barnburners refused to give such a pledge. The National Convention resolved to admit both delegations upon an equal footing, but the Barnburners withdrew, while the Hunkers also declined to take any further part in the proceedings, maintaining, however, their pledge to support the nominees. The convention nominated Lewis Cass of Michigan for the presidency, a Northern man with Southern principles, who at first had favored the Wilmot Proviso and then solemnly recanted. To spare the feelings of the North, the convention refused to adopt a resolution offered by Yancey of Alabama, which substantially indorsed Calhoun's doctrine that slavery could not constitutionally be excluded from the territories. A delegate from Georgia desired to offer a resolution condemning the Wilmot Proviso, but was persuaded to desist. The platform denounced the abolitionists, but expressed itself on the slavery question in generalities conveniently vague.

The National Convention of the Whigs met on June 7 at Philadelphia. Many of Clay's supporters were still full of hope. A majority of the Whigs being in favor of the Wilmot Proviso, it was believed that Clay's speech and resolutions on the Mexican war would naturally have attracted them. It was found, too, that, while General Taylor had among the delegates many warm friends, there was also a very determined, and even bitter, opposition to a candidate who did not represent any principles or policies. But on the first ballot Clay not only failed to receive the vote of Ohio, of whose enthusiastic support he had been assured, but even a majority of the Kentucky delegation voted for Taylor. That was a fatal blow. Taylor had 111 votes, Clay 97; the rest were divided between General Scott, who received the vote of Ohio, and Webster. On the fourth ballot Taylor had 171, a majority over all, and Clay only 32. The bulk of his votes had gone over to his successful rival. Millard Fillmore was nominated for the vice-presidency.

Many delegates were greatly dissatisfied with Taylor's nomination. Some of them offered resolution after resolution to make it mean something, — that the candidate should declare himself as the exponent of Whig principles; that one of those principles was: No extension of slavery by conquest, etc. But all these resolutions were shouted down amid the wildest excitement. Charles Allen and Henry Wilson of Massachusetts then left the convention, declaring that they ceased to be members of the Whig party, and would do all in their power to defeat its candidates. Upon Wilson's call, a meeting of dissatisfied delegates and others was held, to consider steps to be taken for the purpose of organizing the anti-slavery element for action. A convention to meet in August at Buffalo was resolved upon. The National Convention of the Whigs adjourned in great confusion, without having adopted any platform.

Thus both parties avoided taking any clear position on the one great question which most concerned the future of the republic. The Demo cratic Convention had rejected strong pro-slavery resolutions in order to save its chances at the North. The Whig Convention had shouted down anti-slavery resolutions to save its chances in the South. The Democratic party, which contained the bulk of the pro-slavery element, tried to deceive the North by the nomination of a Northern man with Southern principles. The Whig party, whose ruling tendencies were unfriendly to slavery, tried to deceive the South by silencing the anti-slavery sentiment for the moment, and by nominating a Southern man who had not professed any principles at all.

Clay was deeply mortified. Some of his friends had cruelly deceived him, especially those who had promised him the enthusiastic support of Ohio. Neither had he thought it possible that in a crisis the vote of the delegates from Kentucky would fail him. He felt keenly that, in a defeat in which he had been abandoned by his own State, his prestige had suffered. But more than this. The party which he had built up, of which he had been proud, and which had always professed to be proud of him, had thrown him aside for a man who had only at the eleventh hour called himself a Whig, and who did not profess to know anything of Whig principles. He saw in the conduct of his party a confession of moral bankruptcy. He could not persuade himself that the Whig principles of old were not the things in which the country just then took much interest, and that, as to the great question of the day, the Whig party was sharply divided in itself. The old chief retired to his tent. One of the seats for Kentucky in the Senate of the United States having become vacant before the expiration of the term, the governor offered him the executive appointment to the place. Clay promptly declined. Without hesitation he informed his friends, who expressed anxiety as to his attitude, that he would do nothing against, nor anything to support, General Taylor's candidacy.

"I have been much importuned from various quarters," he wrote to a committee of Whigs at Louisville, "to indorse General Taylor as a good Whig, who will, if elected, act on Whig principles and carry out Whig measures. But how can I do that? Can I say that in his hands Whig measures will be safe and secure, when he refuses to pledge himself to their support? When some of his most active friends say they are obsolete? When he is presented as a no-party candidate? When the Whig Convention at Philadelphia refused to recognize or proclaim its attachment to any principles or measures, and actually laid on the table resolutions having that object in view?"

He did not conceal the personal feelings aroused in him by the treatment he had received: "Ought I to come out as a warm and partisan supporter of a candidate who, in a reversal of our conditions, announced his purpose to remain a candidate, and consequently to oppose me, so far as it depended upon himself? Tell me, what reciprocity is this? Magnanimity is a noble virtue, and I have always endeavored to practice it; but it has its limits, and the line of demarkation between it and meanness is not always discernible." If any great principles were at stake, he said, he would, in spite of it all, engage in the contest. But he feared that the Whig party was dissolved, and had given way to a mere personal party, having that character as much as the Jackson party had it twenty years before. There was something pathetic in this appeal of the old leader: "I think my friends ought to leave me quiet and undisturbed in my retirement. I have served the country faithfully and to the utmost of my poor ability. If I have not done more, it has not been for want of heart and inclination. My race is run. During the short time which remains to me in this world, I desire to preserve untarnished that character which so many have done me the honor to respect and esteem."

He remained true to his resolution not to take part in the canvass on either side. At a late period of the campaign, General Taylor formally accepted a nomination for the presidency from a Democratic convention in South Carolina, which preferred him to the Democratic candidate, avowedly because Cass, as a Northern man, could not be trusted with regard to slavery, while General Taylor, as a Southern man, was undoubtedly safe. Then many indignant Northern Whigs, especially in New York, attempted to organize a movement against Taylor with Clay at its head. But Clay peremptorily forbade the use of his name.

Clay was by no means alone dissatisfied with Taylor's nomination. The Whig politicians, who expected to make for Taylor an easy "star-and-stripe campaign," found unforeseen difficulties in their way. Many of the old Whigs continued to believe that their party should remain the representative of certain principles; that it still had a mission to perform; and that it should be led by statesmen. The bestowal of its highest trust and honor upon one who, whatever his merits as a soldier and a gentleman, frankly confessed himself ignorant of the great duties to the discharge of which he was to be commissioned, provoked their anger and contempt. Not only a large number of Clay's friends were so affected, but of Webster's too. Webster himself declared that Taylor's nomination was "one not fit to be made," and only at a late period of the campaign he was moved by unceasing party pressure to make a few speeches for the Whig candidate.

Of greater significance was the defection of a portion of the anti-slavery element in the Whig party, who in Massachusetts went by the name of "Conscience Whigs," and who counted strongly also in New York and Ohio. But, while this defection was avowedly intended to punish the Whig party and to defeat Taylor, the turn which the anti-slavery movement took in the campaign served to save him. The Liberty party had held a convention in October, 1847, and nominated for the presidency John P. Hale, an anti-slavery Democrat representing New Hampshire in the Senate of the United States. But, in order to unite the anti-slavery elements for a common effort, they were willing to attend the general anti-slavery convention at Buffalo in August, which had been planned immediately after Taylor's nomination. In June large mass meetings of those opposed to the extension of slavery took place, without distinction of party, at Worcester in Massachusetts, and Columbus in Ohio, which passed resolutions protesting against the spread of slavery, and appointed delegates to the Buffalo convention. Meanwhile the Barnburner wing of the Democratic party of New York, whose delegates had withdrawn from the Democratic National Convention at Baltimore, met at Utica, and nominated Martin Van Buren as their candidate for the presidency, upon a platform vigorously condemning the extension of slavery into the territories. But, while this sentiment was sincerely cherished by many of those taking part in that movement, there is no doubt that by many others the anti-slavery current of the time was merely used as a convenient weapon, in the war of Democratic factions, to avenge Martin Van Buren and his following upon the Democratic party for the "wrong" he had suffered by his defeat in the Democratic National Convention of 1844. However, the Barnburners counted in their ranks the best talent of the Democratic party in New York, — such men as John A. Dix, Sanford E. Church, Samuel J. Tilden, Dean Richmond, C. C. Cambreleng, Azariah Flagg, Benjamin F. Butler, John Van Buren, Preston King, William Cullen Bryant, James S. Wadsworth, Abijah Mann, Ward Hunt, George Opdyke, and others. The Barnburners, too, resolved to be represented at the anti-slavery convention at Buffalo on August 9.

That meeting was a great event. Many thousands attended it. The moralist, profoundly convinced of the righteousness of his cause, met there with the practical politician. Benjamin F. Butler of New York reported a platform which declared that slavery was a mere state institution; that Congress had no more power to make a slave than to make a king; that the national government should relieve itself of all responsibility for slavery; that Congress should exclude slavery from all free territory; that the answer to the issue forced upon the country by the slave power should be: No more slave States; no more slave territory; no more compromises with slavery; freedom for Oregon, California, and New Mexico. The great battle-cry, "Free soil, free speech, free labor, and free men!" was hailed with shouts and tears of enthusiasm. The names of John P. Hale and of Martin Van Buren were submitted to the convention for nomination as candidates for the presidency. Martin Van Buren received a large majority on the first ballot. Charles Francis Adams was nominated for the vice-presidency. The old anti-slavery men present accepted the result. The enthusiasm of the convention had in it a glow of religious fervor quite uncommon before in political gatherings.

But there was after all something grotesque, if not repulsive, in the selection of Martin Van Buren for the leadership of an anti-slavery movement. It no doubt attracted many Democrats whose feelings on slavery would, without it, not have been strong enough to take them out of their party line. But, as soon as the first excitement was over, many anti-slavery Whigs, who had been inclined to favor the Buffalo nominations, began to remember Martin Van Buren's career with regard to the subject of slavery; and they quietly dropped off and rejoined their old party, finding a ready excuse in the fact that anti-slavery men so earnest and able as William H. Seward vigorously supported Taylor, and represented him as a man who, although a slaveholder himself, was by no means disposed to propagate slavery. The Buffalo movement, therefore, making serious inroads into the Democratic party in New York, while drawing comparatively little of its force from the Whigs, redounded to Taylor's benefit.

It produced an important effect in another direction: it frightened members of Congress. The Oregon bill, involving the right of the slaveholder to take his property into that territory, had agitated Congress for months. At last, on August 13, under the fresh impression made by the great demonstration of Northern anti-slavery sentiment at Buffalo, a bill was passed in effect excluding slavery from Oregon.

Both parties during the presidential campaign denounced the Free Soilers with extreme bitterness as renegades and traitors. A new moral power, which exposes and puts to shame current insincerities, is always treated with contumely by those whose consciences are uneasy. The Whigs, who derived the greatest benefit from the Buffalo movement, seemed to be even more incensed at it than the Democrats, probably because their canvass was the more insincere. The Southern Whigs pictured General Taylor as a better pro-slavery man than Cass, while the Northern Whigs pretended that their candidate was in favor of the Wilmot Proviso. Such a trick may succeed, as it did succeed in 1848; but a party which constantly needs such tricks to achieve success, or to maintain its existence, cannot last. The Whigs carried the presidential election. General Taylor had the electoral votes of fifteen States, among which were eight of the South. But it was the last triumph of the Whig party. As soon as the slavery question became the absorbing issue, the Whig party could not remain together if the Southern Whigs were for and the Northern Whigs against slavery. The next presidential election left it a mere wreck, and a few years more buried even its name.

The Free Soil party, too, as organized at Buffalo, was short lived. It did not carry any State, but received nearly three hundred thousand votes. In New York Van Buren had more votes than Cass. The Democratic faction opposed to him suffered a disastrous overthrow. That accomplished, a large number of the Van Buren Democrats, and among them some of their leading men, renewed their allegiance to their old party, looking upon the revolt of 1848 as a mere political episode. Many of the Whigs, who had voted for Van Buren to avenge Clay, also returned to the fold. But, while the coalition fell to pieces, the vital principle of the Free Soil movement survived, to be obscured by a temporary reaction, and then to rise up again in final triumph.

CHAPTER XXVI

THE COMPROMISE OF 1850

When during the presidential campaign Clay entreated his friends to leave him undisturbed in his retirement, he meant undoubtedly what he said. But after a short rest his interest in public affairs naturally revived to new activity.

The strife about slavery growing constantly more embittered and threatening, some thinking men in the South, who in the general excitement had kept their temper, asked themselves whether slavery was really the economical, moral, and political blessing its hot-blooded devotees represented it to be; and here and there, mainly in the border slave States, voices in favor of emancipation began to be heard again, some in mere whispers, some in more courageous utterance. Especially in Kentucky, where in the spring of 1849 a convention to revise the state constitution was to be elected, the subject became the theme of public discussion. It was the same cause which fifty years before had called forth young Henry Clay's first efforts; and now the old statesman of seventy-two lifted up his voice for it once more. In January, 1849, he went to New Orleans, and from there he sent a letter on emancipation, addressed to Richard Pindell of Lexington, but intended for the people of Kentucky. That part of the letter which exposed the absurdity of the reasons usually brought forward to justify slavery might well have come from the pen of a lifelong abolitionist. If slavery were really a blessing, he reasoned, "the principle on which it is maintained would require that one portion of the white race should be reduced to bondage to serve another portion of the same race, when black subjects of slavery could not be obtained; and that in Africa, where they may entertain as great a preference for their color as we do for ours, they would be justified in reducing the white race to slavery in order to secure the blessings which that state is said to diffuse." In the same style he punctured the argument that the superiority of the white race over the black justified the enslavement of the inferior. "It would prove entirely too much," said he. "It would prove that any white nation which had made greater advances in civilization, knowledge, and wisdom than another white nation would have the right to reduce the latter to a state of bondage. Nay, further, if the principle be applicable to races and nations, what is to prevent its being applied to individuals? And then the wisest man in the world would have a right to make slaves of all the rest of mankind." There was in this something of Benjamin Franklin's manner of pointing an argument. Clay had evidently written it with zest.

He deeply lamented that emancipation had not been accomplished before, and hoped it might not long be delayed. In his opinion, emancipation should be gradual. He proposed that all slave children born after 1855 or 1860 should be free when reaching the age of twenty-five years, then to be hired out under the authority of the State for a period of not exceeding three years, in order to earn a sum sufficient to pay the expenses of their transportation to Liberia, and to provide them an outfit for six months after their arrival there. Their offspring were to be free from their birth, but to be apprenticed until the age of twenty-one, and also to go to Liberia.

This, surely, was a very slow process; and his favorite scheme of transportation to Liberia, based upon his firm belief that the two races could not possibly live together in a state of freedom, could hardly bear examination in point of practicability as well as of justice. The advanced anti-slavery men of the time criticised the plan with great severity. But the principal merit of the letter lay in the fact that Clay, as a slaveholder, and as the foremost citizen of a slave State, proposed a plan of emancipation in any form, accompanying it with such radical reasoning on the general subject of slavery; and that merit was great. As to the practical effect of the plan, had it been adopted, Clay was certainly not wrong in suggesting that, the work once begun, a general disposition would exist to accelerate and complete it. But it was not

THE COMPROMISE OF 1850

adopted. On the contrary, the discussion served only to intensify the determination of the slave-holding interest to maintain itself at any cost, and to rally the South in the struggle against the growing anti-slavery tendency in the North.

But Clay's public activity was not to be confined to the writing of letters. There could scarcely have been a stronger proof of the hold he had upon the people of Kentucky than that the legislature elected him by a unanimous vote to a seat in the Senate of the United States for a full term, at the time when the discussion on emancipation was beginning, and he was known to cherish sentiments so distasteful to a majority of those whom he was to represent. He forgot his vows of retirement and accepted the charge. It was after all natural that, to a man so accustomed to the excitements of public activity and to leadership, quiet retirement, especially at a period of life when it threatened to be final, should have had its horrors.

There seems to have been a feeling in Kentucky as if he, in a position of power, could avert the dangers threatening the country. He himself, however, did not then appreciate the seriousness of the coming crisis. He did not yet understand that the slavery question was overshadowing all else. On December 19, 1848, when his return to the Senate began to be spoken of, he wrote to Thomas B. Stevenson: —

"Greeley writes me from Washington that the Free Soil question will be certainly adjusted at this session, on the basis of admitting the newly acquired territory as one or two States into the Union. Should that event occur, it will exercise some influence on my disposition to return to the Senate, should the office be within my power. It would leave none but the old questions of tariff, internal improvements, etc., on which I have heretofore so often addressed both houses of Congress."

But the Free Soil question was not so easily adjusted. When Congress met in December, 1848, the last session under Polk's presidency, it had to confront a state of things unexpected a year before. The discovery of rich gold mines in California had attracted thither from all parts of the country a sudden and unexampled emigration, increasing in volume from day to day. In a few months a population gathered there strong enough in numbers to authorize the organization of a state government. In any event, the character of that population and the adventurous nature of its pursuits rendered the establishment of some legal authority peculiarly pressing. Polk, therefore, strongly urged that the provisional military rule in New Mexico and California, which ought to have ceased with the war, should be superseded by legally organized territorial governments. As to the slavery question, he recommended the extension of the Missouri Compromise line. Various schemes were proposed in Congress, provoking hot debates between pro-slavery and anti-slavery men. The excitement was increased by vigorous protests from the inhabitants of New Mexico and Califor-

THE COMPROMISE OF 1850 321

nia against the introduction of slavery there; by an attempt on the part of Calhoun to organize a distinctively Southern party; and by threats that the Union would be dissolved in case the North insisted upon the exclusion of slavery from the new conquests; until finally, the impossibility of an agreement becoming evident, the thirtieth Congress adjourned, leaving the decision of the great question to its successor.

President Taylor's inaugural address did not announce a distinct policy with regard to the absorbing problem. His cabinet consisted of four Whigs from slaveholding States, of whom only one, Crawford of Georgia, the secretary of war, belonged to the extreme pro-slavery faction; and of three Northern Whigs, one of whom, Collamer of Vermont, the postmaster-general, was known as an anti-slavery man. The composition of the cabinet, therefore, indicated no settled purpose. But in April, 1849, Taylor sent a confidential agent to California to suggest to the people the speedy formation of a state constitution and government, without, however, advising what should be done with regard to slavery. Upon his arrival that agent found that the inhabitants of California, following the call of General Riley, the military governor, had already taken the matter in hand. A convention to frame a state constitution met on September 1, 1849, and completed its work on October 13. The Constitution contained a prohibition of slavery, which had been adopted by a

VOL. II.

unanimous vote of the convention, including fifteen members who had migrated to California from the slave States. The Constitution was ratified by a popular vote of 12,066 against 811. President Taylor, who wished to meet Congress with the governments to be instituted in the newly acquired territories as accomplished facts, and hoped that the people of New Mexico too would take the task into their own hands, instructed the military officers commanding there not to obstruct, but rather to advance, popular movements in that direction.

The slaveholding interest watched these proceedings with constantly increasing alarm. The territories taken from Mexico were eluding its grasp. Instead of adding to the strength of the South, they would increase the power of the free States. It was a terrible shock. The mere anticipation of it had brought forth suggestions of desperate remedies. In May, 1849, a meeting at Jackson, Mississippi, had resolved that a state convention be held to consider the threatened rights and interests of the South. That state convention met, and issued an address to the Southern people proposing a Southern "popular convention," to be held on the first Monday in June, 1850, at Nashville. The cry of disunion was raised with increasing frequency and violence. Many meant it only as a threat to frighten the North into concession. But there were not a few Southern men also who had regretfully arrived at the conclusion that the dissolution of the Union was necessary to the salvation of slavery. On the other hand, while every Southern legislature save one denounced the exclusion of slavery as a violation of Southern rights, every Northern legislature save one passed resolutions in favor of the Wilmot Proviso.

This was the state of things when, in December, 1849, Clay arrived at Washington to take his seat in the Senate. His relations with Taylor were those of formal civility. Clay did not expect, as he wrote, to " find much favor at court ; " but the President had offered his son, James Clay, the mission to Portugal " in a handsome manner," and the offer had been accepted. Clay sternly resented the insinuation which was reported to have been made by a member of the cabinet, that the appointment of his son would make him, as a senator, obedient to the administration. His reappearance in Washington was by no means welcome to all. It seems to have been especially dreaded by some Southern statesmen. When Clay's election to the Senate began to become probable, in December, 1848, Alexander H. Stephens wrote to Crittenden, then governor of Kentucky : " That ought to be averted if it can be done ; more danger to the success of General Taylor's administration is to be dreaded from that source than from all others." Jefferson Davis, too, then a senator from Mississippi, feared it no less. " I regret exceedingly," he wrote to Crittenden in January, 1849, " to see that Mr. Clay is to return to the Senate. Among many reasons is one in which I know you will sympathize, — the evil influence he will have on the friends of General Taylor in the two houses of Congress." Clay's disposition, on the other hand, when he went to Washington, was not belligerent. "I shall go there," he wrote to Stevenson, "with a determination to support any Whig measures for which I have heretofore contended, and in a state of mind and feeling to judge fairly and impartially of the measures of the administration. I shall not place myself in any leading position either to support or oppose it. But I shall rather seek to be a calm and quiet looker-on, rarely speaking, and, when I do, endeavoring to throw oil upon the troubled waters." He did not foresee that he would at once be in a position of leadership, speaking more than ever before during any session, not at all about old Whig measures, but constantly on the one great question which the old statesman was so reluctant to recognize as the controlling question of the day.

Clay was at heart in favor of the Wilmot Proviso. In August, 1848, he explained in a letter to Stevenson how he thought the newly acquired territories ought to be treated. The retrocession of Mexico and California, which was urged by some Whigs and anti-slavery men, he did not think practicable. But, as to slavery in the territories, the South, he thought, should "yield the point in dispute." The same idea he elaborated at length in a letter to James E. Harvey written a few days later. The North, in his opinion, was over-apprehensive, because, whether admitted or excluded, slaves could not be kept in the new territories. But, even if the South were right in its demand, it ought to yield for other reasons. "The South," he said, "has had the executive government in its hands during the most part of the time since the Constitution was adopted. Its public policy has generally prevailed. The annexation of Texas, and the consequent war with Mexico, were results of Southern counsel. The very exceptionable mode of that annexation was exclusively Southern. From the commencement of the government, we had, prior to the last acquisition, obtained Louisiana, Florida, and Texas, and all these (with the exception of the least valuable part of Louisiana) were theatres of slavery, and augmented the political power arising from slavery. Large portions of the Northern population also feel and believe that their manufacturing interests have been sacrificed by Southern domination." In consideration of all this, he thought, the South ought "magnanimously to assent" to the exclusion of slavery from the new territories.

But of what would happen, if the South refused to accept the interdiction of slavery in the territories, this was Clay's conception: "It [the interdiction of slavery] will nevertheless prevail; and the conflict, exasperated by bitter contention and mutual passions, will either lead to a dissolution of the Union, or deprive it of that harmony which alone can make the Union desirable. It will lead to the formation of a sectional and Northern party, which will, sooner or later, take permanent and exclusive possession of the government." These were the ideas Clay brought with him to Washington, in December, 1849.

The opening of the session was inauspicious. For three weeks a struggle about the speakership convulsed the House of Representatives. The slavery question formed the subject of furious debates, during which members almost came to blows. At last Cobb of Georgia was elected. President Taylor sent his message to Congress on December 24. As to the burning question, he simply announced the fact that the people of California, "impelled by the necessities of their political condition," had framed a state constitution and would soon apply for admission as a State, and he recommended their wish to the favorable consideration of Congress. He expected the people of New Mexico would shortly take the same course, and hoped that, "by awaiting their action, all causes of uneasiness might be avoided, and confidence and kind feeling preserved." In other words, California and New Mexico should be received without further question, even as free States, if the people thereof so desired. In a special message of January 21, 1850, Taylor declared that he had favored prompt action by the people of the new territories, without attempting to exercise any influence as to what that action should be concern-

THE COMPROMISE OF 1850 327

ing slavery. He again urged as prompt as possible a disposition of the matter, in order to put an end to the prevailing excitement, adding that any attempt to deny to the Californians the right of self-government, in a matter peculiarly affecting themselves, would inevitably be regarded by them as an invasion of their rights, and, upon the principles of the Declaration of Independence, the great mass of the American people would sustain them.

General Taylor was a slaveholder, and his sympathies had always been with his class. In 1847 he had written a letter to his son-in-law, Jefferson Davis, in which he declared that he would respect the feelings of the free States, but not permit, if he could prevent, any encroachments upon the rights of the slaveholding States; that he would be willing to have the slavery question freely discussed, but, if any practical attempts were made to deprive the slave States of their constitutional rights, he was also willing that the South should "act promptly, boldly, and decisively, with arms in their hands if necessary, as the Union in that case will be blown to atoms, or will be no longer worth preserving." But Taylor was also a thoroughly honest and simple-minded man; and, when the Southern hotspurs now told him that the constitutional rights of the slaveholding States were actually encroached upon by the proposed admission of California as a free State, he demurred. He had not fathomed Calhoun's metaphysics. If he understood that the interest of slavery required a larger number of slave States, he felt also that there were other rights involved in the question. He could not be persuaded that, if California and New Mexico desired to come into the Union as States without slavery, it would, if they were otherwise qualified to become States, be right to refuse them admission.

The attitude of the President was severely censured, not only by Southern Democrats, but also by Southern Whigs. They fiercely charged him with an unconstitutional assumption of power in suggesting to the Californians and New Mexicans to take steps preparatory to the formation of state governments, and not a few of them denounced him as a "traitor to the South." Instead of allaying the excitement, Taylor's message rather increased it. The slavery question affected the consideration of almost all other subjects, however seemingly remote. In the Senate, for instance, a motion was made to accord the privilege of the floor to the famous temperance apostle, Father Mathew. This compliment to a distinguished foreigner found fierce opposition on the ground that, years ago, he had put his name, together with that of Daniel O'Connell, to an anti-slavery appeal, — an opposition which Clay earnestly deprecated, saying that the advocates of slavery would rather hurt than help their cause by pushing it forward on every possible occasion. The threats of disunion became so frequent and so loud, that the republic seemed to be actually in immediate danger of disruption.

Clay, upon his arrival at Washington, found " the feeling for disunion among some intemperate Southern politicians" stronger than he had expected; but he thought the masses were still sound, and he therefore urged his friends in Kentucky to "get up large, powerful meetings of both parties to express in strong language their determination to stand by the Union." Early in January he wrote that, in case of the adoption of the Wilmot Proviso, for which he thought there was a large majority in the House and a small one in the Senate, the extremists of the South declared themselves openly for a dissolution of the Union, and that he was considering " some comprehensive scheme of settling amicably the whole question in all its bearings." The purpose to attempt a settlement by a plan of his own became confirmed as his anxiety grew lest the disunion sentiment should spread by contagion, and as the bills and propositions brought forward in a disjointed way appeared only still more to increase the prevailing confusion. What happened to him now was what had happened to him so frequently before. Where he was, the minds of his associates seemed to turn instinctively to him for leadership; and the old man who had come to the Senate with the intention of remaining " a calm and quiet looker-on," and of " rarely speaking," soon found himself engaged in the most arduous parliamentary campaign of his life, those in Jackson's time not excepted.

Never had there been a Senate with so splendid an array of talent, and so great a number of names that were then, or were destined to become, famous throughout the land. The three stars of the first magnitude, Clay, Webster, and Calhoun, met once more, and for the last time, on the same theatre of action, and around them Benton, Mangum, Badger, Berrien, Sam Houston, Rusk, King of Alabama, Jefferson Davis, Henry S. Foote, Cass, Butler of South Carolina, Hunter and Mason of Virginia, Daniel S. Dickinson, Stephen A. Douglas, Pierre Soulé, Jesse D. Bright, John Davis of Massachusetts, Thomas Corwin, Hannibal Hamlin, Truman Smith, John P. Hale, and two men who owed their election to the campaign of 1848, — William H. Seward of New York and Salmon P. Chase of Ohio, who grasped the slavery question, in all its moral, social, and political aspects with a breadth of understanding, and treated it with an enthusiastic but calm fearlessness of spirit, startling and puzzling the old statesmen before them. It was the anti-slavery statesmanship of the rising generation.

To this Senate Clay, on January 29, 1850, unfolded his " comprehensive scheme of adjustment." His object was to save the Union, and he reasoned thus: The Union is threatened by the disunion spirit growing up in the South. That disunion spirit springs from an apprehension that slavery is not safe in the Union. The disunion spirit must be disarmed by concessions calculated to quiet that apprehension. These concessions must be such as not to alarm the North. In planning his compromise, he had these troubles to deal with : 1. The South was bitterly opposed to the admission of California as a free State, because it would break that rule by which formerly new States had been admitted only in pairs, one free State and one slave State. It would thus disturb the balance of power between free and slave States in the Senate, and substantially give the North the benefit of the conquests made in the Mexican war. But the admission of California as a free State, its people having declared themselves against the introduction of slavery, was so clearly right in itself that it could hardly be put in question. 2. As to New Mexico and Utah, the remainder of the territory obtained by conquest, the North insisted upon the application of the Wilmot Proviso, the absolute exclusion of slavery. But the Southern hotspurs declared that if the Wilmot Proviso were adopted, the Union should be dissolved at once. 3. Texas claimed as her western boundary the course of the Rio Grande. This would have included the larger part of New Mexico; and, as Texas was a slave State, while New Mexico under the Mexican law had no slavery, the recognition of the Rio Grande boundary would have transformed a large free territory into a part of a slave State, to be used in the future for the formation of new slave States. A much narrower boundary was insisted upon by Northern, and also, upon historical grounds, by some Southern men; but the Texans proclaimed their determination to enforce their claim by the sword if necessary. 4. The South complained that the constitutional obligation to return fugitive slaves from one State to another was not fulfilled by the North, and that, therefore, more stringent legislation must be insisted upon, while the catching of fugitive slaves was especially odious to the Northern people. 5. The North continued to agitate the abolition of slavery in the District of Columbia, and of the slave trade between the different slave States, while the South insisted that such measures would be subversive of their rights and dangerous to their security.

To meet these difficulties Clay proposed, in a set of resolutions to be followed by appropriate bills, a series of measures intended to compromise all conflicting interests and aspirations. The first declared that California should be speedily admitted as a State, — of course with her free-state constitution; the second, that, as slavery did not by law exist and was not likely to be introduced in any of the territories acquired from Mexico, Congress should provide territorial governments for New Mexico and Utah, without any restriction as to slavery, — thus sacrificing the Wilmot Proviso, — without, however, authorizing slaveholders to take their slaves there, — thus adjourning the slavery question as to those territories to a future day; the third and fourth, that a boundary line between

Texas and New Mexico should be fixed, giving to Texas but little of the New Mexican territory she claimed, but granting her a certain sum of money for the payment of that part of her public debt for which, during her independent existence, her customs revenue had been pledged; the fifth, that it was inexpedient to abolish slavery in the District of Columbia without the consent of Maryland, etc.; the sixth, that the slave trade in the District should be prohibited; the seventh, that a more effectual fugitive slave law should be enacted; and the eighth, that Congress had no power to prohibit or obstruct the trade in slaves between the slaveholding States. The preamble declared the purpose of these resolutions to be "for the peace, concord, and harmony of these States, to settle and adjust amicably all existing questions of controversy between them, arising out of the institution of slavery, upon a fair, equitable, and just basis."

This was Clay's plan of compromise. The admission of California was to be made acceptable to the South by giving slavery a chance in Utah and New Mexico, and by the enactment of a more efficient fugitive slave law. The Northern people were to be reconciled to the abandonment of the Wilmot Proviso as to Utah and New Mexico, and to a more efficient fugitive slave law, by the admission of California as a free State, and by the abolition of the slave trade in the District of Columbia. With the South, said Clay in a short speech accompanying the resolutions, the question was one of interest, with the North one of sentiment, and on neither side would there be any sacrifice of principle; but, he added, it was easier to make a concession of sentiment than of interest, — an utterance which plainly proved that Clay indulged in pleasing delusions, not, perhaps, as to the enactment of the compromise, but as to its ultimate effects, if enacted.

Although he deprecated immediate debate, and admonished senators to consider his plan calmly before forming their opinion, there was at once a rattling fusillade of objections and protests from Southern men, Whigs as well as Democrats. Jefferson Davis, who thought that the scheme conceded nothing to the South, and demanded as a minimum the extension of the Missouri Compromise line to the Pacific Ocean, with a provision establishing slavery to the south of that line, called forth from Clay a remarkable answer. "Coming from a slave State, as I do," said Clay, "I owe it to myself, I owe it to truth, I owe it to the subject, to say that no earthly power could induce me to vote for a specific measure for the introduction of slavery where it had not before existed, either south or north of that line. Sir, while you reproach, and justly too, our British ancestors for the introduction of this institution upon the continent of America, I am, for one, unwilling that the posterity of the present inhabitants of California and New Mexico shall reproach us for doing just what we reproach Great Britain for doing to us."

THE COMPROMISE OF 1850

This was a noble declaration, no doubt sincere; and yet, by his second resolution, he proposed to open the way for the introduction of slavery into Utah and New Mexico, where it did not exist. It is true, he did not believe it would ever go there, but, by providing for territorial governments without the exclusion of slavery, he gave it a chance, and that chance was to commend the acceptance of the compromise to the South. He either deceived the South or he deceived himself. In fact, he deceived himself, for the chance he gave to slavery led to an act of the territorial legislature in 1859 sanctioning slavery in New Mexico.

On February 5 Clay supported his plan of adjustment with a great speech. The infirmities of old age began to tell upon him. Walking up to the Capitol, he asked a friend who accompanied him, "Will you lend me your arm? I feel myself quite weak and exhausted this morning." He ascended the long flight of steps with difficulty, being several times obliged to stop in order to recover his breath. The friend suggested that he should defer his speech, as he was too ill to exert himself that day. "I consider our country in danger," replied Clay; "and if I can be the means in any measure of averting that danger, my health and life is of little consequence." When he arrived at the senate chamber, he beheld a spectacle well apt to inspire an orator. For several days his intention had been known to address the Senate on February 5, and from far and near — from Baltimore, Philadelphia, New York, Boston, and places still more distant — men and women had come in great numbers to hear him. The avenues of the senate chamber were buzzing with an eager multitude who in vain struggled to gain access to the thronged galleries and the equally crowded floor. When Clay arose to speak, an outburst of applause in the chamber greeted him. The noise was heard without, and the great crowd assembled there raised such a shout that the orator could not make himself heard until the officers of the Senate had gone out and cleared the entrances. Clay's speech occupied two days. With a faltering voice he began, but gradually he recovered his strength; and the elevation of his sentiments, the sonorous flow of his words, and the lofty energy of his action, enchanted his audience to the last. There was a pathetic interest added to the old charm; for his hearers felt that this manifestation of strength was owing only to a supreme effort of a strong will over failing powers, and that this effort might be his last. On the second day of the speech some of his fellow senators, observing that he overtaxed himself, interrupted him repeatedly with suggestions of an adjournment, but he declined, feeling uncertain whether he would be able to go on the next day. When he had concluded, a great throng of friends, men and women, rushed toward him to shake his hand and to kiss him.

His speech was an appeal to the North for concession, and to the South for peace. He asked the

North whether the enactment of the Wilmot Proviso would not be an unnecessary provocation, since there was no slavery existing in the territories acquired from Mexico, and no probability of its introduction. Why not, then, give it up for the sake of harmony? He reminded his Southern friends that all the great acquisitions of territory — Louisiana, Florida, and Texas — had " redounded to the benefit of the South," and pointed out the injustice of their " pressing matters to disastrous consequences," when, for the first time, the attempt was made to introduce acquired territories without slavery. He emphatically denied the right of any State to secede from the Union, and the possibility of peaceable secession. " War and dissolution of the Union are identical," he exclaimed ; " they are convertible terms ; and such a war ! " With prophetic words he foretold them their isolation in case of an armed conflict.

" If the two portions of the confederacy should be involved in civil war, in which the effort on the one side would be to restrain the introduction of slavery into the new territories, and on the other side to force its introduction there, what a spectacle should we present to the contemplation of astonished mankind ! An effort to propagate wrong ! It would be a war in which we should have no sympathy, no good wishes, and in which all mankind would be against us, and in which our own history itself would be against us ! "

His feelings told him the truth. Southern men indeed, counted upon British support in case of secession; and it may be said that, when eleven years later secession came, in a certain sense they had such support. But it is nevertheless true that, when the governments of Great Britain and France were inclined to recognize the Southern Confederacy as an independent power, it was the abhorrence of slavery prevailing among civilized mankind, their own people included, more than any other influence, that restrained them, and kept the Southern Confederacy in its fatal isolation.

The debate which followed called forth all the great men of the Senate. On March 4 Calhoun appeared, gaunt and haggard, too ill to speak, but still full of that grim energy with which he had been for so many years defending the interests of slavery, calling them the rights of the South. His oration was read to the Senate by Mason of Virginia. Calhoun's mind was narrow, but within its narrow sphere acute. He saw with perfect clearness that slavery could not be saved within the Union, and that every compromise putting off the decisive crisis only made its final doom all the more certain. A year or two before, he had written to a member of the Alabama legislature that, instead of shunning the issue with the North on the slavery question, it should be courted. " I would go even one step farther," he wrote, " and add that it is our duty to *force* the issue on the North. We are now stronger than we shall be hereafter, politically and morally. Unless we bring on the issue, delay to us will be dangerous indeed.

THE COMPROMISE OF 1850

It is the true policy of those who seek our destruction." From the pro-slavery point of view, Calhoun was unquestionably right. The slaveholding States would have been more able to hold their own in 1820 than in 1850, and more in 1850 than they proved to be in 1861.

Calhoun's speech against Clay's plan of adjustment was his last great manifesto. He argued that the Union could not endure without a perfect equilibrium between the slaveholding and the free States; that this equilibrium had been disturbed by the growth of the free States; that this growth had been brought about by legislation favorable to the North and inimical to the South, — the anti-slavery Ordinance of 1787, the Missouri Compromise, the revenue laws oppressive to the planting interest; that the equilibrium would be lost beyond all hope by the admission of California and the exclusion of slavery from the newly acquired territories; that the admission of California was the test as to whether the South ever could expect justice; that, unless the South received justice, the Union would fall to pieces; that to preserve the Union the equilibrium must be restored, and that this could be done only by an amendment to the Constitution restoring to the South the power of protecting herself. As to what that amendment to the Constitution should be, Calhoun did not express himself clearly. It was subsequently revealed that he meant an amendment providing for the election of two presidents, one from the slaveholding and one from the free States, each one to have the veto power with regard to the legislation of Congress, — a fantastic, impossible scheme.

There he sat, the old champion of slavery, himself the picture of his doomed cause, — a cause at war with the civilization of the age, vainly struggling against destiny, — a cause which neither union nor disunion, neither eloquence in council, nor skill in diplomacy, nor bravery in battle, could save: there he sat, motionless like a statue, with the hand of death upon him; his dark eyes flashing with feverish lustre from beneath his knitted brows; listening to his own words from another's mouth, and anxiously watching on the faces of those around their effect, — words of mournful despair, heralding the coming fate, and, without hope, still trying to avert it by counseling impossible expedients. Four weeks later Calhoun closed his eyes forever, leaving his cherished cause to its doom. Clay and Webster were among those who strewed flowers of eulogy upon his grave.

On March 7 Webster spoke. His speech was one of the sensations of the time. The anti-slavery men of New England had hoped that Webster would take in Congress the leadership of the opponents of slavery extension. Webster's past career gave good reasons for this hope, but the expectation was disappointed. Webster had always condemned slavery; now he paraded an array of excuses for its continued existence. He had opposed the annexation of Texas because of slavery;

THE COMPROMISE OF 1850 341

now he laid great stress upon the right of Texas to form out of its territory four new slave States. He had claimed the Wilmot Proviso as his thunder; now he opposed its application to Utah and New Mexico, because he thought slavery was excluded from them by the laws of nature and the ordinance of God, and he censured those insisting upon the proviso because they offered to the South a needless taunt and humiliation. He denounced the abolitionists because they had done nothing useful or good, but only aggravated the evils of slavery. He admitted that the free States had not done their duty in returning fugitive slaves, and declared himself ready to support an effective fugitive slave law. He denounced peaceable secession as an impossibility, and closed with an appeal for the Union.

The effect produced by the "seventh of March speech" on the anti-slavery men, especially in New England, was painful in the extreme. They saw in it the fall of an archangel. They denounced it as a flagrant abandonment of principle, and a profligate bid for the presidency. Their indignation was still more inflamed when Webster shortly afterwards visited Boston, sneered at the anti-slavery movement as an agitation based upon a "ghastly abstraction," and told his constituents that Massachusetts should "conquer her local prejudices." But those went too far who charged Webster with having originated a pro-slavery reaction at the North. Webster's speech was rather a symptom than a moving cause. While the excitement among that portion of the Northern people who took a constant interest in public affairs remained as great as ever, it had for some time been abating among those who became publicly active only on occasion. This did not escape the observation of Southern men. Already, on December 5, 1849, Alexander H. Stephens wrote to his brother: "The North is beginning to count the cost, — not the Free Soilers, but the mercantile class. I shall not yet despair of the republic." He judged correctly. The country was prosperous. The flow of gold from California, present and prospective, seemed to increase the opportunities of enterprise and gain. The field of profitable operations was constantly expanding on all sides. Thus grew from day to day the number of those who feared to see these opportunities disturbed by a great national crisis. The threats of disunion and civil war, so vociferously put forth by the Southern hotspurs, had their effect. Timid patriotism was frightened, and the commercial spirit wanted some settlement of the pending difficulties, without being very exacting.

Such a current of feeling is apt to work by a sort of atmospheric contagion, and could not fail to make itself felt in Congress. Of the Democratic Free Soilers, many sought the sheltering roof of the party whose main force was Southern, and the Whigs were divided. In January the Wilmot Proviso had still a majority in the House of Representatives; in February a resolution embodying it was laid on the table by a majority still larger. The anti-slavery tide was manifestly receding, Webster's speech being, not the origin of the backward movement, but only a part of it — indeed a helping, but not a starting force. The disunion declamations of Southern men, too, gradually lost much of their fierceness, and the general temper of the public mind in both sections of the country grew steadily more favorable to a compromise. The anti-slavery men were as unable to prevent it as the hotspurs of the South. But what they could do was, to answer Calhoun's parting cry of despair with the proclamation that the future was surely theirs.

On March 11 Seward spoke. He insisted upon the prompt and unconditional admission of California, emphatically declaring that he would consent to no compromise upon a question of right. He would not hamper the statesmanship of the future by any compromise whatever. No political equilibrium between freedom and slavery, he maintained, was possible, because if apparently restored to-day it would be destroyed again to-morrow. The moral sense of the age, he boldly proclaimed, would never permit the enforcement of a law making it the duty of Northern freemen to catch the fugitive slaves of Southern slaveholders. He denied that the Constitution recognized property in man. The Constitution, he affirmed, devoted the public domain to union, justice, defense, welfare, and liberty, and it was devoted to the same noble ends by "a higher law than the Constitution." How could wise and patriotic men, he asked, when founding institutions, social and political, for countless millions, contemplate the establishment of human bondage as one of them? If slavery, limited as it then was, threatened to subvert the Constitution, how could wise statesmen think of enlarging its boundaries and increasing its influence? He would therefore bar its expansion by all legal means. Climatic conditions were not sufficient to prevent attempts at the introduction of slavery; and wherever he found a law of God or of nature disregarded, he would vote to reaffirm it with all the sanction of civil authority. He put the final issue clearly before the slaveholders and the compromisers. The threats to dissolve the Union did not dismay him. The question was "whether the Union shall stand, and slavery, under the steady, peaceful action of moral, social, and political causes, be removed by gradual voluntary effort and with compensation, or whether the Union shall be dissolved and civil war ensue, bringing on violent but complete and immediate emancipation." "I feel assured," he added, "that slavery must give way, and will give way, to the salutary instructions of economy, and to the ripening influences of humanity; that emancipation is inevitable, and is near; that it may be hastened or hindered; and that, whether it shall be peaceful or violent depends upon the question whether it be hastened or hindered; that all measures which fortify slavery or extend it, tend to the consummation of violence; all that check its extension and abate its strength, tend to its peaceful extirpation."

A fortnight later Chase followed in a similar strain. "It may be," he said, "you will succeed here in sacrificing the claims of freedom by some settlement carried through the forms of legislation. But the people will unsettle your settlement. It may be that you will determine that the territories shall not be secured by law against the ingress of slavery. The people will reverse your determination. It may be that you will succeed in burying the ordinance of freedom. But the people will write upon its tomb, 'I shall rise again.' And the same history which records its resurrection may also inform posterity that they who fancied they killed the proviso, only committed political suicide."

Such utterances were received by Southern men with explosions of anger, or an affectation of contempt; by the compromisers, with emphatic protests. Even some of the more timid among the opponents of slavery were frightened by words so bold. About Seward's "higher law," of which the Democrats took advantage to brand him as a traitor to the Constitution, many Northern Whigs shook their heads in alarm. Clay was very indignant at so high-handed a way of dealing with his "comprehensive scheme of adjustment," and spoke, in a letter to a friend, of "Seward's late abolition speech" as likely to cut him off from all intercourse with the administration, as it had "eradicated the respect of almost all men from him." Webster mentioned it sneeringly as Governor Seward's "great and glorious speech," and complained to his friends of the slavery discussion obstructing the consideration of the tariff and other important measures, adding that he thought no history showed " a case of such mischief arising from angry debates and disputes, both in the government and the country, on questions of so very little real importance." This appears amazingly short-sighted by the lights of to-day. But it was by no means surprising that the old statesmen should have recoiled from the startling predictions of Seward and Chase. They had all their lives moved in a circle of ideas in which the alternative of speedy emancipation by a peaceable process, or speedy, violent, and complete emancipation as a result of civil war, had hardly been thought of. That alternative had always appeared to them as a choice between an impossibility on one side and a horror on the other; and when now in their old age they were told that the choice must be made, and that without much delay, it was but natural that they should struggle against the new idea with desperation, determined that the dreaded final crisis should at least not be permitted to come while they were alive, and that they should fall back once more upon the statesmanship of anodynes and palliatives. History has demonstrated that Seward and Chase understood the nature of the distemper and read the future, which Clay and Webster did not. This time, however, the old statesmen were still to have their way.

On February 13 President Taylor had laid before Congress the Constitution of California. On the 14th Foote of Mississippi had offered in the Senate a resolution to refer the case of California and all pending propositions concerning slavery, among them Clay's resolutions and a similar set introduced by Bell of Tennessee, to a select committee of thirteen senators who were to report a plan of settlement. Foote's resolution, withdrawn once and then renewed after two months of debate, embracing the whole slavery question, was adopted on April 18. Clay was elected chairman of the committee, which had among its members the foremost men of the Senate, excluding, however, the leading representatives of the anti-slavery sentiment. On May 8 the committee submitted a report consisting of three bills and an elaborate argument.

Clay's course with regard to the admission of California had been very unsteady. His resolutions embodying his "comprehensive plan of adjustment" were certainly open to the construction that all the essential points contained in them were, as parts of a great compromise, to form one legislative measure. But when the Constitution of California was received, Clay declared himself ready to vote for the admission of California separately and immediately. He "did not think it right" that this admission should be confounded or combined with other things. He did not even think that the different resolutions he had offered should be referred to one committee. It was his plan, he said, that they should be acted upon one by one. From this position he gradually drifted away, moved by the pressure brought upon him by Southern men, who insisted that the admission of California as a free State, uncoupled with other measures, would be highly offensive to the South, and might lead to the immediate dissolution of the Union; in any event, it would meet with bitter, perhaps unconquerable, opposition. By April 5 Clay was so far staggered that he thought the coupling of the admission of California with provisions for territorial governments, and for the adjustment of the Texas boundary, would not be improper; and soon afterwards he found the combination not only desirable, but necessary for harmony and peace. To the objection that to make the admission of California dependent upon extraneous conditions would be an indignity to the State, he replied that California should be proud of the opportunity to contribute to the pacification of the country by a little patience on her part.

In accordance with this idea, the first of the bills reported by the committee provided for the admission of California, the organization of territorial governments for New Mexico and Utah without

THE COMPROMISE OF 1850

any restriction as to slavery, and a proposition to Texas of a northern and western boundary with a compensation in money; the second, originally drawn by Mason of Virginia, provided for the capture and delivery of fugitive slaves; and the third bill prohibited the introduction of slaves from adjacent States into the District of Columbia for sale, or to be placed in depot for the purpose of subsequent sale or transportation to other and distant markets. The report also contained a declaration that any new States to be formed out of the territory of Texas should, when fit for admission, be received with or without slavery, as their constitutions might determine. There had been grave disagreements in the committee. Scarcely any member was fully satisfied with the report; but the accompanying argument promised that the adoption of the measures submitted would effect an amicable settlement of all the pending controversies, and "give general satisfaction to an overwhelming majority of the people of the United States."

But no sooner was the first of the three bills, on account of the multiplicity of its subjects derisively called "the Omnibus Bill," before the Senate, than it turned out that the combination of different propositions in one measure, apparently necessary to give the bill the character of a compromise, was also an element of weakness. There were those who would vote for the admission of California, but not for the territorial governments without the exclusion of slavery; there were those who would vote for the territorial governments, but not for the Texan boundary; and those who would not vote for the admission of California in any combination. In other words, it appeared probable that, while each of the different propositions might receive a majority of votes, the different majorities would be composed of different sets of men, and the combined measure would receive no majority at all, on account of the opposition of different men to different parts of it. The anti-slavery men insisted upon the admission of California and territorial governments with the Wilmot Proviso. The extreme pro-slavery men, led by Jefferson Davis, Butler, Mason, and Soulé, would not only not accept the admission of California, but demanded a positive recognition of the right of slaveholders to take their slave property into the territories. Rusk of Texas would not vote for any bill reducing the area claimed by Texas; and Benton opposed the compromise because it yielded to Texas too much of the territory belonging to New Mexico, and because it made the admission of California dependent upon the passage of other measures. While Clay's plan was supported by such Northern men as Webster, Cass, Douglas, and Cooper, and by such Southern Whigs as Badger and Bell, other Southern Whigs took as violently hostile an attitude as the Southern Democrats; and the various elements of opposition, so utterly divergent in their ultimate aims, threatened,

THE COMPROMISE OF 1850

if combined, to prove more than strong enough to accomplish its defeat.

But that was not all. Clay also found President Taylor against him. While the threats of disunion coming from Southern men stimulated Clay's compromising propensity, they stirred the fighting spirit of the old general. He thought that California had a right to demand prompt admission; and when some of the Southern hotspurs told him that the South would not tolerate the admission of California as a free State, but would break up the Union, he answered with much emphasis that such language was treasonable, and that, if in enforcing the laws he should find it necessary, he himself would take command of the army and put down rebellion with a strong hand. He also thought that New Mexico might remain under the military government left by the war, until her people should be ready to do as the Californians had done. On April 23 the military governor of New Mexico actually issued a proclamation calling a convention of delegates to frame a state constitution; and when, on the other hand, the governor of Texas, by virtue of the claim of Texas to all of New Mexico east of the Rio Grande, demanded the withdrawal of the federal troops, and threatened to drive them away with Texan militia if not removed, the President sent word to the military commandant in New Mexico to repel force by force, informing him that, if necessary, he, General Taylor, would be there himself. As to the boundary question, he did not think it his business either to recognize or to deny the claims of Texas; but he considered it his duty, until Congress should have disposed of the matter, to keep things *in statu quo*, and to maintain the public peace against any disturber.

Such being his feelings, Clay's compromise measure found little favor in his eyes. He looked upon any compromise as a concession to a revolutionary and treasonable spirit; and to Senator Hannibal Hamlin, who informed him that he considered the "Omnibus Bill" wrong in principle and that he would do his best to defeat it, he replied: "Stand firm; don't yield; it means disunion, and I am pained to learn that we have disunion men to contend with; disunion is treason." And, with an expression of emphasis sometimes heard among old soldiers, he added that, if they really attempted to carry out their scheme of disunion, "they should be dealt with by law as they deserved, and executed."

The "President's policy," therefore, was to admit California as a State immediately and unconditionally, and to leave New Mexico under the military governor, and Utah, perhaps, under such a government as the Mormons had set up for themselves, until the people of those territories should have formed state constitutions and applied for admission, when the new States should be promptly received; and this, he hoped, would come about very soon. The administration was in a somewhat isolated position; but whatever influence it possessed among members of Congress, and upon public opinion, it employed in favor of this policy and against the compromise. In one respect this plan was weak. The population of New Mexico could not be compared with that of California, either in point of numbers or in point of character. In neither respect was it fit to form a state government. Military rule in a territory could be justified only as a temporary expedient, to be superseded as soon as possible by a legally constituted civil authority. The establishment of regular territorial governments in the newly acquired territories was therefore decidedly called for. Clay further objected to the President's policy that in other respects it stopped short of the requirements of the situation. As he expressed it in one of his numerous speeches on the subject: "Here are five bleeding wounds [counting them upon the fingers of his left hand]: first, there is California; there are the territories, second; there is the question of the boundary of Texas, the third; there is the fugitive slave law, the fourth; and there is the question of the slave trade in the District of Columbia, fifth. What is the plan of the President? Is it to heal all these wounds? No such thing. It is only to heal one of the five, and to leave the other four to bleed more profusely than ever by the sole admission of California, even if it should produce death itself." Whereupon Benton sarcastically remarked that Clay would have found more bleeding wounds if he had had more fingers. Clay complained feelingly that the President, instead of aiding him in pacifying the country, adhered exclusively and persistently to his own plan, regardless of consequences. But Taylor could not be moved. He was determined to the fighting point, and would have signed a bill with the Wilmot Proviso in it, had it been presented to him. The influence he exercised was, therefore, rather on the anti-slavery side. Thus, although the current of popular sentiment ran in favor of a compromise, the practical difficulties Clay had to contend with seemed to be well-nigh insuperable.

But two events happened which essentially changed the aspect of things. On the first Monday in June the dreaded Nashville Convention met. Instead of sending forth fierce threats of disunion in case the extreme demands of the South were not fully complied with, as the Southern hotspurs had hoped, the convention, following more moderate counsels, passed resolutions, indeed, vigorously denouncing the Wilmot Proviso and all other anti-slavery heresies, but at the same time expressing confidence that Congress would find a way to do justice to the South. It is true it also adopted an address in which the sentiments of the "fire-eaters" found their expression, and which soundly denounced Clay's comprehensive plan of adjustment. But on the whole the convention produced the impression that the Southern people were divided in sentiment, and that the Union possessed

THE COMPROMISE OF 1850

a good many friends among them. The effect all this had upon Congress was not to strengthen the Southern extremists, whose main capital consisted in the terror spread by their threats of disunion and war, but rather to discourage Southern opposition to a compromise.

The other event of importance was the sudden death of President Taylor, who, on the Fourth of July, had exposed himself to an unusually hot sun, and then, on the 9th, succumbed to a violent fever. The Vice-President succeeding him in his office, Millard Fillmore, a man of fair abilities but little positiveness of character, had, before his election, passed as a Wilmot Proviso Whig. It has been widely believed that his jealousy of Seward, who easily outstripped him as a competitor for the leadership of the Whig party in New York, induced him to take his position on the other side. But it is by no means improbable that he favored Clay's compromise from natural inclination; for he was one of those men who, when put into positions of great responsibility, will avoid all strong measures, thinking that to be "the safe middle course."

The old cabinet resigned immediately after Taylor's death. Upon the advice of Clay, supported by Mangum, Fillmore appointed Webster secretary of state. The Treasury Department he gave to Thomas Corwin of Ohio, who had been a very earnest anti-slavery man, but gradually became one of the most conservative of Northern Whigs. John J. Crittenden of Kentucky was made attorney-general. He had lost Clay's favor in 1848 by failing to support him for the presidential nomination; but Clay now "acquiesced" in his appointment. "My relations with Mr. Fillmore are perfectly friendly and confidential," he wrote to one of his sons. He had now the administration on his side. It employed its whole influence in favor of the compromise. Still the battle of words continued.

On July 22, nearly six months after the introduction of his resolutions, and two and a half months after the Committee of Thirteen had presented its report, Clay made his closing speech. Ever since January 28, he had been on the floor almost day after day, sometimes so ill that he could hardly drag his tottering limbs to the senate chamber. So he had toiled on, answering objections and arguing, and pleading, and expostulating, and appealing, and beseeching, with anxious solicitude, for the Union, and for peace and harmony among all its people. He had thrown aside all sectional spirit. "Sir," he exclaimed once, "I have heard something said about allegiance to the South. I know no South, no North, no East, no West, to which I owe any allegiance." Whatever may be said of the wisdom of his policy, his motives had never been more patriotic and unselfish. He was no longer a candidate for the presidency. Some of his friends had, indeed, again approached him with inquiries whether he would permit his name to be put forward in 1852, but he had firmly de-

Thos Corwin

THE COMPROMISE OF 1850

clined. There was no longer any vulgar ambition disturbing him. The old man felt that his endeavors must find their reward in themselves. "I am here," he said, "expecting soon to go hence, and owing no responsibility but to my own conscience and to God." Neither had he approached the problem to be solved with his old dictatorial spirit. Time and again he had assured the Senate that he was not wedded to any plan of his own, and that he would be most grateful for the suggestion of measures more promising than those proposed by him as to the pacification of the country. He had sacrificed the Wilmot Proviso, the adoption of which would have accorded best with his natural impulses. He had made concession after concession to the defenders of slavery, much against his sympathies. And now, seeing his scheme of adjustment after all in great danger of defeat, he once more poured out all his patriotic fervor in a last appeal: —

"I believe from the bottom of my soul," he said, "that this measure is the reunion of the Union. And now let us discard all resentments, all passions, all petty jealousies, all personal desires, all love of place, all hungering after the gilded crumbs which fall from the table of power. Let us forget popular fears, from whatever quarter they may spring. Let us go to the fountain of unadulterated patriotism, and, performing a solemn lustration, return divested of all selfish, sinister, and sordid impurities, and think alone of our God, our country, our conscience, and our glorious Union."

His patriotism was, however, not all meekness. In the same speech he severely censured the abolitionists as reckless agitators, and denounced the Southern fire-eaters for their disunion tendencies, reflecting especially upon a member of the Nashville Convention, Rhett of South Carolina, who, after his return to Charleston, had in a public meeting openly proposed to hoist the standard of secession. When Clay had finished his appeal for peace and union, Barnwell of South Carolina, Calhoun's successor, rose and declared his dissatisfaction with Clay's remarks, "not a little disrespectful to a friend" whom he held very dear, and upon whose character he then proceeded to pronounce a warm eulogy, intimating that the opinions held and expressed by Mr. Rhett might possibly be those of South Carolina. Clay was quickly upon his feet. "Mr. President," he replied, "I said nothing with respect to the character of Mr. Rhett. I know him personally, and have some respect for him. But, if he pronounced the sentiment attributed to him of raising the standard of disunion and of resistance to the common government, whatever he has been, if he follows up that declaration by corresponding overt acts" — the old man's eye flashed and his voice rang out in a thundering peal — "he will be a traitor, and I hope he will meet the fate of a traitor!" Like an electric shock the word thrilled the audience, and volleys of applause broke forth from the crowded galleries.

When order was restored, Clay continued: —

THE COMPROMISE OF 1850 359

"Mr. President, I have heard with pain and regret a confirmation of the remark I made, that the sentiment of disunion is becoming familiar. I hope it is confined to South Carolina. I do not regard as my duty what the honorable senator seems to regard as his. If Kentucky to-morrow unfurls the banner of resistance unjustly, I never will fight under that banner. I owe a paramount allegiance to the whole Union, — a subordinate one to my own State. When my State is right — when it has a cause for resistance, when tyranny, and wrong, and oppression insufferable arise — I will then share her fortunes ; but if she summons me to the battlefield, or to support her in any cause which is unjust, against the Union, never, *never* will I engage with her in such a cause!"

The echo of these words was heard eleven years later, when the great crisis had come.

After Clay's closing speech the voting began. Several Southern senators, who at first had been bitterly opposed to Clay's plan, had gradually become persuaded. But the compromise had to suffer a disheartening defeat before achieving its victory. Amendments were offered in perplexing profusion. The Omnibus Bill was disfigured almost beyond recognition. At last, after a series of confusing manipulations, Clay himself incautiously accepted an amendment offered by a senator from Georgia, that, until a final settlement of the Texas boundary was effected with the assent of Texas, the territorial government of New Mexico should not go into operation east of the Rio Grande. As this was virtually delivering over New Mexico to Texas, the whole provision concerning New Mexico was struck out by the aid of friends of the compromise; and when on July 31 the bill was passed, there was nothing left in the "Omnibus" but the establishment of a territorial government for Utah. All the rest had been amended out of it. The compromise seemed to be lost.

The next day Clay appeared in the Senate once more to avow his devotion to the Union, and to defy its enemies; for he feared that, the compromise having failed, it might now be impossible to save it without the employment of force. "I stand here in my place," he said, "meaning to be unawed by any threats, whether they come from individuals or from States. I should deplore, as much as any man living or dead, that arms should be raised against the authority of the Union, either by individuals or by States. But if, after all that has occurred, any one State, or the people of any State, choose to place themselves in military array against the government of the Union, I am for trying the strength of the government." The galleries broke out in applause, which was checked by the presiding officer, and Clay proceeded: —

"Nor am I to be alarmed or dissuaded from any such course by intimations of the spilling of blood. If blood is to be spilt, by whose fault is it to be spilt? Upon the supposition I maintain, it will be the fault of those who raise the standard of disunion and endeavor to prostrate this government; and, sir, when that is done, so long as it please God to give me a voice to express my sentiments, or an arm, weak and enfeebled as it may be by age, that voice and that arm will be on the side of my country, for the support of the general authority, and for the maintenance of the power of this Union!"

The enthusiasm of the galleries became so demonstrative, that the presiding officer was obliged to ask the senator from Kentucky to sit down until order could be restored.

He warned the disunionists, who expressed the belief that the army, commanded in so large a part by officers from Virginia, South Carolina, and other Southern States, would not draw their swords, that they would find themselves gravely mistaken. And, to leave no shadow of a doubt as to his conception of true loyalty to the Union, he said: —

"The honorable senator speaks of Virginia being my country. This Union is my country; the thirty States are my country; Kentucky is my country, and Virginia no more than any other of the States of this Union. She has created on my part obligations and feelings and duties toward her in my private character which nothing upon earth would induce me to forfeit or violate. But even if it were my own State, — if my own State lawlessly, contrary to her duty, should raise the standard of disunion against the residue of the Union, — I would go against her; I would go against Kentucky in that contingency, much as I love her."

Thus, believing his compromise to have been defeated, he defied the enemies of the Union to do their worst, proclaiming himself ready to fight, even against his own State, for the integrity of the republic. At last, on August 2, mortified, exhausted, broken in health, he gave up his leadership and went to Newport to rest and recuperate. Then, in Clay's absence, that proved true which had been frequently urged against the Omnibus Bill, namely, that measures which could not be adopted when lumped together, might be adopted separately. The Texas boundary bill passed the Senate first, under the pressure of peculiar urgency. On August 6 the President informed Congress that the governor of Texas had called the legislature together for the purpose, as was reported, of taking measures for the occupation of New Mexico east of the Rio Grande by force; and that force would have to be repelled by force, unless the national government came to a friendly understanding with Texas. Accordingly the Senate made haste. A bill proposing to Texas a boundary cutting down New Mexico somewhat more than Clay had intended, and offering the sum of ten million dollars for the surrender of the claim of Texas, — the sum originally intended by Clay, but not mentioned in the Omnibus Bill, because Clay feared it might cause stock speculations, — passed the Senate promptly.

Next came a bill to admit California. It was adopted in the Senate on August 12 by a vote of 34 to 18. The senators from Virginia, South Carolina, and Florida, and one each from Tennessee, Louisiana, Mississippi, and Missouri, ten in all, signed a protest setting forth that the admission of California as a free State destroyed the equal rights of the slaveholding States in the confederacy; that it was "contrary to former precedent, and to the spirit and intent of the Constitution;" that it was part of a policy "fatal to the peace and equality of the States" they represented, which "must lead, if persisted in, to the dissolution of that confederacy, in which the slaveholding States have never sought more than equality, and in which they will not be content to remain with less."

On August 15 the bill to establish a territorial government in New Mexico was passed, providing that New Mexico, when fit to be received as a State, might come in with or without slavery, as her Constitution should then determine; and that in the mean time cases involving title to slaves in the territory should go for decision to the Supreme Court of the United States. On August 26 the Senate passed the Fugitive Slave Bill, but in a form more unfavorable to the negro than that in which it had been reported by Clay's committee; a provision giving the person captured as a fugitive slave the benefit of a trial by jury as to his status in the State in which the claimant resided was struck out.

The Texas boundary bill created a great stir in the House of Representatives. As the prospect of such legislation with a grant of money in it grew brighter, Texas scrip rose in the market. About the middle of June it had gone up from 10 per cent. to 50. In case the bill passed, the scrip was not unlikely to rise to par. A large and active lobby gathered in Washington. It was currently reported that millions of Texas securities were in the hands of members of Congress and officers of the government, high and low. Millions could be gained by the passage of the bill. On September 4 the bill was referred to the committee of the whole by a majority of two votes. Its fate looked doubtful. The third reading was refused by a majority of forty-six. Its defeat seemed certain. A reconsideration was moved, pending which the House adjourned. The next day the reconsideration was carried by a majority of fifty-six. An amendment adding to the bill a provision for a territorial government in New Mexico, which had been defeated the day before, was then adopted. But again the House refused the third reading by a majority of eight. Again a reconsideration was moved, but declared out of order by the speaker. Pending an appeal from that decision the House adjourned. The next day the speaker elaborately defended his decision, but that decision was, on the appeal, overthrown by a majority of thirty-eight. The floor of the House was swarming with lobby agents, and amid boisterous demonstrations of delight the third reading was ordered by a majority of ten, and the bill then passed. The House had never presented a more repugnant and alarming spectacle. But the speaker, at least, had done his duty and kept his hands clean. Texas scrip rushed up to par. The other bills sent down by the Senate passed easily.

When Clay returned to Washington in the last week of August, he found that the Senate had carried out the whole programme laid down in his compromise resolutions seven months before, except the interdiction of the slave traffic in the District of Columbia. After a long debate, in which Clay with great emphasis expressed his expectation that slavery would pass away in the District, adding that he was glad of it, that bill, too, passed and became a law. The compromise of 1850 was then substantially complete.

On September 6, Clay wrote to one of his sons: "I am again getting very much exhausted. I wish I had remained longer at Newport, where I was much benefited. I shall as soon as possible return home, where I desire to be more than I ever did in my life." The deep longing of the old man for home, and to be with his wife, had been pervading his letters to his family ever since the beginning of the session. And now, after the tremendous fatigue he had gone through, and from which his health never recovered, that yearning was stronger than ever. At last, on September 30, Congress adjourned, after one of the longest and most arduous sessions on record, and Clay took home with him the consciousness of having done his duty and accomplished a great work. His mind had not been troubled like Webster's, who, as if he had never been clearly convinced of having followed his true convictions of right, sought in the result a justification of his conduct. On September 10, when the passage of the compromise bills in the House seemed secured, Webster wrote to a friend: "Since the 7th of March there has never been an hour in which I have not felt a crushing weight of anxiety and responsibility. I have gone to sleep at night and waked in the morning with the same feeling of eating care; and I have sat down to no breakfast or dinner to which I have brought an unconcerned or easy mind. It is over. My part is acted, and I am satisfied. It is a day of rejoicing here such as I never witnessed. The face of everything is changed. You would suppose nobody had ever thought of disunion. All say they always meant to stand by the Union to the last." And two days afterwards: "Truly, it was not till Mr. Eliot's election [the election to Congress of a compromise Whig in Boston] that there was any confidence here that I was not a dead man."

Not a single moment during the whole struggle did Clay ever fear that he might be a "dead man." No doubt as to whether he was right had ever disturbed his sleep or clouded his waking. He had remained true to his old convictions as to the methods by which the Union could be preserved. During the progress of the debate he had repeatedly changed his tactics, but not essentially his attitude. He had always believed in the statesmanship of compromise, and, as always, so in this crisis. Seeing in the South the principal danger to the Union, he insisted upon concessions on the part of the North to avert that danger. Of such concessions he gave the example by sacrificing his own inclinations as to the Wilmot Proviso, and by accepting in the Committee of Thirteen some modifications of his plan which were distasteful to him. His inmost feelings would indeed repeatedly break forth. Unequivocally he threw the theory of a necessary equilibrium between the free and the slave States to the winds, and almost exultingly recognized the inevitable and constantly growing superiority of the North. If slavery was ultimately to succumb, he was far from regretting its inevitable fate. But he sincerely believed that by compromise measures he could keep the two antagonistic forces at peace, so that the final deliverance might effect itself in the way of a quiet, gradual development without disturbing the Union. In this he erred ; but it was an honest error of judgment, not a conscious self-deception for the occasion.

The compromise of 1850 was perhaps the best that could be made under the circumstances to effect a temporary truce. But no compromise could have been devised to keep the antagonistic forces of freedom and slavery permanently at peace. Calhoun was perfectly right in his conclusion that slavery, in order to exist with security in the Union, must rule it. It needed controlling political power, — more slave States, more representation, an absolute veto upon all legislation hostile to it. If slavery could not obtain this within the Union, and still desired to live, it had to try its fortunes outside. Calhoun's great error was to believe that slavery could survive at all in the nineteenth century. But those who believed like him — and every Southern man who was unwilling to give up slavery would finally accept his conclusions — naturally saw in the admission of California an almost fatal blow to their cause. By that act, the last bulwark they held in the government, the numerical equality between free States and slave States in the Senate, and the resulting veto power of a united South, was overthrown. No arrangement could permanently satisfy them that did not secure to them beyond peradventure a speedy increase of the number of slave States. This they understood well. They, therefore, insisted that the Missouri Compromise line should be run through the newly acquired territories to the Pacific Ocean, and that south of that line slavery should be secured by positive enactment, — or that all laws and usages existing in those territories which prohibited slavery should be declared invalid by act of Congress, in order to give free access to slavery.

But all these things the compromise failed to do. Clay emphatically refused his assent to any measure legislating slavery into free territory. He did, indeed, make some important concessions. His original resolutions contained a declaration that

THE COMPROMISE OF 1850

slavery did not exist by law, and was not likely to be introduced, in the acquired territories. That declaration he gave up. In the Committee of Thirteen he also very reluctantly accepted the duty of reporting an amendment that the territorial legislatures should "have no power to pass any law in respect to African slavery," which was adopted. And finally another amendment passed providing that the territories in question, when fit to be received as States, should be admitted with or without slavery, as their respective constitutions might determine. But what did all this mean? Clay argued that, if in the newly acquired territories slavery actually existed, it could not be abolished, or, if it did not exist, it could not be introduced by any act of the territorial legislature. Did slavery exist in New Mexico and Utah? Clay insisted that it did not; the champions of slavery, that it did, — that, if indeed it ever had been abolished by Mexican law, the Constitution of the United States, being by the act of acquisition spread over the territories, superseded that Mexican law, and carried with it the right of the slaveholder to take and hold his "property" there. This doctrine Clay most emphatically denied. But, as opinions differed upon all these points, the compromise proposed that these differences should be referred for decision to the Supreme Court of the United States. This could not permanently satisfy the South, for it gave no security. It provided only for a lawsuit with an uncertain prospect. Neither could it satisfy the North, for by implication it discountenanced the exercise of the power of Congress with regard to slavery in the territories. It introduced in the discussion of the problem that dangerous explosive, the "principle of non - intervention," which four years later served to justify the repeal of the Missouri Compromise, and then brought the forces of slavery and free labor to confront one another in arms on the plains of Kansas. Thus this part of the compromise of 1850, instead of settling anything, only unsettled the compromise of 1820.

An equally prolific source of mischief was the Fugitive Slave Law. No doubt a large number of slaves had in the course of time escaped from the South and found shelter in the North. No doubt the Northern States had been remiss in performing their constitutional obligations as to the return of fugitives, for in some of them the enforcement of the existing law was actually obstructed by state legislation. No doubt the South had in this respect occasion to complain. But an institution like slavery was naturally exposed to such losses. It would have been prudent to bear them in silence. It was certainly most unwise to make laws calculated to bring the most odious features of slavery home to a free people naturally impatient of its existence. This the Fugitive Slave Law did in a very provoking form. It gave United States commissioners the power, by summary process, to turn over a colored man or woman claimed as a fugitive slave to the claimant. It excluded from the evidence the testimony of the defendant. It "commanded" all good citizens, whenever summoned, to aid in the prompt and effective execution of the law, including the capture of the fugitive. It made the United States marshal liable for the full value of the slave, if a recaptured fugitive escaped from his custody. Whoever knowingly harbored or concealed a fugitive slave to prevent his recapture was to be punished by fine and imprisonment.

Such a law could not pacify; it could not be executed without galling men's moral sense and the pride of free manhood among a people who thought slavery a great wrong, and who would never consider it sinful to help on a poor fugitive seeking his freedom. When first proposing his compromise scheme, and repeatedly during the debate, Clay had remarked that to the Northern people the question was one of sentiment, while to the South it was one of interest, and that it was easier to make a concession of sentiment than of interest. It is an important historical fact that the sentiment prevailing at the North concerning slavery never was understood by the Southern people. They regarded it as a sickly notion of visionary philanthropists, or as the outgrowth of horrible stories told in the North about the South, and artfully used by designing politicians, or as an itching desire to meddle with other people's business. They never appreciated it as the great moral force which it was, and which in the very nature of things would not yield to any compromise. Slaveholder as Clay was, and kind and considerate to his slaves, taking generous care of their well-being, he, with all his anti-slavery instincts and impulses, never fully comprehended the feeling of abhorrence with which the non-slaveholding world looked at the unjust power held by one man over another. But for the business of catching fugitive slaves he himself had no taste. In the course of the debate he said that while he had, with great pleasure, several times given his services as an attorney to negroes trying to prove their freedom, he had only once, very reluctantly, appeared against one to oblige a near friend, and then only after having become perfectly satisfied that the negro really was a slave. And now the Fugitive Slave Law was to make the citizens of the free States do for the slaveholders what not a few of the slaveholders were too proud to do for themselves. Such a law could not but fail. But then it would increase the exasperation of the slaveholders by its failure, while exasperating the people of the free States by the attempts at enforcement. Thus the compromise of 1850, instead of securing peace and harmony, contained in the most important of its provisions the seeds of new and greater conflicts.

One effect it produced which Calhoun had clearly predicted when he warned the slaveholding States against compromises as an invention of the enemy; it adjourned the decisive conflict until the superiority of the North over the South in population and material resources was overwhelming, and, as it happened, until a party, and at its head a man, held the helm of affairs, whose anti-slavery principles and aims made it sure that the cause of the mischief would not in any form survive the issue of the struggle.

CHAPTER XXVII

THE END

AT first Clay's expectations as to the pacificatory effect of the compromise seemed to be justified. The strain of popular excitement, which had been long and severe, was followed by a reaction of lassitude, in many cases degenerating into the very fanaticism of repose. In November, 1850, the adjourned Nashville Convention met again, and passed resolutions which, although unfavorable to the compromise, were comparatively temperate in tone. Moreover, the number of States represented, as well as that of the delegates representing them, was small. The governors of South Carolina and of Mississippi carried on an animated correspondence about the steps to be taken to sever their States from the Union, but the friends of the compromise appealed to the people and defeated the disunionists in the elections. In Georgia a state convention adopted a platform which did, indeed, not wholly approve of the compromise, but accepted it as a basis of settlement and pacification, and spoke much of fidelity to the Union, while, at the same time, resolving that either of five things — namely, the abolition of slavery in the District of Columbia "without the consent and petition of the slaveholders thereof," any act suppressing the slave trade between the slave States, any refusal to admit as a State any Territory because of the existence of slavery therein, any act prohibiting the introduction of slaves into New Mexico and Utah, and any act repealing or materially modifying the Fugitive Slave Law — would be resisted by the State of Georgia, "even, as a last resort, to a disruption of every tie which binds her to the Union." This was indeed Unionism of the conditional species, and a keen observer would easily discern beneath it all a profound distrust and disquietude as to the future, apt to yield in any exciting crisis to the appeals of the determined minority of disunionists, who, after all, judged correctly of the demands which slavery must of necessity ultimately make.

But for the time being a large majority of the Southern people were evidently averse to a violent rupture. Some of the most influential public men of the South, who had vociferously threatened disunion while the compromise measures were pending, such as Alexander H. Stephens, Toombs, Cobb, Clemens, and others, now busied themselves to quiet the fears of their constituents, representing the compromise as a victory of Southern firmness, and as an assurance of future peace and harmony.

At the North, too, the compromise seemed to be acquiesced in by an overwhelming majority of the people as a permanent settlement; and there might have been a possibility for a few years of repose but for the immediate effect of one of the compromise laws. Slaveholders and their agents appeared in the free States to test the virtue of the new Fugitive Slave Act. According to trustworthy estimates, there were about twenty thousand escaped slaves living in the Northern country. Many of them had married free colored women, and reared families of children on free soil. The appearance of the "man-hunter" threw them into fearful consternation. Some of them were captured and carried off to the South. In a few cases it turned out that the persons so captured and carried off were not fugitive slaves at all, but freemen, and these had to be released. In several instances the law was executed with a harshness and cruelty which shocked the popular heart. An outcry arose, not only from colored people and anti-slavery men, but from persons who, although they had so far taken little interest in the matter, now felt their human sympathies and their moral sense insulted by the things they witnessed among themselves. The anti-slavery men took advantage of this change of feeling, and meetings were held in Northern cities ringing with denunciations of the Fugitive Slave Law as an outrage to the dignity of human nature, and as an attempt to carry slavery into the heart of the free North.

As this current of sentiment grew in power, the advocates of the compromise became alarmed lest the efforts at general pacification should be defeated by a revolt of public opinion against the Fugitive Slave Law. They found it necessary to stir up a public sentiment on their side. A systematic agitation was set on foot. An immense meeting, called by merchants of New York, in which the formation of a " Union party " was foreshadowed, opened the campaign. Similar demonstrations followed in Boston and many other cities. Foremost in that agitation was Daniel Webster, and wherever he appeared he spoke with the zealous bitterness of a recent convert. The measures forming the great compromise were put before the people as no less binding than additions to the Constitution would be. And, as usually the point most sharply attacked is most hotly defended, the binding force of the Fugitive Slave Law was insisted upon with such exceptional urgency as if the catching of fugitive slaves had become the main constitutional duty of the American citizen. This could not fail to react.

Clay made a speech in response to an invitation from the Kentucky legislature, in which, adhering to his theory that the principal object to be kept in view was to quiet the dangerous excitement at the South, he represented the compromise as "substantially a Southern triumph," inasmuch as California would have been admitted under any circumstances, while the establishment of territorial governments in New Mexico and Utah without the Wilmot Proviso, and the enactment of the Fugitive Slave Law, were in accordance with the wishes of the South. He roundly berated the Southerners who were not satisfied with the adjustment, and denounced the meeting at Nashville as a second Hartford Convention.

He was not without great anxiety. When the thirty-first Congress reassembled in December, 1850, he availed himself of the earliest opportunity confidently to affirm that general peace and quiet reigned throughout the land, and that this session would remain undisturbed by the slavery question. But in January, 1851, he and forty-four other senators and representatives betrayed their nervousness by issuing a very singular manifesto. They declared that sectional controversy upon the subject of slavery could be avoided only by strict adherence to the compromise; that they intended to maintain that settlement inviolate, and that they would not support for the office of president or vice-president, or senator or representative in Congress, or member of a state legislature, any man, of whatever party, who was not known to be opposed to any disturbance of the compromise, and to the renewal of the agitation of the slavery question. Those who thought such a threat of excommunication necessary could not have been very confident that the public opinion of the country would remain strong enough in favor of the compromise to restrain ambitious politicians from interfering with it.

Indeed, the slavery discussion began again in the House of Representatives with the opening of the session. The members had hardly taken their seats when Giddings of Ohio violently denounced the proceedings which had taken place under the Fugitive Slave Law. In the Senate it was Clay himself who, presenting petitions for the more effectual suppression of the African slave trade, spoke eloquently of the abominations of that traffic, and of the beneficent results which would follow if measures were taken to transport free negroes to Liberia. He also introduced a resolution looking to the adoption of more adequate measures to prevent the employment of American vessels in the slave trade. Hale of New Hampshire replied, on behalf of the Free Soilers, that, while he and his friends were so rudely reproved for agitating the matter of slavery, it ill comported with the position taken by the compromisers, if Clay, their chief, reopened the agitation by expressing such pious and humane sentiments about a cognate subject. This sarcasm had all the more point as just then the manifesto had appeared threatening those who should reopen the agitation with exclusion from office.

Suddenly in February, 1851, the news arrived that in Boston the execution of the Fugitive Slave Law had been successfully resisted by force. A fugitive slave named Shadrach had been rescued by a crowd of colored people from the hands of a deputy marshal of the United States in the court-room. In Washington the report created an almost incredible excitement. It could hardly have been greater had Massachusetts made an attempt to secede from the Union. Clay at once introduced a resolution in the Senate calling upon the President for what official information he had of the occurrence, and to inquire what measures he had taken concerning the matter, and whether any further legislation was required. Feeling as if he had staked his character upon the healing effects of the measure, Clay was greatly disturbed. He confessed himself "shocked" and "distressed," even beyond his power of expression, at the "sacrilegious hands" which had "seized the sword of justice." The President issued a formal proclamation, commanding all officers of the government, civil as well as military, and requesting all good citizens, to rally round the law of the land, and to aid in securing its enforcement. He also sent a message to the Senate, communicating the information called for, assuring Congress that he would exert all the powers of the government to enforce the law, and recommending that he be given larger facilities in calling out the militia of the States in case of resistance to the lawful authorities.

The speech with which Clay received that message proved that his wrath at the liberators of Shadrach had been mainly roused by his anxiety lest the occurrence at Boston should rekindle the dangerous excitement at the South which the compromise had just, to some extent, succeeded in quieting. He did, indeed, not spare the abolitionists who aimed at disunion and incited law-breaking, and he was especially severe in his denunciation of the English philanthropist, George Thompson, the "foreign hireling," as Clay called him, who had come to America "in order to propagate his opinions and doctrines with regard to the subversion of one of the institutions of this country." But he evidently made it the main object of his speech to persuade his Southern friends that, after all, the Fugitive Slave Law was, on the whole, faithfully executed in the free States, and that, therefore, there was no just reason for complaint or apprehension. He passed in review several cases in which fugitive slaves had been returned without difficulty. In fact, he knew of but this one instance of obstruction. "I heard," said he, "with great regret the remarks made by the senator from Virginia [who had complained], because I do not coincide with him in the facts upon which his remarks were founded, and I think they may have a tendency to produce ill effects where there is already too much disposition in the public mind to be operated upon disadvantageously to the Union."

Anxiously he admonished his Southern friends not to be too exacting. They could really not expect to recover the runaways without some trouble and expense. As all laws were occasionally evaded, so would this be, especially as it was a law "to recover a human being who owes service as a slave to another," and as, "besides the aid and the sympathy which he will excite from his particular situation, he has his own intellect, his own cunning, and his own means of escape at his command." Indeed, the South should be satisfied. He was sure the President and the cabinet were " immovably determined " to carry out the law, and to employ all the means in their power to that end; and the people would aid them. In his opinion the " compromise had worked a miracle." The agitation about the Wilmot Proviso had disappeared; also that about California, and about slavery in the District of Columbia. The compromise had " made thousands of converts among the abolitionists themselves." Peace and good feeling had been produced by it surpassing his " most sanguine expectations." Only a few ultraists were still restless, but the people would frown them down. If necessary, however, to quiet the apprehensions of his Southern friends, and to prevent the repetition of such occurrences as the liberation of Shadrach still more effectually, he would willingly see the President authorized to dispense with the proclamation required by existing law, when, in anticipation of a disturbance in connection with the arrest of a fugitive slave, he should call the militia or the army of the United States into service.

A majority of the Southern senators accepted Clay's sanguine view of things. But those who still insisted that the Fugitive Slave Law would never be sure of effectual enforcement unless the Northern people themselves enforced it with cordiality and zeal, as they would enforce a law of

THE END 383

their own, were, after all, right. The anti-slavery men in the Senate said nothing to encourage Clay's hopes, as, indeed, they could not in justice to their own feelings and those of the people they represented. But when Clay, in the course of the debate, classed them with the abolitionists aiming at disunion, Chase rebuked him with great force and dignity, declaring that, while they would restrict slavery within the limits of the slave States, and " not allow it within the exclusive jurisdiction of the national government," their fidelity to the Union was immovable. But, on the whole, the sanguine view prevailed. The judiciary committee of the Senate, to which the President's message was referred, reported that no change of the law concerning the President's power to call out the militia was required.

It was the last session of Congress in which Clay was active, and he found opportunity to speak some parting words about the "old Whig policies," which once had been among the great inspirations of his public endeavors. When presenting some petitions he commended to the Senate the consideration of the tariff question in these faltering accents: "I will take occasion to say that I hope that now, when there is apparent calmness upon the surface of public affairs, — which I hope is real, and that it will remain without disturbing the deliberations of Congress during the present session, — for one, I should be extremely delighted if the subject of the tariff of 1846 could be taken up in a liberal, kind, and national spirit; not with any purpose of reviving those high rates of protection which at former periods of our country were established for various causes, — sometimes from sinister causes, — but to look deliberately at the operation of the tariff of 1846; and, without disturbing its essential provisions, I should like a consideration to be given to the question of the prevention of frauds and great abuses, of the existence of which there is no earthly doubt. We should see whether we cannot, without injury, without prejudice to the general interests of the country, give some better protection to the manufacturing interests than is now afforded." From the great champion of the "American system" this request had a diffident, melancholy sound. It was a very faint echo of past struggles.

During the last days of the session he broke a lance for a river and harbor bill, appropriating $2,300,000, which had come up from the House, and was in danger of being defeated by a determined minority in the Senate. The interests of the great West, the necessity of improving the Mississippi, and the rights of the majority, were the texts of his arguments. But his appeals were in vain. The subject of the tariff was not taken up for consideration, and the river and harbor bill succumbed to parliamentary tactics. Clay's last official act was a refusal to accept the "constructive mileage," a "called session" of the Senate beginning immediately after the adjournment of

Congress for the consideration of executive business, and senators holding themselves entitled to compensation for traveling expenses as if between the adjournment of Congress on March 4 and the opening of the "called session" on the 5th they had journeyed to their homes and returned to Washington.

Clay's health was seriously impaired. A severe cough tormented him, of which his physicians did not seem to know the cause. "I have finally concluded," he wrote to his wife, "to return by Cuba and New Orleans. The great difficulty I have felt in coming to the conclusion has been my long absence from you, and my desire to be with you. But my cough continues; although I do not lay up, my health is bad, and the weather has been the worst of March weather. I hope that I may be benefited by the softer climate of Cuba. I expect to go on the 11th from New York in the steamer Georgia. And I think my absence from home will not be prolonged beyond a month; that is, the middle of April."

But the climate of Cuba did not meet his hopes. His cough continued to distress him. During the summer of 1851 he remained at Ashland, watching the course of events and corresponding with his friends. Again he was addressed by overzealous admirers who desired to bring him forward as a candidate for the presidency in 1852. The ambition of others pursued him when his own was dead. He declined absolutely. "Considering my age," he wrote to Daniel Ullmann, "the delicate state of my health, the frequency and the unsuccessful presentation of my name on former occasions, I feel an unconquerable repugnance to such a use of it again. I cannot, therefore, consent to it."

But another call came which could not be wholly declined. Late in the summer Clay received from a committee of citizens of New York an urgent invitation to visit that State for the purpose of repelling the attacks to which the compromise was exposed. "We have a well-founded conviction," they said, "that the great body of the American people are in favor of maintaining and enforcing the compromises of the Constitution; nevertheless, in the resolutions and addresses adopted at conventions lately assembled around us, we have seen with regret, as well as alarm, that the question of adherence to the compromise measures is avoided or evaded, that modification and amendment are declared to be requisite, and repeal itself admissible. It is evident, therefore, that there requires to be more generally diffused a spirit that will not hold communion with those who advance and support doctrines in relation to the great national adjustment fatal to the future peace and harmony of the Union." In other words, the people were to be persuaded no longer to read the resolutions and addresses of Free Soilers or anti-slavery Whigs, and no longer to listen to the speeches of men who disliked the Fugitive Slave Law. So delicate and fragile, then, was the compromise of 1850 in the opinion of its friends that it must be carefully sheltered against any breeze of a hostile public opinion. To this end Clay was called upon to address meetings in the State of New York. Webster had already been in the field for months. In May, 1851, going from Buffalo to Albany, he delivered a series of speeches, in which he called the anti-slavery men insane people actuated by selfish motives, and denounced the violation of the Fugitive Slave Law as treason. He also spoke at Capon Springs, in Virginia, where he amused the Southern people by deriding the "higher law." Although these efforts were by no means without effect, they could not cure the trouble. The charm of Clay's presence, too, was wanted; but the exertion would have been beyond his power. On October 3 he responded to the invitation in a long letter, which was his last appeal to the American people.

He expressed his regret that his impaired health would not permit him to address his fellow citizens of New York in person. He had hoped, not that the compromise measures would have the unanimous concurrence of the people, but that they would be supported by a commanding majority. That hope, he thought, had not been disappointed. There was still local dissatisfaction, but it gradually yielded to patriotic considerations. He recognized that the Fugitive Slave Law was the sore point. But, with two exceptions, it had been everywhere enforced; and he confidently anticipated that the opposition to it in the North would cease. What was the reason of his solicitude concerning that law?

"The necessity [he wrote] of maintaining and enforcing that law must be admitted by the impartial judgment of all candid men. Many of the slaveholding States, and many public meetings of the people in them, have deliberately declared that their adherence to the Union depended upon the preservation of that law, and that its abandonment would be the signal of the dissolution of the Union. I know that the abolitionists (some of whom openly avow a desire to produce that calamitous event) and their partisans deride and deny the existence of any such danger; but men who will not perceive and own it, must be blind to the signs of the times, to the sectional strife which has unhappily arisen, to the embittered feelings which have been excited, as well as to the solemn resolutions of deliberative assemblies unanimously adopted. Their disregard of the danger, I am apprehensive, proceeds more from their desire to continue agitation than from their love of the Union itself."

Of the "resolutions and addresses adopted at conventions lately assembled," which had so much disturbed the gentlemen inviting him, he had only to say that "we must make some allowance for human frailty and inordinate pride of opinion;" that "many persons at the North had avowed an invincible hostility to the Fugitive Slave Law;" that they might become gradually convinced of the necessity of accepting it for the sake of the Union, only looking for a decent line of retreat; but that if the agitation should be actually continued, his confidence was unshaken in the great body of the Northern people that they would "in due time, and in the right manner, apply an appropriate and effectual corrective."

In the South, too, he saw much "to encourage the friends of the Union." But it was there, after all, that he discovered the real source of the danger threatening the republic. The main part of his letter he devoted to an elaborate review and refutation of the arguments with which nullification and secession were sought to be justified, exposing the absurdity of the theory underlying them, and the criminality of any attempt to carry that theory into practice. If such an attempt were made, he insisted, then "the power, the authority, and the dignity of the government ought to be maintained, and resistance put down at every hazard." He closed with a glowing eulogy on the glories and the benign effects of the Union.

The gentlemen from New York had probably desired a paper of a different character, for almost its whole argument was addressed, not to the North, but to the South. The discussion of the secession doctrines preached at the South occupied four fifths of its space. It was one more of his characteristic efforts to disarm the disunion tendency at the South, to that end opposing the anti-slavery tendency at the North not seldom at a sacrifice of his own feelings.

Such anti-slavery leaders as Seward and Chase

undoubtedly understood far better than Clay what the ultimate result of the conflict between slavery and free labor must be. But he saw more clearly than they did the immediate seriousness of the disunion movement at the South. A majority of the Southern people, and even of Southern public men, while determined to maintain slavery, still sincerely wished to avoid the disruption of the Union, and eagerly clutched at all sorts of delusive hopes. But a very active minority, undeceived by the temporary appearance of harmony, stood always ready to take advantage of any failure of the vaunted adjustments, and they were sure ultimately to exercise the strongest influence, because they had the logic of the situation on their side. They, however, underestimated the moral power of the Northern anti-slavery sentiment in case of a crisis. In fact, the compromise itself had encouraged the two extremes to underestimate each other as to their decision and courage. Many Southerners had vociferously threatened that they would rather dissolve the Union than permit the admission of California as a free State, and then quietly accepted the compromise. Northern anti-slavery men, therefore, concluded that the Southern threats of disunion were, after all, mere bluster without any real determination behind it. Every Northern legislature had passed fierce resolutions insisting upon the Wilmot Proviso, and when Southern men then saw the North accept the compromise, which did not exclude slavery from the territories, in order to pacify the South, they concluded that the South might have obtained much more if it had threatened more, and that the North, for the purpose of preserving peace and of making money, would yield anything and everything if the South only put on a bolder front.

Clay had gradually learned to understand the South well. He knew that the hotspurs were terribly in earnest, and that, in spite of the old attachment to the Union still existing, "the bold, the daring, and the violent," as he wrote to S. A. Allibone in June, 1851, might eventually "get the control and push their measures to a fatal extreme." What he did not appreciate was the character of that "sentiment" which he had asked the Northern people to sacrifice in order to soothe the feelings of the South. He failed to feel that the natural impulses of generosity and the moral pride of the Northern people would inevitably rebel against the Fugitive Slave Law; and he did not see that, by leaving the question of slavery in the territories unsettled, the compromise had only for a short time adjourned the final struggle which he endeavored to avert.

Although his health was not perceptibly improved when the opening session of the thirty-second Congress approached, he went to Washington hoping to take an active part in its deliberations. But it was not to be. Only once did he feel strong enough to go to the senate chamber. Then he remained confined to his rooms at the National

Hotel, a very ill man. But public affairs did not cease to break his repose. Early in the winter he received a visit from Horace Greeley, who informed him of the disturbing effect produced by the Fugitive Slave Law upon the people of the Northern States. Clay deplored that in framing that act no greater care had been taken so to shape its provisions as to spare the feelings of the citizens of the free States, but he thought it unadvisable now to attempt a change of the law.

From his sick chamber, Clay also gave his last warning counsel to the American people. It was when he spoke to Louis Kossuth.

The revolutionary movements in Europe, beginning in the early spring of 1848, had awakened the heartiest sympathies in America, none more than the struggle of the Hungarian people for national independence. In 1849 President Taylor had dispatched a special agent to Hungary to inquire whether the situation of that country would justify its recognition as an independent state. But when that agent arrived there, the intervention of Russia had already rendered the Hungarian armies unable to hold the field. The Austrian minister at Washington, Chevalier Huelsemann, made the sending of the special emissary the subject of formal complaint. Webster, then secretary of state, replied with the famous "Huelsemann letter," which electrified the national pride of the American people. Kossuth, the late "governor" of revolutionary Hungary, escaped into the Turkish dominions,

THE END

and the Sultan refused to surrender the fugitive to the Austrian government. The President of the United States was authorized by a joint resolution of the two houses of Congress, in March, 1851, to send an American man-of-war to the Mediterranean for the purpose of bringing Kossuth to America. Kossuth, accompanied by other Hungarian exiles, embarked on the United States frigate Mississippi on September 10. He spent a short time in England, where he was received with very great enthusiasm, and early in December he arrived at New York. The cause he represented appealed powerfully to the sympathies of a free people; and his own romantic history, his picturesque and impressive presence, and the intellectual richness of his oratory, gorgeous with Oriental luxuriance of phrase, and poured forth with the most melodious of voices and peculiarly captivating accents in a language not his own, fascinated all who saw and heard him. At once he confessed that he had come to enlist the government and the people of the American republic in the cause of his country. He hoped to renew the struggle of Hungary for national independence, and to find in the United States not only sentimental, but " operative," sympathy in the shape of " financial, material, and political aid."

The warm interest which the President and Congress had manifested in his fate, as well as the demonstrations of enthusiasm with which the people greeted him everywhere on his triumphal progress from place to place, were well calculated to encourage in him the hope that the American republic might abandon her traditional policy of non-entanglement, and take an active part in the struggles of his country. In fact, however, scarcely anybody thought soberly and seriously of casting aside the principles so impressively taught in Washington's Farewell Address, to embroil this republic in the turmoils and vicissitudes of the struggles disturbing the old world. But this secret conviction found little expression among those with whom Kossuth came into personal contact. Even at a banquet given in his honor at Washington, where Webster, the secretary of state, and several of the most prominent senators spoke, many of the speeches might have been interpreted as meaning that, if the American republic were not ready at once to throw overboard the principles of foreign policy faithfully adhered to from the beginning, it was only watching for a proper occasion to do so.

Kossuth had in his orations frequently mentioned Clay's name as that of the great advocate of South American independence and of the Greek cause. He solicited an interview with the old statesman, and Clay received him in his sick-chamber. Clay spoke to the distinguished visitor with cordial kindness and respect, but also with a frankness which excluded all misunderstanding. He assured Kossuth that Hungary, in her struggle for liberty and independence, had his liveliest sympathies. "But, sir," he added, "for the sake of my country you must allow me to protest against the policy you propose to her." As to the practical results of giving "material aid" to the Hungarian people in their struggle, he explained that war would probably be the consequence; that the United States could not carry on a land war on the European continent; that a maritime war would "result in mutual annoyance to commerce, but probably in little else;" that, "after effecting nothing in such a war, and after abandoning our ancient policy of amity and non-intervention in the affairs of other nations," the American republic would have justified European powers " in abandoning the terms of forbearance and non-interference" which they had so far preserved toward the United States; that, "after the downfall, perhaps, of the friends of liberal institutions in Europe, her despots, imitating and provoked by our fatal example," might turn upon us in the hour of our weakness and exhaustion; and that, while "the indomitable spirit of the American people would be equal to the emergency," yet the consequences might be terrible enough.

"You must allow me, sir [he continued], to speak thus freely, as I feel deeply, though my opinion may be of but little import as the expression of a dying man. Sir, the recent subversion of the republican government of France (by Louis Napoleon's *coup d'état* of the 2d of December, 1851), and that enlightened nation voluntarily placing its neck under the yoke of despotism, teach us to despair of any present success for liberal institutions in Europe. They give us an impressive warning not to rely upon others for the vindication of our principles, but to look to ourselves, and to cherish with more care than ever the security of our institutions and the preservation of our policy and principles. Far better is it for ourselves, for Hungary, and for the cause of liberty, that, adhering to our wise, pacific system, and avoiding the distant wars of Europe, we should keep our lamp burning brightly on this Western shore, as a light to all nations, than to hazard its utter extinction amid the ruins of fallen and falling republics in Europe."

This was not what Kossuth had come to hear. But it was what the American people really thought when sobered from the fascination of Kossuth's presence, and what other American statesmen would have said to him had they frankly expressed their sentiments.

The excitements preceding the presidential election, too, invaded the sick-chamber to draw from the dying man an expression of opinion which might be used in the contest then going on between various aspirants to the Whig nomination for the presidency. Clay's views as to the prospects of the Whig party were not sanguine. In June, 1851, he had written to Ullmann: "I think it quite clear that a Democrat will be elected, unless that result be prevented by divisions in the Democratic party. On these divisions the Whigs might advantageously count, if it were not for those which exist in their own party. It is, perhaps, safest to conclude that the divisions existing in the two parties will counterbalance each other. Party ties have no doubt been greatly weakened generally, and in particular localities have been almost entirely destroyed."

What he said about party disintegration was undoubtedly true. But that disintegration was far more advanced among the Whigs than among the Democrats. The Whigs had substantially lost their old programme, without uniting upon a substitute. The question of the day was to them only an element of division. The Northern anti-slavery Whigs, under the leadership of such men as Seward, remained in the party hoping to win the mastery of it. But that would have driven away the Southern Whigs, and thus rendered the existence of the party as a "national organization" in the geographical sense of the term impossible. Under the circumstances then existing, an anti-slavery party could only be a sectional party. To retain the Southern Whigs in the organization required concessions to slavery of which the compromise of 1850 might be regarded as the minimum. As to the vitality of the Whig party in its national character, the question was whether the Northern Whigs would accept and support the compromise in good faith. No doubt, Clay's prestige at the North as well as at the South, Webster's authority with his followers, and still more the desire of peace among the business community, prevailed upon many Northern Whigs, who might otherwise have strayed away, to acquiesce in the compromise. But the tendency adverse to it was, with a great many other Northern Whigs, too strong to yield to management.

When the thirty-second Congress assembled in December, 1851, an effort was made to unite the Whig members of the House in declaring the compromise a "finality;" but of the eighty-six Whig members only forty or fifty attended the caucus, and of these one third voted to lay the resolution on the table. Although it was adopted, only a minority of the members committed themselves in its favor. Similar efforts were made in the Senate and the House of Representatives, the principal effect of which consisted in a revival of the slavery discussion. The Southern Whigs were willing to accept the compromise as a "finality" until it should be found that slavery needed more protective legislation, while a large portion of the Northern Whigs refused to see in the compromise any adjustment at all. When on the 9th of April the Whig members of Congress held a caucus to fix upon time and place for the National Convention, and a "finality" resolution was laid upon the table, several members seceded from the meeting; and on the next day eleven Southern Whigs published an address declaring that no candidate for the presidency could have their support whose principles were not plainly defined, and who did not openly accept the compromise as they accepted it.

The discussion of the question whether the compromise was to be a finality had a strong flavor of the grotesque, for the very character of the discussion afforded the strongest proof that it was not, and could not be, an irreversible adjustment. Also the effort to unite the Whigs upon the basis of the compromise made manifest that the party could not be so united. There were in it too many men who had opinions of their own and clung to them. The task of the managers, who had to put the party in array for a presidential campaign, could not have been more perplexing. There seemed to be but one way to hold it together with the least prospect of success, — to find a candidate who possessed the confidence of both wings in a sufficient degree to harmonize them for a common effort. They tried another expedient, with disastrous result. The most prominent aspirants in the field were Daniel Webster and General Scott. By his seventh of March speech, and the bitter attacks upon the antislavery men which followed, Webster hoped to have won the confidence and support of the South. He also counted upon the active support of the administration, it being understood that Fillmore would under no circumstances himself be a candidate, and that Webster was his favorite. In both respects Webster was disappointed. The South did not trust him. His seventh of March speech had generally been looked upon as a change of attitude on his part, as an abandonment of his original principles. As he had thus changed once, so he might change again; and Webster appeared too large a man to be easily controlled. Moreover, while Webster still had many admiring followers in the North, it was thought that his change of attitude had only exasperated the more determined anti-slavery Whigs, and that, therefore, the great "fallen archangel" would by no means be a strong candidate in his own section. General Scott was the favorite of the anti-slavery Whigs, and, as such, suspicious to the Whigs of the South. Indeed, it was feared that, if Webster and Scott remained the only candidates in the field, the party might fall to pieces even before the time for the convention arrived.

The Southern Whigs, and those who consulted their tastes, therefore looked for a more available man, and found him in Fillmore, who had not only, as president, won the confidence of the Southern Whigs by zealously employing his whole power to enforce the compromise measures, but who possessed also a certain popularity with the mercantile element at the North. Neither did the anti-slavery Whigs dislike to see Fillmore brought forward as a candidate, for they thought that the efforts made for him would serve to hold the party together, while at the same time dividing the opposition to their own favorite, General Scott. Thus Fillmore was persuaded to enter the list of candidates, — much to Webster's disgust, who would have given vent to the bitterness of his disappointment had not party friends interposed. But the friendship between President and secretary of state was blighted, especially since Webster saw some reason to believe that Fillmore used the patronage of the government for the furtherance of his own candidacy.

While this war of ambitions was raging, Clay, from his sick-bed, advised his friends to support Fillmore. This advice was interpreted as an unkind thrust at Webster, prompted by motives of personal unfriendliness. The past relations of the two old statesmen were eagerly harrowed up to find the reason for what was called Clay's vindictive spirit. But those who attributed his conduct to such causes undoubtedly wronged him. Mean vindictiveness was not in his nature. His very enemies would hardly have charged him with a want of magnanimity. Whenever he had said or done anything that looked otherwise, it was in the heat of a conflict. The ambition, too, which in younger years might have excited his jealousy of a rival, had ceased to warp his feelings. He was now at peace with the world, expecting soon to leave it; and there could be none but reasons of the public good to inspire his mind. His motives for recommending Fillmore lay on the surface. Fillmore had from the beginning approved, and then as president faithfully executed, the compromise measures. His administration was fully identified with them. If elected he would simply continue in the old course. Clay considered him a man of national principles, who, not by mere promises, but by acts, had won the confidence of the

South, and who would, therefore, disarm the disunion feeling still active there; and, as a Northern man, too, enjoying in a large measure the respect of his own section, perhaps the only candidate capable of saving the Whig party. These expectations were disappointed, but nothing could have been more natural than that he should entertain them.

The Democratic National Convention met at Baltimore on June 1. In the Democratic ranks also there had been much dissension on the "finality" question, but it was more easily subdued by party discipline; and as the Southern interest was predominant in the Democratic organization, and the enforcement of the Fugitive Slave Law was insisted upon by the South, for the time being, as the principal part of the compromise not yet assured, the Democratic party, as the irony of fate would have it, gradually assumed the position of the special representative and champion of Clay's compromise. After a long struggle, the Democratic Convention nominated for the presidency Franklin Pierce of New Hampshire, a Northern man with Southern principles, and declared in its platform that the Democratic party would "abide by and adhere to a faithful execution of the acts known as the compromise measures settled by the last Congress, — the act for reclaiming fugitives from service or labor included."

The Whigs held their National Convention at the same place on June 10. It first adopted a platform declaring " that the series of acts of the thirty-first Congress — the act known as the Fugitive Slave Law included — are received and acquiesced in by the Whig party of the United States as a settlement, in principle and substance, of the dangerous and exciting questions which they embrace; and, so far as they are concerned, we will maintain them, and insist on their strict enforcement, until time and experience shall demonstrate the necessity of further legislation, to guard against the evasion of the laws on the one hand, and the abuse of their powers on the other, not impairing their efficiency ; " and, further, to frown down "all further agitation of the question thus settled, as dangerous to our peace," etc. This was the platform as the Southern Whigs desired it; and then, after many ballots, the results of which were peculiarly humiliating to Webster, who never received more than thirty-two votes, and among them not one from the South, the convention nominated for the presidency General Scott, the favorite of the anti-slavery Whigs. Thus the South had the platform, and the North the candidate; and by such means the party was to be held together. But no sooner was the result known than several Southern delegates declared that they would not agree to support the candidate unless he unequivocally accepted the platform together with the nomination.

While these things were going on, Clay was on his death-bed, growing weaker and weaker from day to day, the end coming fast. He still took interest enough in the affairs of the world to receive reports from the convention, and to express his satisfaction with what had been done.

In one respect he won the greatest triumph of his life at the close of it. Both political parties, his opponents as well as his friends, adopted his measures as the very foundation of their policy. The genius of statesmanship, it would seem, could hardly have achieved a triumph more complete.

This the eyes of the dying man were still permitted to see. But what they did not see was that this triumph would be speedily followed by the complete collapse of the policy he had advocated; that the peace effected by his "adjustment" would prove only a hollow truce, bearing in itself the germs of conflicts more terrible than his imagination had ever conceived; that the Fugitive Slave Law would be the greatest propagator of abolitionism which Machiavelian ingenuity could have devised; that his non-intervention with regard to slavery in New Mexico and Utah would soon serve as sponsor for Douglas's Kansas-Nebraska Bill, and thus bring slavery and free labor face to face, musket in hand, for a deadly conflict on the plains of the West; that a new school of statesmanship was rising up which, to save the republic and its free institutions, would throw compromise to the winds; and a new generation of statesmen, who, with tremendous effect, would lead into battle for liberty and Union that very "sentiment" which he, appreciating neither its character nor its force, had asked the people of the North to sacrifice for the sake of the Union. There they were already when he, tottering with age and bowed down by illness, cast his last look into the senate chamber, — in Daniel Webster's chair Charles Sumner, the champion of the anti-slavery conscience, joining hands with Seward, the philosophical anti-slavery politician; and Benjamin F. Wade, the very embodiment of defiant courage, sent by Ohio as the colleague of Salmon P. Chase.

Some portentous things Clay might have seen even before he closed his eyes: his party hopelessly divided in sentiment, and doomed to destruction in consequence of the very measures of peace with which he had sought to save the Union, vainly trying to prolong its existence by giving the South the platform and the North the candidate; Southern Whigs, in spite of the platform, repudiating its action because of the candidate, and Northern Whigs uselessly striving to save the candidate by repudiating the platform. He might have foreseen how the people would spurn the whole nauseous bargain by giving the Democrats, who had at least the merit of greater straightforwardness, an overwhelming majority of electoral votes; how the Whig party would suffer not only defeat, but annihilation, and how appropriate would be the epitaph suggested for it by a grim popular humor: "Here lies the Whig party, which died of an effort to swallow the Fugitive Slave Law."

Clay, although terribly exhausted by his tormenting cough, lingered on longer than his physicians and attendants expected. Devoted friends surrounded him, and in his last days two of his sons were at his bedside. While he was still able to write or dictate letters, he repeatedly said that, as the world receded from him, he felt his affections more than ever centred on his children and theirs, and that he would be glad to get home once more. He professed himself perfectly composed and resigned to his fate. On May 8 his son Thomas wrote to his wife: "Had you seen, as I have, the evidences of attachment and interest displayed by my father's friends, you could not help exclaiming, as he has frequently done: 'Was there ever man had such friends!' The best and first in the land are daily and hourly offering tokens of their love and esteem for him." He remained a winner of hearts to his last day. He died on June 29, 1852, in the seventy-sixth year of his age. On July 1 the members of the Senate and the House of Representatives, together with the city authorities, militia companies, and civic associations, accompanied his remains from the National Hotel to the senate chamber, where, attended by the President of the United States, the cabinet, and the officers of the army and navy, the funeral services took place. The remains were then taken to his beloved Kentucky, the funeral cortége passing through Baltimore, Wilmington, Philadelphia, the principal places in New Jersey, New York, Albany, Ithaca,

THE END

Syracuse, Rochester, Buffalo, Cleveland, Cincinnati, Louisville, everywhere the people assembling by thousands to do the last honor to Henry Clay. On July 10 his ashes were laid to rest at Lexington, where now an imposing monument marks his tomb.

Not only the halls of Congress, but the whole country resounded with obituary eulogy of the dead statesman. It was more than ordinarily the voice of genuine feeling that spoke. The bereaved affection of his personal friends broke out in loud lament. Even among his opponents the brilliancy of his talents, coupled with so knightly a character, had won a warm-hearted admiration, which found ample utterance. Every patriotic man in the land proudly called him a great American. Nobody wished to remember his faults, or to be over-critical in the praise of his virtues and in the estimation of his public services. It was not at all surprising that, as his enthusiastic nature had always appealed to the emotions, the most generous impulses of the popular heart should have followed him to the grave.

Henry Clay himself had by no means been indifferent to the fame he would leave behind him. In his correspondence there are frequent symptoms of his solicitude as to his place in the history of his country. Nine months before his death, in a letter to Daniel Ullmann, he made some suggestions concerning the inscription to be put upon a large gold medal which his friends in New York caused to be struck in commemoration of his public services. The inscription, as amended by him, read thus: —

SENATE, 1806.
SPEAKER, 1811.
WAR OF 1812 WITH GREAT BRITAIN.
GHENT, 1814.
SPANISH AMERICA, 1822.
MISSOURI COMPROMISE, 1821.
AMERICAN SYSTEM, 1824.
GREECE, 1824.
SECRETARY OF STATE, 1825.
PANAMA INSTRUCTIONS, 1826.
TARIFF COMPROMISE, 1833.
PUBLIC DOMAIN, 1833–1841.
PEACE WITH FRANCE PRESERVED, 1835.
COMPROMISE, 1850.

These were the salient points of his career which Clay himself desired most to be remembered. Singularly enough, the policy of internal improvements was not named in this enumeration, and it is a significant fact that the longest and bitterest of his political struggles — that for the Bank of the United States against Jackson — could not be mentioned in the list of his public services; nor would his efforts to be made president of the United States, which had so intensely engaged his mind and heart, fit a record of the things he was proud of.

But, however incomplete, that record showed how large a place Henry Clay had filled in the public affairs of the republic during almost half a century of its existence. His most potent faculty has left the most imperfect monuments behind it.

He was without question the greatest parliamentary orator, and one of the greatest popular speakers, America has ever had. Webster excelled him in breadth of knowledge, in keenness of reasoning, in weight of argument, and in purity of diction. But Clay possessed in a far higher degree the true oratorical temperament, — that force of nervous exaltation which makes the orator feel himself, and appear to others, a superior being, and almost irresistibly transfuses his thoughts, his passions, and his will into the mind and heart of the listener. Webster would instruct and convince and elevate, but Clay would overcome his audience. There could scarcely be a more striking proof of his power than the immediate effect we know his speeches to have produced upon those who heard them, compared with the impression of heavy tameness we receive when merely reading the printed reports.

In the elements, too, which make a man a leader, Clay was greatly the superior of Webster, as well as of all other contemporaries, excepting Andrew Jackson. He had not only in rare development the faculty of winning the affectionate devotion of men, but his personality imposed itself without an effort so forcibly upon others that they involuntarily looked to him for direction, waited for his decisive word before making up their minds, and not seldom yielded their better judgment to his will-power.

While this made him a very strong leader, he

was not a safe guide. The rare brightness of his intellect and his fertile fancy served, indeed, to make himself and others forget his lack of accurate knowledge and studious thought; but these brilliant qualities could not compensate for his deficiency in that prudence and forecast which are required for the successful direction of political forces. His impulses were vehement, and his mind not well fitted for the patient analysis of complicated problems and of difficult political situations. His imagination frequently ran away with his understanding. His statesmanship had occasionally something of the oratorical character. Now and then he appeared to consider it as important whether a conception or a measure would sound well, as whether, if put into practice, it would work well. He disliked advice which differed from his preconceived opinions; and with his imperious temper and ardent combativeness he was apt, as in the struggle about the United States Bank, to put himself, and to hurry his party, into positions of great disadvantage. It is a remarkable fact that during his long career in Congress he was in more or less pronounced opposition to all administrations, even those of his own party, save that of Jefferson, under which he served only one short session in the Senate, and that of John Quincy Adams, of which he was a member. During Madison's first term, Clay helped in defeating the re-charter of the United States Bank recommended by Gallatin as secretary of the treasury; and he became a firm supporter of Madison's administration only when, as to the war against Great Britain, it had yielded to his pressure. No fault can be found with him for asserting in all important things the freedom of his opinion; but a less impetuous statesman would have found it possible to avoid a conflict with Monroe, and to maintain harmonious relations with General Taylor.

On the other hand, he never sought to organize or strengthen his following by the arts of the patronage-monger. The thought that a political party should be held together by the public plunder, or that the party leader should be something like a paymaster of a body of henchmen at the public expense, or that a party contest should be a mere scramble for spoils, was entirely foreign to his mind, and far below the level of his patriotic aspirations.

It has been said that Clay was surrounded by a crowd of jobbers and speculators eager to turn his internal improvement and tariff policies to their private advantage. No doubt those policies attracted such persons to him. But there is no reason for suspecting that he was ever in the slightest degree pecuniarily interested in any scheme which might have been advanced by his political position or influence. In no sense was he a money-maker in politics. His integrity as a public man remained without blemish throughout his long career. He preserved an equally intact name in the conduct of his private affairs. In money matters he was always a man of honor, maintaining the principles and the pride of a gentleman. The financial embarrassments which troubled his declining days were caused, not by reckless extravagance, nor by questionable speculations, but by the expenses inseparable from high public station and great renown, and by engagements undertaken for others, especially his sons. He was a kind husband and an indulgent father. There is ample evidence of his warm solicitude as to the welfare of his children, of his constant readiness to assist them with his counsel, and of his self-sacrificing liberality in providing for their needs and in aiding them in their troubles. The attacks made upon his private character touched mainly his occasional looseness in his social intercourse and his fondness for card-playing, which, although in his early years he had given up games of chance, still led him to squander but too much time upon whist. Such attacks injured his character because they were not unfounded; and it appears by no means improbable that charges of this kind, striking a vulnerable point, may, in spite of the enthusiastic devotion of many of his friends, which was ready to overlook or forgive any shortcoming, have had something to do with what was called his ill luck as a candidate for the presidency.

The desire of so distinguished a political leader to be president was natural and legitimate. Even had he cherished it less ardently, his followers would have more than once pushed him forward.

But no one can study Clay's career without feeling that he would have been a happier and a greater man if he had never coveted the glittering prize. When such an ambition becomes chronic, it will be but too apt to unsettle the character and darken the existence of those afflicted with it by confusing their appreciation of all else. As Cæsar said that the kind of death most to be desired was "a sudden one," so the American statesman may think himself fortunate to whom a nomination for the presidency comes, if at all, without a long agony of hope and fear. During a period of thirty years, from the time when he first aspired to be Monroe's successor until 1848, Clay unceasingly hunted the shadow whose capture would probably have added nothing either to his usefulness or his fame, but the pursuit of which made his public life singularly restless and unsatisfactory to himself. Nor did he escape from the suspicion of having occasionally modified the expression of his opinions according to supposed exigencies of availability. The peculiar tone of his speech against the abolitionists before the campaign of 1840, his various letters on the annexation of Texas in 1844, and some equivocations on other subjects during the same period, illustrated the weakening influence of the presidential candidate upon the man; and even his oft-quoted word that he would "rather be right than be president" was spoken at a time when he was more desirous of being president than sure of being right.

But, on the whole, save his early change of position on the subject of the United States Bank, Clay's public career appears remarkably consistent in its main feature. It was ruled by the idea that, as the binding together of the States in the Union and the formation of a constitutional government had been accomplished by the compromising of diverse interests, this Union and this constitutional government had to be maintained in the same way; and that every good citizen should consider it his duty, whenever circumstances required it, to sacrifice something, not only of his material advantages, but even of his sentiments and convictions, for the peace and welfare of the common republic.

Whatever Clay's weaknesses of character and errors in statesmanship may have been, almost everything he said or did was illumined by a grand conception of the destinies of his country, a glowing national spirit, a lofty patriotism. Whether he thundered against British tyranny on the seas, or urged the recognition of the South American sister republics, or attacked the highhanded conduct of the military chieftain in the Florida war, or advocated protection and internal improvements, or assailed the one-man power and spoils politics in the person of Andrew Jackson, or entreated for compromise and conciliation regarding the tariff or slavery; whether what he advocated was wise or unwise, right or wrong, — there was always ringing through his words a fervid plea for his country, a zealous appeal in behalf of the

THE END

honor and the future greatness and glory of the republic, or an anxious warning lest the Union, and with it the greatness and glory of the American people, be put in jeopardy. It was a just judgment which he pronounced upon himself when he wrote: "If any one desires to know the leading and paramount object of my public life, the preservation of this Union will furnish him the key."

INDEX

ABERDEEN, LORD, mentions desire of England to abolish slavery, ii. 248; his dispatch used by Calhoun to justify annexation of Texas, 249.

Abolitionists, difference between their view of slavery and that of Clay, i. 306, 307; rise of, ii. 71, 72; form societies, their demands, 72, 73; not at first successful in agitation, 73; denounced by South, their suppression demanded, 74; mobs against, in North, 75; elements of opposition to, 75, 76; their true character and heroism, 76, 77; never attain popularity, 78; their effect upon the North, 78; petition Congress to abolish slavery in District of Columbia, 79; attempt to exclude their publications from mail, 82, 83; in spite of disclaimer, held by South to instigate slave revolt, 83, 84; denounced by Jackson, 84; Calhoun's bill to exclude their publications from mail, 85; growth of movement, 153; lose influence by running into abstract speculations, 153; their cause now goes on by itself, 153; and enters politics, 154; begin to exercise political influence, 163; oppose Whigs more bitterly than Democrats, 163, 164; denounce Clay, 164; considered very dangerous by Clay, 164; Clay's attacks upon, 165–168, 170, 232; petition for dissolution of Union, 233; attempts of Clay to discredit, 236; condemn Clay's Raleigh letter, 246; relations with Liberty party, 254; criticise Clay's plan of emancipation, 318; denounced by Clay for disturbing compromise, 381; denounced by Webster, 387.

Adair, Gen. John, resigns seat in United States Senate, i. 35, 47.

Adams, Charles Francis, nominated for Vice-President at Buffalo convention, ii. 312.

Adams, John, errors of Federalists during his administration, i. 32.

Adams, John Quincy, receives Russian offer of mediation, i. 99; nominated peace commissioner, 100, 101; his character and abilities, 102, 103; disapproves of Clay's convivial habits, 104; describes lack of harmony in commission, 104; quarrels with Clay over fisheries and Mississippi navigation, 110, 111; describes Clay's certainty of British desire for peace, 111; describes Clay's ill-temper, 112, 113; quarrels with Clay over custody of papers, 113; acquiesces in Clay's wish to present article on impressments, 115; describes Clay's dissatisfaction with treaty, 115, 116; regrets too great conviviality at Ghent, 123; negotiates commercial convention in England, 123, 124; appointed secretary of state by Monroe, 141; enmity of Clay toward, 149; describes Monroe's annoyance at Clay's attacks, 150; justifies Jackson's campaign in Florida, 152; tells story of Clay's gambling losses, 160; on proposal to displace Clay as speaker, 161; concludes treaty with Spain acquiring Florida and settling Louisiana boundary, 162, 163; reluctant to abandon Texas, 164; describes conversation with Clay on recognition of South American republics, 169, 170; considers them unfit for self-government, 170; on significance of Missouri question,

174; approves of Missouri Compromise, 198; willing to divide Union into free and slave countries, 198, 199; describes Clay in an unfriendly manner, 201; condemns Clay's loose public morals, 202; controls foreign policy of Monroe's administration, 210; candidate for presidency, his career and character, 226; his political puritanism, 226–228; refuses to work for himself, 227; suggests supporting Jackson for Vice-President, 232; receives eighty-four electoral votes, 232; early determination of Clay to use influence for, 238, 239; accused in anonymous letter of bargaining with Clay, 242; evidence of his diary against any bargain and corruption story, 247, 248; visited by Clay's friends, 247; and by Webster and Clay, 247; his election secured by Clay, 248; offers Clay State Department, 249; question of propriety of his action, 249–251; his impartiality in choosing officers, 249; offers Crawford Treasury Department, 249; wishes to offer Jackson War Department, 250; questionable appearance of the transaction, 250, 251; previous enmities of Clay with, 251; his controversy with Russell not upheld by Clay, 251; inaugurated, 254; congratulated by Jackson, 255; his administration the last of old school, 258; his policy in nominating officers, 258; his cabinet, 258; appoints King minister to England, 259; plan of Sterret to insult, 259, 260; refuses to remove Sterret, 260; his reasons, 260, 261; his rigidly consistent policy, 261; sees formation of a Southern party, 265; makes far-reaching suggestions as to internal improvements, 265, 266; his constitutional doctrines, 266, 267; announces appointment of envoys to Panama Congress, 267; his cautious attitude toward South America, 268, 269; attacked by Randolph, 273; by Jackson, 276; describes bitter feeling in Congress, 278; attacked by Duff Green, 280; refuses to punish intriguing officials, 281; refuses to dismiss McLean, 282; slandered in campaign of 1828, 288; does not expect to win, 288; defeated in election, 288; his civil service policy not the only cause of defeat, 289; his defeat inevitable, 289, 290; destroys chances by his severity and coldness, 292; inspired by Clay with interest in Panama Congress, 294; issues retaliatory proclamation against England, 298; does not object to negotiations with England regarding return of fugitive slaves, 307; his friendly relations with Clay during administration, 309; eulogizes Clay after 1828, 310; depressed by defeat in election, 311; his election causes break in Republican party, 312; not opposed on grounds of principle, 313; accused of Federalism by opposition, 315; his connections with Federalist and Republican parties, 317; hated by Federalists on account of his changing sides, 317; his followers from Whig party, 319; supported by anti-Masons, 342; on importance of anti-Masonic movement, 345; describes Clay's dogmatic leadership, 360, 361; on committee to investigate United States Bank, 374; makes a minority report, 374; considers Jackson about to yield to nullifiers, ii. 6; describes Clay's opinion of Indians, 59; begins struggle for right of petition, 82; condemns attitude of Jackson toward Mexico, 94; describes superiority of Clay over Calhoun in debate, 149; on enmity between Clay and Webster, 175; on Clay's "crowing" too much, 192; on Tyler's legal status as President, 201; answers Tyler's veto severely, 227; wishes to continue to defy Tyler, 227; secures repeal of gag rule, 233; presents disunion petition, 233; attempt to censure, 233; his bitter defense, 233, 234; votes against Mexican war bill, 284; his death in House of Representatives, 298.

INDEX

Adams, Dr. William, English peace commissioner, i. 105; on commission to treat concerning commerce, 124.

Alexander, Emperor of Russia, offers to mediate between England and United States, i. 99; unable to help in 1814, 106; looked upon by Americans as "benevolent uncle," 270; asked to urge Spain to recognize independence of colonies, 271; arbitrates claim for slave compensation in favor of United States, 300.

Alien and Sedition Laws, opposition to, in Kentucky, i. 31-33.

Allen, Charles, bolts Whig party, ii. 306.

Allibone, S. A., letter of Clay to, on danger of disunion, ii. 391.

Ambrister, Robert, executed by Jackson, i. 152; case debated in Congress, 153-157.

America, Central, Clay's treaty with, i. 299.

Anderson, Richard C., envoy to Panama Congress, i. 293; death, 293.

Anti-Masons, their origin, i. 341, 342; support Adams in 1828, 342; hold balance of power in New York, 343; spread over North, 343; denounced by Clay, 343, 344; nominate Wirt for President, 344; wish Clay to withdraw, 344; their strong membership, 345; carry Vermont in 1832, 383.

Anti-slavery movement of Revolution, i. 27-29; its theoretical character and slight results, 28; feeble in Kentucky, 30; practically dead in 1820, 172, 173; continues to exist feebly, ii. 71.

Arbuthnot. See Ambrister.

Armstrong, John, protests against French seizures of American ships, i. 74.

Ashburton, Lord, negotiates with Webster, ii. 218, 279.

Astor, John J., relieves Treasury in 1813, i. 99.

Atkinson, Simeon, compared with Kremer by Webster, i. 243.

Austin, Moses, founds colony in Texas, ii. 88.

BADGER, GEORGE E., secretary of navy, ii. 191; meeting of cabinet at his house, 213; in Senate of 1849, 330; supports Clay's compromise, 350.

Bankrupt law, recommended by Van Buren, ii. 134; repealed, 222.

Banks, state, their growth after lapse of first United States Bank, i. 131; cause inflation and suspension, 131, 132; deposits distributed among, by Taney, ii. 29, 51; rivalry among, for deposits, 52; great expansion of, 52; expand loans and circulation, 116; enormous increase of, 117; play part in land speculation, 118; amount of government deposits in, 120; doubt as to safety of, 120; bill to protect deposits in, 121; arbitrary treatment of, by government, 122; obliged to contract loans in order to distribute surplus, 123; embarrassed by specie circular, 125; suspend specie payments in 1837, 128; failure of pet bank scheme admitted by Van Buren, 133; removal of deposits from, denounced by Whigs, 138; process of resumption of specie payments by, 143, 144.

Bank of United States, history of the first, i. 62, 63; opposition to its re-charter, 63; upheld by Gallatin, 64; opposed by Gallatin's enemies in Senate, 64; held unconstitutional by Clay, 64-66; defeated, 66; second one proposed by Dallas, 132; bill to charter, its features, 132; opposed by Federalists, supported by Republicans, 133; argument of Clay in behalf of, 133-135; doubts of Jackson as to policy of re-chartering, 347, 353; secures sound currency in South and West, 352; its able management, 352; cause of Jackson's hostility to, 353, 354; attacked and slandered by kitchen cabinet, 354; supported in Congress, 355; failure of Jackson to stir opinion against, 355, 356; report of Secretary McLane in favor of, 355, 356; advised by Whigs against any compromise with Jackson, 356; its officers wish to keep it out of politics, 356; determination of Clay to use it against Jackson, 356, 357; eulogized by Whigs in platform, 357, 358; petitions for re-charter, 358; favorable reports on, 373; attacked by Benton, 374; investigated, 374; report of committee condemns, 374; re-charter bill vetoed, 375, 376; determination of Jackson to crush, 375; denounced by Jackson as a dangerous monopoly, 376; Clay's arguments of 1811 against, used by Jackson, 376, 377; defended in Senate, 377; Democrats obliged to choose between it and Jackson, 378, 379; its veto thought by Clay to ruin Jackson, 379, 380; aids Whig campaign, 382; Clay's blunder in dragging it into politics, 383, 384; withdrawal of deposits from, suggested by Kendall, ii. 26; deposits in, voted safe by House, 26; suspected by Jackson of corruption, 26; refusal of Duane to remove deposits from, 27, 28; popular objections to removal, 28; Jackson's "paper to the cabinet," 28; deposits removed from, by Taney, 29; curtails loans, 29; denounced by Jackson in message, 30; removal of deposits from, defended by Taney, 30, 31; debate on, in Senate, 32-37; petition against attack upon, presented to Senate, 37, 38; held by Jackson responsible for distress, 40; grows increasingly unpopular, 47, 48; resolutions against in House, 48; discussion of its character, 49-52; at first nonpartisan, 49; its capacity for mischief, 49; driven by Jackson to use power in defense, 50; really unsuitable to a democratic country, 50, 51; inferior to Chase's system, 51; first contracts, then expands loans, 116, 117; its re-charter advocated by Webster and Clay after panic of 1837, 142; its subsequent career and failure, 143, 144; Tyler's doubtful position on, 202, 203; third one recommended by Ewing, 205, 206; bill to incorporate, passed by Congress, 206; vetoed by Tyler, 206; popular mandate for, claimed by Clay, 208, 209; attempt to pass a charter agreeable to Tyler, 209, 210; again vetoed, 210; probable good results of Tyler's veto, 210, 211; killed by veto, 211; not mentioned in Whig platform, 256; abandoned as obsolete by Clay, 300.

Barbour, James, proposes a convention to dissolve the Union, i. 196, 197; secretary of war under Adams, 258; disapproves Adams's position on internal improvements, 266.

Barbour, Philip P., defeated for speakership by Clay, i. 204.

"Barnburners," in New York, their leaders, ii. 304; advocate Wilmot Proviso, 304; withdraw from Democratic Convention, 305; nominate Van Buren for President, 311; their motives, 311; attend Free Soil Convention, 312; return to Democratic party, 315, 342.

Barnwell, Robert W., defends Rhett against Clay, declares secession sentiments to be those of South Carolina, ii. 358.

Barry, William T., postmaster-general under Jackson, i. 330.

Bayard, James A., superior in reasoning to Clay, i. 48; nominated peace commissioner, 100, 101; holds to opinions stubbornly, 104.

Bayard, Richard H., against expunging resolution, ii. 102; against distributing fourth installment of surplus, 136.

Bebb, Governor William, assures Clay he can carry Ohio, ii. 299.

Bell, John, supports repeal of four years' term act, ii. 69; secretary of war, 191; introduces compromise resolutions, 347; supports Clay's compromise, 350.

Benton, Thomas H., canvasses for Clay in 1824, i. 228; told by Clay of intention to support Adams, 238; asserts that "demos krateo" principle requires election of Jackson, 240; his admiration of Clay's

INDEX

"high-toned" duel with Randolph, 274, 275; in error as to origin of Jackson's hostility to bank, 353; attacks bank in Senate fruitlessly, 355; advocates cheap public lands, 370; criticises Clay's plan to distribute proceeds of sale of public lands, 371, 372; draws up charges against bank, 374; defends Jackson's veto, 378; tells Democrats they must choose between bank and Jackson, 379; wrangles with Clay, 379; on Verplanck's tariff bill, ii. 8; describes popular approval of compromise tariff, 20; his dreaded "money king," 33; describes Van Buren during Clay's appeal, 39; opposes resolutions condemning Jackson's protest, 43; supports repeal of four years' term act, 69; on date of beginning of slavery debate, 71; his campaign to expunge resolutions of censure, 100; his expunging motion, 100, 101; claims popular will demands it, 101, 102; on Clay's speech, 104; finds it difficult to hold party together, 104, 105; denounces "bank ruffians," 106; introduces specie resolution into Senate, 124; on effect of specie circular, 125; satirized by Clay, 207; comments on Clay's valedictory, 226; attempt of Tyler to conciliate, by appointing Fremont to office, 239; claims to have been tricked into voting for Texas annexation resolution, 272; in Senate of 1849, 330; his reasons for opposing Compromise, 350; ridicules Clay's "bleeding wounds," 353.

Bentzon, ——, plays cards with Clay, i. 104.

Berlin Decree, issued, i. 69; said to be revoked, 74, 87.

Berrien, John M., attorney-general under Jackson, i. 330; consults with Tyler's cabinet concerning bank, ii. 209; in Senate in 1849, 330.

Beverly, Carter, describes Jackson's statement of bargain story, i. 282, 283; writes to Clay retracting his share in bargain story, 285.

Biddle, Nicholas, refuses to dismiss Mason to please Jackson, i. 354; wishes to keep bank out of politics, 354; delighted with Jackson's veto message, 379; accused by Jackson of causing distress, ii. 40; his management of bank at first excellent, 49; resigns presidency of bank, prosecuted, 144; his death, 144.

Birney, James G., significance of vote for, in 1840, ii. 190; nominated for President in 1843, 254; his character and principles, 255; relations with Clay, 255; his vote in New York gives State to Polk, 265.

Blair, Francis P., letter of Clay to, on presidential election of 1824, i. 236; letter of Clay to, on Adams and Jackson, 239; on charges of bribery, 248; supplants Green in kitchen cabinet, 346; turned against Clay through "relief" movement in Kentucky, 346; edits the "Globe," 347; suggests removal of deposits, ii. 26.

Bolivar, Simon, his eulogistic letter to Clay, i. 295; gloomy reply of Clay to, 295, 296.

Bonaparte, Napoleon, invades Spain, i. 58; issues Berlin and Milan decrees, 69; wishes to force United States into war with England, 70; issues Rambouillet decree, 74; orders Champagny to declare to United States the revocation of Berlin and Milan decrees, 74; refuses reparation for captures under Rambouillet decree, 76; causes fictitious decree revoking Berlin and Milan decrees to be shown, 87; Republicans accused of subserviency to, 90; his retreat from Moscow, 99; his downfall leaves England free to crush United States, 106.

Boone, Daniel, his career in Kentucky, 113.

Branch, John, secretary of navy under Jackson, i. 330.

Brazil, treaty of Clay with, i. 299.

Bright, Jesse D., in Senate in 1849, ii. 330.

INDEX

Brooke, Francis, Clay's correspondence with, in 1824, i. 229; letters of Clay to, on Jackson, 239, 241; on charges of corruption, 248; letter to, on acceptance of State Department, 252, 253; letter of Clay to, on Anti-Masons, 344; letter of Clay to, on rejection of Van Buren's nomination, 369; letter of Clay to, on nullification proclamation, ii. 8; letter of Clay to, on life at Ashland, 24; letter describing Clay's journey, 25; letter on alliance with Calhoun, 46; letter to, on plan to oppose Van Buren, 131; letter to, on Calhoun, 163; letter to, on necessity of attracting Democrats, 174; letter to, on spoils, 194; on retiring from Senate, 222.

Brooke, Robert, studies of Clay with, i. 8, 10.

Bryant, William Cullen, tries to support Polk and oppose Texas, ii. 259, 271; a Barnburner, 312.

Buchanan, James, refuses to corroborate Jackson's story of Clay's attempt at a deal, i. 284; his letter called a vindication by Jackson's friends, 286; votes against repeal of four years' term, ii. 69; moves to receive abolition petitions, but reject the prayer contained, 80; votes for Calhoun's bill to exclude abolition matter from mails, 86; reports resolution indorsing Jackson's attitude toward Mexico, 95; supports expunging resolution, 102; satirized by Clay, 207; secretary of state under Polk, 273; asks Mexico if it will receive an envoy with full powers, 276; affirms right to whole of Oregon, but offers forty-ninth parallel, 280, 281; on refusal, threatens to insist on all of Oregon, 281.

Burr, Aaron, his Western scheme, i. 34; motion to arrest, on charge of unlawful enterprise against Spain, 34; asks Clay for counsel, 35; upheld by popular sympathy, 35; explains at length his schemes, 35, 36; asserts that Jefferson supports him, 36; defended by Clay, 36; later anger of Clay with, 37; repulsed by Clay in 1815, 37.

Bush, ——, assaulted by Daviess, i. 33; action of Clay in behalf of, 34.

Butler, Benjamin F., appointed attorney-general, ii. 29; a Barnburner, 312; reports platform at Buffalo Convention, 312.

Butler, Andrew P., in Senate in 1849, ii. 330; leads extreme pro-slavery wing, 350.

CALHOUN, JOHN C., one of the war Republicans, i. 78; leader of new school, 128, 129; supports protection in 1816 to help cotton interest, 130; leads in advocating internal improvements, 137; his loose construction of Constitution, 137; secretary of war under Monroe, 142; urges punishing Jackson for lawlessness, 152; withdraws from candidacy for President, 223; supported for Vice-President by Jacksonians, 232; elected Vice-President, 233; begins to organize pro-slavery party, 265; relations of Green with, 346; quarrel of Jackson with, 348; his friends driven from administration, 348; secures rejection of Van Buren's nomination by casting vote, 369; advocates nullification in "Address to South Carolina," ii. 2, 3; his argument, 3; repeats manifesto in 1832, 3, 4; resigns vice-presidency, 8; elected to Senate, 8; conferred with by Clay as to compromise tariff, 11; his reasons for preferring Clay's bill to Verplanck's, 12–14; not alarmed by Jackson's threats, but by popular support to administration, 13; prefers Clay's bill because avowedly a compromise, 13, 14; opposes home valuation amendment, 16; forced by Clayton to vote for it, 17; with Clay and Webster in opposition to Jackson, 30; supports resolutions condemning Jackson's protest, 43; galls Clay by repeating nullification principles, 46; his alliance with Clay unnatural, 46; reports abuses in executive patronage, 61, 62; advocates resolution to compel President to give reasons for removal, 62; supports repeal of four years' term act, 69; denounces abolition petitions, and moves not to receive them, 79; holds that Congress is unable to declare what publications are incendiary, 84; wishes government to follow States, 84; introduces bill to exclude abolition matter from mails in States where it is prohibited, 85; his doctrines denounced by Whigs, 85, 86; his bill defeated, 86; favors immediate annexation of Texas, 92; opposes expunging resolution, 102; his view of distribution of surplus as a loan, 121, 122; moves amendment to sub-treasury bill, 137; dissolves alliance with Clay in public letter attacking Whigs, 145; his personal debate with Clay and Webster, 146-149; claims a consistent "record," 147; describes his triumph over Clay in 1833, 147; attacked by Clay in return, 147, 148; inferior as an orator to Clay, 148; his account of compromise of 1833 at variance with facts, 148; never a Whig, 149; origin of his change in principles, 149; his one aim to strengthen slavery, 150; disingenuous arguments, 150; unable to remain silent on slavery, 155, 156; introduces resolutions defending slavery and condemning opposition, 156, 157; demands a test vote, 157; doubtful of his ability to maintain slavery in Union, 157, 158; repudiates Clay's resolutions on slavery, 161; refuses to yield an inch to North, 161, 162; his resolutions amended and adopted, 162; weakness of his position, 162; suspected by Clay of ambition to lead South, 163; eulogizes Clay's speech against abolitionists, 168; asserts slavery to be a blessing, 169; offers resolutions protesting against liberation of Enterprise slaves, 170; ridiculed by Clay, 207; shakes hands with Clay after valedictory, 226; accepts State Department from Tyler solely to annex Texas, 241; makes half-promise to protect Texas during negotiations, 241; knows his position to be false, 241, 242; submits treaty and Aberdeen's dispatch to Senate, 248; holds annexation necessary to prevent abolition of slavery, 249; works to prevent nomination of Van Buren, 251; negotiates concerning Oregon, 280; declines arbitration, 280; dreads war with England and wishes compromise, 282; introduces resolutions asserting necessity of slavery in territories, 302; rejects squatter sovereignty, 303; insists on right of slaveholders under Constitution to take slaves into territories, 304; attempts to organize a Southern party, 321; meets Clay for last time in Senate, 330; his last oration read to Senate by Mason, 338; wishes to force issue, 338, 339; argues that only by complete equilibrium can Union be maintained, 339; his position hopeless, 340; his death, 340; right in his belief of danger to slavery, 367; his error, 368.

California, preparations to seize, in 1845-1846, ii. 276, 277, 278; seized by Fremont, 285; discovery of gold in and settlement of, 320; organization of, proposed by Polk, 320; protests against introduction of slavery, 320, 321; forms a state constitution prohibiting slavery, 321, 322; admission of, urged by Taylor, 326, 327; declared inevitable by Clay, 331; admission proposed in compromise of 1850, 332; demanded by Seward, 343; constitution of, referred to select committee, 347; Clay's policy toward, 347, 348; admitted over protest of slave States, 362, 363.

Cambreleng, C. C., a Barnburner, ii. 311.

Canada, conquest of, expected by Clay, i. 79, 86; failure of attempts to invade, 86, 87; invasion of, denounced by Quincy, 89; attack upon, defended by Clay, 97; attempt of House to secure return of fugitive slaves from, 300; "Patriot war" in, ii. 151.

Canning, George, succeeded by Wellesley, i. 73; haughty attitude towards United States, 298; death, 298.

Cass, Lewis, congratulates Clay on vindication from Kremer's slander, i. 257; moves inquiry into condition of army and navy, ii. 281; nominated for presidency, 305; his position on Wilmot Proviso, 305; distrusted by South Carolina, 309; defeated in election, 314; in Senate in 1849, 330; supports Clay's compromise, 350.

Castlereagh, Lord, his letter to Foster on Orders in Council, i. 84; letter of Liverpool to, on American war, 108; congratulates Liverpool on Peace of Ghent, 118; said by Clay to dictate Monroe's policy, 166.

Champagny, announces revocation of Berlin and Milan decrees, i. 75.

Charles X., resents Jackson's language concerning claims on France, ii. 53.

Chase, Salmon P., his banking system superior to the United States Bank, ii. 51; leads at Liberty convention of 1843, 255; in Senate in 1849, 330; his statesmanship, 330; asserts purpose to persevere even if Wilmot Proviso be shelved, 345; understands future better than old statesmen, 347.

Cherokees, opposed by Jackson in dispute with Georgia, i. 347; aid to their emigration advocated by Clay, ii. 59-61.

Chesapeake, attacked by Leopard, i. 71; captured by Shannon, 105.

Cheves, Langdon, one of war Republicans, i. 78; favors increased navy, 80; successful president of second bank, 352.

Choate, Rufus, in campaign of 1840, ii. 187.

Church, Sanford E., a Barnburner, ii. 311.

Civil service, administration of, by Adams, i. 258; refusal of Adams to dismiss his enemies from, 259-261, 281, 282; not the cause of Adams's overthrow, 289, 290; traditional method of treatment from Washington to Adams, 333, 334; turned over to his friends by Jackson, 335-336 (see Spoils System); ruined by Jackson's policy, 338; resolution to repeal four years' term in, and to require reasons for removal from, 62; debate as to powers of President and Senate over, 62-65, 67, 68; corruption in, caused by spoils, 184, 185.

Clay, Cassius M., works for Clay in 1844, ii. 264.

Clay, Henry, conflicting opinions concerning, i. 1, 2; lack of good biography, 2; ancestry, 2, 3; birth, 2; schooling, 3, 4; "mill-boy of the slashes," 4; placed by stepfather in Denny's store, 4; appointed clerk of chancery court, 5; his appearance, manners, and reading habits, 5, 6; becomes clerk for Wythe, 6; instructed in literature and law by Wythe, 6; decides to enter law, 8; studies with Brooke and obtains license, 8; introduced into society, 9; organizes a club, 9; irreproachable behavior in, 9; removes to Kentucky, 9; his slender equipment for the law, 10; ability to seem well-informed, 11; effects of his education on his character and career, 11, 12; later regrets it, 12; ready to enjoy frontier society, 18; joins a debating club, 18; anecdote of his first speech, 19; his modest ambitions, 19; gains success at bar, 20; anecdotes of his pleading in murder cases, 20, 22; accepts office of attorney for the commonwealth, 22; secures condemnation of a negro slave, 22, 23; regrets his success and resigns from office, 23; his success in civil cases, 23; lack of thorough study prevents his attaining eminence, 23; love of sport and of gaming, 23; his training in oratory, 24; marries, his family, 24; his popularity and its sources, 25, 26; lovable characteristics, 25; his strong hold upon Kentucky, 26; advocates emancipation in 1799, 27; his courage in taking unpopular side, 30; never regrets his action, 30, 31; denounces Alien and Sedition laws, 32, 33; his speech at Lexington, 33.

In Kentucky Legislature. Elected in 1803, 33; gains leadership in eloquence, 33; defies Colonel Daviess, 34; applied to by Burr for counsel when attacked by Daviess, 35; accepts with hesitation, 35; asks Burr for written statement of his doings, 35; convinced by Burr's reply, 36; later mortified at his connection with Burr, 37; refuses him his hand, 37.

In United States Senate. Appointed to fill an unexpired term, 36; his legal ineligibility, 38; his status not questioned, 38; enters at once into business, 39; his audacity, 39; advocates measures in favor of bridges and canals, 39, 40, 46; the champion, although not the originator, of internal improvements, 40, 45; represents Western feeling, 45, 46; asserts constitutionality of internal improvements, 46, 47; his enjoyment of his senatorial term, 47; described by Plumer, 47, 48; argumentative character of his oratory, 48.

In Kentucky Legislature. Reelected to Assembly, chosen speaker, 49; opposes a motion to repudiate British law as any authority, 50; his eulogy upon the common law, 50; introduces resolutions upholding embargo and Jefferson's administration, 51; advocates resolution to wear only clothes of domestic manufacture, 51; duel with Marshall, 52; first advocacy of protection, 52.

In United States Senate. Appointed to fill unexpired term, 52; his speech advocating home market, 52, 53; does not desire to foster manufactures, 53, 54; wishes simply independence of foreign countries, 54; discusses methods of encouragement, 55; his position not different from that of Gallatin, 57; introduces bill granting preëmption rights to public lands, 57; and bill to regulate trade with Indians, 57; advocates occupation of West Florida, 59; his argument for the American claim, 59, 60; attacks opponents as defenders of monarchy and unpatriotic friends of England, 60, 61; by his bold attitude toward England gains leadership, 61, 62; moves censure of Pickering, 62; embodies "Young America," 62; opposes re-charter of bank, 64; his reasons, 64; argues its unconstitutionality, 64–66; really responsible for its defeat, 66.

In House of Representatives. Elected to Congress, 67; prefers House to Senate, 67; as leader of younger Republicans, chosen speaker, 68; participates frequently in debate, 68; his associates, 78; gives House committees into control of war party, 79; advocates an increase in army, 79; urges war with England, 79; expects conquest of Canada, 79; does not desire an aggressive navy, 80; wishes to build one for defense, 81; wisdom of his position, 81; gets assistance of Western members, 81, 82; urges an embargo upon Madison, 82; his demands for war, 83; denies having compelled Madison to favor war, 84; silences Randolph, 84; effect of his enthusiasm in Kentucky, 86; his appointment as general-in-chief considered by Madison, 88; his retention in Congress urged by Gallatin, 88; bitterly attacked by Quincy, 90; replies, outline of his speech, 91–98; defends administration from charge of wantonly making war, 91; points out inconsistency of Federalists, 92; defends Jefferson from Federalist attacks, 93; taunts Federalists with disunion plots, 93, 94; explains why England was attacked instead of France, 94; defends continuance of war upon impressment issue alone, 95–97; urges renewed exertions against Canada, 97; effect of his speech on the country, 98; appointed peace commissioner by Madison, 101 ; tries in Congress to "fire the national heart," 191 ; resigns position and goes on peace mission, 101.

Peace Commissioner. His colleagues, 102; contrast with Adams, 103, 104; expects English to recede from extreme demands, 109 ; quarrels with Adams, 110 ; willing to abandon fisheries with English navigation of Mississippi, 110 ; confident throughout that English wish peace, 111 ; his conduct during negotiations criticised by Adams, 112, 113 ; loses his temper frequently, 113 ; quarrels with Adams over custody of papers, 113; especial reasons for his irritation, 113; downfall of his hopes in making war, 114; willing to see negotiations fail, 114; suggests breaking off, 115 ; tries to discuss impressment, 115; willing for three years more of war, 115; at last minute wishes to resist, 115, 116 ; signs treaty reluctantly, 116 ; fears peace will be unpopular, 118 ; becomes satisfied with result of war, 119; justifies his course in connection with it, 121, 122 ; enjoys social life at Ghent, 122, 123 ; instructed to negotiate treaty of commerce, 123; hesitates to go to London, 123 ; ready to go after hearing of battle of New Orleans, 123 ; in French society, remark to Madame de Staël, 124; in negotiations at London, 124 ; returns to America, his reception, 125.

In the House of Representatives. Elected in 1815, 125; declines mission to Russia, 126 ; declines War Department, 126; reëlected speaker, 126; leader of new school of Republicans, 128; explains its programme in speech on direct taxes, 128 ; opposes reduction of taxes in order to prepare for possible war, to begin internal improvements, and protect manufactures, 128, 129 ; uses war argument to justify protection in 1816, 131; his defense from charge of inconsistency in favoring bank, 133–135 ; has difficulty in avoiding his own constitutional objections, 134, 135 ; virtually admits error, 135 ; also abandons constitutional theories, 136; but does not adopt Federalist ground, 137 ; advocates permanent fund for building canals and roads, 137, 138 ; votes to increase pay of Congressmen, 139; loses popularity on this account, 139 ; has difficulty in securing reëlection, 139, 140; anecdote of his canvassing, 139; votes to repeal the pay act, 140; candidate for secretary of state under Monroe, 141; disapproves of Adams's appointment, 141; declines other offices, 141 ; keenly disappointed and angry with Monroe and Adams, 141 ; reëlected speaker, 142 ; his speech on internal improvements, 143–145 ; advocates construction of constitution adequate to country's future growth, 143, 144 ; emphasizes importance of Union, 144; condemns strict construction, 144; prefers consolidation to separation, 145 ; this speech summarizes his creed, 145 ; criticises Monroe's arguments against internal improvements, 146; displeases by showing resentment, 146; said to have favored South American States solely to annoy Monroe, 147; injustice of this statement shown by his earlier actions in their behalf, 147; demands repeal of neutrality law, 147 ; urges recognition of insurgents, 147 ; opposes sending commissioners to investigate, 148 ; his speech in favor of recognition, 148, 149; denies danger from Spain, 149; unable to lead House, 149; displeases by his personal attacks on Monroe and Adams, 149; alarms Monroe, 150; really injures his cause, 150; condemns Jackson's campaign in Florida, 153 ; not personally an enemy of Jackson, 153; fears his motives in censuring him may be misconstrued, 153; makes an elaborate effort to disclaim personal feelings,

154 ; outline of his speech, 155-157 ; censures Jackson's treatment of Arbuthnot and Ambrister, 155 ; and his outrages on Spain, 156 ; urges supremacy of law, 157 ; ability of speech, 157 ; its weak points, 157 ; fails to realize popularity of a military hero, 157 ; defeated in his attempt to censure Jackson, 159 ; temporary decline in Clay's popularity, 160 ; his gambling habits, 160, 161 ; announces intention of abandoning them, 161 ; proposal to displace him as speaker, 161 ; his retention advised by Monroe, 162 ; reëlected and resumes opposition, 162 ; condemns Adams's treaty with Spain, 163 ; introduces resolutions against the treaty, 164 ; condemns administration for abandoning Texas claim, 165 ; defeated, 165 ; continues to urge recognition of Spanish-American republics, 165 ; condemns administration for subservience to England, 166 ; glowing description of South America, 166, 167 ; renews attack and secures passage of resolutions, 167 ; gains popularity in South America, 168 ; his attitude due to sympathetic character, 168 ; persuades himself by his own rhetoric, 169 ; his conversation with Adams, 169, 170 ; his view really superficial, 171 ; but popular with masses, 171 ; opposes and uses casting vote against prohibition of slavery in Arkansas, 177 ; not the "father" of the Missouri Compromise, 178 ; prominent in debate but not leader, 178 ; a strong defender of slavery and States' rights, 179 ; supports compromise, 180 ; uses position as speaker to override Randolph and save bill, 180; 181 ; evidently abandons earlier anti-slavery professions, 181 ; inconsistency in his condemnation and advocacy of slavery, 182 ; leaves Congress for a year to mend private affairs, 182 ; urges a claim upon Monroe, 183 ; on returning to House, assumes leadership in Missouri question, 186 ; argues that Missouri clause against free negroes need not bar its admission under the compromise, 186-189 ; urges conciliation, 187 ; brings in a report aiming to appease both sides, 188, 189 ; defeated by extremists, 189 ; reports resolution avoiding difficulty over counting Missouri's electoral vote, 190 ; baffles attempt of Floyd and Randolph to force question during counting of vote, 191 ; moves a special committee and selects members, 192 ; succeeds in carrying a compromise resolution, 192 ; his success due to personal exertions and skill, 192, 193 ; praised by Adams, 193 ; approached by Randolph with proposal for secession, 197 ; advises against it, 197 ; dreads disunion, 197 ; gains great distinction by conduct during struggle, 200 ; Adams's estimate of his character, 201 ; never charged with official corruption, 202 ; more national than sectional, 202.

Candidate for the Presidency. Retires from Congress, 202 ; retained as counsel for Bank of United States in Ohio and Kentucky, 202 ; stands for sound money in Kentucky, 203 ; reëlected to Congress and to speakership in 1823, 204 ; confessed candidate for presidency, 204 ; popular interest in his career in Congress, 204 ; opposes granting a pension to mother of Commodore Perry, 205 ; his courage in taking unpopular side, 206 ; attacks Monroe's position on internal improvements, 206-208 ; upholds constitutionality of building roads and canals, 207 ; urges demands of the West, 207, 208 ; revives memory of his opposition to Monroe, 208 ; supports motion to send an agent to Greece, 209 ; offers resolution embodying Monroe doctrine, 209 ; agrees with administration, 210 ; his resolution criticised as dangerous, 211 ; makes a blustering reply, 211 ; imprudence of his language as a candidate, 211, 212 ; supports, in 1820, an attempt to increase tariff rates, 214 ;

assumes championship of protective tariff bill in 1824, 214; growth of his opinions since 1816, 214; makes a brilliant speech, 214–218; describes distress, advocates home market, 215; calls protection "the American system," 216; urges agricultural States to submit to temporary loss, 216; strong and weak points in speech, 216; absurd economic statements, 217; success of speech, 218; replied to by Webster, 218; gains a triumph in passage of bill, 219, 220; sarcastic remarks of Webster on his phrase, "American system," 220, 221; nominated for presidency by Kentucky and other state legislatures, 228; canvasses actively all over country, 228; correspondence with Benton, Porter, and others, 228, 229; urges on friends but refuses to make promises, 229, 230; refuses suggested coalition with Crawford, 230; does not hesitate to avow opinions, 230; campaign attacks upon, 231; said by Jackson men to be planning coalition with Crawford, 232; denies it, 232; receives thirty-seven electoral votes, 232; excluded from consideration in House, 233; keenly disappointed at defeat, 233; loses vote of Louisiana by a trick, 233; remarks of Van Buren on, 233, 234; welcomes Lafayette to House of Representatives, 234, 235; friendship with Lafayette, 235; able by his influence in Congress to decide choice of president, 236; describes solicitations of friends of other candidates, 236, 237; former haughty conduct of Jackson toward him, 237; attempts of Jackson's friends to bring about a reconciliation, 237, 238; receives frequent civilities from Jackson, 238; decides early to throw influence for Adams, 238; unmoved by instructions of Kentucky legislature to vote for Jackson, 238; his objections to Crawford, 239; considers Jackson unfit for presidency, 239; his opinion of Adams, 239; not bound by Benton's *demos krateo* principle, 240; denounced by Jacksonians for not supporting Jackson, 241; accused in anonymous letter of having offered a bargain to Jackson and Adams, 242; publishes a fiery card in reply, 242; discovers Kremer to be author of slander, 243; demands an investigation in the House, 244; rejects a disclaimer offered by Kremer, 245; inner history of intrigue against, 246; his friends urge his appointment upon Adams, 247; has interview with Adams, 247; the bargain charge a mere calumny, 248; his intense indignation, 248; secures choice of Adams, 248; offered secretaryship of state, 249; his fitness for position, 249; doubtful propriety of his accepting, 250; his known rivalry with Adams, 250, 251; danger of his seeming to justify bargain story, 251; reasons leading him to accept offer, 252; led by desire to secure presidential succession, 253; thanked by House for his career as speaker, 253; stands as greatest speaker in history of House, 254; attempt to prevent his confirmation in Senate, 254; efforts of Jackson against, 254; asks in vain for a formal inquiry, 254, 255; no tangible charges made against, 255; publishes an elaborate refutation, 256; regrets having threatened to challenge Kremer, 256; congratulated upon successful vindication, 256, 257; continues to be thought guilty by people, 257.

Secretary of State. Urges Adams to punish office-holders for openly opposing administration, 260; disapproves of Adams's extreme impartiality, but does not favor partisan removals, 262; removes family to Washington, 262; at public dinners, keeps explaining bargain story, 262; afflicted by death of daughters, 262; hopes that excitement of campaign has died down, 263; insulted by a friend of Jackson's, 263; indirectly attacked by Jackson in accepting nomination for presidency, 264; doubtful concerning Adams's doc-

INDEX 429

trine of internal improvements, 266; enthusiastic over proposed Panama Congress, 268; urges acceptance of invitation to participate, 268; his cautious instructions to envoys, 269; instructs Middleton to urge Emperor of Russia to persuade Spain to recognize independence of former colonies, 271; attacked by Randolph as "blackleg," 273; his duel with Randolph, 274; comments of Webster and Benton upon, 274, 275; not a real duelist, 275; suffers from ill-health, 276; enthusiastically received in Kentucky, 276; continues to explain away bargain story, 276; bitterly attacked by opposition in nineteenth Congress, 278; urges Adams to remove McLean, 282; again accused of bargain by Beverly and Jackson, 282, 283; thinks he has discovered a responsible author of slander, 283; calls upon Jackson for proof, 283, 284; exonerated by Buchanan, Jackson's witness, 284; calls upon friends who also disclaim any bargain, 284, 285; congratulated at final collapse of slander, 285; continues to be slandered by Jackson and his friends, 285, 286; public and private character assailed during campaign, 288; tries to bear Adams's defeat with composure, 293; leaves office with Adams, 293; review of his career as secretary of state, 293–308; disappointed at failure of Panama Congress, 294; disappointed in nature of Spanish-American republics, 294; expresses his feelings to Bolivar, 295, 296; fails to purchase Texas, 296; in commercial diplomacy, follows idea of reciprocity, 297; dealings with England, 298, 299; replies to Canning, 298; concludes numerous treaties, 299; secures settlement of slave indemnity with Great Britain, 300; instructs Gallatin to offer surrender of deserters for return of fugitive slaves, 300, 301; not a thoroughly pro-slavery man, 302; vacillates between anti- and pro-slavery opinions, 302; favors recognition of Hayti, 302; not alarmed at negro legislators at Panama Congress, 302; favors colonization of free blacks, 303; in speech before colonization society, urges its practicability, 303, 304; condemns slavery vigorously, 304; justifies agitation for its amelioration, 305; contrast between this speech and other acts, 305, 306; inability of abolitionists to appreciate his state of mind, 306; lack of clearness in his views on slavery, 307; ability of his state papers, 307; finds office labor irksome, 308; suffers ill-health, 308; worried by attacks on character, 308; feels his acceptance of State Department to be a mistake, 308; on continued good terms with Adams, 309; dissuaded by Adams from resigning, 309; declines Adams's offer of place on Supreme Bench, 310; eulogized by Adams, 310; talks of retirement, but continues to think of presidency, 311; asks Everett if he can gain Eastern States, 311.

In Retirement. Recognized chief of National Republican party, 325; his capacity for leadership, 325–329; assumes lead habitually on all occasions, 326; success of his oratory, 326; not a profound speaker, but a great debater, 326–327; his manner, 327; immense effects produced, 327, 328; crushes Marshall in joint debate, 328; his gallantry and brilliancy, 328; social attractiveness, courtesy, generosity, and charm, 328, 329; supported by industrial elements, 329; hated by Jackson, 329, 330; his enemies given cabinet positions by Jackson, 330; his influence dreaded by Jackson in State Department, 330, 331; his friends removed from office, 331; at public dinner, deplores election of Jackson as dangerous to liberty, 331, 332; regrets inability of people to perceive danger, 332; denounces Jackson's spoils system, 336, 337; declines to return to Congress or to enter Kentucky legislature, 339; enjoys farm life, 339; continues to plan for next election, 339; thinks Jackson cannot hold followers together, 339; rejoices in popular enthusiasm, 339, 340; makes tours in West, 340; received everywhere with cannon and brass bands, 340 ; describes his triumphs, 341; has high hopes for 1832, 341; looked upon as inevitable opponent of Jackson, 341; letter of Webster to, 341; declines to commit himself on anti-Mason issue, 343; thinks anti-Masonry not a political question, 343; hopes anti-Masons will drift to his support, 344; reiterates opposition to movement, 344; prefers Jackson to an anti-Masonic president, 344 ; alienates Kendall and Blair, who now support Jackson, 346; applauds Webster's reply to Hayne, 348; demand for his presence in Congress, 349; letter of Webster urging him to enter Senate, 349; reluctantly accepts, 349, 350; his election bitterly opposed by Jacksonians, 350; chosen by a small majority, 350.

In United States Senate. His nomination by National Republicans a foregone conclusion, 351; urges immediate re-charter of bank in 1832, 356; thinks a veto by Jackson will ruin his chances, 357; nominated for presidency, 357; his blunder in forcing bank charter as issue in campaign, 358; arranges a caucus of protectionists, 360; lays down programme for party, 360; wishes to reduce revenue without interfering with protection, 360; insists on home valuation, 361; introduces resolution embodying his views, 361; makes two speeches on the tariff, 361-364; condemns distribution of surplus revenue, 362; historical arguments in favor of tariff, 362; denounces nullification, 362, 363; makes a bitter attack on Gallatin for his free trade memorial, 363, 364; his previous dealings with Gallatin, 364, 365; later practically adopts Gallatin's plans, 365; succeeds in passing tariff of 1832, its effects, 366; leads opposition to confirmation of Van Buren as minister to England, 367; holds him responsible for "spoils system," 368; thinks Van Buren ruined, 369; obliged by a trick of opponents to consider, in committee on manufactures, a proposal to reduce price of public lands, 369; reports on public lands, 370; advocates maintenance of price and distribution of proceeds among States, 371; his scheme criticised by Benton, 372; unable to foresee expansion of country, 372; thinks question of public lands will long outlast protection, 373; damaged as candidate by his position, 373; his own argument against bank in 1811 used by Jackson in veto message, 376, 377; denounces veto message, 377; condemns Jackson's use of veto power, 378; has wrangle with Benton, 379; thinks veto will ruin Jackson, 379; nominated by a "young men's" convention, 381; sanguine of success up to the end, 382, 383; badly defeated, 383; ruins his cause by three grave blunders, 383; exasperates South by tariff of 1832, 383; forces the bank question into party politics, 383, 384; believes he can stir up enthusiasm for a moneyed corporation, 384; doubts sincerity of Jackson's nullification proclamation, ii. 7, 8; offers a compromise tariff in 1833, 10; appalls protectionists by advocating gradual reduction of duties to twenty per cent., 10, 11; prepares scheme with Calhoun, 11; avows necessity of compromising to avert danger of abolition of protection, 11, 12; also dreads civil war, 12; and hesitates to trust Jackson with power of Force Bill, 12; his bill preferred by Calhoun because professedly a compromise, 13; defends tariff as a protective measure, 14, 15; tries to defend himself from charge of compromising with nullifiers, 15, 16;

INDEX 431

moves home valuation amendment in Senate to satisfy manufacturers, 16; intercedes with Clayton to save Calhoun from humiliation, 17; makes final appeal for compromise, 17-19; denies charge of ambition, 18; his bill substituted for Verplanck's in the House, 19; gains credit as "pacificator," 20; fails to realize that slavery, not tariff, was the real cause of difficulty, 21; affirms supremacy of national government, 22; last encounter with Randolph, 22, 23; his Land Bill passed and vetoed by Jackson, 23; describes life at Ashland, 24, 25; describes his journey through North and East, 25; at a disadvantage compared with Jackson in nullification affair, 25; unites with Webster and Calhoun in opposing Jackson's bank policy, 30; offers resolution demanding whether the President's paper read to the cabinet was genuine, 31; introduces resolutions condemning Jackson's removal of Duane, and Taney's removal of deposits, 32; accuses Jackson of wishing a despotism, 33; holds theory that Treasury Department is responsible to Congress, not to the President, 35; his view of Taney's action, 36; refers to Gallatin with respect, 36; his resolutions debated and adopted, 37; introduces joint resolution requiring restoration of deposits, 37; appeals melodramatically to Van Buren to describe to Jackson the ruin caused by removal of deposits, 38, 39; behavior of Van Buren toward, 39; censures Jackson's dictatorial theories of the presidency, 43; lays down rules to follow in coercing Jackson, 43; compares Whigs of 1834 with those of 1770, 45; galled by enforced cooperation with Calhoun, 46; tries in vain to separate bank question from that of Jackson's behavior, 47; although defeated, gains parliamentary honors, 52; undertakes to prevent Jackson's message from bringing on war with France, 56; reads report on French relations to Senate, 56, 57; affirms intention to insist on claims, and disavows apparent menace, 56, 57; offers resolution not to undertake reprisals upon France, 57; modifies it so as to spare Jackson's feelings, 57; his credit in bringing about a peaceful conclusion, 58; thinks Indians unfit to become citizens, 59; presents memorial in behalf of Cherokees oppressed by Georgia, 60; introduces resolutions to allow Indians to defend rights in courts, 60, 61; in debate on power of President to remove officials, 62; proposes resolution to limit power of President to remove, 63; supports proposition to require reasons for removal, 64, 67, 68; shows inadequacy of constitutional protection against spoils system, 64, 65; does not foresee share of Senate in spoils system, 65; afflicted by death of a daughter, 70; again introduces land bill, 70; opposes refusal to receive anti-slavery petitions, 80; but does not advocate their reference to a committee, 80; offers an amendment giving reasons for opposing abolition in the District of Columbia, 81; fails to obtain support, 82; admits power of Congress to abolish in the District of Columbia, 82; denounces Calhoun's bill to permit exclusion of anti-slavery matter from mails in South, 85, 86; thinks it unconstitutional, 86; desire of Madison that he may compromise slavery matters, 87; begins to doubt wisdom of compromise of 1833, 87; his positions with regard to Texas, 87, 88; attacks Adams in 1820 for abandoning claim to Texas, 87; in 1827 wishes to purchase it, 88; reports resolution to recognize independence of Texas when it is apparent, 92; warns against hasty action, 93; secretly alarmed at raising slavery question, 93; deprecates harsh attitude of administration toward Mexico, 95; does not vote on resolution to recognize independence of

INDEX

Texas, 95; mortified at finding Whigs looking for some other candidate for presidency, 96, 97; thinks himself the only man capable of uniting party, 97; discusses chances of competitors, 97, 98; favors Harrison as candidate, 98; thinks of retiring, 98, 99; feels unable to prevent downward course, 99; declares intention not to serve, yet accepts second election to Senate, 99; again introduces land bill, 100; favors international copyright, 100; condemns expunging resolutions, 103, 104; comment of Benton on his speech, 104; triumph of Jackson over, in carrying the expunging resolutions, 106; defeated in every respect by Jackson, 106; feels keenly the degradation of Senate, 107; considers so-called deposit of surplus in 1837 a gift, 122; on effect of the specie circular, 125; prepares to lead opposition to Van Buren, 131, 132; proposal to nominate him for 1840, 132; his letter in reply, 132, 133; deplores calling of extra session, 135; insists upon continuance of distribution of surplus, 135; votes against bill to withhold fourth installment, 136; opposes vainly an issue of treasury notes, 137; leads opposition to sub-treasury scheme, 138; considers Jackson's attack on bank the cause of panic, 139; thinks sub-treasury plan dangerous to popular liberties, 139, 140; his solemnity in describing dangers, 141; probably sincere in his statement, 141; thinks a new bank would restore prosperity, 142, 143; not willing to have a bank unless supported by people, 143; offers resolution to receive notes of resuming banks for public dues, 143; carries on personal debate with Calhoun, 146; begins by criticising Calhoun's alliance with Van Buren, 146; controversy as to which won in 1833, 147; appears better than Calhoun in the altercation, 148; has stronger side of argument, 148, 149; willing to admit change of opinion, 150; on permanent tariff, 151; denounces British in Caroline affair, 151; advises caution in boundary disputes with England, 152; advises moderation towards Mexico, 152; queries as to abolition movement in the North, 154; moves to refer petitions to Committee on District of Columbia, 155; denies that slavery is not a subject for argument, 155; votes for Calhoun's resolutions on slavery, 159; urges necessity of Union, 159, 160; offers resolutions denying power of Congress to interfere with slavery in States, and condemning abolition elsewhere and its agitation as inexpedient, 160, 161; stirs Calhoun's anger by not affirming right of protection for slavery, 161; succeeds in securing adoption of his resolutions as substitutes for Calhoun's, 162; suspects Calhoun of ambition, 163; his view of danger to Whig party from abolitionists, 164; loses popularity with slaveholders, 164; makes a speech to "set himself right" with South, 165; his least creditable performance, 165; attacks abolitionists, 165–168; denies possibility of emancipation, 166; asserts right of property in slaves, 167; asserts dangers of any kind of emancipation, 167; opposed to slavery in abstract, 167; defends himself from charge of inconsistency, 168; praised in a patronizing way by Calhoun, 168, 169; unable as a presidential candidate to reply, 169; eulogized by Preston, 170; later regrets Calhoun's resolutions protesting against the liberation of slaves in Enterprise case, 170; votes for the resolutions, 171; endeavors as candidate to conciliate all elements of oppositions, 173; promises to adhere to tariff of 1833, 173; considers internal improvements no longer necessary, 173; a bank inexpedient until clearly demanded, 173; considers partisan use of government patronage dangerous, 173; endeavors to conciliate dissatisfied Democrats,

INDEX 433

174; intrigues in Virginia senatorial election in favor of Rives, 174; wishes to placate Tyler by making him Vice-President, 174; estranged from Webster, 175; opposed by his friends, 175; letter of Harrison to, on his candidacy, 175, 176; elements of opposition to, 176; warned by Porter of opposition in New York, 176; visits New York, 177; his withdrawal suggested by Thurlow Weed, 177; his vacillations as to candidacy, 178; determines to remain in the field, 178; prevented by a trick from receiving delegates from New York, 178, 179; skill used in preventing his nomination at National Convention, 179; defeated after several days' manœuvring, 180; anger of his friends, 180; praised by opponents, 180; writes letter advising harmony and submission, 181; his rage at news of defeat, 181, 182; justified in his chagrin, 182; mortified at consciousness of vain sacrifices, 183; relates anecdote of Democratic party proscription, 184; supports Whig candidates in campaign, 187; lays down programme of party, 187-189; advocates limitation of executive, 188; reform of currency, 188; doubtful about a bank, 189; contented with tariff of 1833, 189; use of public lands for revenue, 189; abandonment of internal improvements, 189; economy and an end to abolition agitation, 189; declines offer of secretaryship of state, 190; advises Harrison to appoint Webster and trust no malicious reports, 191; his friends in cabinet, 191; moves repeal of sub-treasury act, 191; his triumphant speech, 191, 192; considers election a popular mandate to repeal sub-treasury, 192; again urges in vain his land bill, 192; criticised by Adams for "crowing" over Van Buren, 192; overwhelmed by requests from office-seekers, 193; his support requested for a New York manager, 193, 194; resolves to have nothing to do with spoils, 194; considers himself more important than Harrison, 194, 195; corrects Harrison's inaugural address, 195; persuades Harrison to call an extra session, 195; requested by Harrison to communicate henceforth by writing, 195; replies denying any dictation, 195, 196; rupture probably caused by New York politicians, 197; leaves Washington much embittered, 197; his relations to Tyler before 1841, 199, 200; considers Tyler not a full President, 201; in doubt as to Tyler's principles, writes him a letter, 202; asked by Tyler to frame a bank so as to avoid all objections, 203; determines to lead Congress without regard to Tyler, 205; proposes six objects to be attained at extra session, including repeal of sub-treasury act, a bank, a tariff, 205; secures repeal of sub-treasury act, 205; introduces and secures passage of bill incorporating bank, 206; ridicules Democratic congratulations to Tyler on his bank veto, 207; attacks Tyler, asserting that bank was main issue of last election, 208; asserts that he had been confident of Tyler's support, 208; accuses Tyler of inconsistency, 209; disclaims any further responsibility for a bank bill, 209; secures passage of bill to distribute proceeds of sale of public lands, 211; urges that action will relieve indebted States, 212; opposes in vain an amendment suspending distribution when tariff duties rise above twenty per cent., 213; concerts with members of cabinet, their resignation, 213; his "doom" announced by Tyler to Webster, 214; resolves to take Whig party away from Tyler, 214, 216; ridicules Tyler's personal following, 216; means to make breach between Tyler and Whigs irreparable, 216; grows increasingly imperious in his leadership, 219; wishes to limit debate, 219; fails in attempt to control Senate, 219;

wishes to lay on the table petitions against his measures, 220; fails to lead Whigs to victory in local elections, 220; attributes Whig defeats to Tyler, 220; determines to retire from Senate, 222; his speeches intended to guide followers in future, 222; opposes repeal of bankrupt act in vain, 222; offers amendments to Constitution to check executive power, 222; extravagant opinion of veto power, 222, 223; ill-considered nature of his proposals, 223; introduces resolutions to reduce expenses, 224; admits failure of compromise tariff, and advocates increase of duties, 224; continues to insist on distribution of sales of public lands, 224; his valedictory on leaving the Senate, 225; its impressiveness, 225; honored by adjournment of Senate, 225, 226; greets Calhoun, 226; comments of Benton on, 226; effect of his departure, 226; advises Congress not to yield to Tyler's vetoes, 227; his distribution scheme finally abandoned, 228.

In Retirement. Candidate for Presidency. Replies to letters of invitation, 229; welcomed in Kentucky, 229; extravagantly eulogized by constituents, 229, 230; renominated by Whigs in various States, 230; greeted with demonstrations, 230; petitioned by Mendenhall to liberate his slaves, 231; his skillful reply, 231, 232; advises abolitionists to begin charity at home, 232; scores a great apparent triumph, 232; his generous conduct to Giddings when censured, 235; thinks abolitionists more dangerous to country than slavery extremists, 236; seeks to discredit them, 236; visits the Southwest, 242; character of his journeys, 242; his speeches, 243; his gifts, 243; distinguished visitors, 243; on good personal terms with Van Buren, 243, 244; entertains Van Buren at Ashland, 244; supposed to have agreed with him to keep Texas question out of politics, 244; or to oppose it, 244; hopes at first question will not be forced upon country, 244; at Raleigh learns of treaty of annexation, 245; writes a public letter, 245, 246; denies any claim to Texas, 245; objects to a war for Texas, 246; opposes annexation as disturbance of existing balance, 246; and as certain to meet with great opposition, 246; by this letter arouses displeasure of extremists of both sides, 246; his reasoning satisfactory to bulk of Northern Whigs, 247; nominated with enthusiasm for presidency, 250; receives overtures for reconciliation from Webster haughtily, 250; publicly praised by Webster, 251; his relations with Birney prior to 1844, 255; in campaign, returns to position of 1840 regarding a bank, 256; accused by Democrats of wishing to repeal tariff of 1842, 258; forced to explain again the old bargain story of 1824, 259; in a position, owing to Raleigh letter on Texas, to receive full Northern support, 260; yields to demands of Southern Whigs, 260; writes to Miller disclaiming any desire to placate abolitionists in his disapproval of Texas, 261; writes again that slavery question ought not, as a temporary issue, to prevent annexation of Texas, 261, 262; commits a blunder in these letters, 262; denounced by Liberty party as slaveholder and gambler, 262; strengthens their attacks by his Alabama letters, 263, 264; tries in vain to explain the letters away, 264; discourages Whigs by his mistake, 265; loses election through New York Liberty vote, 265, 266; damaged also by unpopularity of Frelinghuysen, 266; ruins his own chances, 266; deeply cast down by his defeat, 267, 268; receives letters and visits of condolence, 269; suffers business embarrassments, 269; saved by gifts from admirers, 270; attends meeting of American Colonization Society, 270; description of enthusiasm over him, 271; cited as authority in 1845 for illegality of cession of territory without consent of both houses of Congress, 281; during war, continues to receive popular testimonials, 287; afflicted by death of son at Buena Vista, 288; becomes member of Episcopal Church, 288; in 1847 makes a speech on the war, 290-292; condemns the origin of war, 290; warns against annexing Mexico, 291; offers resolutions calling for a generous peace and disavowal of slavery propaganda, 291, 292; his policy echoed by Whigs in other States, 292; continues to regard himself as candidate for presidency, 292; yet cautious about committing himself, 293; regarded by many of admirers as unsuitable candidate, 293; has grown stale as an aspirant, 293; abandoned even in Kentucky, 294; admired by General Taylor, 294; disgusted at movement in favor of Taylor, 296; regards nomination of a military chieftain as a violation of Whig principles, 296, 297; announces intention to remain passive, 297; visits Washington to plead before Supreme Court, 297; determines not to withdraw name from convention, 297; complains of Taylor movement in Kentucky, 297; present at death of Adams, 298; receives great public demonstrations on Northern journey, 298; abandons cool attitude, 298; assents publicly to use of name in National Convention, 299; expects Taylor to withdraw, 299; startled at Taylor's letter announcing purpose to remain a candidate, 299; does not appreciate decay of old issues, 300; upholds them in letter to Ullman, 300; at Whig convention his supporters still hope to nominate him, 305; fails to receive vote of Ohio, 305; defeated for nomination by Taylor, 306; deeply mortified at failure, 307; and at abandonment by Kentucky, 307; considers Whig party morally bankrupt, 307; declines nomination to Senate, 308; refuses to support Taylor's candidacy, 308; considers election a merely personal one, 308, 309; refuses to allow use of name by Northern Whigs against Taylor, 309; writes letter advocating emancipation in Kentucky constitution, 316, 317; skill of his argument against slavery, 317; proposes gradual emancipation with colonization, 318; merits of his plan, 318; elected to Senate, 319; his return thought necessary to avert public dangers, 319; does not yet understand seriousness of crisis, 319; expects speedy settlement of Free Soil question, 320.

In United States Senate. Takes seat in Senate, 323; his relations with Taylor, 323; his return dreaded by Southern leaders, 323; determines not to seek leadership, 324; personally favors Wilmot Proviso, 324; thinks South ought to admit it, 325; points out continuous domination of South at Washington, 325; thinks that if South persist, it will cause its own overthrow, 325, 326; deprecates Southern discourtesy to Father Mathew, 328; urges friends to get up Union mass meetings in Kentucky, 329; begins to plan some scheme to prevent a dissolution of the Union, 329; again assumes leadership, 329; brings forward his compromise, 330; plans to appease South without alarming North, 330, 331; difficult questions to be faced by him, 331, 332; features of the compromise, 332, 333; proposes to admit California, abandon Wilmot Proviso, compensate Texas for smaller boundaries, prohibit slave trade in District of Columbia, make a new fugitive slave law, 332, 333; thinks North better able to make concessions, 334; deprecates immediate debate in vain, 334; in reply to Davis, avows unwillingness to sanction slavery in new Territories, 334; yet really does so by his compromise, 335; advocates compromise in a great speech, 335-338; his feeble health, 335; popular interest in speech, 336; appeals for peace and harmony, 337; denies possibility of peaceable secession, 337; foretells isolation of South in such a struggle, 337; answered by Calhoun, 338; indignant at Seward's anti-slavery speech, 345, 346; reports from select committee, 347; at one time willing to admit California at once, 347, 348; later led to couple it with other compromise measures, 348; reports omnibus bill, and others embodying compromise, 348, 349; hampered by Taylor's belligerent attitude, 351; his compromise opposed by Taylor, 352; condemns Taylor's policy as inadequate, 353; the "bleeding wounds" remark, 353; his compromise denounced by Nashville Convention, 354; advises Fillmore to appoint Webster secretary of state, 355; exercises influence with administration, 356; makes his closing speech, 356; disclaims any sectional spirit, 356; no longer a candidate for presidency, 356; no longer attempts to dictate, 357; his concessions to slavery made unwillingly, 357; urges union above all things, 357; condemns fire-eaters, 358; denounces disunion as treason, 358; asserts paramount allegiance to the Union, not the State, 359; incautiously accepts amendment damaging the Texas boundary compromise, 359; thinking compromise lost, urges that disunion be met by force, 360; promises his support to national government against the South, 651; gives up leadership and retires, 362; his measures subsequently passed, 362-365; returns to Senate, and advocates passage of bill prohibiting slave trade in District of Columbia, 365; desires rest and home, 365; satisfied with his part, 365, 366; advocates compromise for the sake of Union, not for the sake of the South, 367; his error, 367; refuses to introduce slavery into free territory, 368; but abandons any protection to New Mexico, 369; his opinion that slavery does not exist in New Mexico denied by South, 369; fails to comprehend the feelings of Northern anti-slavery men, 372; in speech to Kentucky legislature represents compromise as a Southern triumph, 377; denounces Nashville Convention, 378; joins with other Congressmen in promising to support no man for office who does not oppose disturbance of compromise, 378; introduces petitions for suppression of African slave trade, 379; sarcastic reply of Hale to, 379; introduces resolution calling for information concerning Shadrach rescue, 380; denounces abolitionists, especially Thompson, 380, 381; tries to persuade South that law is executed faithfully, 381; insists that compromise has worked a miracle, 382; accuses Chase of desiring disunion, 383; suggests doubtfully a consideration of tariff, 383, 384; advocates river and harbor bill, 384; refuses to accept constructive mileage, 384; his ill-health causes voyage to Cuba, 385; returns to Ashland, 385; obliged again to refuse proposal to run for presidency, 385, 386; invited to visit New York to uphold compromise, 386; writes a letter in reply, 387; condemns abolitionists for disturbing compromise, 388; thinks Fugitive Slave Law must and will be enforced, 388, 389; condemns nullification and secession, 389; understands temper of South better than Seward and Chase, 390, 391; fails to understand spirit of North, 391; tries to resume attendance at Senate, 391; remains at National Hotel, 392; discusses Fugitive Slave Law with Greeley, 392; interview with Kossuth, 394; explains impossibility of United States aiding Hungary, 395; doubts future of liberalism in Europe, 396; thinks Whig chances poor in election of 1852, 396; considers party ties weakened, 397; advises friends to support Fillmore for nomination, 401; not led through enmity to Webster, 401; considers Fillmore as identified with compromise, 401; satisfied with nomination of Scott upon compromise platform, 404; his principles adopted by both parties, 404; lives to see collapse of Whig party, 405; his last illness, 406; attentions of friends, 406; his death and funeral services, 406, 407; chorus of eulogy upon, 407; suggests inscription for medal, 407, 408; omits mention of internal improvements and bank from list of achievements, 408; comparison of his oratory with Webster's, 409; superior as leader to all contemporaries except Jackson, 409; lack of sound political foresight, 410; rashness in politics, 410; inclined to be in opposition, 410, 411; not a spoilsman, 411; personally incorruptible, 411; his family life and private character, 412; effect of presidential ambition on his career, 412, 413; his apparent equivocations, 413; consistency of his devotion to Union, 414; his lofty patriotism, 414, 415.

Characteristics. General views, i. 1, 2, 103–104, 325–329, ii. 408–415; unfriendly view of, i. 350; his own view, 408; brilliancy, i. 200, 328; convivial habits, i. 104, ii. 412; courage, i. 34, 206, 230, 275, 328, ii. 165, 260, 316, 358, 361; depression, liability to, i. 233, 234, ii. 98, 99, 267, 307; descriptions of, by Plumer, i. 47, 48; by Adams, i. 112, 113, 201, 310; devotion of friends to, i. 1, 2, ii. 270, 287, 293, 407; diplomatic ability, i. 307, ii. 56; education, i. 4, 6, 8, 10–12; enthusiasm, i. 79, 83, 86, 98, 101, 103, ii. 191; frankness, i. 328, ii. 150; farm life, fondness for, ii. 25; gaming habits, i. 104, 160, 161, ii. 412; generosity, i. 25, ii. 17, 59; imperiousness, i. 103, 113, ii. 219, 220, 250, 410; imprudence, i. 212, 325, ii. 208, 262; integrity, i. 202, ii. 194, 411; jealousy, i. 146, ii. 296; leadership, i. 61, 191, 192, 200, 325, 326, 383, 384, ii. 219, 321, 409–411; legal ability, ii. 20–22, 23; oratorical ability, i. 19, 24, 25, 33, 48, 157, 169, 200, 234, 326–328, ii. 148, 231, 336, 409; personal appearance, i. 25; self-confidence, i. 39, 62, 325, ii. 366, 410; sensitiveness, i. 308, ii. 96, 107, 197, 307; social qualities, i. 9, 18, 25, 103, 328, ii. 412; superficiality, i. 11, 157, 168, ii. 410; sympathy, i. 23, 25, 329; temper, i. 103, 113, ii. 147, 148, 181, 182, 219, 229, 307; vindictiveness, i. 149, 150, 169, ii. 191, 192.

Political Opinions. Abolitionists, ii. 165–168, 232; Alien and Sedition Laws, i. 32; Arkansas, slavery in, i. 177; Bank of United States, i. 64–66, 133–135, 356–358, ii. 173, 189, 408; bargain and corruption story, i. 241–243, 250–252, 255–257, 282–286, 308; California, admission of, ii. 347–348; colonization of free blacks, i. 303, 304, ii. 378, 379; common law, i. 50; compromise of 1833, ii. 17, 18, 22, 146, 147; compromise of 1850, ii. 330–334, 335–338, 353–357, 366, 367; Constitution, i. 136, 137, 138, 143–145, 186, 207; copyright, international, i. 100; debate, freedom of, ii. 219; Democratic party, ii. 33; District of Columbia, abolition in, i. 81, 82; disunion, i. 197, ii. 22, 160, 337, 358, 359, 360, 361, 389; dueling, i. 34, 52, 242–244, 256, 274, ii. 152; England, i. 60, 61, see war of 1812; election of 1824, 238–240; Europe, republican institutions in, ii. 395–396; expunging resolution, ii. 103, 104; Federalists, 92, 93; fisheries, i. 110, 111; France, i. 83, 92, 94, ii. 56; Hungarian intervention, ii. 394; impressment, i. 95, 96; Indians, i. 57; internal improvements, i. 39, 40, 45–47, 129, 138, 143–145, 207, ii. 173, 189, 384; mail, abolition papers in, ii. 85, 86; manifest destiny, ii. 290–292; Mississippi navigation, i. 110, 111; Missouri Compromise, i. 178, 179, 180, 181, 182, 186–193; navy, i. 80, 81, 129; nullification, ii. 15, 389; offices, appointment to, i. 260–262,

ii. 63-65, 173, 188, 222; Panama Congress, i. 268; paper money, i. 203, 204; pensions, i. 205; petition, right of, ii. 80, 151, 155; presidential ambition, i. 141, 146, 151, 228, 229, 230, 253, 311, 341, 349, ii. 18, 97, 132, 133, 169, 170, 173, 178, 181, 292, 356, 385, 408, 412-413; protection, i. 51, 52-55, 57, 129, 214-219, 360-364; ii. 14, 173, 189, 227, 383; public lands, i. 57, 370, 371, ii. 23, 70, 100, 157, 189; Republican principles, i. 128, 129; slavery, i. 27, 31, 167, 177, 179, 181, 182, 302-306, ii. 159-161, 167, 168, 171, 231, 317, 334, 379; South American republics, i. 147-149, 271; Spain, Adams's treaty with, i. 163-165; sub-treasury, ii. 139-141, 191; Texas, i. 164, 165, ii. 87, 88, 92, 93, 244-246, 261, 262; Treasury Department, ii. 35, 36, 188, 222; treaty of Ghent, i. 110-116, 122; treaty power, i. 164; Union, i. 144, 145, 202, ii. 18, 356-359, 360, 361, 414, 415; veto power, i. 378, ii. 188, 222; war of 1812, i. 78, 79, 83, 86, 91, 94-98, 113, 114, 121, 122; war with Mexico, ii. 290, 292; West Florida, i. 59-62; Whig party, ii. 188, 296, 307-309, 396; Wilmot Proviso, ii. 324, 325.

Clay, Colonel Henry, killed at Buena Vista, ii. 287, 288.

Clay, James, appointed minister to Portugal by Taylor, ii. 323.

Clay, John, father of Henry Clay, his character and death, i. 3.

Clay, Mrs. John, mother of Henry Clay, i. 1; her character, 3; refuses money from Tarleton as compensation for property taken, 3; marries Captain Watkins, 4; removes to Kentucky, 9.

Clay, Thomas, describes Clay's friends, ii. 406.

Clayton, John M., in debate on Jackson's bank veto, i. 377; threatens to defeat compromise tariff unless Calhoun vote for all parts of it, ii. 17; supports repeal of four years' term act, 69; opposes expunging resolutions, 102; against distributing fourth installment of surplus, 136; declines nomination for Vice-President, 181; in campaign of 1840, 187.

Clemens, Jeremiah, represents compromise as a Southern victory, ii. 375.

Clinton, De Witt, candidate for presidency, i. 223; declines mission to England, 259.

Clinton, George, defeats re-charter of bank, i. 66.

Cobb, Howell, elected speaker in 1849, ii. 326; represents compromise as a Southern victory, 375.

Coleman, Dr. L. H., letter of Jackson to, on tariff, i. 225.

Collamer, Jacob, postmaster-general under Taylor, an anti-slavery Whig, ii. 321.

Colonization of free negroes, its purpose, i. 303; reasons for support of, 303; advocated by Clay in 1827 as practicable, 303, 304.

Compromise of 1850, planned by Clay, ii. 329; his reasoning as to its necessity, 330, 331; difficulties to be settled by, 331; resolutions to settle, introduced by Clay, 332-334; how each side is to be appeased, 333; attack upon, in Senate, 334; Clay's speech in behalf of, 335-338; Calhoun's speech against, 338-340; Webster's seventh of March speech for, 340, 341; speech of Seward against, 343-345; speech of Chase on, 345; introduction of Omnibus and other bills, 348, 349; elements of opposition to, 350; opposition of Taylor to, 351, 352; Clay's "bleeding wounds" speech, 353; aided by Fillmore's administration, 356; Clay's speech for, 357-359; destruction of Omnibus Bill, 359, 360; last speech of Clay on Union, 360-362; passage of Texas Boundary Bill in Senate, 362; admission of California by Senate, 362; establishment of territorial government in New Mexico, 363; passage of Fugitive Slave Bill, 363; passage of Texas Boundary Bill by House, 364; completed by passage of bill prohibiting slave trade in District of

INDEX 439

Columbia, 365; discussion of its statesmanship, 367-373; fails to settle question of slavery in territories, 368-370; exasperates North by Fugitive Slave Law, 370; by adjourning conflict, gives North the victory in 1861, 373; generally accepted in 1850 as a settlement, 374-376; agitation in favor of, in North, 377; declared to be a final settlement by Congressmen, 378; its success announced by Clay, 382, 387; voted a finality by a minority of Whig Congressmen, 398; upheld by both party conventions, 402, 403; its collapse later, 404.

Congress, defeats re-charter of bank, i. 66; adopts non-importation and embargo, 71; repeals embargo for non-intercourse, 73; offers to repeal non-intercourse against either country recalling orders or decrees, 74; feebleness of its policy, 77; led by Clay to increase army and navy, 79-81; receives John Henry letters, 82; renews embargo, 82; declares war, 85; adopts tariff of 1816, 131; and charters second bank, 133; passes bill for internal improvements, 138; votes to increase pay of members, 139; repeals vote, 140; urged by Monroe not to act hastily on Spanish treaty, 163; debate in, on admission of Missouri, 175-177; admits Arkansas without prohibiting slavery, 177; debate in, on Missouri Compromise, 177, 178; debate in, over Missouri Constitution, 184-189; controversy in, over counting Missouri's electoral vote, 189-191; successful management of Clay to avoid an outbreak, 190, 191; finally admits Missouri by a narrow vote, 191, 192; passes bill authorizing plans for roads and canals, 208; controlled by enemies of Adams's administration, 286; passes tariff of 1828, 286; supports bank, 355; passes tariff of 1832, 366; reports favorably to bank, 373; passes re-charter bill, 375; debates Verplanck tariff bill, ii. 8; passes compromise tariff and force bill, 19, 20; parties on bank question in, 30; its relation to Treasury Department, 34-36; adjourns, 44; passes act reducing duties on French wines, 54; asked by Jackson for authority to make reprisals on France, 54; recommended by Jackson to exclude French shipping and goods, 58; passes bill to distribute surplus to States, 70, 121; passes bill to protect deposits in banks, 121; passes bill to recall specie circular, 126; passes bill for fourth installment of surplus, 136; debates and passes sub-treasury bill, 138; extravagance in, 185; controlled by Whigs, 205; repeals sub-treasury act, 205; passes bills to charter bank, 206, 210; passes Clay's land bill, 211; passes provisional tariff bill, 226; finally passes bill to suit Tyler, 228; forced by Tyler to abandon Clay's land bill, 226-228; declares war begun by act of Mexico, 284; passes tariff of 1846, 284; restores sub-treasury system, 284; congratulates Europe on revolutions of 1848, 304; influenced by Free Soil movement to organize Oregon, 313; debates slavery in territories, 320, 321; not alarmed by Nashville Convention, 355; completes compromise, 365; adjourns, 365; authorizes President to bring Kossuth to America in man-of-war, 393; honors Clay's memory, 406.

Connecticut, repeals "black laws," ii. 154.

Constitution, question of its relation to internal improvements, i. 44, 45; amendment suggested by Jefferson, 45; Clay's view of, as justifying internal improvements, 46, 47; held by Clay not to justify bank, 64-66; later held to justify second bank, 133-135; broad construction of, by Clay, 136, 145; relation to internal improvements, 142-144, 206-208; relation of treaty power to cession of territory, 164; relation to Missouri Compromise, 180; in relation to free negro clause of Missouri Constitution, 184; in relation to Benton's *demos krateo* principle, 240; amendment proposed by Jackson to prevent official "corruption," 264; doctrine of Adams as to internal improvements, 266, 267; amendments to, introduced into Senate, 275, 276; Jackson's view of its interpretation, 378; Calhoun's theory of nullification, ii. 3; Clay's theory of Treasury Department, 34, 35; held by Jackson to forbid Senate's censure, 40, 41; relation to power of President to dismiss from office, 62–65; its relation to power of Congress over slavery in States, 73; its relation to exclusion of abolitionist documents from mail, 84–86; in relation to expunging resolutions, 102; discussion of Jackson's attitude toward, 109, 110; resolutions of Calhoun concerning its necessary protection of slavery, 156, 157; amendment proposed by Clay, 222, 223; in relation to Texas annexation, 240–242, 272; Calhoun's theory of slavery in territories, 302.

Cooper, James, supports Clay's compromise, ii. 350.

Copyright, international, favored by Clay, ii. 100.

Corwin, Thomas, in campaign of 1840, ii. 187; in Senate in 1849, 330; secretary of treasury, 355; becomes a conservative, 355.

Cotton culture, its effect on slavery, i. 173.

Craig, Sir James, connection with Henry letters, i. 82.

Crawford, W. H., candidate for presidency, his career and character, i. 223; a partisan manager, 223; nominated by Republican caucus, 223; coalition of Clay with, suggested by Van Buren, 230; charged with corruption, 231; and with bargaining with Clay, 232; receives 41 electoral votes, 232; reasons for Clay's refusal to support, 238, 239; declines Adams's offer of Treasury Department, 249; letter of Clay to, on Adams, 309.

Creeks, defeated by Jackson, i. 106.

Creole case, ii. 234; resolutions of Giddings concerning, 234, 235.

Crittenden, J. J., told by Clay of intention to support Adams, i. 238; opposes expunging resolutions, ii. 102; against fourth distribution of surplus, 136; attorney-general under Harrison, 191; tribute of Clay to, on leaving Senate, 225; on effect of Clay's departure from Senate, 226; advised by Clay not to yield to Tyler, 227; letter of Clay to, on Texas annexation, 244, 247; believes Clay cannot be elected, 293; letter of Davis to, on Clay's return to Senate, 323; attorney-general under Fillmore, 356; relations with Clay, 356.

Cuba, attacks upon, to be discouraged by Panama Congress, i. 270; revolutions in, opposed by slaveholders, as liable to throw it into hands of England, 270.

Cumberland Road, begun, i. 43; consent of States to, 45; veto of bill to establish toll-houses on, by Monroe, 206.

Curtis, Edward, his appointment as collector at New York desired by Weed, ii. 193; an able party manager, 193, 194; works for Webster against Clay, 194; offers to abandon Webster for Clay, 194; anxiety of Weed to secure offices for, 194; Clay's opinion of, 196; question of his appointment causes rupture between Clay and Harrison, 197; appointed collector, 197.

Dallas, A. J., proposes protective duties, i. 130; his ideas followed in tariff of 1816, 131; proposes a revival of Bank of United States, 132.

Dallas, George M., nominated for vice-president, ii. 252.

Daschkoff, ——, offers Russian mediation to Madison, i. 99, 100.

Daviess, Colonel Joseph Hamilton, assaults Bush, i. 33; attacked by Clay, challenges him, 34; moves to compel attendance of Burr at court to answer charges, 34; a Federalist and unpopular, 35.

INDEX 441

Davis, Jefferson, regrets Clay's return to Senate, ii. 323; letter of Taylor to, on slavery, 327; in Senate in 1849, 330; opposes Clay's compromise and calls for extension of Missouri Compromise line, 334; opposes admission of California, and demands recognition of slavery in territories, 350.

Davis, John, nominated for Vice-President, ii. 230; in Senate in 1849, 330.

Deacon, Peter, Henry Clay's schoolmaster, i. 4, 10.

Debt, national, its extinction approaches in 1830, i. 347.

Delaware, votes for Clay in 1832, i. 383.

Democratic party, begins as Jacksonian opposition to Adams, i. 265; determines to break down administration, 265; opposes Panama mission, 273; continues to oppose all administration measures, 275; its violent language against Adams, 276–280; organizes a machine, 280, 281; succeeds in defaming Adams, 281; unmoved by Clay's destruction of bargain story, 286; controls twentieth Congress, 286; its slanders against Adams, 288; carries election, cause of its success, 290–292; a personal party at outset, 313; gradually controlled by South, 316; claims to be orthodox Republican party, 317; its resemblance to the Jeffersonian Republican party, 318; on the whole, considered successor of Republicans, 319; composed of farmers and poorer classes, 320; its despotic leadership by Jackson, 322, 323, 325; demands share of offices, 335; considers spoils system democratic, 337, 338; opposes Clay's election to Senate, 350; favors bank in 1829–1830, 355; endeavors to entrap Clay, 369, 370; called upon by Benton to choose between bank and Jackson, 378, 379; nominates Van Buren at Jackson's dictation, 380; follows Jackson's policy against bank, 380, 381; denounces bank, 381; derides the "Young Men's Convention," 381; grows enthusiastic over Jackson's struggle against bank, 382; damaged by bank excitement in elections of 1834, ii. 46; regains popularity, 47, 48; nominates Van Buren for President at Jackson's dictation, 96; elects Van Buren easily, 98; demands expunging of censure of Jackson, 100; its success held by Benton to prove popular demand for expunging, 101; members of, reluctant to vote for expunging resolutions, 103,105; Van Buren's leadership of, 129, 130; reaction against, after panic of 1837, 131, 183; proposes issue of treasury notes, 136; secession of conservative faction from, 145; renominates Van Buren, 183; damaged by spoils system, 184, 185; and by reaction against Jackson's rigid rule, 185; defeated, 189; congratulates Tyler on bank veto, 207; gains in elections of 1841, 220; aids in passage of tariff of 1842, 228; dissensions in, 251; position of Van Buren in, 251; its national convention defeats Van Buren by two-thirds rule, 252; advocates reoccupation of Oregon and reannexation of Texas, 252; resignation of Tyler in favor of, 253; embarrassed by insignificance of Polk, 256; equivocal position of, on tariff, 257; in Pennsylvania poses as defender of tariff against Whigs, 258; Northern members of, oppose annexation of Texas and vote for Polk, 259; possibility of anti-Texas members supporting Clay, 260; elects Polk through Liberty vote in New York, 265; its other frauds, 265, 266; declares for "fifty-four forty or fight," 280; movement in, to annex Mexico, 290; main strength of, in South, 301; dislikes slavery question, 302; its national convention admits both Hunkers and Barnburners, 305; nominates Cass, 305; rejects Calhoun's doctrine as to slavery in territories, 305; denounces abolitionists, 305; damaged by Free Soil movement, 313; denounces Free Soilers, 314; defeated in election, 314; expected

442 INDEX

by Clay to win in 1852, 396; in national convention, advocates compromise and nominates Pierce, 402.

Denmark, treaty of Clay with, i. 299.

Denny, Richard, services of Clay in his store, i. 4.

Detroit, surrender of Hull at, i. 86.

Dickinson, Daniel S., originates plan of "squatter sovereignty," ii. 303; leader of Hunker faction, 304; in Senate in 1849, 330.

Diplomatic history, relations of United States to Engand and France, i. 68; failure of Jefferson's foreign policy, 68, 69, 71; Monroe's treaty, 71; Erskine's mission to United States, 73; Jackson's mission, 73; outbreak of war of 1812, 85, 87; attempt at Russian mediation, 99, 100; treaty of Ghent, 102-119; mission of Clay, Adams, and Gallatin to negotiate treaty of commerce, 123, 124; Adams's treaty acquiring Florida and settling Louisiana boundary, 162, 163; treaty not ratified by Spain, 163; finally adopted, 165; negotiations of Clay relative to West India trade, 297, 298; conclusion of treaty in 1827 by Gallatin, 298; negotiations over compensations for slaves taken, 300; attempt of Clay to induce England to return fugitive slaves, 300, 301; negotiations with France over depredation claims, ii. 53; treaty with, 53; mission of Livingston to France, 54, 55; break of diplomatic relations, 55; renewed negotiations and second break, 58; mediation of England, 58; relations with Mexico in 1836, 94, 95; negotiations leading to Ashburton treaty, 218, 237; negotiations of Upshur and Calhoun leading to treaty of annexation with Texas, 238-242; treaty of annexation signed, 245; rejected, 260; annexation by joint resolution, 272-274; negotiations with Mexico over Texan boundary, 274-278; mission of Slidell to Mexico, 277; Oregon negotiations with England, 278-283; negotiations of Calhoun and Pakenham, 280; negotiations of Buchanan, 281; final compromise on forty-ninth parallel, 282, 283; events preceding war with Mexico, 283, 284.

Distribution of surplus, voted by Congress, ii. 70, 121; reasons for, 120; its effects, 122, 123; first two payments, 127; third payment, 128; fourth payment advised against by Van Buren, 134; demanded by Whigs, 135, 136; how used by States, 135, 136; bill for its payment passed, 136.

District of Columbia, abolition of slavery in, demanded by abolitionists, ii. 73; petitions for, 79; opposed by Clay's resolutions, 81, 82; position of Van Buren on, 130; resolutions of Calhoun and Clay on, 156, 160, 161; slave trade in, to be abolished in compromise of 1850, 333.

Disunion, movement toward, in New England, i. 82, 99, 106; killed by treaty of Ghent, 121; threatened by South in Missouri debate, 176; 186; alarms Northern men into supporting South, 195; its possibility in 1820, 196; planned for by South, 197; considered possible by Clay, 197; by J. Q. Adams, 198; no idea of coercion against, in 1820, 198, 199; not advocated in 1832, ii. 5; discredited by Jackson's proclamation and by Force Bill, 22; threatened by South unless abolitionists are put down, 75; threatened by South Carolina in 1844, 252; threatened in 1849 by South in case of exclusion of slavery from territories, 321; threatened with increased violence in 1850, 328, 329; opposed by Clay, 329; denounced by Clay and Webster as impossible without war, 337, 341; forcible resistance to, threatened by Taylor, 351, 352; duty of its suppression asserted by Clay, 358, 359, 361, 389; discussed in South Carolina and Mississippi, but defeated in elections, 374; last appeal of Clay against, 389.

Dix, John A., leader of Barnburners, ii. 304, 311.

Douglas, Stephen A., supports application of Missouri Compromise line

INDEX 443

to Texas, ii. 272; in Senate in 1849, 330; supports Clay's compromise, 350.

Duane, William J., appointed secretary of treasury, ii. 27; expected by Jackson to remove deposits, 27; opposes removal as dangerous and wishes congressional action, 27; unmoved by Jackson's arguments, 28; defies kitchen cabinet, 28; refuses to yield or resign, 29; dismissed, 29.

EATON, JOHN H., moves not to assent to clause in Missouri Constitution against free negroes, i. 184; manages reconciliation of Jackson and Clay, 238; real author of Kremer's letters, 246; secretary of war, 330; forced by Jackson to support Van Buren for Vice-President, 380.

Eaton, Mrs. "Peggy," controversy over, in Jackson's cabinet, i. 338, 367.

Election of 1824, i. 221-248; description of candidates, 222-228; Jackson's campaign, 226; Clay's campaign, 229, 230; proposed coalitions, 230; campaign slanders, 231, 232; vice-presidential candidates, 232; electoral vote, 232, 233; intrigues to settle vote of House, 236-238; constitutional power of House, 240; the bargain story, 241-247; real relations of Clay and Adams, 247; election of Adams, 248; further history of bargain story, 282-286.

Eliot, Samuel A., his election pleases Webster, ii. 366.

Ellmaker, Amos, nominated for Vice-President by Anti-Masons, i. 344.

Embargo, adopted against England, i. 71; its effect, 72; repealed, 73; renewed as war measure, 82.

England, relations with, in Jefferson's first term, i. 40; animosity against, in West, 49; denounced in Kentucky, 51; supposed to be intriguing for West Florida, 58; fear of, denounced by Clay, 61; Orders in Council of, against France, 69; intends to crush out neutral trade, 70; impresses American seamen, 70; commercial warfare of Jefferson against, 71-73; disavows Erskine, 73; agrees to withdraw orders in case France withdraws decrees, 75; refuses to withdraw orders, 76; reluctance of Madison toward war with, 77; desire of West for war with, 78; declaration of war against, 85; repeals Orders in Council, 87; its successes in War of 1812, 86, 87, 98, 99; rejects Russian mediation, 100; offers to treat directly, 100; wishes to isolate American commissioners, 102; continued successes in 1813-1814, 105, 106; free, after fall of Napoleon, to crush United States, 106; considers Americans to be suing for peace, 107; abates extreme demands in view of Continental situation, 108, 109; anxious for peace, 111; dissatisfied with treaty, 118; negotiates commercial convention, 124; refuses to open questions of impressment or blockade, 124; its influence on Monroe's administration denounced by Clay, 166; pointed to by Clay as example of benefits of protection, 217; negotiations with, over West India trade, 297; offers privileges on condition of reciprocity, 297, 298; prohibits intercourse with West Indies, 298; mission of Gallatin to, 298; concludes treaty in 1827, 298, 299; agrees to pay lump sum for slaves carried off in 1813, 300; refuses proposed return of fugitive slaves, 301; mediates between France and United States in 1836, ii. 58; effect of crisis of 1836 in, upon America, 127; Ashburton treaty with, 237; rumors of intention to secure emancipation in Texas, 238, 248, 249; mediates between Texas and Mexico, 239; occupies Oregon jointly with United States, 278; negotiates as to boundary, 279; negotiations of Calhoun and Pakenham, 280; offers arbitration, 280, 281; danger of war with, 281; declines forty-ninth parallel, 281; then proposes it, 282; concludes treaty, 283; its aid hoped for by South in case of secession, 337.

Enterprise case, Calhoun's resolutions on, ii. 170.

Era of good feeling, characteristics of, i. 140, 221; decay of parties in, 282, 312.

Erie Canal, begun, i. 44.

Erie Lake, victory of, i. 105.

Erskine, David M., exceeds instructions and is recalled, i. 73.

Eustis, William, offers resolution admitting Missouri on condition of expunging article against free negroes, i. 186.

Everett, Edward, asked by Clay as to his chances of carrying Eastern States, i. 311; in campaign of 1840, ii. 187.

Ewing, Thomas, on Jackson's bank veto, i. 377; supports resolutions of censure, ii. 37; supports Calhoun's report on executive patronage, 62; votes for repeal of four years' term act, 69; opposes expunging resolution, 102; taunts Jacksonians, 103; in campaign of 1840, 187; secretary of treasury under Harrison, 191; recommends a bank, 206; authorized by Tyler to confer with Congress concerning a bank, 209; resigns, 214.

FEDERALISTS, commit blunders during John Adams's administration, i. 31, 32; alarm masses by seeking to silence opposition by law, 32; break up as a party during Jefferson's administration, 41; jealous of West, 59; deny claim to West Florida, 59; censured by Clay, 59, 60; denounce war in 1812, 83; support increase of navy, 89; attack conduct of war, 89, 90; incur suspicion of lack of patriotism, 91; denounced by Clay, 92-94; practically disappear after War of 1812, 126; oppose tariff of 1816, 130; oppose bank, 133; vote for King in 1816, 140; disappear as national organization, 221; propitiated by letter of Jackson, 225; convention of, nominates Jackson, 226; given offices by Adams, 259; join Whig party as a rule, 317.

Fessenden, William Pitt, vice-president of "young men's" convention, i. 381.

Field, David Dudley, opposes annexation of Texas, but supports Polk, ii. 259.

Fillmore, Millard, nominated for Vice-President, ii. 306; succeeds Taylor, 355; his character, favors Clay's compromise, 355; his cabinet, 355, 356; aids Clay, 356; informs Senate of danger of collision in New Mexico, 362; issues proclamation in Shadrach case, 380; his support expected by Webster, 399; supported by Southern Whigs, 400; supported by Clay, 401; identified with compromise measures, 401.

Financial History, see Bank, Tariff; distress of Treasury during War of 1812, i. 99; suspension of specie payments after war, 131, 132; paper-money craze in Kentucky, 203; events leading to crisis of 1819, 212, 213; prevalence of "cheap money" theories, 213; excitement over removal of deposits, ii. 29, 30, 37; distress petitions, and delegations, 37, 40; causes for speculation in Jackson's time, prosperity and high foreign credit, 115; expansion of loans by "pet banks," and others, 116; banking mania, 117; land speculation, 117-119; part played by banks in, 118; growth of surplus, 119, 120; alarm created by, 120; bill to protect deposits, 121; and to deposit surplus with States, 121; difficulties of banks in contracting loans to carry out distribution act, 123; shifting of specie, 123; issuance of "specie circular," 125; its paralyzing effect on land payments, 125; dangerous tightness of market, 126; refusal of Jackson to rescind specie circular, 126; first two payments of surplus, 127; collapse of prices in 1837, 127; growing bankruptcy, 128; collapse of banks and suspension of specie payments, 128; refusal of Van Buren to recall specie circular, 131; passage of fourth installment, 136; issue of treasury notes, 137; indebtedness of States in 1841, 212; threatened repudiation, 212; proposal of Congress to assist States, its error, 212; failure of Clay's land bill to act, 213; increase of public debt, 221; difficulties in placing loan, 221; deficit, 221.

Fisheries, debate over, in treaty of Ghent, i. 110; quarrels between American envoys over, 110, 111.

Flagg, Azariah, a Barnburner, ii. 312.

Florida, debate as to United States's claim to, i. 58; negotiations over, 58; troubles in, 58; claim to, asserted by Madison, 59; debate over, in Senate, 59–62; Indian troubles in, 151; career of Jackson in, 151, 152; acquired by Adams's treaty, 162; its seizure proposed, 163; abolition in, opposed by Clay, ii. 161, 162.

Floyd, John, moves to count electoral vote of Missouri in 1820, i. 190; ready for a decision by force, 191; ruled out of order by Clay, 191; extravagant attacks on Adams's administration, 279, 280; receives electoral vote of South Carolina in 1832, 383.

Foote, Henry S., in Senate in 1849, ii. 330; offers resolution for select committee to settle slavery question, 347.

Force Bill, demanded by Jackson, ii. 9; passed by Senate, 17; final passage and signing, 20.

Forsyth, John, moves appointment of committee to investigate Kremer's charge against Clay, i. 244.

Forward, Walter, secretary of treasury, suggests increase in tariff, ii. 221.

Foster, A. J., letter of Castlereagh to, on Orders in Council, i. 84.

Fox, Charles James, his oratory compared to Clay's, i. 327.

France, commercial warfare of, against England, i. 69; its aggressions on American commerce, 74; its perfidious conduct regarding decrees, 74–76, 87; attempts to force United States into war with England, 75, 87; continues to seize American vessels, 76; complained of by Madison, 77; an example, according to Clay, of benefits of protection, 217; negotiations over claims of United States against, ii. 53; refuses to pay, 53; makes treaty agreeing to pay, 53; but still refuses to make appropriations, 54; threatened by Jackson, 54; recalls its minister and dismisses Livingston, 55; danger of war with, 55; soothing language to, of Clay's report in Senate, 56, 57; action against, refused by Senate, 57; pacified by Clay's resolution, passes appropriation on condition of explanations of Jackson's message, 58; again angered at Jackson's message, refuses payment, 58; recalls representative, 58; pacified by English mediation, 58; war with, averted by Clay, 58, 59; mediates between Texas and Mexico, 239; Clay's opinion of Napoleon's *coup d'état* in, 395.

Franklin, Benjamin, his example referred to by Clay to justify emancipation, i. 31.

Free Soil party, movement of Whigs toward, ii. 306, 310; joined by Liberty party, 311; by Barnburners, 311; formed at Buffalo convention, 312; nominates Van Buren, its platform, 312; loses support of anti-slavery Whigs, 313; causes organization of Oregon, 313; denounced by old parties, 314; causes defeat of Cass, 314; dissolves, 315; its principle remains, 315.

Frelinghuysen, Theodore, votes for repeal of four years' term act, ii. 69; nominated for vice-president, 250; his unpopularity damages Clay, 266.

Fremont, John C., appointed to command Oregon expedition, to propitiate Benton, ii. 239; discovers passes in Rocky Mountains, 279; takes possession of California, 285.

Frenchtown, defeat of Winchester at, i. 98.

446   INDEX

Fugitive slaves, negotiations of Clay and Gallatin concerning their return by England, i. 300, 301; necessity of comprising, in compromise, law for their return, ii. 332, 333; passage of law, 363; denunciation of law in North, 376; its necessity as alternative to disunion urged by Clay, 388; enforcement of law demanded by Democratic and Whig conventions, 402.

GAINES, GENERAL, begins Seminole war, i. 151; ordered by Jackson to enter Texas, ii. 91; recalled, 91.

Gallatin, Albert, makes elaborate report on internal improvements, i. 46; makes report on manufactures, suggesting various methods of encouragement, 55-57; practically agrees with Clay, 57; wishes re-charter of bank, 63; refutes charges against bank, 64; opposed by Smith coterie, 64; dissuades Madison from making Clay commanding general, 88; nominated peace commissioner, 100, 101; becomes guiding mind of commission, 105; tries in vain to interest Emperor of Russia on behalf of United States, 106; has difficulty in maintaining peace between Adams and Clay, 110, 113; negotiates treaty of commerce in London, 123, 124; one of Republican triumvirate, 127; his diplomatic career, 128; proposes to assist Greece, 209; withdraws from nomination for vice-president, 231; declines mission to Panama Congress, 293; minister to England, 298; his share in negotiations over Orders in Council of 1826, 298; renews convention of 1815, 298; instructed to propose return of fugitive slaves, 300; does so in a perfunctory way, 301; on Clay's improvement in office, 308; advocates revenue tariff, 359; denounced as an alien at heart by Clay, 363; his career and patriotism, 364, 365; pained at Clay's bitter attack, 365; his suggestions practically adopted by Clay, 365, 366; quoted as authority on banking by Clay, ii. 36; leads in effort to resume specie payment, 143.

Gambier, Lord, English peace commissioner, i. 105.

Garrison, William Lloyd, begins agitation for immediate abolition, ii. 72; mobbed in Boston, 75; his heroism, 77.

Georgia, upheld by Jackson against Supreme Court, i. 347; nominates Clay in 1842, ii. 230; adopts compromise as provisional basis of settlement, 374, 375.

Giddings, Joshua R., offers resolutions justifying slaves in Creole case, ii. 234; censured, and resigns, 235; thanked by Clay for his firmness, 235; reëlected, 235; denounces Fugitive Slave Law, 379.

Girard, Stephen, aids Treasury in 1813, i. 99.

Goderich, Lord, on English commercial treaty commission in 1814, i. 124; prime minister, 298.

Goulburn, Henry, English peace commissioner, i. 105; on commercial treaty commission, 124.

Gouverneur, Samuel L., asked not to send abolitionist documents, turns to postmaster-general for instructions, ii. 83.

Granger, Francis, an anti-Mason, i. 345; nominated for vice-president, ii. 98; postmaster-general, 191.

Greece, revolts against Turkey, i. 208; sympathy for, in United States, 208, 209.

Greeley, Horace, describes office-seekers in 1841, ii. 193; on evil effect of Clay's Alabama letter, 264; describes probable slavery compromise to Clay, 319; informs Clay of unpopularity of Fugitive Slave Law, 392.

Green, Duff, slanders Adams's administration, i. 280; ejected from kitchen cabinet, 346.

Grundy, Felix, one of war Republicans, i. 78.

HALE, JOHN P., nominated by Liberty party, ii. 310; defeated at Buffalo

INDEX 447

convention, 312; in Senate of 1849, 330; sarcastic reply to Clay in 1851, 379.

Hamilton, Alexander, his leadership compared to that of Clay and Jackson, i. 321.

Hamilton, Colonel James A., appointed by Jackson to hold State Department until arrival of Van Buren, i. 331; describes indifference of Jackson to fitness in his officials, 338.

Hamlin, Hannibal, in Senate in 1849, ii. 330; conversation with Taylor on compromise, 352.

Hampton, Wade, fails to attack Montreal, i. 105.

Hanseatic League, treaty of Clay with, i. 299.

Harrison, General W. H., retreats in 1813, i. 98; wins battle of Thames, 105; nominated for president in 1836, ii. 98; favored by Clay, 98; favored by Webster over Clay, 175; his advantages as a "military hero," 175; writes modest letter to Clay, 175, 176; united upon by opposition to Clay, 176; his character and career, absence of Whig principles, 185, 186; his grievance against Jackson, 186; "log cabin and hard cider," 186; elected president, 189; tries to avoid interview with Clay, 190; offers cabinet places to Clay and Webster, 190; advised by Clay to trust in his frankness, 191; his cabinet, 191; rebukes Clay for dictatorial tone, 195; his address influenced by Clay, 195; at Clay's suggestion, calls extra session of Congress, 195; tells Clay to communicate henceforth by writing, 195; reply of Clay to, 195-197; intends to keep promises of reform, 197; issues circular prohibiting official interference in elections, 197, 198; his death, 198.

Hart, Lucretia, marries Clay, i. 24; letter of Clay to, ii. 385.

Hart, Thomas, letters of Clay to, on Burr, i. 37; on life in Washington, 47.

Harvey, James E., letter of Clay to, on slavery in territories, ii. 324, 325.

Hayne, Robert Y., Webster's reply to, i. 347.

Hayti, recognition of, deprecated by Adams and Clay at Panama Congress, i. 269, 270; wished by Clay in 1825, 302.

Henderson, General James P., sent by Texas as special envoy, ii. 240; arrives in Washington, 241; deceived by Calhoun, 241, 242.

Henry, John, his mission to New England, i. 82; sells letters to Madison, 82.

Henry, Patrick, in 1773, writes letter deploring his situation as slave-owner, i. 27, 28, 306.

Herrera, President of Mexico, wishes Slidell to delay arrival, ii. 277; overthrown by revolution, 278.

"Higher Law," referred to by Seward, ii. 344; denounced as treason by Democrats, 345; ridiculed by Webster, 387.

Hill, Isaac, in kitchen cabinet, i. 346; complains to Jackson of Mason as president of branch bank, 353.

Holy Alliance, arraigned by Webster, i. 209; defied by Clay, 211.

Horsey, Outerbridge, denies claim of United States to West Florida, i. 59; criticised by Clay, 60.

House of Representatives, defeats recharter of bank, i. 66; preferred by Clay to Senate, 67; its character in 1811, 67; elects Clay speaker, 68; led by Clay and war Republicans, 79; refuses to debate war, 84; vote in, for war, 85; debate in, on conduct of war, 89-98; reëlects Clay speaker, 101, 126; strength of parties in, 126; again reëlects Clay, 142; adopts resolutions on internal improvements, 145; defeats Clay's motion to recognize South American insurgents, 150; debates resolution censuring Jackson, 153; rejects the resolution, 159; reëlects Clay speaker in spite of proposal to lay him aside, 162; rejects Clay's resolutions on Spanish treaty, 165; adopts Clay's resolution to recognize South American republics, 167;

rejects appropriation for ministers, 167; passes bill admitting Missouri without slavery, 177; finally adopts Missouri Compromise, 178, 180; debate in, on admission of Missouri, 185; rejects bill to admit Missouri, 185; rejects resolution forcing Missouri to change Constitution, 186; report of Clay to, on Missouri Constitution, 188, 189; rejects Clay's attempt to conciliate, 189; trouble in, over right to count Missouri's electoral vote, 189-191; managed by Clay, 191; finally votes to admit Missouri, 192; elects Clay speaker in 1823 over Barbour, 204; debates proposed pension to Perry's mother, 205; debates bill authorizing President to plan a system of internal improvements, 206-208; debates Greek question, 211; debates tariff of 1824, 214-219; passes bill, analysis of vote, 219; has to choose president in 1825, 236; led by Clay, 236; intrigues in, 236-238; attempt of Benton to persuade, 240; appoints committee to investigate Kremer's bargain story, 244; refusal of Kremer to testify before, 245; elects Adams president, 248; thanks Clay for services as speaker, 254; passes appropriations for Panama mission, 273; bitter struggle in, between Jacksonians and Adams men, 287; asks president to negotiate with England for return of fugitive slaves, 300; affirms constitutionality of bank and defeats resolution against re-charter, 355; committee of, reports declaring bank unsound, 374; passes bill to re-charter bank, 375; debates Verplanck tariff, ii. 8, 9, 19; substitutes Clay's compromise for Verplanck bill, 19; votes that deposits are safe in bank, 26; controlled by Democrats, 30; rejects resolution to restore deposits, 37; passes resolutions against return of deposits and renewal of charter, 48; defeats Clay's land bill, 70; votes to recognize Texas when it has a civil government, 93; investigates administration of civil service, 184; abandons gag rule, 233; attempts to censure Adams, 233, 234; censures Giddings, 234, 235; carried by Democrats in 1842, 237; passes joint resolution annexing Texas, 272; debates and passes Wilmot Proviso with two-million bill, 286; again passes Wilmot Proviso, but yields to Senate, 286; struggle in, over speakership, 326; defeats Wilmot Proviso, 343; passes Texas boundary bill, disgraceful scenes, 363-365; debates Fugitive Slave Law, 379.

Houston, Sam, goes to Texas to cause rebellion, ii. 90; relations with Jackson, 90; deteats Santa Anna, 91; asks Upshur if United States will protect Texas by force during negotiations, 239; rejects armistice with Mexico, 240; in Senate in 1849, 330.

Hudson, George, grandfather of Henry Clay, i. 3.

Hülsemann, Chevalier, complains of American emisary to Hungary, ii. 392; reply of Webster to, 392.

Hull, William, surrenders at Detroit, i. 86.

Hungary, revolts against Austria, ii. 392; sympathy of United States for, 392; attempt of Kossuth to get aid for, 393, 394; opinions of Clay on, 394-396.

"Hunkers," in New York, reject Wilmot Proviso, ii. 304; pledge to support Democratic nominees, 304, 305; defeated by Barnburners, 314.

Hunt, Washington, on damaging effect of Clay's Alabama letter, ii. 264.

Hunt, Ward, a Barnburner, ii. 312.

Hunter, Robert M. T., in Senate in 1849, ii. 330.

IMPEACHMENT, its suggested use against a president, for corrupt removals from office, shown to be impossible, ii. 64, 65.

Impressment, its exercise by England, i. 70; after repeal of Orders in Council, remains cause of war of 1812, 88; speech of Clay on, 95-97;

excluded from treaty of peace, 109, 117.
Indiana, journey of Clay in, ii. 230.
Indians, quiet during Jefferson's first term, i. 40; bill to regulate trade with, 57; Clay's opinion of, ii. 59; Clay urges aid to Cherokees in removing west of Mississippi, 59–61.
Ingham, Samuel D., secretary of treasury under Jackson, i. 330; compliments bank, 353; corresponds with Biddle concerning Mason, 354; later confesses how kitchen cabinet turned Jackson against bank, 354.
Internal improvements, favored from outset by Clay, i. 39, 40; demanded by West, 43; by Eastern cities, 44; question of their constitutionality, 44, 45; urged by Jefferson, 45; report on, urged by Clay, and made by Gallatin, 46; advocated by Calhoun, 137, 138; vetoed by Madison, 138; held unconstitutional by Monroe, 142; defended by Clay, 143–145; bill for, vetoed by Monroe, 206; debated in House, 206–208; advocated in widest sense by Adams, 265, 267; not a party issue, 313; bill for, vetoed by Jackson, 317; bill for, vetoed by Polk, ii. 284; last effort of Clay for, 384.
Ireland, ruined, according to Clay, by absence of protection, i. 217.

JACKSON, ANDREW, gains successes over Creeks in 1813, i. 106; receives authority to attack Seminoles, 151; his campaign in West Florida, 151, 152; his treatment of Arbuthnot and Ambrister, 152; supported by Adams, partially justified by cabinet, 152; attacked by Clay in Congress, 153, 155–157; unnecessary character of Clay's attack upon, 157; his popularity as a military hero, 158; resolutions to censure rejected, 159; received everywhere as a "vindicated hero," 159, 160; letter of Monroe to, on Louisiana boundary, 164; candidate for president, 224; his civil and military career, 224, 225; unfit for executive office, 225; campaign for, 225, 226; writes various politic letters, 225; elected senator, 226; nominated in various ways, 226; called a murderer by opponents, 231; his managers announce coalition of Crawford and Clay, 232; supports Calhoun for vice-president, 232; suggested for vice-president by Adams, 232; receives ninety-nine electoral votes, 232; on bad terms with Clay, 237; attempts to become reconciled, 237; meets him at dinner, offers various courtesies, 238; refusal of Clay to support, 239; question as to his asserted plurality of popular vote, 239–241; his friends attack Clay bitterly, 241; his managers use Kremer as a tool to defame Adams and Clay, 246; not willing to receive offer of War Department from Adams, 250; wishes Clay's nomination rejected by Senate, 254; writes letter to Swartwout on subject, 254; declines to bring charges before Senate, 255; votes against confirmation, 255; congratulates Adams, 255; begins to repeat on journey home the corruption story, 255; popularly thought to have been cheated out of election, 257; nominated for president by Tennessee, 263; accepts in letter promising to reform corruption at Washington, 263, 264; his followers determine to break down Adams's administration, 265; asserts the question at issue to be the people versus the administration, 277; his campaign in 1827, 279, 280; denounced by Adams's friends, 282; repeats bargain story publicly, 283; called upon by Clay for proof, 283; points to Buchanan as witness, 284; his story denied by Buchanan, 284; does not retract or reply, but later repeats story, 285; his friends continue to believe and assert story, 286; abused in campaign of 1828, 288; elected, 288, 289; his followers form new opposition party, 312, 313, 317; his protectionist sentiments, 313; discussion of his char-

450 INDEX

acter and sources of leadership, 322-325; his ignorance, 322; masterfulness, 322; considers party his army, 323; intense seriousness, 323; his popularity, 323, 324; intolerance of opposition, 324; certainty of rectitude, 325; his hatred for Clay, 329, 330; chooses his cabinet from Clay's enemies, 330; determined not to leave State Department under Clay's influence, orders Hamilton to hold it until arrival of Van Buren, 330, 331; attacked as a military despot by Clay, 332; his popularity with ignorant masses, 333; announces purpose to reform administration, 334, 335; lack of excuse for his removing officials, 335; fills offices with his friends, 335; denounced by Clay, 336; honestly thinks himself to be reforming government, 337; utterly indifferent to fitness of candidate, 338; characteristics of his cabinet, 338; his downfall expected by Clay, 339; supported by Masons, 342; preferred by Clay to an anti-Masonic president, 344; his kitchen cabinet, 345, 346; his first message to Congress, 347; vetoes "Maysville Road" bill to show hostility to internal improvements, 347; favors Georgia against Supreme Court in Cherokee case, 347; his "Union" toast, 348; hostility to Calhoun, 348; his cabinet resigns, 348; appoints a new cabinet, 348; nominated for second term, 348; queries constitutionality of bank in first message, 353; not at first an enemy of bank, 353; mind poisoned against bank by kitchen cabinet, 354; renews attack on bank in subsequent messages without effect, 355; not inclined to push matters to a decision, 356; hope of Clay to ruin, by forcing bank upon, 357; denounced in Whig platform for attacking bank, 358; at first a protectionist, later favors a revenue tariff, 359, 360; his proposed reduction of duties opposed by Clay, 360; his friendship for Van Buren, 366; nominates him minister to England, 367; not led to adopt spoils system by Van Buren, 368; determines to revenge rejection of Van Buren's nomination, 369; without any definite public land policy, 370; believes all charges against bank, 375; determines to crush bank as a political enemy, 375; not hindered by opposition in his own party, 375; vetoes bank, his message, 376, 377; condemns the bank as unconstitutional monopoly, 376; quotes Clay's own words, 376, 377; declares indifference to Supreme Court decision, 377; denounced by Whig leaders in Senate, 377, 378; defended by Benton, 379; his veto message derided by Whig papers, 379, 380; not formally renominated, 380; selects Van Buren for vice-president, 380; his veto popular with masses, 381; supported by Democrats without exception, 381; popularity of his attack on bank, 382, 384; signs tariff of 1832, ii. 2; his mild references to opposition in message of 1832, 5, 6; thought by Adams to be on point of surrendering to South Carolina, 6; issues proclamation against nullification, 6, 7; intimates use of force, 7; stirs enthusiasm in North, 7; criticised as "too ultra" by Clay, 8; asks for authority to coerce South Carolina, 9; dislike of Clay to give him military power, 10; story of his threat to hang Calhoun, 13; signs compromise tariff and Force Bill, 20; importance of his assertion of supremacy of general government, 22; kills Clay's Land Bill by pocket veto, 23; makes triumphant tour in North, 24; surpasses Clay in popularity, 25; resolves to destroy bank, asks investigation, 26; considers bank an agency of corruption, 26; reconstructs cabinet, 27; appoints Duane, an opponent of bank, to Treasury Department, 27; objection of his friends to removal of deposits, 27, 28; unmoved by opposition, 28; urges Duane in vain,

INDEX

28; reads to cabinet paper written by Taney taking responsibility, 28, 29; dismisses Duane and appoints Taney, 29; announces to Congress removal of deposits and assails bank, 30; snubs Senate for demanding copy of paper read to cabinet, 32; asserts responsibility to people alone, 32; resolutions of censure moved against, 32; accused by Clay of aiming at tyranny, 33; discussion of legality of his action toward Treasury Department, 33-36; condemned in Clay's appeal to Van Buren, 38, 39; considers distress due to bank, 40; sends protest against censure to Senate, 40, 41; affirms president to be direct representative of people, 40; denies right of Senate to judge his conduct, 40; fallacy of his arguments, 41, 42; dangerous character of his doctrines, 42, 43; does not probably realize their full bearing, 42; denounced by Clay as a would-be despot, 43; his protest condemned by Senate, 43; all his nominations rejected by Senate, 44; does not lose but gains popularity by attack on bank, 47, 52; continues to denounce and harass bank, 48; his attack at first wanton, 49; later justified, 49-52; his methods of attack indefensible, 51, 52; urges claims upon France with vigor, 53; recommends reprisals to force French Chambers to appropriate money, 54; effect of his message in France, 55; his message deprecated by Clay, 55, 56; his language explained away, 57; refuses to apologize, although disclaiming menace, 58; causes renewed rupture with France, 58; recommends exclusion of French vessels, 58; gains popularity by his language, 58; causes demoralization by appointments, 61; attacked by Clay for appointments, 64, 65; reluctant to sign distribution bill, 70; denounces abolitionists, suggests prohibiting incendiary publications in the mail, 84; tries to purchase Texas, 90; complicity with Houston's schemes in Texas, 90; instructs Gaines to be ready to aid Texans, 91; adopts mild tone toward Mexico, 94; declares Mexico has given cause for war, and asks power to resort to reprisals, 94; selects his successor, 96; debate over Benton's resolutions to expunge censure of, 101-105; his tyranny described by Clay, 103, 104; his joy over expunging resolutions, 106; his complete triumph over Clay, 106, 107; contradictory views of, 107; estimate of his character and good points, 108; dangers of his policy, 108-110; his assumption of sole popular representation the same as Napoleon's, 110; irrevocably damages American government, 111; violence during his administration, 111, 112; approves assaults upon his enemies, 112; suggests distribution of surplus, later repents, 119; gives reasons why he should not have signed bill, 121; at first pleased by land sales, 124; later distrusts speculation, 124; issues specie circular ordering only coin to be received for public lands, 125; vetoes bill rescinding specie circular, 126; escapes discredit of panic, 129; his financial policy attacked by Whigs, 137; called by Clay cause of panic, 139; reaction against his severe discipline, 185; writes letter in favor of Texas annexation, 239; tries to break force of Van Buren's letter against annexation, 248; renews, in 1844, the charge of bargain against Clay, 258, 259; orders exploration of Oregon, 279.

Jackson, F. J., his mission to United States, i. 73.

Jefferson, Thomas, aided by Wythe in revising laws of Virginia, i. 7; a student in Wythe's office, 7; effect of his reforms upon Virginia aristocracy, 8; leads opposition to Alien and Sedition laws, 32; said by Burr to approve his schemes, 36; receives Burr's letter to Clay, 37;

INDEX

success of his policy of attracting moderate Federalists, 41; announces successful expedition of Lewis and Clarke, 42; apprehends private jobbery from internal improvements, 45; advocates a constitutional amendment to justify them, 45; later favors Cumberland Road, 45; eulogized in Kentucky resolutions, 51; failure of his peaceful foreign policy, 68; rejects Monroe's treaty, 71; calls extra session of Congress to pass embargo, 71; his unfitness for conflict, 72; welcomes end of term as a deliverance, 72; leaves all responsibility to Madison, 73; defended against Quincy by Clay, 91, 93; unable to carry out his own Republican principles, 127; his position as sage of Monticello, 127, 128; his alarm over Missouri controversy, 193; his position as party leader, 321; his policy regarding offices, 334; suggests distribution of surplus, ii. 119.

Johnson, Andrew, tenure-of-office act under, ii. 63; elected to Congress, 290.

Johnson, Reverdy, in campaign of 1840, ii. 187.

Johnson, Richard M., deplores Clay's imprudence as a candidate, i. 211, 212; defeated by Clay for Senate, 350.

Johnston, J. S., correspondence of Clay with, in 1824, i. 229, 230.

KANE, J. K., letter of Polk to, on tariff, ii. 257.

Kearney, General Philip, seizes New Mexico, ii. 285.

Kendall, Amos, teacher in Clay's family, describes the way to be popular in Kentucky, i. 17; in kitchen cabinet, 346; quarrels with Clay, 346; suggests to Jackson removal of deposits, ii. 26; approves exclusion of abolition matter from mails, although unlawful, 83.

Kent, Joseph, opposes expunging resolution, ii. 102.

Kentucky, explorations of Boone in, i. 13; settled mainly from Virginia, 14; description of frontier society in, 14–18; education in, 16, 17; constitutional convention of, 27; emancipation movement in, 27; its unpopularity, 30; opposes Alien and Sedition laws, 31; sympathy in, for Burr, 35; career of Clay in legislature of, 49–52; movement to abolish use of English law, 50; effect of Clay's opposition, 50; adopts resolutions denouncing England and supporting Jefferson, 51; demands admission of Missouri with slavery, 177; paper-money craze in, 203; struggle over constitutionality of relief acts, 203, 346; supports Clay for presidency in 1823, 204, 228, 233; instructs members of Congress to vote for Jackson, 238; votes for Jackson in 1828, 293; elects Clay to Senate, 350; votes for Clay in 1832, 383; enthusiasm for Clay in, ii. 229; grows weary of Clay as a candidate, 294; movement in, for Taylor, 295; discusses emancipation, 316–319; rejects Clay's plan, 319; elects Clay to Senate, 319; wishes him to compromise dangers, 319.

King, Preston, leader of Barnburners, ii. 304, 311.

King, Rufus, Federalist candidate for presidency, i. 140; appointed minister to England, 259; replaced by Gallatin, 298.

King, William R., votes against repeal of four-years' term, ii. 69; in Senate in 1849, 330.

Kitchen cabinet of Jackson, i. 346, 348; turns Jackson against bank, 354; suggests removal of deposits, ii. 26.

Kremer, George, avows authorship of bargain story against Clay, i. 243; his character, impossibility of Clay's fighting with, 243; his excitement over appointment of investigating committee, 244; sends a disclaimer to Clay, 244; refuses to testify before committee, 245; description of his use as tool by Jackson's managers, 246; contempt of Clay for,

INDEX 453

252; his address to constituents repeating charges of corruption, 254.

Kossuth, Louis, escapes into Turkey, ii. 392; brought to America in man-of-war, 393; his enthusiastic reception, 393; tries to get aid from United States, 393; speech of Webster at banquet to, 394; interview with Clay, 394; Clay's advice to, 394-396.

LAFAYETTE, MARQUIS DE, letter of Washington to, on slavery, i. 29; his visit to America and reception, 234; welcomed by Clay to Congress, 234, 235; his friendship for Clay, 235.

Lands, public, bill of Clay concerning preëmption of, i. 57; report of Clay on, 370, 371; Benton's report on, 371, 372; exaggerated importance of, to Clay, 372; bill to distribute proceeds of, passed, ii. 23; vetoed by Jackson, 23; Clay's bill again passes Senate, but fails in House, 70; Clay's bill fails again, 100; wild speculation in, 117-119, 124; specie circular issued concerning payments for, 125; collapse of speculation in, 127, 128; proposal to reduce price of, 152; Clay's bill to distribute proceeds of, passed, 211; fails to operate, 213; its amendment urged by Clay, 224; Clay's bill incorporated in tariff of 1842, 226; vetoed twice by Tyler, 226, 227; finally abandoned, 228.

Leigh, Watkins, declines nomination for vice-presidency, ii. 181.

Lemoyne, F. J., vote for, in 1840, ii. 190.

Letcher, Robert P., urges Adams to give Clay an important place, i. 247; moves substitution of Clay's compromise for Verplanck bill, ii. 19; letter of Crittenden to, on Clay's leaving Senate, 226.

Lewis, Major William B., manages Jackson's candidacy, i. 225; in kitchen cabinet, 346; opposes removal of deposits, ii. 27.

Lewis and Clark, their expedition to the Pacific, i. 42.

Lexington, founded, i. 16; society and culture of, 16-18.

Liberty party, casts seven thousand votes for Birney and Lemoyne, ii. 190, 254; its origin and character, 254; differs from abolitionists, 254; brought into prominence by Texas question, 255; its national convention in 1843, leaders and candidates, 255; attacks Clay rather than Polk, 262, 263; its reasons not illogical, 263; receives anti-slavery Whigs after Clay's Alabama letters, 264; its vote in New York gives election to Polk, 265, 266; nominates Hale in 1847, 310; attends Free Soil Convention, 311.

Lincoln, Abraham, compared to Jackson and Clay, i. 321; elected to Congress in 1846, ii. 289.

Liverpool, Lord, does not desire to prolong American war, i. 108; congratulated by Castlereagh on peace of Ghent, 118.

Livingston, Edward, secretary of state under Jackson, i. 348; minister to France, ii. 27; his instructions to insist on payment of claims, 54; reports Louis Philippe's suggestion to Jackson, 54; given his passports, 55.

Long, James, attempts to make Texas independent, ii. 88.

Louis Philippe, makes treaty concerning American claims for French depredations, ii. 53; fails to secure an appropriation from Chambers, 54; suggests to Livingston that Jackson use earnest language, 54.

Louisiana, effect of its purchase on country, i. 42; explored by Lewis and Clark, 42, 43; claimed to contain West Florida, 58; electoral vote taken from Clay by a trick, 233.

Lovejoy, Elijah P., murdered in Illinois, ii. 75.

Lowndes, William, one of War Republicans, i. 78; advocates increased navy, 80; reports bill to reduce war taxes, 128; supports tariff of 1816 in cotton interest, 130; defends Spanish treaty of 1819

INDEX

against Clay, 165; moves admission of Missouri, 185; calls upon House to preserve peace in Missouri, 185.

Lundy, Benjamin, his career as abolitionist, ii. 71.

McLane, Louis, secretary of treasury, i. 348; submits report to Congress in favor of bank, 355; recommends turning over proceeds of sale of public lands to States, 370; made secretary of state, ii. 27.

McLean, John T., postmaster-general under Adams, i. 258, 259; intrigues against Adams, 281; his dismissal urged in vain by Clay, 282.

Madison, James, issues proclamation asserting claim to West Florida, i. 58, 59; attacked by Federalists, 59; appeals vainly to England against Orders in Council, 71; left by Jefferson with responsibility of facing England, 73; issues proclamation reopening commercial intercourse with England, 73; accepts Napoleon's assertion of revocation of decrees, 75; complains at continued French aggressions, 77; advises preparations for defense against England, but really hopes for peace, 77; throughout life like a timid old man, 78; willing to follow policy of Congress, 78, 79; submits John Henry letters to Congress, 82; at Clay's suggestion, recommends an embargo, 82; renominated for president, 84; not forced into war policy for fear of losing nomination, 84; simply swept by current, 84; on cause of war, 84; sends war message, 85; wishes to make Clay commander-in-chief, 88; reëlected president, 89; defended by Clay against Quincy, 91; accepts offer of Russian mediation, 100; nominates peace commissioners, 100, 101; accepts offer of direct negotiations, 100; authorizes commissioners to accept *status ante bellum*, 109; offers Clay War Department, 126; unable to hold party to old principles, 128; vetoes internal improvement bill, 138; his reasoning as to removals from office discussed by Clay, ii. 64; wishes Clay to compromise abolition discussion, 86, 87.

Maine, its admission coupled with that of Missouri to preserve balance of power, i. 177; nominates Clay for president, ii. 230.

Mangum, W. P., votes for repeal of four-years' term, ii. 69; in Senate of 1849, 330; advises Fillmore to appoint Webster secretary of state, 355.

Mann, Abijah, a Barnburner, ii. 312.

Manufacturers, demand more protection, i. 213; organize lobby against compromise tariff, ii. 16; demand home valuation, 16; reconciled to tariff, 20; dread influence of abolitionists on South, 75; demand protection in 1842, 226, 227.

Marcy, William L., defends Van Buren's conduct on ground that "to victors belong spoils," i. 368; leader of Hunker faction, ii. 304.

Marshall, Humphrey, opposes resolutions to support Jefferson, i. 51; denounces Clay's resolutions as claptrap, 51; duel with Clay, 52.

Marshall, John, a student in Wythe's law office, i. 7; congratulates Clay on vindication from Kremer's attack, 257.

Marshall, Tom, anecdote of his inability to answer Clay, i. 328.

Maryland, emigrants from, in Kentucky, i. 14; passes law permitting emancipation, 28; demands admission of Missouri with slavery, 177; votes for Clay in 1832, 383; nominates Clay for president, ii. 230.

Mason, Jeremiah, president of branch bank at Portsmouth, complained of to Jackson, i. 353, 354.

Mason, J. Y., in Senate in 1849, ii. 330; reads Calhoun's speech to Senate, 338; draws Fugitive Slave Act, 349; demands recognition of slavery in territories, 350.

Massachusetts, votes for Clay in 1832, i. 383; denounces gag rule, ii. 153.

INDEX 455

Massachusetts Anti-Slavery Society, denies intention to incite slaves to revolt, ii. 83.

Mathew, Father, compliment to, opposed on ground of his having signed anti-slavery petition, ii. 328.

Mendenhall, a Quaker, presents petition asking Clay to emancipate slaves, ii. 231 ; Clay's skilful reply to, 231, 232.

Mexico, scheme of Burr against, i. 34 ; boundary treaty with, 299 ; grants land to Americans in Texas, ii. 88 ; forbids importation of slaves, 88 ; attaches Texas to Coahuila, 89 ; emancipates slaves, 89 ; excludes Texas from emancipation decree, 89, 90 ; prohibits immigration into Texas, 90 ; revolutions in, 90 ; revolt of Texas from, 90, 91 ; refuses to recognize independence of Texas, 91 ; aggressive conduct of Jackson toward, 94 ; desire to force a quarrel with, 94, 95 ; position of Clay on claims against, 152 ; arbitration treaty with, to settle claims, 236 ; declares annexation of Texas to be a declaration of war, 239 ; objections of Clay to a war with, 245 ; negotiates a peace with Texas, 273 ; breaks off diplomatic relations with United States, 274 ; war with, not necessary, 274 ; occupation of territory claimed by, ordered by United States, 275, 276 ; refuses to receive Slidell as plenipotentiary, 277, 283 ; revolution in and bankruptcy of, 278 ; accused by Polk of invading United States, 284 ; war with, begun, 284 (see War with Mexico); territorial cessions from, expected by Polk, 285 ; crushed in 1847, 290 ; its annexation demanded by Democrats, 290 ; signs treaty of Guadalupe Hidalgo, 301 ; recognizes Rio Grande as boundary, and cedes California and New Mexico, 301.

Middleton, Henry, describes Clay's gambling fortunes, i. 160.

Milan Decree, i. 69 ; said to have been revoked, 74, 87.

Miller, Stephen F., letters of Clay to, on Texas annexation, ii. 261, 262.

Mississippi, English right to navigate, in treaty of Ghent, i. 110.

Missouri, its admission petitioned for, i. 172 ; anti-slavery amendment to bill authorizing a state government, 172 ; fails of admission in fifteenth Congress, 177 ; coupled with Maine in sixteenth Congress, 177 ; compromise concerning, moved by Thomas, 177, 178 ; adopts Constitution prohibiting entrance of free negroes, 183 ; debate in Congress over it, 184-189 ; question of counting its electoral vote, 189-191 ; finally admitted by a close vote, 192 ; votes for Clay in 1824, 233.

Missouri Compromise, proposed by Thomas, i. 177 ; adopted, 178 ; relation of Clay to, 178 ; dissatisfaction with, among extremists, 184 ; successful in appeasing discord, 193, 194 ; discussion of its significance, 194 ; a victory for slavery, 194 ; discussion of its statesmanship, 195, 196 ; possible results of exclusion of Missouri as a slave State, 196 ; actually prevents dissolution of Union, 196, 199, 200 ; its line proposed for new territories, ii. 320, 334, 368.

Monroe, James, his treaty with England rejected by Jefferson, i. 71 ; offers Clay mission to Russia, 126 ; elected president, 140 ; the last of Virginia dynasty, 140 ; selects Adams for secretary of state, 141 ; offers Clay War Department and mission to England, 141 ; enmity of Clay towards, for not giving him secretaryship of state, 141 ; sends message announcing objections to internal improvements, 142 ; suggests a constitutional amendment, 142 ; criticised sharply by Clay, 146 ; appoints commissioners to investigate South American republics, 147 ; asks for appropriation for their expenses, 148 ; disturbed at Clay's systematic opposition, 150 ; annoyed at Jackson's outrages in Florida, 152 ; enmity toward, disavowed by Clay, 154 ; advises against attempt to displace Clay as speaker, 162 ;

sends message to Congress dissuading from action on Spanish treaty, 163; advises against insisting on Texas in Louisiana boundary treaty, 164; recommends recognition of insurgent South American republics, 168; reëlected president, 189, 190; vetoes bill to establish toll-gates on Cumberland Road, 206; doubts constitutionality of internal improvements, 206; attacked by Clay, 206; signs bill to plan internal improvements, 208; expresses sympathy with Greeks, 209; his message establishing Monroe doctrine, 210; letter of Jackson to, on appointments to office, 225.

Monroe doctrine, resolution of Clay's, embodying, i. 209, 210; supported by Clay, 210; in connection with Panama Congress, 268, 269.

Morgan, Captain William, exposes Freemasonry, i. 341; his disappearance, 342.

Morris, Thomas, nominated for vice-presidency, ii. 254.

Morse, S. F. B., completes telegraph between Baltimore and Washington, ii. 253.

Murphy, William S., announces that United States will protect Texas during negotiations, ii. 240; disavowed by Nelson, 240.

NAPOLEON III., LOUIS, success of his *coup d'état* causes Clay to despair of republican institutions in Europe, ii. 395.

Nashville Convention, called by Mississippi State Convention to consider interests of South, ii. 322; denounces compromise and Wilmot Proviso, but does not advocate secession, 354; at second session adopts moderate resolutions, 374; denounced by Clay, 378.

National Republicans. See Whig Party.

Native American movement, damages Clay in 1844, ii. 266; nominates Taylor for presidency, 295.

Navy, opposed by West, i. 80; advocated by Clay, 80-82; its successes in war of 1812, 87, 98; mismanaged, 98.

Nelson, John, attorney-general, disclaims promises made by Murphy, ii. 240; but offers to concentrate troops near Texas, 241.

New England, emigrants from, in Ohio, i. 13; mission of Henry to, 82; disunion movement in, 82, 85, 89; grows increasingly hostile, 99, 106; opposes tariff of 1816, 130; opposes tariff of 1824, 219; supports Adams for president, 226; favors tariff of 1828, 286; supports Adams in 1828, 288; appalled at Webster's seventh of March speech, ii. 341.

New Mexico, conquered by Kearney, ii. 285; territorial organization of, proposed by Polk, 320; protests against introduction of slavery, 321; urged by Taylor to form a state constitution, 322, 326; to be organized without Wilmot Proviso by compromise of 1850, 332; its claim against Texas upheld by Taylor, 351; weakness of Taylor's policy toward, 352, 353; government in, established, 363; argument of Clay as to impossibility of slavery in, 368, 369.

New Orleans, battle of, i. 117, 118.

New York, emigrants from, in Ohio, i. 13; spoils system in, 333; rise of anti-Masons in, 342; election of Clay delegates to Whig convention prevented by Weed, ii. 176-179; Whigs of, support Clay for president in 1844, 230; Liberty vote in, decides election against Clay, 265, 266; struggle in, between Hunkers and Barnburners, 304, 305; decides election of Taylor over Cass, 314; Clay invited to visit, to repel attacks on compromise, 386.

Nicholas, George, denounces Alien and Sedition acts with Clay, i. 33.

Niles, Hezekiah, analyzes vote for tariff of 1824, i. 219; describes campaign of 1824, 232; fears violence in election of 1828, 278; letter of Clay to, on election of 1828, 293; astonished at compromise tariff, ii. 10, 11; on party name of Whigs, 45;

INDEX 457

describes popular violence during Jackson's time, 111, 112.
Nominations, how made, prior to 1824, i. 222; use of national conventions in 1831, 351.
Non-importation, used against England, i. 71; and against France, 73; raised, then resumed, 73; revived against England, 75.
North, its attitude toward slavery in 1820, i. 173; surprised at excitement of South over anti-slavery restriction in Missouri, 174; attacks slavery in debate on Missouri, 175; legislatures of, demand exclusion of slavery from Missouri, 176; held together against slavery by sentiment only, hence defeated, 178; disgusted at Missouri Constitution, 184; wishes to refuse to count Missouri's electoral vote, 189; denounces nullification, ii. 7; Jackson's tour in, 24; Clay's rival journey in, 25; alarmed at abolition agitation, 73; mobs in, against abolitionists, 75; elements in, opposed to abolitionists, 75, 76; how affected by abolitionists, 78; unwilling to put them down by law, 78; begins to take anti-slavery ground, 153; reluctant to follow Calhoun, 158, 159; begins to grow anti-slavery, 235; protests against Texas annexation, 236; instructs senators and representatives to sustain Wilmot Proviso, 286; unpopularity of war and of Polk's diplomacy in, 289; advocates Wilmot Proviso, 302, 323; considered by Clay over-anxious, 325; possibility of its being driven to form a sectional party seen by Clay, 325, 326; opposes Texas's claim to part of New Mexico, 331; urged by Clay to give up sentimental opposition to compromise, 334, 337; beginning of reaction in, favoring compromise, 341-343; alarmed by disunion cry, 342; exasperated by Fugitive Slave Law, 370-372; its feeling against slavery not understood by South, 371; denounces Fugitive Slave Law, 376; movement in, to suppress anti-slavery agitation, 377, 378, 386, 387; underestimates purpose of South, 390; considered weak by South, 391; strength of its "sentiment" underestimated by Clay, 391.
North Carolina, emigrants from, in Kentucky, i. 14, 16; Whigs in, nominate Clay for president, ii. 230.
Northwest Ordinance, anti-slavery clause of, i. 28, 29.
Nullification, movement for, begins, i. 347; formulated by Calhoun, ii. 2, 3; Southern attitude toward, 5; proclamation of Jackson against, 7; denounced in North, 7; not negatived by compromise measures, 21; subsequent debate of Clay with Calhoun concerning, 148, 149.

O'CONNELL, DANIEL, connection of Father Mathew with, ii. 328.
Ohio, its settlement, character of emigrants, i. 13; votes for Clay in 1824, 233; triumphal journey of Clay in, 340, 341; anti-Whig influence of abolitionists in, ii. 164; Whigs of, nominate Clay for president, 230; sends Wade to Senate, 405.
Opdyke, George, a Barnburner, ii. 312.
Orders in Council, their policy, i. 69, 70; their effect, 70; refusal of England to recall, 75, 76; repealed too late to prevent war, 87, 88; not alluded to in treaty of peace, 117.
Oregon, question concerning, postponed by Clay, i. 299, 300; caution concerning advised by Clay, ii. 153; re-occupation of, demanded by Democratic Convention, 252; joint occupation of, 278; exploration and settlement of, 279; demanded by West, 280; forty-ninth parallel rejected by England, 280, 281; "fifty-four forty or fight," 280; negotiations of Calhoun and Buchanan concerning, 280, 281; claimed by Polk, 280, 281; abandonment of extreme claims to, by Polk under influence of South, 282; Senate advises acceptance of forty-ninth parallel, 282; treaty concerning, ratified, 283; bill to organize with Wil-

INDEX

mot Proviso defeated in Senate, 303; votes against slavery, 303; organized in 1848, 313.

PAKENHAM, English minister, negotiates with Calhoun concerning Oregon, ii. 280; offers to arbitrate, 280; declines forty-ninth parallel, 281; again proposes arbitration, 281.

Panama Congress, announced to Congress by Adams, i. 267; warmly supported by Clay, 268; its purposes, 268; how regarded by Adams and Clay, 269, 271; opposed by slaveholders, 271, 272; and by Adams's enemies, 272; popular in country, 272; failure of, 293, 294.

Paredes, Arrillaga, supplants Herrera in Mexico, ii. 278; refuses to receive Slidell under threat, 283.

Parish, David, aids Treasury in 1813, i. 99.

Patriot war, Clay's opinion of, ii. 151.

Patterson, Robert, founds Lexington, i. 16.

Pennsylvania, emigrants from, in Ohio, i. 13; in Kentucky, 14, 16; enthusiastic for war in 1812, 83, 85; suggests national nominating convention, 222; conventions in, nominate Jackson, 226; supports Jackson vigorously, 289; spoils system in, 333; tariff campaign of Democrats in, in 1844, 257, 258.

Pensacola, seized by Jackson, i. 152.

Perry, O. H., wins battle of Lake Erie, i. 105; bill granting pension to his mother opposed by Clay, 204, 205.

Petition, right of, discussed in Congress, ii. 79-81, 82, 154, 155, 163, 233.

Phelps, Mrs., saved by Clay in murder case, i. 20.

Pickering, Timothy, denies claim of United States to Florida, i. 59; his censure moved by Clay, for quoting confidential document of Senate, 62.

Pierce, Franklin, nominated for presidency in 1852, ii. 402.

Pindell, Richard, letter of Clay to, on emancipation, ii. 317, 318.

Pinkney, William, joins Monroe in making treaty with England, i. 71.

Plumer, William, describes Clay in 1806, i. 47, 48; impressed by his oratory, 48.

Poindexter, George, wins and loses eight thousand dollars from Clay, i. 160; offers resolution denouncing Jackson's protest, ii. 41; votes for repeal of four-years term, 69.

Poinsett, Joel R., minister to Mexico, i. 293; instructed to attend Panama Congress, 293; instructed to propose purchase of Texas, 296.

Polk, James K., introduces resolutions that deposits should not be restored, ii. 48; nominated for president, 252; jeered at as insignificant by Whigs, 256; reputed a free-trader, 257; writes a letter favoring protection, 257; asserted in Pennsylvania to be a protectionist, 258; saved from losing votes, as an annexationist, by Wright's candidacy, 259; attitude of Liberty party toward, 262; carries New York and wins election, 265, 266; accepts Tyler's annexation of Texas, 273; determines to seize Rio Grande as boundary, 274; appoints Slidell envoy to Mexico, 276; claims the whole of Oregon, 280; recommends termination of joint occupancy, 281; declines arbitration, 281; declines to assume responsibility of accepting compromise, 282; submits draft of treaty to Senate, 282; advised to accept, 283; sends message to Congress announcing war with Mexico, 284; vetoes a river and harbor bill, 284; asks two millions for negotiations, 285; renews demand, 286; repels people by his equivocal diplomacy, 289; urges organization of new territories and extension of Missouri Compromise line, 320.

Porter, General Peter B., correspondence of Clay with, in 1824, i. 228; describes Clay's chances for New York support for nomination in 1843, ii. 176, 177; tries to secure Clay's support for nomination of

INDEX

Curtis as collector in New York, 193; letter of Clay to, on reconciliation with Webster, 250.
Porto Rico. See Cuba.
Prentiss, Sargent S., in campaign of 1840, ii. 187.
Presidency, held by Jackson to be "direct representative of people," ii. 40, 42; dangers of this theory to republican institutions, 109, 110.
President, frigate, attacks Little Belt, i. 76.
Preston, William, votes for repeal of four-year term, ii. 69; opposes expunging resolution, 102; describes extravagance of Congress in 1835, 121; against distributing fourth installment of surplus, 136; his anger at Clay's attack on nullification, 149; aids Clay in preparing speech against abolitionists, 165; eulogizes Clay for consulting him, 170; in campaign of 1840, 187; moves adjournment of Senate on Clay's retirement, 225.
Protection, first resolution of Clay in favor of, i. 51; war argument of Clay for, 52, 53; not designed to encourage manufactures, 53, 54; methods of encouragement suggested, 55; report of Gallatin on, 55-57; argument of Clay for, in 1816, 131; demand for, after crisis of 1819, 213; embodied in tariff of 1824, 214; argument of Clay for, 214-218; called the "American" system, 216; argument of Webster against, 218, 219; opposed by South after 1820 as inimical to slave labor, 314, 315; agitation against, in South Carolina, 358; favored by Jackson, 359, 360; Clay's argument for, in 1832, 361-364; not considered permanent by Clay, ii. 173; no longer an issue in 1848, 300.
Prussia, Clay's treaty with, i. 299.

QUAKERS, oppose slavery, ii. 71, 80; praised by Clay for moderation, 232.
Quincy, Josiah, makes bitter attack upon conduct of war of 1812, i. 89, 90; calls invasion of Canada a buccaneering exploit, 89; accuses administration of wishing war on any pretext, 90; and of subserviency to France, 90; makes mistake of seeming unpatriotic, 91; reply of Clay to, 91-98.

RAMBOUILLET decree, i. 74.
Randolph, John, offers resolution against war with England, i. 84; overridden by Clay as speaker, 84; opposes protection as benefiting North at expense of South, 130; moves to reconsider Missouri Compromise, 180; his motion defeated by Clay through a trick, 180, 181; represents extreme Southern view, 189; insists on House facing Missouri issue, 191; ruled out of order by Clay, 191; votes against Missouri Compromise, 192; urges Clay to lead a secession movement, 197; abuses Clay and Adams, 273; his duel with Clay, 274, 275; toast at public dinner to, 278; favors colonization of free blacks, 303; comes to Senate while dying, to hear Clay, ii. 22; last meeting with Clay, 22, 23.
Reciprocity in commercial privilege, basis of Clay's treaties, 297.
Republican party, rise of war party in, i. 67, 68; its leaders, 78; favors France and wishes war with England, 78; carries Madison with it, 84; censured by Quincy for conduct of war, 90; accused of subserviency to Bonaparte, 90; defended by Clay, 91-98; incapacity of, in conduct of war, 98, 99; adopts Federalist principles, 126-128; decay of old Jeffersonian views in, 127; new leaders of, 128; programme for, laid down by Clay, 128, 129; ready to support bank in 1816, 132, 133; its loose construction not the same as that of Federalists, 136, 137; falls to pieces in election of 1824, 223, 312; its connection with Democratic party, 318.
Rhett, R. B., proposes secession, ii. 358; defended by Barnwell, 358; denounced as a traitor by Clay, 358.
Rhode Island, votes for Clay in 1832, i. 383.

Richmond, Dean, a Barnburner, ii. 311.

Riley, General, calls convention to frame constitution for California, ii. 321.

Rives, William C., supports expunging resolution, ii. 102; opposes sub-treasury, 145; his reëlection favored by Clay, 174.

Rochester, W. B., correspondence of Clay with, in 1824, i. 228.

Romanzoff, Count, offers Russian mediation between England and United States, i. 99.

Rush, Richard, secretary of treasury under Adams, i. 258; an anti-Mason, 345.

Rush, Thomas J., in Senate in 1849, ii. 330; opposes any bill reducing area of Texas, 350.

Russell, Lord John, calls Polk's language to Oregon "blustering," ii. 280.

Russell, Jonathan, appointed peace commissioner, i. 101; plays cards with Clay, 104; his ability, 104; under Clay's influence, 104; controversy with Adams, 251.

Russia, attempts to mediate between United States and England, i. 99, 100, 106; asked to urge Spain to abandon colonies, 271; arbitrates question of compensation for slaves, 300.

SACKETT'S HARBOR, American success at, i. 105.

Sanford, Nathan, supported for vice-president by Clay's friends, i. 232.

Santa Anna, General, tries to conquer Texas, ii. 90; defeats and massacres Americans, 91; defeated and captured by Houston, 91; promises to procure recognition of Texan independence, 91; intrigues with Polk's administration, 285; allowed to reënter Mexico, 285; makes renewed efforts at defense, 287; defeated by Scott, 287.

Sargent, Epes, on Clay's dislike to put military power in Jackson's hands by Force Bill, ii. 12.

Sargent, Nathan, on Clay's gambling habits, i. 160, 161; describes Clay's rupture with Harrison, ii. 195; describes grief of Whigs at Clay's defeat in 1844, 267.

Scott, Winfield, his candidacy in 1840, ii. 179; writes to Clay deprecating jealousy, 179; used by Weed to keep delegates from Clay, 179; discovers the deception, 180; leads enterprise against Vera Cruz, 286, 287; defeats Santa Anna and captures Mexico, 287; receives vote of Ohio in Whig convention, 306; candidate for nomination in 1852, 399; supported by anti-slavery Whigs, 400; nominated for president, 403; attitude of Southern Whigs toward, 403.

Sedgwick, Theodore, opposes Texas annexation, but favors election of Polk, ii. 259.

Seminole war, i. 151.

Senate of United States, appointment of Clay to, i. 38; does not question Clay's eligibility, 38; discusses protection, 52; debate in, over claim to West Florida, 59; debates bank, 64, 65; defeats re-charter of bank, 66; vote in, for war, 85; ratifies Florida treaty with Spain, 165; strikes anti-slavery clause out of Missouri bill, 177; couples admission of Missouri with that of Maine, 177; rejects amendment prohibiting slavery in Missouri, 177; passes resolution against free negro clause in Missouri Constitution, 185; withdraws from joint convention to count electoral vote of Missouri, 190; coöperates with Clay in final settlement of Missouri question, 192; attempt of Jackson to prevent Clay's ratification by, 254, 255; objects to Adams's proposed mission to Panama Congress, 271; confirms nominations, 273; debate in, on power of president to send ministers without consent of Senate, 273; reports in favor of bank, 355; adopts Clay's tariff resolution, 366; debates Van Buren's nomination as minister to England, 367, 368; rejects his nomination, 369; debates public land

INDEX

policy, 372; passes Clay's land bill, 373; passes bill to re-charter bank, 375; debate in, on Jackson's veto, 377; fails to pass bill over veto, 379; discusses Force Bill, ii. 9; passes it, 17; passes compromise tariff, 20; controlled by Whigs, 30; passes resolution concerning "paper read to cabinet," 31; snubbed by Jackson, 32; debates resolutions of censure on Jackson and Taney, 32-37; passes resolutions of censure, 37; passes joint resolution ordering return of deposits, 37; receives distress petitions in favor of bank, 37, 38; its censure denounced by Jackson in protest, 40, 41; debates Jackson's protest, 41-43; refuses to put protest on journal, 43; rejects all of Jackson's nominations, 43, 44; refers French relations to Clay's committee, 56; resolves to take no action against France, 57; debate in, on removals from office, 62-65, 67, 68; later growth of "courtesy of," 65; votes to repeal four-years' term, 68; passes Clay's land bill, 70; debates Calhoun's bill to exclude anti-slavery matter from mails, 85, 86; defeats it, 86; debates Texan independence, 92-93; votes to recognize Texas, 95; debates relations with Mexico, 95; controlled by Democrats, 100; debates expunging resolutions, 101-105; passes them, 105, 106; debates Calhoun's and Clay's resolutions on slavery, 156-162; continues to lay petitions on table, 163; refuses to repeal sub-treasury act, 192; Clay's farewell to, 225, 226; rejects annexation treaty, 260; induced to pass annexation resolution by a trick, 272, 273; gives "notice" to England, 282; consulted by Polk in advance as to Oregon treaty, 282, 283; advises Polk to accept forty-ninth parallel, 282; rejects Wilmot Proviso, 286; rejects bill to organize Oregon with exclusion of slavery, 303; reëlection of Clay to, 319; debate in, on compliment to Father Mathew, 328; eminent membership of, in 1850, 330; debates Clay's compromise scheme, 334, 335-345; renewed debates on Foote's resolution, 347; opposition in, to Omnibus bill, 350; defeats Omnibus bill, 359, 360; passes Texas boundary bill, 362; passes other bills of compromise, 363; passes bill prohibiting slave-trade in District of Columbia, 365; resolutions against slave trade introduced by Clay, 379; considers Shadrach case, 379, 380; debate in, on compromise, 382, 383.

Sergeant, John, opposes admission of Missouri as a slave State, i. 185; envoy to Panama Congress, 293; nominated for Vice-President, 293; consults with Tyler's cabinet concerning bank bill, ii. 209.

Seward, William H., an anti-Mason, i. 345; said to favor Clay in 1839, ii. 177; supports Taylor, 313; in Senate of 1849, 330; his speech against compromise, 343-345; appeals to higher law, 344; predicts inevitable fall of slavery, 344, 345; denounced for higher law, 345; sneered at by Webster, 346; understands future better than old statesmen, 347; jealousy of Fillmore toward, 355.

Shadrach, rescued from United States deputy marshal, ii. 379.

Shepperd, ——, tart remark on Clay's apparent popularity, ii. 271.

Slavery, its influence in Kentucky, i. 14, 15; movement to abolish, in Kentucky, 27; movement against, during Revolution, 27, 28; abolished in South American States, 167; strengthened by cotton culture, 172, 173; defended by South as beneficial and necessary, 175; attack of North upon, in Missouri debate, 175; strengthened by Missouri Compromise, 194; not directly the subject of politics after 1821, ii. 71; attacked by abolitionists, 72, 73; powers of Congress over, according to abolitionists, 73; defended by South, 74; introduced into Texas, 88; abolished in Mexico, 89; not admitted by South to be cause of inferior growth, 154; unable to stand free debate, 155; Calhoun's resolutions concerning, 156, 157; Smith's resolutions on, 158; Clay's resolutions on, 159-161; deplored as necessary by Clay, 167, 168; great moral revolution in favor of, expected by Calhoun, 169; doctrine of, in territories, held by Calhoun, 302; squatter sovereignty theory advocated by Dickinson, 303; its fall foreseen by Calhoun, 338-340; ruin predicted by Seward and Chase, 343-345; justice of Seward's view of, 346; impossibility of saving by compromise, 368.

Slave trade, abolition provided for in Constitution, i. 28; its prohibition fails to weaken slavery, 172.

Slidell, John, appointed envoy to Mexico, ii. 276; instructed to buy disputed territory and California, 277; in Mexico, insists on opening negotiations at once, 277; difficulty over his commission, 277; threatens to leave, 277; demands to be received, 283.

Sloat, Commodore John D., ordered to seize California on declaration of war, ii. 276.

Smith, Robert, an enemy of Gallatin, and hence of bank, i. 64.

Smith, Truman, moves anti-slavery and Unionist amendments to Calhoun's slavery resolutions, ii. 158; in Senate of 1849, 330.

Soulé, Pierre, in Senate of 1849, ii. 330; leads extreme pro-slavery wing, 350.

South, favors war in 1812, 85; supports tariff of 1816 in favor of cotton, 130, 131; decay of philosophical anti-slavery movement in, 172, 173; change of attitude in, toward slavery, 174; alarmed at superior growth of free States, 174; determined to maintain equilibrium in Senate, 174, 175; superior in unity of interest to North, 178; insists upon admission of Missouri without further question after adoption of compromise, 184; demands counting of Missouri's electoral vote, 189; learns its power over North, 195; would probably have seceded in 1820, 196; its plans for disunion, 196, 197; opposes tariff of 1824, 219; its reasons, 220; opposes insurrections in Cuba as disquieting to slavery, and rendering Cuba liable to seizure by England, 270; aims to control foreign policy in favor of slavery, 272; dissatisfied with tariff of 1828, 287; votes for Jackson in 1828, 288; favors colonization, 303; its new policy toward slavery after 1820, 314; gains leadership in Jackson party, 316; journey of Clay in, 340; opposes tariff, 361, 366; Clay's blunder in repelling, by tariff of 1832, 383; its complaint against tariff, ii. 1, 2; abandons hope of aid from Jackson, 2; does not favor South Carolina in 1832, 4, 5; on the whole, approves Jackson's proclamation, 7; encouraged by result of nullification to terrorize North, 21; alarmed by Turner's insurrection, 73, 74; and by English emancipation of slaves, 74; praises slavery as a moral good and denounces abolitionists, 74; demands that North silence them, 74, 75; exasperated at refusal of North to suppress abolitionists by law, 79; endeavors to prevent circulation of abolition literature in mails, 82, 83; accuses abolitionists of inciting slaves to revolt, 83, 84; looks to Texas for more slave territory, 89, 90; demands annexation of Texas, 89; rejoices at battle of San Jacinto, 92; urges recognition of Texan independence, 92; land speculation in, 119; collapse of prices in, 127; depressed at superior growth of North, 154; commercial convention in, ascribes inferiority to tariff and demands free trade, 154; refuses to recognize slavery as true cause, 154; refuses to let slavery rest, 233; agitated by supposed English plots in Texas, 238; journey of Clay through, 242; displeased with Clay's Raleigh letter on Texas, 246; agitates for annexation, 251; defeats

INDEX 463

Van Buren in Democratic convention by two-thirds rule, 252; increasing excitement in, 260; not won by Clay's Alabama letters, 262; opposes war with England, 282; denounces Wilmot Proviso, 286; adopts Calhoun's theory of slavery in territories, 302; threatens secession in 1849, 321; alarmed at action of California, 322; movement in, to call Nashville Convention, 322; increasing demand for secession, 322, 323; dreads return of Clay to Senate, 323; thought by Clay to be likely to yield point at issue, 324, 325; its long domination at Washington pointed out by Clay, 325; unable to persuade Taylor to oppose free States, 327, 328; denounces Taylor, 328; aim of Clay to placate South by compromise, 330, 331; urged by Clay to be satisfied and not demand all, 337; its failure in case of secession predicted, 337; terrifies North by cry of disunion, 342; does not understand Northern attitude against slavery, 371, 372; averse to a rupture on the whole, 375; accepts compromise, 375; said by Clay to have won a triumph in the compromise, 377, 378; efforts of Clay to appease, after Shadrach case, 381; urged not to expect too much from North, 381, 382; demands that North enforce Fugitive Slave Law, 382; last appeal of Clay to, 389; its serious purpose understood by Clay, 390, 391; underestimated by North, 390.

South Carolina, rise of nullification movement in, against tariff, i. 347, 366; votes for Floyd in 1832, 383; votes to nullify tariff of 1832, ii. 4; prepares to resist federal authority, 4; anti-nullification in, overcome, 4, 5; surrender to, feared by Adams, 6; defies Jackson's proclamation, 8; postpones conflict, 9; prefers Clay's bill to Verplanck's as an avowed concession, 13, 14; really gains by her action, 15, 16; repeals nullification ordinance, 20; denounces Force Bill, 20; claims to have won victory, 21; cries "Texas or disunion," 252; Democratic Convention in, nominates Taylor, 309.

Southard, Samuel L., secretary of navy under Adams, i. 258; supports resolutions of censure on Jackson, ii. 37; votes for repeal of four-years' term, 69; opposes expunging resolution, 102; against distributing fourth installment of surplus, 136; declines nomination for vice-president, 181.

Spain, negotiations with, over Florida, i. 58; invaded by Napoleon, 58; its struggle with revolted colonies, 147, 149; relations of Monroe's administration with, after Jackson's campaign in Florida, 152; treaty of Adams with, ceding Florida, 162; refuses ratification, 163; its decay ascribed by Clay to lack of protection, 217; desire of slaveholders that it retain Cuba, 270; urged to recognize independence of South American republics, 271.

Spanish-American republics, sympathy of Clay with their struggle against Spain, i. 147-149; idealized by Clay, 148, 166, 167; recognition urged by Clay, 166, 167; recommended by Monroe, 168; popularity of Clay among, 168; Adams's opinion of, 169, 170; resolution of Clay concerning, 209 (see Panama Congress); disillusionment of Clay with, 294-296; considered unfit for freedom or self-government, 295, 296.

Spencer, Ambrose, tells Clay abolitionists defeat him in 1844, ii. 265.

Spoils system, used in New York and Pennsylvania, i. 333; applied to national offices by Jackson, 336; denounced by Clay, 337; its justification in eyes of masses, 337, 338; evil effects of, 338; Van Buren condemned as author of, 368; causes alarm among statesmen, ii. 61; condemned in report by Calhoun, 61, 62; proposal to check by requiring reasons for removal, 62; debate on, 62-65; later participation of Senate and House in, 65-67; only to be cured by executive, 67; remarks of Clay on, 67, 68; corruption caused by, 184, 185; discredits Democratic party, 185; continued under Whig party, 193-195; difficulties of Clay with, 193, 194, 197; circular against, issued by Harrison and Webster, 197, 198.

Squatter sovereignty, proposed by Dickinson, ii. 303; rejected by Calhoun, 303.

Staël, Madame de, clever remark of Clay to, i. 124.

States' rights, held by South to be infringed by restriction on Missouri, i. 175, 184; revived by South after 1820 as protection to slavery, 314-316; in Calhoun's doctrine of nullification, ii. 3; held by Calhoun to forbid Congress excluding publications as incendiary, 84, 85; advocated by Calhoun solely to protect slavery, 150, 156.

Stephens, Alexander H., describes popular desire to hear Clay in 1845, ii. 270, 271; fears Clay wishes to run again for president, 297; dreads return of Clay to Senate, 323; anticipates yielding of North in 1849, 342; represents compromise as a Southern victory, 375.

Stephenson, James, his nomination as minister to England rejected by Senate, ii. 44.

Sterret, ——, denounced for planning an insult to Adams, i. 259; his removal urged by Clay, 260; refused by Adams, 260.

Stevens, Thaddeus, an anti-Mason, i. 345.

Stevenson, Thomas B., letter of Clay to, ii. 319, 324.

Story, Joseph, congratulates Clay on vindication from Kremer's slander, i. 257; letter of Webster to, on Clay-Randolph duel, 274.

Sub-treasury, bill establishing, introduced, ii. 137; defeated, then passed, 138; opposition of Clay to, 139-142; extravagant fears of, 140.

Sumner, Charles, succeeds Webster in Senate, ii. 405.

Sumner, Professor W. G., his biography of Jackson referred to, i. 203, 374.

Supreme Court, defied by Jackson in Cherokee case, i. 347; in case of bank, 376, 377.

Swartwout, Samuel, letter of Jackson to, against Clay, i. 254; his defalcation as collector of New York, ii. 184.

Sweden and Norway, treaty of Clay with, i. 299.

TALLMADGE, JAMES, moves anti-slavery proviso to bill authorizing admission of Missouri, i. 172; votes to exclude abolition matter from mails, ii. 86; opposes sub-treasury, 145; declines nomination for vice-president, 181.

Taney, Roger B., attorney-general, i. 348; writes Jackson's paper read to cabinet, ii. 29; appointed secretary of treasury, 29; orders removal of deposits, 29; defends action in report to Congress, 30, 31; his reasons declared unsatisfactory by Senate, 32; his nomination rejected by Senate, 44; subsequently made chief justice, 44.

Tariff, of 1816, demand for, after war of 1812, i. 129, 130; elements of opposition to, 130, 131; carried by South and West, 131; fails to secure complete protection, 212; demand for more protection by manufacturers, 213; ' failure to revise, in 1820, 214; tariff of 1824, reported to House, 214; debate upon, 214-219; passed by Congress, analysis of vote for, in House, 219; supported by Middle States, opposed by East and South, 219; of 1828, carried by Northern and Western States, 286, 287; not a dividing issue between parties in 1828, 313; agitation for and against, in 1830-1831, 347; causes nullification movement, 347; necessity of diminishing, to cut down revenue, 358; free trade meetings against, 359; method of modification laid down by Clay, 360, 361; carried in 1832, 366; its character, 366; increases disgust of South, 366, ii. 1, 2; nullified in

INDEX 465

South Carolina, 4; Verplanck bill debated in House, 8, 9; compromise tariff introduced by Clay, 10; agreed to by Calhoun, 11, 12; Clay's speech in favor of, 11, 14-16; defended, as not being a concession, by Clay, 15; opposed by Webster and others, 16; question of home valuation amendment, 16, 17; the nullifiers forced to vote for home valuation, 17; compromise tariff passed, 19, 20; not considered a protective measure by South, 21; revision suggested in 1841 by Tyler, 221; and by Clay, 224; two bills vetoed because coupled with Clay's land scheme, 226, 227; tariff of 1842 passed, 228; equivocal attitude of Democrats toward, 257; popularity of tariff of 1842 taken advantage of by Democrats, 257; no longer an issue in 1848, 300; its consideration suggested by Clay in 1851, 383, 384.

Tarleton, Colonel, his money refused by Mrs. Clay, as compensation for property destroyed, i. 3.

Taylor, John W., moves prohibition of slavery in Arkansas, i. 177; attacks Clay's defense of slavery, 179.

Taylor, General Zachary, ordered to approach Rio Grande, ii. 274, 275; authorized to construe as war any attempt by Mexicans to cross Rio Grande, 275; reports no expectation of war on part of Mexicans, 275; again ordered to "repel invasion," 275; again asks for instructions, 275, 276; directed to advance whole force to Rio Grande, 278; his movements in Texas, 283; begins hostilities, 283; wins battles, 285; other successes, 286; defeats Santa Anna at Buena Vista, 287; considered by Weed as a possible Whig candidate, 294; his unfitness for office, 294; gradually persuaded to allow candidacy, 295; writes to Clay concerning his willingness to stand aside, 295; nominated by public meetings, 295; considers himself a people's candidate, 295; writes vague letter to satisfy Whig managers, 296; disgust of Clay at his candidacy, 296, 297; in letter to Clay, refuses to withdraw, 299; preferred by some because not a party man, 299; opposition to, in Whig convention, 305; nominated, 306; refusal of Clay to support, 308; accepts nomination from South Carolina Democrats, 309; opposition among Whigs to his candidacy, 309, 310; disgust of Webster, 310; not damaged by Free Soil nomination, 313; different descriptions of, in North and South, 314; elected by South, 314; his inaugural address, 321; his cabinet, 321; sends agent to California to urge formation of state government, 321; wishes New Mexico to organize constitution, 322; relations with Clay, 323; offers James Clay mission to Portugal, 323; sends messages urging admission of California and New Mexico as States, 326, 327; favors slavery and rights of South, 327; but unwilling to refuse admission of California, 327, 328; censured by the South, 328; defies Southern threats and insists on admission of California, 351; orders commander in New Mexico to use force against Texas, 351; opposes compromise as yielding to secession, 352; threatens to hang disunionists, 352; weakness of his plan as to New Mexico, 353; his policy attacked by Clay, 353; unmoved by Clay, ready to sign Wilmot Proviso, 354; his death, 355; sends special agent to Hungary, 392.

Tecumseh, killed at battle of Thames, i. 105.

Telegraph, its use in reporting Democratic national convention, ii. 253.

Tennessee, elects Jackson Senator, i. 226; nominates him for presidency, 226; nominates Jackson again for 1828, 263; his letter of acceptance to, 263.

Texas, claim to, abandoned in Adams's Spanish treaty, i. 162; upheld by Clay, 163, 164; purchase attempted by Clay, 296, ii. 88; colonization of, by Americans, 88; in-

466 INDEX

troduction of slavery into, 88; maintenance of slavery in, desired by South, 88, 89; refuses to obey Mexican decree of emancipation, 89; land speculation in, 90; failure of Jackson to purchase, 90; immigration of Americans into, prohibited, 90; rises against Mexico and declares independence, 90, 91; battles of Alamo and San Jacinto, 91; petitions for its recognition, 92; its recognition discussed in Senate, 92; attitude of Clay toward, 93; finally recognized, 95; proposes annexation, 236, 237; desire of Tyler to annex, 237; rumors of English designs to secure emancipation in, 238; intrigues of Tyler's cabinet in Senate to prepare annexation of, 238, 239; wishes to be assured of protection of United States before negotiating for annexation, 239; fears renewal of hostilities by Mexico, 239; assured of protection by Murphy, sends envoy to treat, 240; rejects armistice with Mexico, 240; promise of protection to, disavowed, 241; equivocal promise of Calhoun to, 241, 242; deceived by promises, 242; agreement of Clay and Van Buren to oppose annexation of, 243, 244; treaty of annexation signed, 245; letter of Clay against, 245, 246; letter of Van Buren against, 247, 248; arguments of Calhoun and Tyler in behalf of, 249; agitation for annexation of, in South, 252; annexation demanded by Democratic convention, 252; the real issue of campaign of 1844, 259; treaty with, rejected by Senate, 260; further letters of Clay upon, 261, 262; popular mandate for, claimed by Tyler in 1844, 271; annexed by joint resolution, 272, 273; negotiates peace with Mexico, 273; rejects peace and accepts annexation, 273, 274; question as to boundary of, 274; see War with Mexico, settled in treaty of Guadalupe Hidalgo, 301; claims part of New Mexico, 331; to be indemnified for abandoning part of claim in compromise of 1850, 333, 349; threatens to occupy part of New Mexico, 351; defied by Taylor, 351, 352; on the point of using force, 362; pacified by passage of boundary bill in Senate, 362; passage of boundary bill by House causes disgraceful speculations, 363-365.

Thames, battle of, i. 105.

Thomas, Jesse B., suggests Missouri compromise, i. 177.

Thomas, Roland, describes appearance of Clay as a young clerk, i. 5.

Thompson, George, denounced by Clay, ii. 381.

Thompson, Richard W., in campaign of 1840, ii. 187.

Thurston, Buckner, resigns seat in Senate, i. 52.

Tilden, Samuel J., a Barnburner, ii. 311.

Tinsley, Colonel, obtains a clerk's place for Clay, i. 5.

Tinsley, Peter, Clay a clerk in his office, i. 5, 10; his office visited by Wythe, 6.

Tippecanoe, battle of, i. 78.

Todd, ——, plays cards at Ghent with Clay, i. 104.

Tompkins, Daniel D., elected vice-president, i. 190.

Toombs, Robert, represents compromise as a Southern victory, ii. 375.

Tracy, Uriah, attacked by Clay, i. 48.

Transylvania University, its foundation, i. 16, 17.

Treasury Department, organized differently from other departments, ii. 34; secretary of, directed to report to Congress, 34; held by Clay to be subject to Congress, not to president, 35.

Treaty of Ghent, place of meeting of commissioners, i. 102; description of American envoys, 102-105; the British envoys, 105; crushing demands of English, 107; determination of Americans to break off negotiations, 107; reluctance of English to abandon peace, 108; resumption of negotiations, 109; agreement upon *status ante bellum*, 109; refusal of English to consider blockade or impressment, 109; submission of Americans to *status ante bellum*, 109, 110; difficulties over Mississippi navigation and fisheries, 110, 111; final agreement, 111; difficulties of American envoys, 112; quarrels between them, 112, 113; dissatisfaction of Clay with treaty, 114-116; terms of treaty, 116; popularity of treaty in United States, 118.

Tucker, Beverly, letter of Wise to, on Webster, ii. 218.

Tucker, Henry St. George, reports resolution on internal improvements, i. 142; describes Madison's desire that Clay compromise slavery question, ii. 86, 87.

Turner, Nat, his insurrection, ii. 74.

Tyler, John, congratulates Clay on vindication from Kremer's slander, i. 257; denounced by Jacksonian papers for approving Clay's conduct in election, 279; tries to explain away action, 279; opposes Force Bill in Senate, ii. 17; votes for repeal of four-year term, 69; nominated for vice-president, 98; resigns rather than vote to expunge resolutions of censure, 100; defeated by Rives for senatorship through Clay's influence, 171; to be appeased by vice-presidency, 174; nominated for vice-president, 181; succeeds Harrison as president, 198; his strict-constructionist record, 199; supports Clay for nomination in 1840, 200; his opinion of Clay, 200; not in reality a Whig, 200; doubt as to his status, 201; considers himself president, 201; advised by his friends as to policy, 201, 202; issues address using Whig phraseology, 202; writes to Clay a doubtful letter as to his policy, 202, 203; in message speaks uncertainly about bank, 203; leaves matter to Congress, 204; intention of Clay to drive, 205; signs repeal of sub-treasury, 205; vetoes bank bill, 206; congratulated by Democratic Senators, 207; his message attacked by Clay, 208; accused by Clay of deception, 208; and of inconsistency in opposing popular mandate, 209; authorizes cabinet to consult with Congress about a new bank bill, 209; dislikes term "bank," 209; vetoes second bank bill, 210; good effects of his action, 210, 211; signs Clay's land bill, 211; his cabinet resigns, 213; rejoices at Webster's determination to remain, 214; hopes to use Webster to ruin Clay, 214; discussion of his quarrel with Whigs, 214-217; not guilty of breaking pledges, 214; his equivocations, 215; his kitchen cabinet, 215; his ridiculous ambitions, 215, 216; quarrel not necessarily inevitable, 216; appoints a new cabinet, 216, 217; exposed by old members of cabinet, 217; denounced by Whig party, 217; fails to profit from Webster's adherence, 217, 218; remains isolated, 220; recommends a revision of tariff, 221; vetoes provisional tariff bill, 226; vetoes permanent tariff bill, 226; censured by Adams, 227; ambitious to secure annexation of Texas, 236, 237; urges it upon Webster, 237; consults friends as to advisability of joining Democrats, 237; reorganizes cabinet, 237, 238; directs Upshur to propose annexation to Texan minister, 238; conciliates Benton by making Fremont commander of Oregon expedition, 239; offers state department to Calhoun, 241; accused by Clay of raising Texas question for political capital, 244; urges annexation of Texas in order to prevent abolition of slavery, 249; tries to purchase Democratic support, 253; expects a popular uprising in his favor, 253; nominated for presidency, 253; withdraws in favor of Polk, 253; on failure of annexation treaty, suggests annexation in some other way, 260; asserts that result of election is a mandate to annex Texas, 271; signs joint resolution of annexation and sends messenger to Texas, 273; mentions Oregon in messages, 279.

INDEX

Tyler, John, Jr., describes scene between Webster and Tyler, ii. 214.
Tyler, Lyon G., on reasons for putting Fremont in charge of Oregon expedition, ii. 239.

ULLMANN, DANIEL, letter of Clay to, on Whig issues, ii. 300; letter of Clay to, declining to be a candidate in 1852, 386; letter of Clay to, on Whig prospects in 1852, 396, 397; letter of Clay to, suggesting inscription for gold medal, 407.
United Provinces of Rio de la Plata, recognition as independent urged by Clay, i. 147, 149.
United States, prosperity of, under Jefferson's first administration, i. 40; controls foreign carrying trade, 41; damaged by Napoleonic struggle in Europe, 49; crushed between Orders in Council and Napoleon's decrees, 70; its contemptible position in 1810-1811, 76, 77; feeling in, concerning war of 1812, 83, 85; military weakness, 85, 86; rejoices over treaty of Ghent, 118, 119; popularity of "military heroes" in, 157, 158; sudden excitement in, over Missouri debate, 176; weakness of Union sentiment in, in 1820, 197-199; possibility of dissolution of, in 1820, 199; sympathy in, for Greece, 208, 209; poorer than Spain or Ireland, according to Clay, 217; Democratic revolution in sentiment of, 290-292, 332; prosperity and contentment of, 332, 333, 352; popularity of compromise tariff in, ii. 20; lawlessness in, during Jackson's administration, 111, 112; prosperity of, during Jackson's terms, 114; sympathy in, for Hungary and Kossuth, 392-396.
Upshur, Abel P., secretary of state under Tyler, ii. 237; zealous advocate of Texan annexation, 238; directed by Tyler to approach Texan minister, 238; formally proposes annexation, 239; unable to assure Houston of military support during negotiations, 239; assures Houston of certain ratification of treaty, 240; killed by "Peacemaker" explosion, 240.
Utah, in compromise of 1850. (See New Mexico.)

VAN BUREN, JOHN, a Barnburner, ii. 312.
Van Buren, Martin, manager for Crawford in 1824, i. 230; suggests coalition of Clay and Crawford, 230; describes Clay's depression after defeat, 233; admits intention to oppose administration in any event, 273; manager of Jackson's campaign, 280; accuses administration of attempts to bribe, 280; selected by Jackson for State Department, 330; unable to enter upon duties at once, 330; elected governor of New York, 343; Jackson's favorite, 366; supports Jackson in Eaton case, 366, 367; nominated minister to England, 367; opposed because he had instructed minister to England to abandon claim to colonial trade, 367; his policy condemned by Clay, 367; denounced by Clay as originator of "spoils system," 368; not in reality its inventor, 368; defended by Marcy, 368; nomination rejected, 369; thought by Clay and Calhoun to be ruined, 369; determination of Jackson to avenge, 369; solemnly appealed to by Clay to tell Jackson of popular misery, ii. 38, 39; his conduct during and after speech, 39; favors Calhoun's bill to exclude abolition papers from mail, 86; nominated for president, 96; elected, 98; his election claimed by Benton to sanction expunging resolution, 101, 102; his character and career, 129-130; owes presidency solely to Jackson, 130; promises to follow Jackson's policy, 130; promises to oppose abolition in District of Columbia, 130; refuses to recall specie circular, 131; calls extra session of Congress, 131; his message of September, 1837, 133; his sound financial recommendations, 133, 134; would confine duty

of government to regulation of coinage, 134, 135; does not plan any union of sword and purse, 142; elements of opposition to, 172, 173; renominated, his unpopularity, 183; discredited by "spoils," 185; and by reaction against Jackson's despotic leadership, 185; defeated in election, 187; declines proposed annexation of Texas, 236; pleasant personal relations with Clay, 243; visits Clay at Ashland in 1842, 244; agrees with Clay to oppose annexation of Texas, 244; writes letter against annexation, 247; remarks of Jackson on, 248; has majority of delegates at Democratic convention, 251, 252; organized opposition of Texas annexationists to, 251; defeated by two-thirds rule, 252; leader of Barnburners, 304; nominated for presidency by Barnburners, 311; nominated by Buffalo Convention, 312; his candidacy an anomaly, 313; repels anti-slavery Whigs, 313; receives more votes than Cass in New York, 314.

Vermont, carried by anti-Masons, i. 383; denounces gag-rule and protests against annexation of Texas, ii. 153, 154.

Verplanck, Gulian C., introduces tariff bill reducing duties, ii. 8; reasons why Calhoun preferred Clay's bill to his, 12-14; not a compromise, 13.

Veto power, Clay's attack on, discussed, ii. 222-223; its value in government, 223.

Virginia, change in society produced by Revolution, i. 8; emigrants from, in Ohio, 13; in Kentucky, 14, 16; adopts laws ameliorating slavery, 28; demands admission of Missouri with slavery, 177; favors nullification, but offers to mediate, ii. 5; instructs Senators to vote to expunge censure of Jackson, 100.

Von Holst, H. C., on the "reign of Andrew Jackson," ii. 107.

WADE, BENJAMIN F., elected to Senate, ii. 405.

Wadsworth, James S., a Barnburner, ii. 312.

Walker, Robert J., presents petition to recognize independence of Texas, ii. 92; offers amendment to joint resolution annexing Texas, giving president option to begin new negotiations, 272.

War of 1812, causes of, 78-84; preparations for, 79, 80; enthusiasm for, in South and West, 83; dreaded in the East, 83; declared by Congress, 85; opposition to, 85; defeat of invasion of Canada, 86, 87; part played by navy in, 87; conduct of, denounced by Federalists, 89, 90; American defeats in 1813, 98; military events in autumn of 1813, 105, 106; negotiations at Ghent, 108-116; discussion of peculiarities of war, 116, 117; battle of New Orleans, 117; discussion as to justification of war, 119-121; on the whole, worth fighting, 120, 121; effect on manufactures, 129.

War with Mexico, advance of Taylor to Rio Grande, ii. 274-276; hostilities begun, 283, 284; victories of Taylor on Rio Grande, occupation of New Mexico and California, 285; intrigues with Santa Anna, 285; further successes of Taylor, 286, 287; Scott's expedition, 286, 287; capture of Mexico, 287; vacillating conduct of Whigs toward, 288, 289; treaty of Guadalupe Hidalgo, 301.

Washington, George, complains of reception of abolition petitions by Virginia legislature, i. 29; his authority used to support bank against Jackson, 377.

Watkins, Captain Henry, marries Henry Clay's mother, his character, i. 4; places Henry Clay in a store, 4; gains for Clay a clerkship in High Court of Chancery, 4, 5; removes to Kentucky, 9.

Webb, James Watson, abandons Jackson for Clay, 1832, i. 383.

Webster, Daniel, opposes protection in 1816, i. 130; opposes bank, 133; offers resolution to send a commissioner to Greece, 209; denounces

470   INDEX

Holy Alliance, 209; his able speech against protection in 1824, 218; contrast with Clay, 218; satirizes the so-called "American system," 220; describes Kremer to his brother, 243; urges Adams not to exclude Federalists from office, wishes mission to England, 247; congratulates Clay on his vindication, 257; sends Clay cheering reports of popular opinion, 263; comments on Randolph-Clay duel, 274; again congratulates Clay on extinguishing bargain slander, 285; on Clay's candidacy in 1832, 341; his reply to Hayne, 347, 348; urges Clay's presence in Congress, 349; a friend of Jeremiah Mason, 354; advises bank officials against trying to suit new charter to ideas of administration, 356; opens debate on Jackson's bank veto, 377; on weakness of nullifying legislation, ii. 4; convinced of a plan for a Southern confederacy, 5; opposes compromise bill, 16; advocates Force Bill in Senate, 17; joins Clay in opposing Jackson's bank policy, 30; supports resolutions of censure, 37; presents "distress petitions," 38; supports resolutions condemning Jackson's protest, 43; supports Calhoun's report on executive patronage, 62; advocates power of Congress to demand reasons for removal, 63; votes for repeal of four-year term, 69; advocates recognition of Texas, lest some European power obtain it, 92; considered a poor candidate for presidency, 97; nominated by Massachusetts, 98; opposes expunging resolution, 102; reads a solemn protest, 105; on effect of specie circular, 126; votes against fourth installment of distribution of surplus, 136; his speech against sub-treasury, 142; agrees with Clay on necessity for a new bank, 142; his part in "personal debate" of Clay and Calhoun, 146; his ambition for presidency, 174; withdraws on account of slender support, 174; ill-will against Clay, 175; favors Harrison, 175; in campaign of 1840, 187; his nomination as secretary of state not opposed by Clay, 191; supported by Curtis, 194; issues circular prohibiting participation of office-holders in politics, 197; authorized by Tyler to confer with Congress regarding a "fiscal corporation," 207; absents himself from meeting of Tyler's cabinet, 213; agrees to remain in cabinet, to Tyler's satisfaction, 214; criticises sudden resignation of colleagues, 215; out of place in Tyler's cabinet, 217; unable to influence Whigs by remaining, 217; incurs odium himself, 218; has to remain in order to carry through boundary negotiations, 218; disliked by Tyler's friends, 218; remains isolated, 218, 219; unable to prevent Massachusetts Whigs from nominating Clay, 230; urged by Tyler to secure annexation of Texas, 237; refuses offer from Texan minister, 237; resigns office, 237; at Whig convention of 1844, 250; returns to Whig party, 250; reconciled with Clay, 250; eulogizes Clay at convention, 251; ignores Oregon question in negotiation with Ashburton, 279; receives vote in Whig Convention of 1848, 306; in Senate in 1849, 330; his seventh of March speech, 340, 341; denounced in New England, 341; considered to have sacrificed principles in hopes of presidency, 341; does not cause but accompanies pro-slavery reaction, 341, 342; sneers at Seward's speech, 346; fails to understand future, 346, 347; supports Clay's compromise, 350; secretary of state under Fillmore, 355; describes his dejection since 7th of March, 366; leads agitation against agitations 377; denounces anti-slavery men, 387; derides "higher law," 387; writes Hülsemann letter, 392; his speech at dinner to Kossuth, 394; effect of his authority upon party, 397; candidate for presidential nomination, 399; fails to conciliate

South, 399 ; expects Fillmore's support, 399 ; angry at Fillmore's candidacy, 400 ; fails to get nomination, 403 ; compared with Clay as an orator and leader, 40C.

Webster, Ezekiel, letter of Daniel Webster to, on Kremer, i. 243.

Weed, Thurlow, an anti-Mason, i. 345 ; says Jackson was willing to re-charter bank with modifications, 356 ; said to favor Clay's nomination in 1839, ii. 177; suggests Clay's withdrawal as unable to carry New York, 177, 178 ; determines to nominate Harrison, 178 ; uses Scott as candidate to keep delegates away from Clay, 179 ; on nomination of Tyler, 181 ; wishes Clay to secure appointment of Curtis as collector, 193; his anxiety over him, 194 ; probably causes rupture between Harrison and Clay in order to secure office for Curtis, 197; organizes a Whig machine to get control of offices, 198 ; letter of Hunt to, on damaging effect of Clay's Alabama letter, 265 ; desires to make Taylor Whig candidate, 294.

Wellesley, Marquis of, succeeds Canning in foreign office, i. 73 ; on superiority of American over English commissioners in 1814, 119.

Wellington, Duke of, opposes demanding cession of land from America in 1814, i. 108 ; proposal to send him to America, Clay's comments, 124.

West, the, opposes Federalists, i. 31 ; influences feeling in Jefferson's administration, 42 ; settlement of, 43 ; demands internal improvements, 45 ; jealousy of Federalists toward, 59 ; opposes navy, 80 ; expansion of, foreseen by Clay, 207, 208 ; supports tariff of 1824, 219 ; supports Jackson in 1828, 288 ; development of, during Jackson's administration, ii. 114, 115 ; demands all of Oregon, 280.

Wheaton, Henry, letter of Madison to, on causes for war of 1812, i. 84.

Whig party, begins in defense of Adams against Jackson, i. 281, 282 ; its struggle in House, 287; begins to defame Jackson, 287, 288; cause of its defeat, 290–292; becomes regular opposition after defeat, 316; claims to be orthodox Republican party, 317 ; continues in a sense the Federalist party, 317 ; differs from Federalists in not being anti-democratic, 318, 319; and in its objects, 319 ; its leaders, 319 ; composed of mercantile and industrial classes, 320 ; welcomes any deserters from Jacksonians, 320, 321 ; better in opposition than in power, 321 ; inferior to Democrats in discipline, 321 ; its select character, 321 ; led by Clay, 325, 341 ; divided by anti-Masons, 341, 345 ; demands Clay's presence at Washington, 349, 350 ; Clay its inevitable candidate, 351 ; its programme, 351 ; advised by Clay to make bank an issue, 357 ; nominates Clay at national convention, declares safety of bank, and demands defeat of Jackson, 358 ; denounces Jackson's veto, 379 ; its campaign literature, 382 ; sanguine of success, 383 ; badly beaten in election, 383 ; causes for its defeat, 383, 384 ; wins in local elections in 1834, ii. 45 ; takes name of Whig, 45 ; receives anti-Jackson Democrats, 46 ; despondent during Jackson's second term, 96 ; considers Clay "unavailable," 96 ; does not hold national convention and scatters vote, 98 ; defeated, 98 ; profits by reaction after panic of 1837, 131 ; demands payment of fourth installment of surplus, 135 ; ridicules Jackson's financial policy, 137 ; denounces sub-treasury bill for removing deposits from banks, 138 ; alliance with, dissolved by Calhoun, 145, 146 ; more bitterly opposed by abolitionists than Democrats, 164 ; aided by various factions against Van Buren, 172 ; division in, between Northern and Southern members, over slavery, 173 ; elements in, opposed to Clay, 176 ; holds national convention, 179 ; management of, to prevent Clay's nomination, 179, 180; nominates Harrison, 180; nominates Tyler for vice-presidency, 181; anger of Clay at its abandonment of him, 182; its debt to Clay, 182, 183; a coalition rather than a party in 1840, 183; adopts no platform, 185; its "hard-cider and log-cabin" campaign, 186, 187; programme for, laid down by Clay, 188, 189; elects Harrison, 189; reasons for its nomination of Tyler, 200; doubtful adherence of Tyler to, 200-204; controls Congress, 204, 205; led by Clay, 205; enraged at Tyler's bank veto, 207; repudiates Tyler after second veto, 213, 214, 216, 217; led by Clay to make breach irrreparable, 216; abandoned by Tyler Democrats, 216; burns Tyler in effigy, 217; displeased with Webster for remaining in Tyler's cabinet, 217, 218; defeated local elections in 1841, 220; exhorted by Clay, 222; follows Clay's precepts in Congress, 226; passes tariff bills with land-sale distribution, 226, 227; enraged at Tyler's vetoes, 227; urged by Clay and Adams not to yield, 227; gives way and abandons land bill, 228; defeated in 1842, 237; regains ground in 1843, 243; accepts Clay's position regarding Texas, 247; its national convention nominates Clay and Frelinghuysen, 250; return of Webster to, 250, 251; disappointed at defeat of Van Buren's nomination, 256; despises Polk and expects easy victory, 256; defied by Democrats to repeal its own tariff of 1842, 258; attacked by Liberty party, 262, 263; damaged by Clay's Alabama letters, 264, 265; hopes for success up to end, 266; prostrated by defeat of Clay, 267; votes in House against annexation of Texas, 272; vacillating conduct of, in regard to Mexican war, 288; gains in elections of 1846, 289; movement to make Taylor candidate of, 294-296; desire of Clay to lead, 296-299; not repelled by Taylor's intention to be a candidate at all events, 299; failure of its old principles, 300; main strength in North, but obliged to conciliate South, 301; dreads slavery question, 302; a majority of, favors Wilmot Proviso, 305; nominates Taylor at national convention, 305, 306; refuses resolutions in favor of Wilmot Proviso, 306; bolt of anti-slavery Whigs from, 306; fails to adopt a platform, 306; refusal of Clay to support, 307-309; disgust of conservative members of, at nomination, 310; helped by Free Soil movement, 313; denounces Free Soilers, 314; duplicity of its campaign, 314; elects Taylor, 314; loses principles without getting new, 397; to retain Southern Whigs, obliged to adopt compromise, 397; fails to attend congressional caucus to declare compromise a finality, 398; efforts to hold party together on compromise, 398, 399; candidates for presidency in, 399-401; urged by Clay to nominate Fillmore, 401; declares compromise a finality and nominates Scott, 403; defeated and goes to pieces, 405.

Whigs, Southern, pro-slavery in sentiment, ii. 164, 173; urge Clay to favor annexation of Texas, 260; urge Taylor as a pro-slavery man, 314; denounce Taylor for advocating admission of California, 328; effort to retain, causes dissolution of party, 397; not won to Webster's support by his speech, 399; support Fillmore for nomination, 400.

White, Hugh L., although a friend of Jackson, votes for repeal of four-year term, ii. 69; considered a possible candidate for presidency, 98; nominated in Alabama and Tennessee, 98; opposes expunging resolution, 102.

Whitman, Dr. Marcus, leads caravan to Oregon, ii. 279.

Whitney, Asa, suggests transcontinental railway, ii. 280.

Whitney, Eli, invents cotton-gin, its effect, i. 173.

Wilkinson, General James, fails in

attack upon Montreal, i. 105; fails in 1814, 106.
William and Mary College, studies of Wythe at, i. 7.
Willis, ——, defended by Clay in murder trial, i. 20, 21; later remark of Clay to, 22.
Wilmot, David, moves proviso against slavery in new territories, ii. 285, 286.
Wilmot Proviso, introduced in 1846, ii. 285, 286; defeated, 286; popular in North in 1847, 302; in campaign of 1848, 304, 305; to be abandoned in compromise of 1850, 332; denounced by Webster in 7th of March speech, 341; voted down in 1850, 343; its revival predicted by Chase, 345.
Wilson, Henry, bolts Taylor's nomination and calls meeting of dissatisfied Whigs, ii. 306.
Wilson, Isaac, opens school in Lexington, i. 16.
Winchester, General James, defeated at Frenchtown, i. 98.
Wirt, William, attorney-general under Adams, i. 258; nominated for president by anti-Masons, 344; favors Clay, but declines to withdraw, 344, 345; receives electoral vote of Vermont, 383.
Wise, Henry A., describes how Whig managers prevented election of Clay delegates in New York, ii. 178; describes Clay's anger at loss of nomination in 1840, 181, 182; reminds Clay of warnings of intrigue, 182; in campaign of 1840, 187; on nomination of Tyler, 200; describes advice given to Tyler by his friends, 201, 202; on origin of Tyler's second veto message, 210; adviser of Tyler, 215; wishes to get rid of Webster, 218.
Woodbury, Levi, secretary of navy, i. 348; complains to Jackson of Mason, president of branch bank, 353; made secretary of treasury, ii. 44.
Worthington, Senator, moves resolutions calling upon Gallatin to report a plan of internal improvements, i. 46.
Wright, Silas, opposes resolutions condemning Jackson's protest, ii. 43; votes against repeal of four-year term, 69; votes to exclude abolition matter from mails, 86; ironical remark to Clay on proposal to repeal sub-treasury, 192; declines vice-presidential nomination, 252; accepts nomination for governor of New York to help Polk, 259.
Wythe, George, chancellor of Virginia, selects Clay to copy decisions of court, i. 6; his kindness toward and elevating influence upon Clay, 6, 8; his career in Virginia, 7; emancipates slaves, 7; other famous students in his office, 7; introduces Clay into good society, 9; directs Clay's reading, 10; his influence turns Clay against slavery, 30.

YANCEY, W. L., his resolution on slavery in territories rejected by Democratic Convention, ii. 305.
Young Men's National Convention, nominates Clay, i. 381, 382.